Gender, Sexuality and Global Politics

Series Editors: **Ali Bilgic**, Loughborough University, UK, **Synne L. Dyvik**, University of Sussex, UK, **Gunhild Hoogensen Gjørv**, UiT The Arctic University of Norway, Norway, **Thomas Gregory**, The University of Auckland, New Zealand and **Swati Parashar**, University of Gothenburg, Sweden

Expanding the boundaries of International Relations, this series reflects on politics globally with innovative and transdisciplinary perspectives.

With a focus on feminist, lesbian, gay, bisexual, trans and queer activism, the series will examine existing hierarchies, practices and power relations, investigating the often violent effects of these on different peoples, geographies and histories.

Also available

Digital Frontiers in Gender and Security
Bringing Critical Perspectives Online
By **Alexis Henshaw**

Queer Politics in Contemporary Turkey
By **Paul Gordon Kramer**

Forthcoming

Queering Kinship
Non-heterosexual Couples, Parents, and Families in Guangdong, China
By **Han Tao**

Bodily Fluids, Fluid Bodies and International Politics
Feminist Technoscience, Biopolitics and Security
By **Jenn Hobbs**

Gender, Identity and Conflict
Theorising Gender, Peace and Security in the Eastern Himalayan Borderland
By **Dipti Tamang**

The Right Kind of Queer
Race, Sexuality, And Gender in Contemporary Constructions of Swedishness
By **Katharina Kehl**

For more information about the series and to find out how to submit a proposal visit
**bristoluniversitypress.co.uk/
gender-sexuality-and-global-politics**

International Editorial Board

Linda Åhäll, University of Gothenburg, Sweden
Terrell Carver, University of Bristol, UK
Shine Choi, Massey University, New Zealand
Bina D'Costa, Australian National University, Australia
Paula Drumond, O Instituto de Relações Internacionais PUC-Rio, Brazil
Cynthia Enloe, Clark University, US
Des Gasper, Erasmus University, Netherlands
Inanna Hamati-Ataya, University of Cambridge, UK
Catarina Kinnvall, Lund University, Sweden
Rauna Kuokkanen, University of Lapland, Finland
Peace Medie, University of Ghana, Ghana
Annie Paul, University of the West Indies, Jamaica
Manuela Picq, Amherst College, US
Vicki Squire, University of Warwick, UK
Cemal Burak Tansel, University of Sheffield, UK
Maria Tanyag, Australian National University, Australia
Cai Wilkinson, Deakin University, Australia

For more information about the series and to find out how to submit a proposal visit
**bristoluniversitypress.co.uk/
gender-sexuality-and-global-politics**

QUEER CONFLICT RESEARCH

New Approaches to the Study of Political Violence

Edited by
Jamie J. Hagen, Samuel Ritholtz
and Andrew Delatolla

First published in Great Britain in 2025 by

Bristol University Press
University of Bristol
1-9 Old Park Hill
Bristol
BS2 8BB
UK
t: +44 (0)117 374 6645
e: bup-info@bristol.ac.uk

Details of international sales and distribution partners are available at bristoluniversitypress.co.uk

© Bristol University Press 2025

British Library Cataloguing in Publication Data
A catalogue record for this book is available from the British Library

ISBN 978-1-5292-2504-4 hardcover
ISBN 978-1-5292-2505-1 paperback
ISBN 978-1-5292-2507-5 ePub
ISBN 978-1-5292-2506-8 ePdf

The right of Jamie J. Hagen, Samuel Ritholtz and Andrew Delatolla to be identified as editors of this work has been asserted by them in accordance with the Copyright, Designs and Patents Act 1988.

All rights reserved: no part of this publication may be reproduced, stored in a retrieval system, or transmitted in any form or by any means, electronic, mechanical, photocopying, recording, or otherwise without the prior permission of Bristol University Press.

Every reasonable effort has been made to obtain permission to reproduce copyrighted material. If, however, anyone knows of an oversight, please contact the publisher.

The statements and opinions contained within this publication are solely those of the editors and contributors and not of the University of Bristol or Bristol University Press. The University of Bristol and Bristol University Press disclaim responsibility for any injury to persons or property resulting from any material published in this publication.

Bristol University Press works to counter discrimination on grounds of gender, race, disability, age and sexuality.

Cover design: Blu Inc
Front cover image: stocksy.com/Laura Stolfi

This book, in its articulation of queer conflict research, addresses a range of sensitive topics, including but not limited to sexual violence and other forms of bodily and psychological harm.

To all the queer and trans family members that we have lost to violence. To our queer and trans family living in conflict today. And to those committed to telling their stories.

Contents

List of Figures   xi
Notes on the Contributors   xii
Acknowledgements   xviii

Introduction: Telling Queer Stories of Conflict   1
Jamie J. Hagen, Samuel Ritholtz and Andrew Delatolla

PART I   Queer Approaches to Conflict Research

1. The 'Queer' in Conflict Research as Subject, Structure, and Method: Initial Epistemological Considerations for the Early Career Researcher   19
   Samuel Ritholtz
2. Queering the Politics of Knowledge in Conflict Research   41
   José Fernando Serrano-Amaya
3. Workshop as Queer Feminist Praxis: Insights from Colombian Queer and Trans Women Organizing for Peace   61
   Jamie J. Hagen

PART II   Queer Methods of Conflict Research

4. The Visual as Queer Method   83
   Dean Cooper-Cunningham
5. Poetry as a Queer Epistemological Method: Disrupting Knowledge of the Lebanese Civil War with Etel Adnan's *The Arab Apocalypse*   107
   Andrew Delatolla
6. Queer Tools for the Ruthless Archive: Methodological Notes on Trans and Queer Exploration in Argentinean Archives   128
   Patricio Simonetto

PART III   Queer Experiences of Conflict Research

7. Researching Queer Lives in the Shadow of North-East Nigeria's Conflict   157
   Chitra Nagarajan

8	Entangled Intimacies, Queer Attachments: Reflections on Fieldwork with a Diaspora of War *Ahmad Qais Munhazim*	179
9	Doing NGO Research with Diverse SOGIESC Refugees in Lebanon, Syria, and Turkey: A Conversation *Zeynep Pınar Erdem, Charbel Maydaa, Henri Myrttinen and Helena Berchtold*	190

Conclusion: Thinking (of) Queer Conflict Research 202
Laura Sjoberg

Resource Guide I: Guide for Good Practices for Researching 218
Queer and Trans Communities in Highly Sensitive Contexts
Cristian González Cabrera, Erin Kilbride, Kyle Knight, Yasemin Smallens and Rasha Younes (Human Rights Watch's LGBT Rights Program)

Resource Guide II: 'The Emotional Work is Part of the 242
Work': Strategies to Maintain Researcher Emotional and
Psychological Safety During Challenging Fieldwork
Maureen Freed

Index 251

List of Figures

4.1	Untitled photograph by Mads Nissen (2013)	84
4.2	Jon and Alex by Mads Nissen (2014)	100
5.1	Etel Adnan, from *The Arab Apocalypse*, p 7	115
5.2	Etel Adnan, from *The Arab Apocalypse*, p 10	117
5.3	Etel Adnan, from *The Arab Apocalypse*, p 11	118
5.4	Etel Adnan, from *The Arab Apocalypse*, p 48	122
6.1	Image of Marina standing	137
6.2	Images of Marina	138
6.3	Image of Arturo	144

Notes on the Contributors

Helena Berchtold (she/her) is a research assistant for MOSAIC, the Middle East and North Africa (MENA) Organization for Services, Advocacy, Integration & Capacity Development. She is also an evaluator with the German Institute for Development Evaluation. Helena has an interest in gender-based violence, gendered aspects of security and migration, and feminist movements. In her work with MOSAIC MENA, she focuses on the experiences of persons of diverse sexual orientation, gender identity, gender expression and sex characteristics (SOGIESC) in Lebanon, Syria and Turkey.

Cristian González Cabrera (he/him) is a researcher in the LGBT rights programme at Human Rights Watch (HRW), where he focuses on Latin America and the Caribbean. Prior to joining HRW, Cristian was a German Chancellor fellow at the Berlin-based European Center for Constitutional and Human Rights (ECCHR), where he supported all aspects of the organization's universal jurisdiction litigation arising out of Colombia and Syria. Before ECCHR, Cristian worked at the San Francisco-based Center for Justice & Accountability (CJA) on Alien Tort Statute and the Torture Victim Protection Act cases in US federal courts arising out of Latin America and the Horn of Africa. A former Fulbright Scholar in Germany, he received his Juris Doctor from UCLA School of Law and his bachelor's degree from Columbia University.

Dean Cooper-Cunningham (he/him) is Assistant Professor in International Relations in the Department of Political Science at the University of Copenhagen. His research brings together feminist and queer theory, critical security studies, and visual theory/methods. His current work focuses on theorizing an international politics of sex and analysing how powerful actors in global politics strategically adopt pro- or anti-queer domestic and foreign policy agendas. Dean places particular emphasis on the radical antinormative and antisocial politics of early queer thought. His work on gender, sexuality, security, and visual and bodily forms of activism has appeared in *The International Feminist Journal of Politics* and *Millennium: Journal of International Studies*, and *Security Dialogue*.

Andrew Delatolla (he/him) is Lecturer in Middle Eastern Studies in the School of Languages, Cultures and Societies at the University of Leeds and a visiting research fellow at the Middle East Centre at the London School of Economics and Political Science. He was previously Assistant Professor in International Relations at the American University in Cairo. His research interests centre on the intersections of race and sexuality in relation to statehood and state formation. His research focuses on the international relations and politics of the Middle East and North Africa (Egypt, Lebanon, Syria, Turkey, and the Ottoman Empire) through an international historical political sociological lens. His current and developing project examines the politics of queer radicalism in disrupting the relationship between statehood and sexual governance.

Zeynep Pınar Erdem (she/her) is a PhD researcher at the Institute for Intercultural and International Studies at the University of Bremen, focusing on the experiences of forced migrants with diverse sexual orientations, gender identities and expressions and sex characteristics (SOGIESC) in Uganda and Lebanon. She has worked as a lawyer, researcher, and consultant on human rights law and humanitarian law, with a specific focus on conflict-related sexual violence, LGBTI rights, and rights of refugees and asylum seekers in Turkey and the Middle East. Pınar has worked for United Nations Population Fund (UNFPA) Turkey, Human Rights Watch, All Survivors Project, and International Centre for Migration Policy Development (ICMPD). She previously worked as a researcher for MOSAIC MENA.

Maureen Freed (she/her) is a UK Council for Psychotherapy (UKCP)-accredited practitioner and supervisor of counselling and psychotherapy. She teaches the clinical component of the University of Oxford MSt in Psychodynamic Practice. She works in private practice in Oxford, UK and for the Rhodes Trust (as Scholar Mental Health Advisor). She has a particular interest in trauma, and is an accredited practitioner of eye movement desensitization and reprocessing (EMDR), a leading trauma therapy.

Jamie J. Hagen (she/her) is Lecturer in International Relations in the School of History, Anthropology, Philosophy and Politics, Queen's University Belfast. She is also founding co-director of the Centre for Gender in Politics. Her research bridges a feminist security studies approach with queer theory to offer a more complete gender analysis of how the implementation of the Women, Peace and Security (WPS) resolutions impact lesbian, gay, bisexual, transgender, and queer (LGBTQ) people living in conflict-related environments. Her ongoing British Academy Innovation Fellowship analyses how the participation of LBTQ women can be improved in peacebuilding processes. Partners on the project include Anupama Ranawana at Christian Aid UK, Colombia Diversa, and Christian Aid Colombia who together are focusing on the participation of LBTQ women in Colombia's first WPS National Action Plan for the implementation of United Nations Security Council Resolution 1325 in Colombia.

Erin Kilbride (she/her) is a researcher in the LGBT rights programme at Human Rights Watch (HRW), investigating human rights violations against lesbian, bisexual, and queer communities. Prior to Human Rights Watch, Erin was the Research Coordinator at Front Line Defenders, providing emergency support to human rights defenders (HRDs) at risk and leading fact-finding missions across Africa, Asia, and the Americas. She has authored investigations into military trials of civilians, targeted killings of HRDs, and sexual violence perpetrated by security forces in Bangladesh, Egypt, El Salvador, Indonesia, Kyrgyzstan, Myanmar, Tanzania, and the US. She recently led the first global investigation into threats and attacks against sex worker rights defenders. Erin has worked on border demilitarization, refugee solidarity, and Search and Rescue with several collectives, and reported on human rights and humanitarian crises for Al Jazeera, NPR, HuffPost, Think Progress, and Middle East Eye. She received her BA in Women's and Gender Studies from Georgetown University.

Kyle Knight (he/him) is a senior researcher on health and LGBT rights at Human Rights Watch (HRW). Previously, he was a fellow at the Williams Institute of the University of California at Los Angeles School of Law, and a Fulbright scholar in Nepal. As a journalist he worked for Agence France-Presse in Nepal and for the UN's humanitarian news service (IRIN), reporting from Burma, Papua New Guinea, Timor-Leste, Bangladesh, Malaysia, and Indonesia. He has worked for UNAIDS, the Astraea Lesbian Foundation for Justice, and in the children's rights and health and human rights divisions at HRW. He sits on the editorial board of the Annals of LGBTQ Public and Population Health Journal. He has a BA in Cultural Anthropology from Duke University and a Master's in Public Health from the London School of Hygiene and Tropical Medicine.

Charbel Maydaa (they/them) is the founder and former director (2014–19) of MOSAIC, a holistic programme committed to the improvement of the health and wellness of LGBTIQ persons in the MENA region. Since 2004 they have been promoting LGBTIQ rights. They are a certified trainer on sexual orientation, gender identity and expression, and sex characteristics, reproductive health/rights, and clinical management for women and men survivors of sexual violence/rape. They have facilitated more than 150 training sessions at national and international levels.

Ahmad Qais Munhazim (they/them), a genderqueer Afghan, Muslim, and perpetually displaced, is Assistant Professor of Global Studies at the Thomas Jefferson University, Philadelphia. As an interdisciplinary scholar, de/colonial ethnographer, and community activist, Munhazim's work troubles borders of academia, activism, and art while exploring everyday experiences of migration and war in the lives of queer and trans Afghans. Currently, Munhazim is preparing their book manuscript based on a de/colonial ethnography of queer and trans Afghans in Afghanistan and Afghan refugees, immigrants, and asylum seekers in the US. Munhazim has published articles, poetry, and non-fictions in the *Journal of Narrative Politics*, *Kohl: A Journal for Body and Gender Research*, *The Oxford Handbook of Global LGBT and Sexual Diversity Politics*, *Antipode*, *We Are Meant to Rise: Voices for Justice from Minneapolis to the World*, *Queer Voices: Poetry, Prose and Pride*, and *The Conversation*. Munhazim, born and raised in Afghanistan and currently exiled in Philadelphia, holds a PhD in Political Science from the University of Minnesota.

Henri Myrttinen (he/him) is a researcher with MOSAIC MENA and has been researching and working on issues of gender, peace, and security, particularly the broadening of the scope to critically examining masculinities, as well as persons of diverse sexual orientation, gender identity and expression (SOGIE). In the Global Challenges Research Fund (GCRF) Hub, he is working with MOSAIC MENA on investigating, better understanding, and responding to the experiences of persons of diverse sexual orientation, gender identity, gender expression and sex characteristics (SOGIESC) impacted by the war in Syria and by displacement, both in Syria and in Lebanon.

Chitra Nagarajan (she/her) is an activist, researcher, and writer who works to build peace and protect and promote human rights, focusing on conflict analysis, climate security, disability inclusion, and protection of civilians. She is part of anti-racist, anti-fundamentalist, feminist, and queer rights movements and integrates intersectional feminist methodologies and principles throughout her work. She co-edited *She Called Me Woman: Nigeria's Queer Women Speak* and her forthcoming book *The World was in Our Hands: Voices from the Boko Haram Conflict* will be published by Cassava Republic Press in Spring 2024.

Samuel Ritholtz (they/them) is Departmental Lecturer in International Relations at the Department of Politics and International Relations at the University of Oxford, in association with St Hilda's College. Previously, they were Part-time Assistant Professor and Max Weber Fellow in the Department of Political and Social Sciences at the European University Institute. Samuel received their DPhil and MSc from the Refugee Studies Centre in the Department of International Development at the University of Oxford.

Their research interests include contemporary political theories of violence, marginality, and war with a focus on LGBTIQ+ experiences of crisis, conflict, and displacement. They have held visiting research fellowships at the Hertie School (Centre for International Security) in Berlin and at the Universidad de los Andes in Bogotá. They have worked for the United Nations, in the Executive Office of the Secretary-General, as well as for human rights organizations in Washington DC, New York, and Buenos Aires. Samuel is the co-author of the forthcoming monograph, *Toward a Queer Theory of Refuge*. Their work has appeared in academic journals such as the *American Political Science Review, Politics & Gender,* and *Global Studies Quarterly* and in media outlets, such as *the Guardian, the Washington Post,* and *Slate*.

José Fernando Serrano-Amaya (he/him) is Associate Professor in the Department of Languages and Cultures, Universidad de los Andes (Colombia). He received his PhD from the University of Sydney (2015) and a Master's in Conflict Resolution (University of Bradford, UK, 2004). He has developed his career as researcher, consultant, and lecturer. He has extensive experience working for NGOs, international cooperation agencies, and state institutions in Colombia. His research interests include gender and sexual violence, peacebuilding, social policies, and knowledge management. He is a lecturer on gender, sexualities, queer studies, and peace studies and is currently researching on pedagogies and politics of reconciliation in Australia, Colombia, and South Africa and on the participation of LGBTQI+ organizations on peacebuilding. His most recent book is *Homophobic Violence in Armed Conflict and Political Transition* (2018).

Patricio Simonetto (he/him) is Lecturer in Gender and Social Policy at the University of Leeds. He previously held a Marie Skłodowska-Curie Individual Fellowship at the Institute of the Americas, University College London. He was previously Research Assistant at the National Council of Scientific and Technical Research (Argentina). He specializes in the social history and culture of sexuality in Latin America and is the author of *Money Is Not Everything: The Purchase and Sale of Sex in Argentina in the Twentieth Century* (2022); *El dinero no es todo: La compra y venta de sexo en la Argentina del siglo XX* (2019), and *Entre la injuria y la revolución: El Frente de Liberación Homosexual en la Argentina* (2017).

Laura Sjoberg (she/her) is British Academy Global Professor of Politics and International Relations at Royal Holloway University of London. Her research addresses issues of gender and security, with foci on politically violent women, feminist war theorizing, sexuality in global politics, and political methodology. She teaches, consults, and lectures on gender in global politics, and on international security. Her work has been published in more than

50 books and journals in political science, law, gender studies, international relations, and geography.

Yasemin Smallens (she/her) is Coordinator in the LGBT Rights Program. Yasemin holds a bachelor's degree in Political Science from Vassar College. Previously she has worked on refugee policy and police surveillance technologies at the Brennan Center, municipal identification cards and voting reform at For the Many, and transgender rights and police reform at the New York Civil Liberties Union. She also worked on the film *Pier Kids: The Life*, which documents the experiences of homeless transgender youth of colour around New York City's piers.

Rasha Younes (she/her) is a senior researcher with the LGBT Rights Program at Human Rights Watch (HRW), investigating abuses against LGBT people in the MENA region. Prior to joining HRW, Rasha was a Thomas J. Watson fellow, where she researched oral tradition as a form of activism in South Africa, Ireland, India, Germany, and the Czech Republic. She has previously worked on women's rights issues for the Clinton Center for Women's Empowerment in Morocco, the Women's Center of Montgomery County, and the Norristown Courthouse in Philadelphia. Rasha was also a Caux Initiatives of Change scholar in Switzerland, a fellow for the Center of Peace and Global Citizenship in Philadelphia, and a researcher for the Arab Council for Social Sciences in Beirut. Rasha holds a master's degree in Social Anthropology from Central European University in Budapest, and a bachelor's degree in Cultural Anthropology from Bryn Mawr College.

Acknowledgements

We are grateful for the LGBTIQ+ community who has helped to support each of us individually as friends, scholars, and in our own queer conflict research. We also acknowledge the feminist, queer, and trans scholars who have come before us, creating a space in activism, policy, and academia for the work in this volume. The International Studies Association LGBTQA Caucus continues to be an especially important community for not only supporting our work but also offering mentorship to queer scholars. We thank the contributors for trusting us with their work. We also thank our reviewer for their support and guidance, and our editors and the editorial team at Bristol University Press. And a very special thanks to Ila Zelmanovitz Axelrod for all of their assistance in completing this volume.

Introduction: Telling Queer Stories of Conflict

Jamie J. Hagen, Samuel Ritholtz and Andrew Delatolla

Amid the growing politicization of LGBTIQ+ identities,[1] it is now more urgent than ever to bring a queer dimension to conflict studies. But even the frame of inquiry, *queer conflict research*, brings with it so many questions. Who is this research for? Who should carry it out? Why should it be studied? For many in international studies, considering LGBTIQ+ lives within the existing literature about peace and conflict is altogether new. Still, given what we as editors recognize as a growing interest in using 'queer methodologies' to better understand conflict, we are motivated to present a diversity of queer approaches for answering these questions. Informed by feminist principles about the emancipatory potential for research, the chapters in this volume tell the stories of LGBTIQ+ people in conflict not only as victims of political violence, but also as experts and agents of change (Basu, 2013). We situate our volume in conversation with existing queer (Otto, 2007; Kollman and Waites, 2009; Waites, 2009; Wilkinson and Langois, 2014) and feminist (Enloe, 1990; Tickner, 1997) international studies scholarship which, while not written as queer conflict research, provides foundational insights for this emerging work.

There are multiple approaches to thinking through how scholars can conduct queer conflict research. For some, queer conflict research means research that disrupts and redefines existing methodological and epistemological frameworks of conflict research by drawing from queer theoretical propositions. For others, queer conflict research means to engage with queer subjects during and after conflict. The concept *queer* as it relates to conflict research needs a degree of flexibility. We build on Cynthia Weber's theoretical insights in *Queer International Relations* where she argues 'by failing to fully take on board the insights of their queer studies colleagues about the possibility and impossibility of producing and deploying sexualized subjectivities, most IR scholars regularly undertheorize how the will to knowledge about sexualities is part of what makes international games of power possible and impossible' (2016: 2). Weber puts queer studies scholarship and IR scholarship in conversation—something we aim to do with queer studies scholarship and IR studies of peace and conflict. As such, queering conflict research can extend beyond the study of LGBTIQ+ people's experiences of political violence during conflict. Indeed, the difficulty behind this volume, as well as its strength, is the breadth of approaches that can be classified as 'queer'. As editors we do not envisage a single approach to queer conflict research, acknowledging there are multiple approaches. Rather than making a definitive claim about what queer conflict research is/is not, thus policing its boundaries, we aim to illuminate why queer conflict research matters. The queer scholars in this volume each take a stance on the 'queer' of their work and, in doing so, they ask how their positionality matters in queer conflict research.

At the same time, there are ethical considerations involved in writing about and working with queer communities in conflict-related contexts, which require careful thought. Notably, queer communities face augmented forms of violence, regardless of geographic location,[2] which at times increase according to their race, gender identity, migration status, disability, and class. These factors must be considered when engaging with LGBTIQ+ communities, reflecting on their experiences, writing academic research, deriving theoretical propositions, and consulting with governments and non-governmental organizations. Therefore, we highlight the epistemological, methodological, and ethical concerns across a variety of approaches to queer conflict research.

With this volume, we seek to provide a cohesive resource for scholars of political violence who are engaged, and seeking to engage, with queer conflict research. We bring together a series of different queer methodological approaches to address the epistemological (what), methodological (how), and ethical (why) issues of queer scholarship in studies on conflict and political violence. Organized into three parts, the volume examines queer approaches to conflict research, queer methods in conflict research, and finally queer experiences of conflict research. In these parts, we examine not only why queer research methods are important for the study of political violence, but also how to apply them, including reflections on the experience of being a queer person conducting this research. The authors included in the volume discuss, explain, and show their different approaches to queer investigations of conflict and violence, using a variety of case studies and diverse methodological approaches. The volume concludes with two resource guides that provide important guidance on how to conduct queer conflict research in a safe and ethical manner.

Situating queer conflict research

While some of the authors in this volume explore the conditions of queer and trans people in situations of conflict and political violence, others engage with 'queer' as an epistemological and theoretical position that shapes the conduct and focus of the research. Notably, in both cases, the authors highlight a concern with the ethical implications of research on conflict and political violence. Moreover, it should be noted that these two forms of engagement are not mutually exclusive: many of the authors in this volume tell the stories of queer people from queer positionalities.

This volume explores a plurality of queer scholarship in conflict research that puts in dialogue the approaches of *mainstream* political science with more *critical* approaches.[3] To date, *mainstream* approaches to contentious queer politics have derived from positivist and postpositivist traditions, thus speaking to a more general political science readership. These interventions in *mainstream* political science often build on more *critical* approaches, together developing a broader research agenda of queer conflict studies. In this emerging field, we underscore the importance of this dialogue between epistemic traditions (those deemed *mainstream* and *critical*) to promote full inclusion of the diverse array of queer forms of analyses that focus on the fine-grain, often qualitative, aspects of LGBTIQ+ lives and experiences. Without this full inclusion, underlying cisheteronormative and endosexist biases go unexamined. As such, to achieve its full intellectual and political promise, queer conflict research must centre queer and trans perspectives at every stage of the research process and in all types of research. This in turn enables us to destabilize norms about gender and sexuality, based on cisgender, heterosexual, and endosexist assumptions along with binary stereotypes about femininity and masculinity. As feminist and queer scholars have shown, with this destabilization, assumptions are revealed, and concepts can be improved (Weber, 2016; Delatolla, 2020; Ritholtz, 2023; Ritholtz and Buxton, 2023). Such a consideration of queer scholarship in conflict research reveals opportunities ignored by more normative approaches.

Queering conflict research can also complicate Western narratives associated with the progress of LGBTIQ+ rights (Delatolla, 2020); illustrating the complex realities that queer people experience. Western narratives of LGBTIQ+ rights often rely on queer people engaging in homonormative demands of visibility of their identities for a cisgender heterosexual audience (Halberstam, 1998; Duggan, 2004; Stryker, 2008). *Coming out* allows society to categorize and classify non-normative bodies and orientations, making them acceptable to heteronormative logics, institutions, and structures of statehood. In reality, queer and trans experience are much more complex than these narrow and normative logics. Visibility and *coming out*, while necessary to be 'seen' by the legal configurations of LGBTIQ+ rights, can expose queer individuals and communities to increased and heightened threats of violence. As such, the queer experience is one that can be understood as the complex navigation of (in)visibility, as it relates to violence and experiences of joy and celebration.

These complex navigations mean queer and trans people also bring a unique lens to how they see conflict, and envision peace. As one example,

Lyra McKee, a lesbian journalist who lived and worked in Belfast, reported on the high rate of suicide within her generation, born during the post-Good Friday Agreement ceasefire in Northern Ireland. While the 1998 Good Friday Agreement brought an end to active armed conflict, the peace process has failed to facilitate some much-needed economic and social transformation in the wake of this ceasefire. In a 2016 article in *The Atlantic*, McKee noted, 'The tragic irony of life in Northern Ireland today is that peace seems to have claimed more lives than war ever did' (2016). Here, McKee points to the violence of the continuing political, economic, and social injustices in the country. She brings an interpersonal, experiential, temporal awareness to her journalism, relying on her own experiences of conflict during peacetime to challenge mainstream narratives. Her 'letter to my 14-year-old self' about coming out as a lesbian was shared widely when just three years later in 2019, at the age of 29, McKee was fatally shot while covering riots in the Creggan area of Derry, Northern Ireland. In the letter she assures herself, and those of us reading her letter, 'It won't always be like this. It's going to get better' (2020: 149).

In upending normative positionalities through queer experience, queering is a way of thinking differently not only about conflict's harmful impacts, but also about the meaning of conflict altogether. In this sense, this volume builds on the work of other queer method texts (Jagose, 1996; Hall and Jagose, 2012; Browne and Nash, 2016; Dadas et al, 2019; Ghaziani and Brim, 2019), to reveal how queer perspectives in research not only foster inclusion but also destabilize core concepts in any field. We follow Browne and Nash's definition of 'queer research' as

> any form of research positioned within conceptual frameworks that highlight the instability of taken-for-granted meanings and resulting power relations. Queer inflected perspectives, approaches and conceptualisations have been taken up, disputed and reworked in different disciplinary contexts, reflecting the traditions of knowledge production in those disciplines (2016: 4).

By engaging in this approach, not only are we able to problematize, disrupt, and expand approaches in existing conflict research, but we are also able to continue the process by reworking concepts, theories, and framings as our intellectual understanding evolves. These different intersectional, and transforming queer positionalities make it impossible to demarcate the boundaries or limits of the 'queer' in queer conflict research. Instead, we aim to highlight the exciting, and limitless, possibilities of adopting a queer lens.

In addition to highlighting an epistemological approach to queer conflict research, one that allows researchers to build a queer theoretical framework of analysis, this volume provides a variety of discussions on research methodologies and methods that include fieldwork, interview practices, cultural analyses, and archival research. It considers the multiple ways that methods and methodologies can be queered, the importance of engaging in queer methodological research, and the ethics of queer methods and methodologies. In writing about queering conflict and political violence, we also engage with queer IR scholarship (Sjoberg and Weber, 2014; Picq and Thiel, 2015; Weber, 2016; Delatolla, 2020), critical security studies (Puar, 2007; Amar, 2014), feminist security studies (Wibben, 2011; Shepherd and Sjoberg, 2012; Shepherd, 2013; Hagen, 2016), studies of sexuality, nationalism, and contentious politics (Peterson, 1999; Canaday, 2009; Ashe, 2018; Nagle and Fakhoury, 2018; Slootmaeckers, 2019; Ayoub, 2015; Tschantret, 2018, 2020), of masculinities (Connell, 2005; Belkin, 2012), as well as feminist literature, which has taken a growing interest in LGBTIQ+ activism as a part of transitional justice (Bueno-Hansen, 2017; Fobear and Baines, 2020; Díaz Calderón, 2021). Critically, the book brings together scholars in a variety of disciplines who are focused on issues of political violence and conflict.

The volume provides a foundation for approaching queer methods and methodologies in the study of political violence and conflict. We are also informed by ongoing research by civil society organizations, such as Human Rights Watch (HRW, 2009; HRW, 2019), International Alert (Myrttinen and Daigle, 2017), Outright International (Outright, 2014; Davis and Stern, 2018), Colombia Diversa (2017, 2020), and Caribe Afirmativo (2019), among others, who have been reporting on the experiences of LGBTIQ+ people in conflict and post-conflict for over a decade and a half. As demonstrated by the chapters in this volume, we also recognize the importance of linking this research with feminist peace research (Cockburn, 2007; Cohn, 2012; Väyrynen et al, 2022) to interrogate assumed foundational concepts about gender and the state, while also developing queer epistemological and methodological questions about how we as researchers see and study political violence.

Queer approaches to conflict research

The contributors within our volume have taken an expansive and creative look at queer conflict. In some instances, the authors find that queer conflict generates new ways of thinking about peace and conflict. In others, authors detail how our understanding of conflict can be reshaped (or *queered*) when informed by the lived experiences of queer people living through and with conflict. Drawing on literature focused on complex humanitarian emergencies, queer IR, and scholarship about the experiences of queer and trans asylum seekers, we understand conflict to exist in spaces far outside of recognized conflict zones. Conflict for many queer people begins in the home. Others may face conflict within their own communities, or in a state-sanctioned homophobic and transphobic backlash exacerbated during times of conflict and post-conflict.

In the first part of the book, we begin by examining some of these various queer approaches to conflict research. It begins with Chapter 1, written by Samuel Ritholtz, who considers the first steps for the early career researcher interested in queer conflict research. Drawing on their own experience as a DPhil student at the University of Oxford in the disciplines of International Development and International Relations, with a focus on refugee and conflict studies, Ritholtz reflects on tensions experienced doing this research and proposes an expansive queer epistemological approach that recognizes the layered knowledge regimes that impact the lives of queer and trans people. Thus, Ritholtz illustrates the value of queer conflict research, despite efforts by some in the discipline to dismiss much of this work as central to international studies.

Chapter 2 is written by José Fernando Serrano-Amaya and addresses knowledge production through a discussion of representation and victimhood in conflict with a focus on the Colombian context. Here, the author examines gender and sexual violence, particularly homophobic violence in the context of political transitions, and questions why some events are brought to people's attention while others are silenced. Serrano-Amaya argues, 'The field of queer conflict research has produced a type of knowledge that challenges standard divisions between areas of expertise and offers a unique opportunity to explore other paths for the development of queer research practices'.

Bringing these questions to the dynamics of queer conflict field research, in Chapter 3, Jamie J. Hagen examines how queer women can be centred in approaches to queer conflict research practice through queer feminist research practices as illustrated by a workshop organized by Colombia Diversa about queering the women, peace, and security agenda in Colombia. Here, Hagen notes how queer women continue to be marginalized in conflict research, even when that research is focused on women and the experience of the LGBTIQ+ community. In putting the spotlight on how a workshop can serve as a queer feminist method, Hagen underscores the importance of building solidarity across feminist and LGBTIQ+ movements in organizing for peace and security.

Queer methods of conflict research

The volume's second part considers the use of various methods to conduct queer conflict research of political violence including the use of visuals, poetry, and archives. This section builds on a queer epistemic position by asking *how* queer individuals experience themselves in the world and *what kind* of knowledge can be produced from these experiences? This makes it possible to develop different queer methodological frameworks to engage with and study the world. Such frameworks allow researchers to ask new questions about the complexities of queer lives and communities, refusing to be simplified into heteronormative or otherwise binary logics of gender and sexuality. It also highlights new critiques of *how* we engage in research, opening novel methods for research.

First, in Chapter 4, Dean Cooper-Cunningham offers visual politics as a method of queer conflict research through an approach to studying (in)security, which includes words, images, and the body as epistemic sites. Through an analysis of visual imagery during an anti-LGBTIQ+ crackdown in Russia, Cooper-Cunningham demonstrates how this 'tripartite word-image-body approach' allows researchers to see and understand security problems specifically—and international politics more broadly—in a more complex and culturally situated manner. Cooper-Cunningham explores how visuals can be made *queer* in the service of queer research, highlighting the importance of seeing the international politics of sex.

Next, Andrew Delatolla in Chapter 5 questions the linearity and causality of existing scientific methods by using poetry as an epistemic method of queer conflict research. He uses the book-length poem of the queer Lebanese-American poet, author, and visual artist Etel Adnan, '*The Arab Apocalypse*' (1989). Delatolla explores how, through this creative process, a queer episteme and positionality of experiencing conflict disrupts discussions in conflict research and brings renewed interventions on the complicated realities of peace and conflict.

In the final chapter of Part II, Patricio Simonetto in Chapter 6, explores different ideas when confronting the 'ruthless archive' to engage in queer research. Focused on trans lives in Argentina, Simonetto interrogates how researchers engage with an archive that is often hostile to queer individuals. From these experiences, Simonetto questions how researchers deal and cope with the language of the archive, the relationship between the researcher and the archival documents, and what happens to cisheterosexed life records when we apply queer perspectives as researchers. Simonetto's contribution reveals not only the challenges of documenting queer and trans lives of the past, but also the challenges to the researcher engaged in this demanding work.

Queer experiences of conflict research

Queer narratives of political violence—of finding care and security within the community—can also reshape an understanding of conflict. The reality is that for many queer and trans individuals, 'peace' does not always mean safety. Thus, when this peace for the queer community is found, it is something to acknowledge. Corey, a queer 47-year-old member of the LGBTIQ+ community living in Colombia, shares the recent peace enjoyed by his community has been something to cherish: 'I feel very happy because we can go out without any problems. Before we were afraid to go out, and if armed groups found us on the street at midnight, they could take us away, torture us, or send us home' (Ritholtz and Stallone, 2022). Corey's town in the Mountains of María was one of the most violent towns for LGBTIQ+ people during the peak of the Colombian Civil War at the start of the 21st century, with violence perpetrated by paramilitary groups, guerrilla groups, and state actors. Today, while this tepid peace is threatened by the growth of organized criminal networks in Colombia, Corey relies on groups such as Caribe Afirmativo, an LGBTIQ+ rights organization that offers safe spaces for LGBTIQ+ people in Colombia while working to transform prejudices, imaginaries, and social/institutional practices around sexual and gender diversity. While these efforts come with the risk that increased visibility for queer people may also result in the increased targeting of the population, because of Caribe Afirmativo's work in promoting tolerance and providing shelter in hostile environments, Corey and the broader LGBTIQ+ community in their town have enjoyed a new-found, if fragile, peace.

The experience of queer and trans individuals like Corey during war demonstrate that security, like peace, is not something that can be declared, but instead must be lived. Queer conflict research informed by scholars of the Colombian civil war, such as Mauricio Albarracín (2011), Nancy Prada (2015, 2019), Samuel Ritholtz (2022), and José Fernando Serrano-Amaya (2017), not only provides much needed nuance about who gets targeted and when (rejecting LGBTIQ+ as a unitary group but finding nuance at the intersections of gender, class, race, and other identities), but also about the different regimes of power that overlap the political. Similarly, Fidelma Ashe (2019) and Moira Duggan (2012) both consider the role of gender and sexuality in relation to nationalism in the conflict in Northern Ireland during the Troubles. Centring queer and trans lives in studies of political violence, such as in the Colombian civil war or the conflict in Northern Ireland, reveals not only a political phenomenon of scapegoating the socially marginal in a country in order for political actors to consolidate power, but also ties it to the dynamics subordinating economic regimes, which rely on this marginalization in order for other elites to consolidate both economic and political power (Chitty, 2020).

We conclude the volume with contributions from authors who are in different ways centring the queer experience to think about queer experiences of conflict research. First, in Chapter 7, independent researcher Chitra Nagarajan examines the ethical considerations surrounding a study aiming to deepen understanding and analysis of the realities, challenges, and resilience of queer people in the highly volatile and insecure context of northeastern Nigeria. In this chapter, Nagarajan highlights how to maximize the benefits for queer people in participatory and non-participatory research of this kind; by addressing the issue of power and knowledge production as well as knowledge sharing, and the importance of ensuring the safety, security, and well-being of participants, researchers, and the queer community at large. The chapter argues that engaging in a queer perspective that negates extractive practices draws attention to the limits of this research and opens a discussion of future possibilities.

Next, in Chapter 8, Ahmad Qais Munhazim explores the intersubjective relationship between the researcher and the researched. Thinking about their own overlapping identities as a queer, Muslim, Afghan asylum seeker, they ask: how are the identities and experiences of a researcher entangled with those of the researched? How do attachments to home and experiences of war and displacement trouble the ethical terrain in the field? Providing a reflexive and honest experiential narrative, Munhazim exposes heteronormative assumptions of racialized, homophobic, conflict-ladened geographies. This chapter explores these questions while advancing a diasporic feminist and queer ethic of intimacy and care.

To complement these considerations put forward by Nagarajan and Munhazim, Chapter 9 focuses on observations and ethical considerations made by non-governmental organizational researchers. As the editors of this volume are all researchers situated in academic institutions, we wanted to reflect on the limitations of the academy in taking queer conflict research forward by providing space for those doing queer conflict research in a different institutional environment. This final chapter includes a grounded insight into this challenge through a conversation co-authored by four collaborators, Zeynep Pınar Erdem, Charbel Maydaa, Henri Myrttinen, and Helena Berchtold who write about the ethical issues of research involving displaced, precarious, and threatened individuals in the Middle East and North Africa (MENA). Together they focus their reflections on their experiences working with MOSAIC MENA—an organization led by activists as well as legal and health experts—to provide specialized and comprehensive services for marginalized groups, to research and advocate for policy reform, develop knowledge and capacities on SOGIESC (sexual orientation, gender identity and expression, and sex characteristic) issues, and engage society in the fight against human rights violations, especially against LGBTIQ+ rights. In an informal dialogue, the four explore some of the benefits and drawbacks, and some of the achievements and frustrations of conducting this research on the ground in Lebanon and Turkey. To conclude, Laura Sjoberg reflects on the contributions of this volume and future of queer conflict research in the context of her trailblazing career as a scholar of gender, sexuality, and war.

A note on the resource guides

In addition to these contributions, we also include two resource guides at the end of the volume to support those engaged in queer conflict research, particularly early career researchers. First, we include a resource guide developed by a team of researchers at the Human Rights Watch (HRW) LGBT Rights Program. HRW documents and exposes abuses based on sexual orientation and gender identity worldwide, including torture, killing and executions, arrests under unjust laws, unequal treatment, censorship, medical abuses, discrimination in health and jobs and housing, domestic violence, abuses against children, and denial of family rights and recognition. With this resource guide, the LGBT Rights Program team build on their decades of experience to offer insight into 'good' practices for conducting research about queer experiences of political violence in a safe and ethical manner.

Recognizing that the ethic of care and intimacy developed by contributions in this volume apply to both the researcher and the researched, we also include a second resource guide on vicarious, or secondary, trauma, which is a unique form of trauma that results from being exposed to the trauma of others. As queer conflict research exposes researchers to upsetting themes that may directly relate to their own lived experience of trauma as queer and trans researchers, we have included this guidance from Maureen Freed, a vicarious trauma expert, psychotherapist, and counsellor at the University of Oxford. We hope that, together, these two research guides aid researchers in conducting safe and ethical research. As researchers, we take on these risks, but there is no glory in experiencing harm. We must protect ourselves as a way to further protect our research collaborators.

Conclusion

Together, the chapters in this volume illustrate that to *queer* conflict research is to make visible stories like those of Lyra and Corey as central to understanding and confronting political violence. This text is the first critical, in-depth discussion on queer methods and methodologies for research on political violence and conflict. It makes a crucial intervention in how queer methods and methodologies can be used and developed for more ethical research. Queer as both an epistemic and methodological framework, then, allows for a consideration of violence at the core of different regimes of power.

In putting this volume together, we have sought to create a foundational text for future students and scholars to refer to that centres a queer positionality in this challenging subject matter. The text engages in discussions of what queer approaches entail, how to engage in a queer approach to the study of conflict, and why these queer approaches are important. The chapters explore a variety of specific methodological approaches, including fieldwork, interviews, cultural analysis, and archival research, as well as broader academic debates, such as how to work with research partners in an ethical manner.

The aim of this volume is to bring scholars together and build on existing scholarship that currently attends to these issues. We hope to provide interested students, researchers, and educators with a series of foundational discussions that reveal the breadth and depth of queer approaches to research on conflict and violence in a single volume. In doing so, this volume contributes to developing a burgeoning field of queer scholarship, reinforcing the insights of feminist and gender approaches, and challenging existing approaches to research on political violence and conflict. The contents of these chapters also show the reader these methods in practice by considering case studies from around the globe. The chapters include examples of doing queer conflict research engaging with queer communities in Colombia, Lebanon, Indonesia, Iraq, Nigeria, Russia, Syria, St Vincent and the Grenadines, Turkey, and within the Afghan diaspora.

This volume is the resource that we wish all existing queer conflict researchers had available at the start of their careers, including us, the editors. Our goal here is to put into writing the decades of wisdom and knowledge that have been built by research on queer and trans lives by queer and trans people throughout the world. While the text cannot cover everything, it can begin a conversation and provide a first resource. We hope the contributions in these pages motivate and challenge the reader, while also deepening their knowledge on the topic of queer conflict research. We further hope that this book serves as one opportunity, of many, for researchers on queer conflict to come together and learn from one another. May we continue to share queer stories of LGBTIQ+ people living with, transforming through, and thinking beyond conflict.

Notes

[1] As authors of this chapter, and editors of this volume, we use the acronym LGBTIQ+ (lesbian, gay, bisexual, transgender, intersex, queer, and others) to describe people with non-hegemonic sexual orientations, gender identities, and sex characteristics (SOGIESC). The authors also use 'queer and trans' as another collective adjective to describe these same populations. This said, we have let each contributor choose the term they want to use to describe these populations; we recognize these identities as culturally situated and deeply personal. For this reason, the book contains a range of different approaches to this question of terminology.

[2] LGBTIQ+ people in the US are four times more likely than non-LGBTIQ+ people to be victims of violent crime (Flores, Langton, Meyer, and Romero, 2020).

[3] We italicize 'mainstream' and 'critical' to recognize these concepts as constructions that result from hierarchies of power in the academy that can legitimize certain epistemic approaches over others. While we do not wish to reinforce this binary, we use these terms to highlight the impact of reifying a certain epistemic approach as the 'norm'.

Acknowledgement

We would like to thank Alyson Price for her review of this piece.

Bibliography

Adnan, E. (1989) *The Arab Apocalypse*, Sausalito: The Post-Apollo Press.

Albarracín, M. (2011) 'Retos Para La Investigación de La Violencia Contra La Población LGBT En El Marco de Conflicto Armado', Bogotá: Universidad de Los Andes, Centro de Investigaciones Jurídicas.

Amar, P. (2014) *The Security Archipelago: Human Security States, Sexuality Politics, and the End Of Neoliberalism*, Durham/London: Duke University Press.

Ashe, F. (2018) *Reimaging Inclusive Security in Peace Processes: LGB&T Perspectives (PSRP Report)*, Global Justice Academy, Edinburgh: University of Edinburgh.

Ashe, F. (2019) *Gender, Nationalism and Conflict Transformation: New Themes and Old Problems in Northern Ireland Politics*, London: Routledge.

Ayoub, P.M. (2015) 'Contested norms in new-adopter states: international determinants of LGBT rights legislation', *European Journal of International Relations*, 21(2): 293–322.

Basu, S. (2013) 'Emancipatory potential in feminist security studies', *International Studies Perspectives*, 14(4): 455–8. Available from: www.jstor.org/stable/44214631

Belkin, A. (2012) *Bring Me Men: Military Masculinity and the Benign Facade of American Empire*, London: Hurst.

Browne, K. and Nash, C.J. (2016) 'Queer methods and methodologies: an introduction', in K. Browne and C.J. Nash (eds) *Queer Methods and Methodologies: Intersecting Queer Theories and Social Science Research*, London: Routledge, pp 1–23.

Bueno-Hansen, P. (2017) 'The emerging LGBTQ rights challenge to transitional justice in Latin America', *The International Journal of Transitional Justice*, 12(1): 126–45.

Canaday, M. (2009) *The Straight State: Sexuality and Citizenship in Twentieth-Century America*, Princeton/Oxford: Princeton University Press.

Caribe Afirmativo (2019) 'Nosotras Resistimos'.

Chitty, C. (2020). *Sexual Hegemony: Statecraft, Sodomy, and Capital in the Rise of the World System*. Durham, NC: Duke University Press.

Cockburn, C. (2007) *From Where We Stand: War, Women's Activism and Feminist Analysis*, New York: Zed Books.

Cohn, C. (2012) *Women and Wars: Contested Histories, Uncertain Futures*, New York: Wiley.

Colombia Diversa (2017) 'Vivir bajo sospecha', *Estudios de Caso: Personas LGBT Víctimas Del Conflicto Armado En Vistahermosa y San Onofre*. Available from: www.colombiadiversa.org/conflictoarmado-lgbt

Colombia Diversa (2020) 'Orders of violence: systematic crimes against LGBT people in the Colombian armed conflict', Bogota: Colombia Diversa. Available from: https://colombiadiversa.org/publicaciones/orders-of-prejudicecrimes-committed-against-lgbt-people-in-the-colombian-armed-conflict/

Connell, R. (2005) *Masculinities* (2nd edn), New Jersey: Wiley.

Dadas, C., Banks, W.P., and Cox, M.B. (eds) (2019) *Re/Orienting Writing Studies: Queer Methods, Queer Projects*, Logan, UT: Utah State University Press.

Davis, L. and Stern, J. (2018) 'WPS and LGBTQ rights', in S.E. Davies and J. True (eds), *The Oxford Handbook of Women, Peace and Security*, New York: Oxford University Press, pp 657–68.

Delatolla, A. (2020) 'Sexuality as a standard of civilization: historicizing (homo)colonial intersections of race, gender, and class', *International Studies Quarterly*, 64(1): 148–58.

Díaz Calderón, J.C. (2021) 'De La Política Queer a La Performance Transfeminista Transfronteriza Guerrillera Andina. Conversación Con PachaQueer', *Revista Interdisciplinaria de Estudios de Género de El Colegio de México*, 7(1): 1–23.

Duggan, L. (2004) *The Twilight of Equality: Neoliberalism, Cultural Politics, and the Attack on Democracy*, New York: Beacon Press.

Duggan, M. (2012) *Queering Conflict: Examining Lesbian and Gay Experiences of Homophobia in Northern Ireland*, Farnham: Ashgate.

Enloe, C. (1990) *Bananas, Beaches and Bases: Making Feminist Sense of International Politics*, Berkeley, CA: University of California Press.

Flores, A.R., Langton, L., Meyer, I.H., and Romero, A.P. (2020) 'Victimization rates and traits of sexual and gender minorities in the United States: results from the National Crime Victimization Survey, 2017', *Science Advances*, 6(40): eaba6910.

Fobear, K. and Baines, E. (2020) 'Pushing the conversation forward: the intersections of sexuality and gender identity in transitional justice', *The International Journal of Human Rights*, 24(4): 307–12. Available from: doi.org/10.1080/13642987.2019.1673980

Ghaziani, A. and Brim, M. (2019) *Imagining Queer Methods*, New York: New York University Press.

Hagen, J.J. (2016) 'Queering women, peace and security', *International Affairs*, 92(2): 313–32.

Halberstam, J. (1998) *Female Masculinity*, Durham, NC: Duke University Press.

Hall, D.E. and Jagose, A. (2012) *The Routledge Queer Studies Reader*, New York: Routledge.

Human Rights Watch (2009) '"They want us exterminated": murder, torture, sexual orientation and gender in Iraq', New York: Human Rights Watch. Available from: www.hrw.org/sites/default/files/reports/iraq0809web.pdf

Human Rights Watch (2019) '"Don't punish me for who I am": systemic discrimination against transgender women in Lebanon', New York: Human Rights Watch. Available from: www.hrw.org/sites/default/files/report_pdf/lebanon0910_pdf.pdf

Jagose, A. (1996) *Queer Theory*, Melbourne: Melbourne University Press.

Kollman, K. and Waites, M. (2009) 'The global politics of lesbian, gay, bisexual and transgender human rights: an introduction', *Contemporary Politics*, 15(1): 1–17.

McKee, L. (2016) 'Suicide among the ceasefire babies', *The Atlantic*, [online] 20 January. Available from: www.theatlantic.com/health/archive/2016/01/conflict-mental-health-northern-ireland-suicide/424683/

McKee, L. (2020) *Lyra McKee: In Her Own Words*, UK: Faber and Faber.

Myrttinen, H. and Daigle, M. (2017) *When Merely Existing Is a Risk: Sexual and Gender Minorities in Conflict, Displacement and Peacebuilding*, London: International Alert.

Nagle, J. and Fakhoury, T. (2018) 'Between co-option and radical opposition: a comparative analysis of the consequences of liberal and corporate power-sharing on gender and LGBT movements in Northern Ireland and Lebanon', *Nationalism and Ethnic Politics*, 18(1): 82–99.

Otto, D. (2007) '"Taking a break" from "normal": thinking queer in the context of international law', *Proceedings of the Annual Meeting (American Society of International Law)*, 101: 119–22.

OutRight Action (2014) *When Coming Out Is a Death Sentence: Persecution of LGBT Iraqis*, New York: OutRight Action.

Peterson, V.S. (1999) 'Sexing political identities/nationalism as heterosexism', *International Journal of Feminist Politics*, 1: 34–65.

Picq, M.L. and Thiel, M. (eds) (2015) 'Introduction: sexualities in world politics', in *Sexualities in World Politics: How LGBTQ Claims Shape International Relations*, London: Routledge, pp 1–22.

Prada, N. (2015) 'Aniquilar La Diferencia. Lesbianas, Gays, Bisexuales y Transgeneristas En El Marco Del Conflicto Armado Colombiano', Bogotá: Centro Nacional de Memoria Histórica.

Prada, N. (2019) 'Ser Marica En Medio Del Conflicto Armado. Memorias de Sectores LGBT En El Magdalena Medio', Bogotá: Centro Nacional de Memoria Histórica.

Puar, J.K. (2007) *Terrorist Assemblages: Homonationalism in Queer Times*, Durham, NC: Duke University Press.

Ritholtz, S. (2022). *Civil War & the Politics of Difference: Paramilitary Violence Against LGBT People in Colombia* (Ph. D. Dissertation, University of Oxford).

Ritholtz, S. (2023) 'Is queer-and-trans youth homelessness a form of displacement? A queer epistemological review of refugee studies' theoretical borders', *Ethnic and Racial Studies*, 46(9): 1854–76.

Ritholtz, S. and Buxton, R. (2023) 'Sanctuary after asylum: addressing a gap in the political theory of refuge', *American Political Science Review*, 117(3): 1166–71.

Ritholtz, S. and Stallone, K. (2022) '"It gives me joy": the LGBT Colombians embracing visibility in town with a legacy of abuse', *The Guardian*, 4 February 2022, sec. World | South America.

Serrano-Amaya, J.F. (2017) *Homophobic Violence in Armed Conflict and Political Transition*, Springer.

Shepherd, L.J. (ed.) (2013) Critical Approaches to Security: An Introduction to Theories and Methods, London: Routledge.

Shepherd, L.J. and Sjoberg, L. (2012) 'Trans-bodies in/of war(s): cisprivilege and contemporary security strategy', *Feminist Review*, 101(1): 5–23.

Sjoberg, L. and Weber, C. (eds) (2014) 'The forum: queer international relations', *International Studies Review*, 16(4): 596–622.

Slootmaeckers, K. (2019) 'Nationalism as competing masculinities: homophobia as a technology of othering for hetero- and homonationalism', *Theory and Society*, 48(2): 239–65.

Stryker, S. (2008) 'Transgender history, homonormativity, and disciplinarity', *Radical History Review*, (100): 145–57.

Tickner, J.A. (1997) 'You just don't understand: troubled engagements between feminists and IR theorists', *International Studies Quarterly*, 41(4): 611–32.

Tschantret, J. (2018) 'Cleansing the caliphate: insurgent violence against sexual minorities', *International Studies Quarterly*, 62(2): 260–73.

Tschantret, J. (2020) 'Revolutionary homophobia: explaining state repression against sexual minorities', *British Journal of Political Science*, 50(4): 1459–80.

Väyrynen, T., Parashar, S., Féron, E., and Confortini, C.C. (eds) (2021) *Routledge Handbook of Feminist Peace Research*, New York: Routledge.

Waites, M. (2009) 'Critique of "sexual orientation" and "gender identity" in human rights discourse: global queer politics beyond the Yogyakarta Principles', *Contemporary Politics*, 15(1): 137–56.

Weber, C. (2016) *Queer International Relations*, Oxford: Oxford University Press.

Wibben, A.T.R. (2011) *Feminist Security Studies: A Narrative Approach*, New York: Routledge.

Wilkinson, C. and Langlois, A.J. (2014) 'Special issue: not such an international human rights norm? Local resistance to lesbian, gay, bisexual, and transgender rights—preliminary comments', *Journal of Human Rights*, 13(3): 249–55.

PART I

Queer Approaches to Conflict Research

1

The 'Queer' in Conflict Research as Subject, Structure, and Method: Initial Epistemological Considerations for the Early Career Researcher

Samuel Ritholtz

Introduction

This chapter, a proposed 'starter guide' for early career researchers interested in queer conflict research, investigates the tensions between discipline, epistemology, and method as it relates to studies at the intersection of queer (and trans) studies and political violence. It proposes an expansive queer epistemological approach that recognizes the layered knowledge regimes impacting the lives of queer and trans people, running the gambit of positivism to postmodernism. In doing so, it reinforces Matt Brim's (2020) assertion: 'the project of queer theory is to explore and respond to the universe of queer need, including the need to reimagine the universe of queer need'.

I begin this chapter with my own personal story of pursuing queer conflict research as a graduate student at the University of Oxford. I then explore different epistemological approaches to queer conflict research. From there, I introduce the concept of queer epistemology through a genealogical consideration of an intellectual predecessor, feminist standpoint theory. I conclude the chapter with suggestions of how to operationalize queer epistemology in queer conflict research through three possible frames for research design: 'queer as a subject', 'queer as a structure', and 'queer as a method'.

Pursuing queer conflict research in the academy

In 2017, as a first-year graduate student, when I told people of my interest in working on queer and trans themes of conflict, I was instructed to go and read Foucault. I loved reading Foucault, questioning core structures of society that perpetuate power, and recognizing knowledge as one of these structures, registered with me (see, for example, Foucault, 1990, 1995, 2003, 2007). As a queer person, I felt the impact of these regimes of knowledge in my everyday life and thus reading Foucault's analysis felt like an academic intervention into my personal world. But, as a scholar, I wasn't sure that a Foucauldian approach suited my own desired approach to social science research. I saw the value in using deconstruction and basing myself in a humanist (or postmodern) epistemology to answer the questions I had regarding my research, namely: why is it that armed actors target people with non-hegemonic sexual orientations and gender identities during conflict? And I further recognized the list of scholars who had effectively taken on such challenges (for example, Rao, 2010, 2020; Wilcox, 2015; Weber, 2016). But despite my love for theory, I found myself drawn to a different literature in conflict research, one more closely tied to the epistemologies of interpretivism and postpositivism. To explore my research question from this epistemic position, I had few places to turn: the scholars of political violence at my university did not focus on queer and trans lives, and those engaging in 'queer studies' based themselves predominantly in the humanities. In dialogue with peers at other universities, I learned that I was not alone in this dynamic. The unfortunate reality is that despite the great interest among students in queer and trans topics in the study of politics, there are few scholars in university faculties who study these themes, particularly at research universities that provide relevant graduate study. I present this chapter, thus, as a first stop for those wishing to engage in research relating to LGBTIQ people in highly violent contexts. It is 'what I wish I had known' when I first started my graduate work and an opening survey of possible epistemological pathways on queer conflict research.[1]

My inspiration to undertake queer conflict research came from my experiences in the academy and outside of it. Before starting graduate school, I spent years working on international human rights issues with the United Nations, the Organization of American States, and various non-governmental organizations. It was during this time as a policy wonk that I realized how research can inform policy, change perspectives, and inspire action.[2] Without strong, cogent research to document the lives of LGBTIQ people in highly violent contexts, the topic stayed by the wayside. In this advocacy space, I saw incredible non-governmental organizations arguing forcefully for the inclusion of LGBTIQ populations in peace and security discussions at the international level.³ These organizations grounded their advocacy in research that revealed the stakes of exclusion. I admired their approaches and sought to return to the academy to develop my own research skills.

Upon my return to graduate studies, I quickly fell in love with academia. I relished taking the time and space to ask difficult questions and to think deeply about a given subject. As I designed my dissertation on anti-LGBTIQ violence during the Colombian Civil War, I was inspired by two related camps of scholars: the incredible work of scholars challenging conflict studies' silence on sexual violence in conflict, including Dara Kay Cohen (2016), Jelke Boesten (2014), and Elisabeth J. Wood (2006); and critical theorists laying bare the epistemic impacts of ignoring identity in knowledge production, including Gayatri Spivak (1985), Iris Marion Young (2011), Patricia Hill Collins (2003), and Sandra Harding (1987). Upon first review, these two camps of scholars seem quite disparate, one associated with feminist and postpositivist approaches to conflict studies and the other with critical epistemologies. But upon closer inspection, it was evident that the latter group's observations and contentions were vital in framing the work of the former group. As such, it was in connecting the work of 'theorists' with 'empiricists' that I realized the analytical potential in centring epistemology (particularly one that is critical or queer) in one's research, no matter one's approach.

Early career researchers interested in this topic must recognize the reality of the field and that certain approaches are privileged over others. Happily, things are changing and there is certainly a broader openness to queer and trans topics in *mainstream* political science,⁴ but this openness is often reliant on the use of dominant epistemological approaches related to arguments of causality based on a positivist epistemic tradition (more on this later). As Phillip Ayoub (2022: 2) documents: 'While we have seen substantial gains over the last two decades, many LGBTIQ scholars and their scholarship still face individual-level and structural discrimination in political science, encompassing active and passive homophobia and transphobia in teaching, getting hired and promoted, gaining access to research funding, and publications.' As such, though times are changing and a new generation of scholarship is legitimizing the study of queer and trans lives in *mainstream* political science, young scholars (and their faculty supervisors) must be aware of the broader academic landscape in which they are connected. Furthermore, given that change is piecemeal and university departments are quite autonomous, it is important not only to know where allies occur within different universities but also the range of positions that universities, and journals, take on the issue. Writing ten years ago, but still prescient today, Marla Brettschneider (2011: 25) observes, 'work in GLBT studies and queer theory is often seen as special interest political science at best and not political science at worst'.[5] In short, queer conflict research is not a 'neutral' endeavour.

My own journey as a graduate student reflects many of the dilemmas faced by early career researchers interested in broader political questions related to queer and trans lives in violent contexts. In doing my doctorate at the University of Oxford, I found myself in a largely supportive but very decentralized environment, which meant that it was up to me to find the support I needed. In 'designing my committee', which at Oxford involves finding one or two supervisors to supervise your doctorate, before building out a broader examination committee, I was met with a range of responses to my desired research. When I first started reaching out to faculty, I was told by a senior professor in *mainstream* political science that my desire to study violence against LGBTIQ people during the civil war was not really politics, but perhaps more appropriate for sociology or gender studies.[6] When I approached a queer scholar in another discipline, I was informed that they did not have the capacity to take on queer studies topics outside of their discipline and was reminded that 'one doesn't have to study queer topics to supervise queer research in politics'. I eventually found two supervisors who knew little of queer politics but were willing to learn and knew what good research looked like.[7] And then, slowly but surely, over the course of my PhD, I built a broader community of supportive conflict scholars with little knowledge of queer studies but who were open to such interventions.

This dynamic had its pluses and minuses: still, it is one opportunity for entry that I would recommend for scholars trying to get through the door. In some ways, it was a difficult arrangement because it meant that I was on my own when it came to learning the existing LGBTIQ scholarship and framing my approach. Graduate school, particularly a PhD, in general, is a difficult solo journey, but that difficulty can be exacerbated when one is exploring new terrain with limited mentorship (Majic and Strolovitch, 2020). In line with other scholars' experiences, I had to look beyond my own university to connect with experts on this topic to help mentor me. But on the plus side, my two supervisors served as a first test in my attempt to frame the study of queer and trans lives in conflict studies towards a more traditional political science audience. Among my committee members, I knew I had a sympathetic audience, which provided a safe environment for me to develop my research, but they were also productively suspicious: was I introducing something new? Was it already being captured by more humanist (or postmodern) studies of conflict? Could they understand my points? My approach?

In crafting intelligible work that defended my points and provided something new, I learned an invaluable lesson in positioning my research for the various 'appropriate' audiences. I also stumbled upon an ontological tension in queer conflict research: whether queering a subject matter simply requires a renewed focus on those with non-hegemonic sexual orientations and gender identities or whether there is a certain epistemological approach required to redress the epistemic silence present in disciplines devoid of queer and trans subjectivities. For students and early career scholars of queer conflict research, this tension persists not only in how they design their research, but also in how they pitch their contributions to a given literature.

Epistemology in queer conflict research

Existing scholarship on queer conflict research shows that there is not one way to do research on queer and trans lives. As such, it is best to mitigate any assumptions of what queer research should look like by taking space to reflect on the epistemic foundation of one's research design in order to be intentional from the start. In this chapter, I apply Donatella Della Porta and Michael Keating's (2008) typology of epistemology to queer conflict research in order to make a claim of pluralism in queer research. I recognize this claim can be contentious given that, in the wake of an unequal and impartial academy, people have strong feelings about what constitutes queer research and often associate it with a particular approach (normally those of interpretive or humanistic epistemologies). In the interest of identifying a wider world of opportunities for early career researchers, I choose not to gatekeep the concept and will let the reader decide what queer means to them. To me, in this chapter, queer conflict research is the study of violent contentious politics as it relates to people of non-hegemonic sexual orientations, gender identities, and sex characteristics.

Many of these epistemological considerations occur at the start of one's graduate-level education, where moments of imposter syndrome-induced, confused head nodding reveal the tacit socialization processes that might push a graduate student towards one epistemological position over another. Unless one is of the 'lucky' few who attends a university that requires instruction in the philosophy of knowledge at the start of the PhD, one might confront a series of situations where jargon is used without introduction. As just one of many personal examples, at the welcome drinks for my master's programme, a faculty member and I had an entire conversation about the dominance of *positivism* in political science, which I understood at the time as the dominance of *positivity* in political science. While I initially left that conversation encouraged that I was entering a field defined by its cheerfulness (reader, I was not), I later realized I was mistaken and victim to this 'hidden curriculum' of epistemology in graduate studies. In this section, I introduce different epistemological approaches to queer conflict research as well as some common terms inherent to the research process.

Three concepts are core to the research process: ontology (the study of being), epistemology (the study of knowledge production), and methodology (the study of research methods). In comparing approaches to social research, Piergiorgio Corbetta (2003: 12–13) refers to these three concepts as the research design's ontological base, epistemological base, and methodological base. The ontological base of a research design is the 'what' being studied. Ontological concerns of research relate to understanding how the subject exists in the world and are thus able to be studied. The epistemological base of a research design relates to the ability to know the subject through the research process. Epistemological concerns thus relate to core questions of the feasibility of producing knowledge on the subject of inquiry. And the methodological base relates to the approaches undertaken in an attempt to know this world. Methodological concerns then relate to the methods undertaken in the study of the subject.

To connect these concepts a bit further, ontology establishes the worldview of the researcher: how things are and can thus be studied.[8] Epistemology then connects these ontological considerations of the world to an approach to knowledge production. One's methodological approach, then, reflects both the ontological and epistemological world in which it is situated. If one thinks that truth can be proven, then one will design research with the goal of proving this truth. If one thinks truth is contextual, then one will design research that outlines and explores the subjective processes that produce this 'truth'. Generally, research designs in social science are often described by two other key terms of the 'hidden curriculum': deductive and inductive research. Deductive research is research that starts with an argument (or hypothesis) that is then defended or *proven* through a research design, often referred to as 'theory-testing'. Inductive research is research that starts with a question that is then explored through a research design that builds to an argument, often referred to as 'theory-building'.[9] While research designs of both types appear in many different epistemological contexts, these two approaches to research are often shorthand for the dominant framings of epistemology in conflict studies—one is either testing theory or building it. Incorrectly, this shorthand is often connected with other binaries, such as deductive reasoning is to quantitative methods as inductive reasoning is to qualitative methods.

These binaries, however, are not necessarily accurate. Plenty of deductive reasoning occurs in qualitative reason and the reverse is true in quantitative research. But these associations introduce conversations on epistemology, which is best articulated by Della Porta and Keating (2008: 23), who identify epistemology as 'the study of the limits of knowledge'. In this framing, epistemology becomes a consideration of what types of knowledge can be produced through this approach and how? From this perspective, Della Porta and Keating introduce four epistemologies present in broader social science: positivist, postpositivist (critical realist), interpretivist, and humanistic (postmodern). These framings fit as a general introduction to different approaches within queer conflict research. These epistemologies are important to understand as they are the foundations of social science research and still serve as organizing principles within departments. Regrettably, these different approaches are neither equal nor neutral with certain approaches being privileged and prioritized over others by many universities with political science departments committed to more *mainstream* approaches. Still, I have found it useful to consider these different approaches in order to better understand the varied options to approach different questions, particularly for early career researchers.[10]

Positivism is an epistemological approach to social science that derives from the 'hard' sciences. Positivists view political phenomena as objective and, thus, knowledge can be captured with the right research design that centres the identification of important (or instrumental) variables to explain the outcome of interest (or dependent variable). As such, positivism relies on identifying causal relationships to explain outcomes, often through quantitative methods.

- Joshua Tschantret is one scholar who uses positivist approaches in queer conflict research. In his piece, 'Cleansing the caliphate: insurgent violence against sexual minorities', Tschantret asks why insurgents target certain groups for extermination. To answer, he identifies three causal mechanisms that are presented as hypotheses. He (2018: 263) then tests these hypotheses using quantitative data 'on violence against sexual minorities by every nonstate actor in the Uppsala Conflict Data Program (UCDP)'. Tschantret then process traces these dynamics of violence by non-state actors in Syria and Iraq to further reveal the causal mechanisms identified by statistical analysis. His focus on causal inference through statistical analysis, as well as his overall deductive (or hypothesis-testing) approach, positions his work within positivism.

Postpositivism, also called critical realism, is similar to positivism in that it believes social phenomena can be captured with the right research design, but to an extent. Postpositivists recognize a certain level of subjectivity in research which impacts the kinds of questions that can be asked and, further, how these questions may be answered. Postpositivists may still use causal inference through quantitative approaches, but they might also pursue causal argumentation through qualitative approaches. Postpositivists often work with mixed-methods research designs, where quantitative approaches are paired with qualitative approaches in recognition of such complexities in research. Postpositivists recognize the social processes that impact knowledge production (in a manner akin to constructivism in international relations), thus weighing heavily the context of research as well as case-study approaches.

- Phillip Ayoub's book *When States Come Out: Europe's Sexual Minorities and the Politics of Visibility* (2016) represents a postpositivist approach to the study of queer contentious politics. In this book, Ayoub sets out to explain the evolution of LGBTIQ rights in Europe and the role of both domestic and transnational politics. He uses a mixed-methods approach that puts into dialogue standard texts from social movements and constructivist international relations literature with other texts from queer studies that relate to this topic but were not common in these literatures. The quantitative section of the research design utilizes statistical analysis developed after extensive qualitative analysis based on interviews, archival materials, and years of fieldwork with the movements he studied. Recognizing the limitations of statistical analysis (or pure quantitative approaches) and thus pairing it with more qualitative approaches is a key aspect of postpositivist epistemologies.

Interpretivism considers reality as both objective and subjective in the sense that one's understanding of a given social or political phenomenon is going to be based on the local context where the phenomena occur, as well as the researcher's own subjectivity (again perhaps a more extreme version of constructivism in international relations). As such, interpretivist scholars do attempt to explain reality but in a way that is grounded in contextual and subjective knowledge.

- An exemplary scholar of interpretive queer conflict research is Cai Wilkinson, whose work on post-soviet states often relies on the recognition that knowledge is contextually situated and produced. In their work 'Putting "traditional values" into practice: the rise and contestation of anti-homopropaganda laws in Russia', Wilkinson considers the weaponization of 'traditional values' towards anti-'homopropaganda' laws in Russia and their argument relies on recognizing the cultural uniqueness of the context (2014). To explore this phenomenon, Wilkinson explores the history and specific discourse that utilized established Russian ideals against queer and trans lives. This approach recognizes its knowledge as subjective and, thus, contextual.

Humanistic approaches, often called postmodern, focus on the subjectivity of knowledge, recognizing that one's understanding of the world is based on a series of meanings that were constructed through both social and political practice. These approaches deny the possibility of understanding an objective knowable reality and instead focus on what regimes of knowledge are produced through subjective processes.

- A formative text on humanistic approaches to queer conflict research is Cynthia Weber's *Queer International Relations* (2016). In this fundamental

work, Weber queers the study of international relations by theorizing why concepts of sexuality and queerness become dismissed from questions of both international politics and international theory. Weber builds on the critical work in global queer studies, such as Jasbir Puar's *Terrorist Assemblages* (2018), to deconstruct core concepts in the field of international relations to demonstrate how questions of gender and sexuality are actually at the core of international relations. In doing so, she reveals how queer studies have already impacted the field of international relations through many post-structural and constructivist ideals.
- Another classic scholar of humanist approaches to queer conflict research is Rahul Rao (2010, 2020), whose work has combined both queer and postcolonial studies to destabilize core ideals in international relations.

Queer epistemology and its intellectual antecedents

To develop the case for what I call a queer epistemology of conflict studies, I present a genealogy of the concept that links it with an intellectual antecedent: feminist standpoint theory.[11] I then consider questions of anti-LGBTIQ violence and injustice in the episteme and finally present a queer approach to the study of knowledge.

Queer epistemology can be understood as part of what Liz Stanley and Sue Wise (1990: 26) call critical epistemology or the 'theory of knowledge which addresses central questions such as: who can be the "knower", what can be known, what constitutes and validates knowledge, and what the relationship is or should be between knowing and being'. Critical approaches to epistemology highlight a normative question within existing theories of knowledge. As such, a queer epistemology of conflict research has the capacity to explore cisheteronormative biases within the discipline from any of the four previously identified epistemic positions. This approach follows in the footsteps of scholars who found that their lived experiences were not reflected in modern thought and thus argued that a wrong was committed against them in their silencing. Gayatri Spivak (1985) labelled this silencing as 'epistemic violence', which recognized the harm in having their own experience denied in the production of knowledge. Kristie Dotson (2011) has identified two pervasive forms of epistemic violence: denying voice to the person as a knower (testimonial quieting) and perceiving an immediate unwillingness or inability to accept the testimony of another (testimonial smothering). This silencing has been labelled 'epistemic injustice' by Miranda Fricker (2007), who argues that by limiting how knowledge is produced, harm is compounded through the continued obviation and silencing of a given community.

To develop queer epistemologies in conflict studies and thus produce queer conflict research, scholars can build on these interventions of feminist standpoint theory. Standpoint theory comes from feminist scholars in the late 20th century who were unsatisfied with the totalizing materialism of historical Marxism (Young, 1980), but still recognized the harm in the accepted neutrality in science, famously referred to as the 'view from nowhere' by Thomas Nagel (1989). These scholars, later known as feminist epistemologists and standpoint theorists, began to question the role of situated knowledge in all disciplines. They 'contended that methods themselves had no inherent epistemological or ontological qualities; rather how they are deployed in the pursuit of certain forms of knowledge produced data that supported feminist ways of knowing, and contested masculinist forms of knowledges' (Browne and Nash, 2016: 11). Sandra Harding (1986: 24), one of the leading scholars of this movement, argued 'that sexism and androcentrism are social biases correctable by stricter adherence to the existing methodological norms of scientific inquiry'. As such, according to Harding, even the most rigorous sciences were not free from bias. To redress this partiality, an epistemological approach had to be developed that took into account 'subjugated' perspectives so as to develop more inclusive methods and methodologies (Harding, 1986; Haraway, 1988). According to Harding, the benefit of research that begins with a consideration of the marginalized is that it can produce new insights into social reality freed from privileged biases (Harding, 1991; Hammers and Brown III, 2004). And notably, this did not require a particular approach to knowledge.

These scholars ultimately produced a new approach known as 'feminist standpoint theory'. Taking an approach from Marxism, which acknowledged the impact of one's perspective or knowledge based on a situated class position, Nancy Hartsock argued for an approach to knowledge from the position of the woman. As explained by Hartsock, 'Women's lives make available a particular and privileged vantage point on male supremacy' (1983: 284). In other words, by exploring a subject through the lens of 'women', one can better see how social structures produce differential impacts on the basis of gender. In this approach, power is understood to be relational, contextual, and situated by actors in social structures (Haraway, 1988; Young, 2011). While this approach was productive in highlighting the unacknowledged impacts of social structures on women, it risked essentializing both the category of women and their experiences to the perspectives of middle- and upper-class white women (Spivak, 1985; Mohanty, 1991; Young, 1994). As such, scholars built on this foundational work as well as the earlier work of Black feminist scholars (Lorde, 1980) to develop an 'intersectional' approach that incorporated broader concepts of gender, sexuality, race, ethnicity, class, and colonial legacy (Crenshaw, 1991; Collins, 2003).

A queer epistemological approach to conflict research can adapt this intersectional approach to recognize how sexuality and gender, as organizing principles of society that preserve hegemonic orders, among other exclusionary social structures, impact the research process as it relates to the study of conflict (Hammers and Brown III, 2004).[12] This approach has the potential to challenge cisheteronormative forms of knowledge by revealing how these assumptions fail to accurately consider the range of queer and trans experience during conflict (Boellstorff, 2010). It can be applied to the range of epistemic traditions outlined in the previous section. As Corie Hammers and Alan Brown III (2004: 95) note: 'Just as feminist researchers have addressed and made us aware of both the androcentric and Eurocentric bias within the research process, so too have queer researchers highlighted for us the heterocentric bias within research.' Interrogations of queer epistemology must balance the question of whether it is enough to produce new knowledge on queer subjects or if the very pursuit of this knowledge must be queer and reflexive, while also challenging heteronormative forms of knowledge (Boellstorff, 2010). For guidance on where to begin with such an approach, much of the work of queer theorists is relevant to scholars of conflict studies. Kath Browne and Catherine Nash (2016: 5) note that 'queer theory challenges the normative social ordering of identities and subjectivities along the heterosexual/homosexual binary as well as the privileging of heterosexuality as "natural" and homosexuality as its deviant and abhorrent "other"'. Queer theorists work with and build on the efforts of scholars of feminist studies to argue that sexuality and gender are organizing principles of society that preserve hegemonic orders and deserve to be interrogated (Wittig, 1989; Sullivan, 2003; Sedgwick, 2008). Influenced by Michel Foucault's (1990) work on sexuality as a historically specific concept that became a source of power-knowledge that restructured society, queer epistemologists investigate the impact of the Foucauldian notions of subjectification and disciplinary power, meaning how the structure of society and its norms relating to sexuality and gender exert control over queer and trans people and how power is exercised through their disciplining.

In centring queer and trans perspectives in conflict studies, early career researchers should not feel a need to prove a bias. Indeed, this could be impossible. Instead, they can follow Rolin's (2009: 219) suggestion that applications of standpoint theory 'urge feminists to reflect on relations of power as a distinctive kind of obstacle to the production of scientific knowledge'. As such: 'The obstacle is not adequately conceptualised as a cognitive bias that a social scientist may be vulnerable to; it is more adequately conceptualised as a social phenomenon that is endemic in the world of power relations' (2009: 219). One way to frame this consideration is through case studies, which can highlight the analytical potential of the approach (Wylie, 2003). By considering the relationship between sexuality, gender, and hegemonic order, scholars conducting conflict research can utilize a queer epistemological approach not only to extend our understanding of queer and trans experiences of conflict but also to explore how norms pertaining to sexuality and gender might further impact cis and straight populations during conflict, thus complicating existing conceptualizations of the concept. How exactly scholars develop their queer epistemological approach, particularly relating to how they incorporate and present their 'standpoint', depends on both their epistemological tradition of choice as well as with whom they view their work to be in dialogue. 'The intended audience', here, serves as a key framing device in terms of the presentation of one's research.

A queer epistemology in political violence studies

Queer epistemology thus becomes a 'choose your own adventure' in designing research. This said, I outline three approaches through which early career researchers can consider developing a queer research design. These frames include '**queer as a subject**', '**queer as a structure**', and '**queer as a method**'. In deciding which frame to use, I suggest two questions for scholars interested in queer epistemological approaches to ask themselves. First, which approach best serves my research questions? Second, which approach speaks to my intended audience?

In **queer as a subject**, the researcher is focusing on queer and trans people (or themes) as their unit of analysis. In this approach, scholars can adopt a myriad of research designs that specifically study queer and trans subjects. By their very nature, these studies can cohere quite closely with an existing literature or methods of the discipline by incorporating a new demographic or social group into the debates of the field. Because of its similarity to many positivist and postpositivist approaches, this approach has the benefit of being familiar to scholars of the discipline that are not necessarily interested or educated on queer and trans topics (that is, *mainstream* political science).[13] But the risk of this approach is that it can essentialize queer and trans experience by treating it as similar to other minority groups without considering its difference appropriately. This manner of engagement risks shallow analysis, missing difficult-to-see dynamics that facilitate exclusion.

A way to avoid this risk of essentialization is to incorporate existing queer scholarship from other epistemological approaches into the concepts being deployed. Recent scholarship in the related field of sexual violence during conflict has done this masterfully in terms of incorporating more humanist feminist scholarship into postpositivist approaches. Elisabeth J. Wood (2006, 2009), Dara Kay Cohen (2016), Amelia Hoover Green (2018), Milli Lake (2022), and Sarah Parkinson (2023) all build on more interpretive and humanist approaches to gender in their (post)positivist approaches to the study of sexual violence.[14] These scholars cite humanist feminist work, present their arguments in a language that is familiar to their positivist peers in political violence studies, and then utilize these insights in order to build concepts and theories. In studies of queer contentious politics, Phillip Ayoub's work also reflects this approach, incorporating humanist queer thought into studies of social movements through a postpositivist research design.

My own dissertation followed this approach to a certain extent; I incorporated humanist studies of anti-LGBTIQ violence during conflict into my own interpretivist analysis of the violent targeting of LGBTIQ people during the Colombian Civil War (Ritholtz, 2022a). The intended audience for this research project was *mainstream* political violence scholars and, as such, I was cognizant that my framing needed to be intelligible to them. While effective in getting a broader public to listen, I have felt that this approach suffers what I call 'the minority burden' of consistently explaining seemingly basic concepts to people with a limited background or interest in the subject matter. The burden has been felt both emotionally and logistically: it can be exhausting to explain the same concepts on repeat or to be forced to justify one's research when others do not, but it can also be challenging to fit the requisite amount of explanation into a journal article that has an 8,000-word limit! Unless, of course, it is a journal open to appendices.

Further, using scholars from other disciplines opens one up to critiques that they are presenting their research to the wrong audience. With that said, this approach can also be exciting because new voices bring in new perspectives. A published piece of my dissertation on the concept of cruelty in conflict studies, though not necessarily on queer topics, utilized critical theorists and interpretive approaches to challenge existing analytical frames popular among positivists in the field (Ritholtz, 2022b). And though a grim subject, the response and conversations that I've had post-publication demonstrate to me that there is broad interest in such an approach.

This consideration of the audience highlights a difficult element of this approach: it can be very difficult to make different epistemologies speak to one another. Gabrielle Bardall et al (2020) have a very helpful way of operationalizing this frame in conflict research. In their piece 'How is political violence gendered?', these scholars cite the strengths and limitations that political violence studies and violence against women in politics studies have respectively. As the authors note: 'Political violence scholarship identifies the discrete attacks that fuel conflict, whereas scholarship on violence against women illuminates how violence maintains the gendered distribution of power throughout society. Each approach has advantages, but also blind spots' (2020: 922). Respectively, to bridge these fields, they suggest focusing on three elements in their analyses of gendered violence—motive, form, and impact. In breaking down these three elements, these scholars can provide more nuance in the dynamics of gendered violence and avoid the risk of oversimplification in these complex dynamics. This approach also allows for the inclusion of more interpretive approaches as both form and impact recognize that sometimes gendered violence doesn't have to be intentional to be worthy of inquiry.

The second approach, '**queer as a structure**', fits more easily with established queer epistemological approaches. In queer as a structure, scholars study how structures of sexuality and gender impact the subject of study. These structural approaches might look at structures of exclusion that facilitate bias or discrimination within a certain thematic area or even within a discipline (recognizing epistemology as a social structure of knowledge). 'Queer as a structure' projects could be of any discipline or epistemological approach but match well with interpretivist (or constructivist) work, where political phenomena can be tied to social structures of sexuality and gender. These projects can be rather flexible in audience as constructivism in international relations leaves open interpretive approaches to the discipline and more critical works regularly deconstruct the structures that facilitate political phenomenon. Though this approach of queer as a structure might find the largest audience, in seeking a middle ground, it risks being maligned by the two main audiences (*mainstream* political science and critical security studies). As such, it is paramount for young scholars to think carefully about with whom their work is in dialogue and to still frame their research in a way that is intelligible to their desired audience. The late scholar, Lee Ann Fujii (2021, 2009), utilized interpretivist approaches powerfully but presented them in a way that made 'traditional' political violence scholars pay attention, namely by detailing her rigorous fieldwork methodology as well as research design and using terminology already established in the literature. Lisa Wedeen's (2015) work on Syria and Yemen is another example of interpretivist work that incorporates much insight from humanist work in an engaging and cross-epistemic matter.

I used this approach of queer as a structure in an article that questioned cisheteronormative bias in the epistemology of refugee studies (which was originally my master's thesis) (Ritholtz, 2023). This approach was effective in pointing out the hypocrisy in a literature that considers itself to be inclusive by revealing the analytical impact of exclusion in core conceptions of the field. Furthermore, the approach is successful in speaking to a broad set of audiences because it pushes scholars of all backgrounds to think about ontological omissions in their own research. With that said, after the many rewrites required to turn my master's thesis into a journal article, I would say that this approach draws the most enthusiasm when the critique is productive, in that its contribution goes beyond identifying a problematic and builds to a new approach or conception in the literature.

The third approach, '**queer as a method**', is perhaps the most established queer epistemological approach in conflict studies. In 'queer as a method', scholars take a given subject and *queer* it. To queer something means to destabilize its orientation from a cisheterosexist gaze, thus fundamentally questioning some core assumptions of the subject. *Queering* something is a form of deconstruction that provides new forms of thinking on a given subject. Browne and Nash explain that to queer is to 'challenge the normative social ordering of identities and subjectivities along the heterosexual/ homosexual binary as well as the privileging of heterosexuality as "natural" and homosexuality as its deviant and abhorrent "other"' (2010: 5). Eve Kosofsky Sedgwick cites 'queering' as a deconstructive approach that identifies 'sites that are peculiarly densely charged with lasting potentials for powerful manipulation' (1990: 10). This approach is the most well-known form of queer epistemology and heralds the work of Foucault that began this piece.

Interestingly, queering something doesn't mean only focusing on queer and trans populations. Instead, it can show how destabilizing core assumptions actually have broader impacts. Current research on queering genocide studies demonstrates this point effectively (Waites, 2018). The benefit of this approach is that it is the standard in more critical approaches to conflict studies as well as critical security studies. As such, undertaking this approach will find a receptive community of queer scholars ready to engage.[15]

In my own experience, it also just feels good to deconstruct concepts taken for granted. As part of a broader book project on queer theory and refugee studies, my co-author Rebecca Buxton and I attempt to rearticulate core concepts in the discipline of refugee studies by centring the experiences and actions of LGBTIQ+ refugees. Rebecca and I have published two chapters of this monograph project (Ritholtz and Buxton, 2021, 2022), which have had positive responses in both academic and policy communities because of how it centres the lives of LGBTIQ+ in situations of forced displacement in concept generation, as opposed to applying existing concepts onto these populations. Laura Shepherd's book *Gender, Violence and Security* (2013) demonstrates the exciting potential of this approach when she deconstructs, through a discourse analysis, the layers of assumption and power in the Women, Peace, and Security agenda at the United Nations. Shepherd's work shows how this approach can have a real impact on policy discussions by revealing assumptions that undergird an entire policy arena.

The risk of this approach is that it may have limited engagement with *mainstream* political science, which can be dismissive of humanist approaches. But luckily, there are welcoming political science communities where early career scholars can find their people.[16] Further, as Rebecca and I experienced in our piece in the *American Political Science Review* (2023), queer deconstruction can be well received in *mainstream* political science journals when it clearly connects with broader debates in the literature of the field. While the current openness to LGBTIQ subjects in *mainstream* political science journals may be a temporary phenomenon, the growing salience of anti-LGBTIQ politics in far-right governance and coalition-building reinforces the importance of studying this phenomenon. While these disciplinary dynamics should not influence one's research approach too heavily, it is an important consideration for early career researchers when considering departments, journals, and associations.

Conclusion

In this chapter, I attempt a first introduction to queer and trans research in conflict studies in the form of a 'how to think about epistemology' guide. Excitingly, this is an area of research with lots of energy and innovation. Regrettably, it is also an area of research that has been maligned by many *mainstream* political science departments and journals because of histories of cisheterosexist exclusion. In recognition of this reality, the chapter began with a survey of epistemologies in queer conflict research, showcasing the range of epistemological approaches that exist on the subject matter. From there, it introduced the concept of queer epistemology to the reader, which is an approach to knowledge that focuses on redressing cisheterosexist bias in the production of knowledge, from a range of epistemological approaches. From there, I presented a few queer epistemological approaches in conflict studies, introducing three approaches, or frames, that might broadly relate to standard epistemologies of social science but are more appropriately tied to methodology or research design. These three frames—'queer as a subject', 'queer as a structure', and 'queer as a method'—provide early career researchers with a first way of thinking about how to design productive research in queer conflict studies.

While this chapter has been presented as a first guide in navigating the different epistemologies of queer conflict research, it has also revealed much of the politics of knowledge production present in conflict studies and political science. The production of knowledge on queer conflict research is by no means an apolitical process and this chapter has made it clear that what becomes prioritized or valued is a result of intersecting privileges and exclusions. The epistemic questions presented in this chapter directly relate to tensions in the ethical production of knowledge on queer and trans lives and reveal what is at stake in doing queer conflict research. Epistemology, beyond being the bedrock of any research, is inherently tied to the politics of queer and trans lives. What is studied is what becomes visible. As such, in the pursuit of inclusive forms of knowledge, there is inherently a pursuit of justice.

Notes

[1] The tone and inspiration of this piece come from Kristin Luker's brilliant book *Salsa Dancing in the Social Sciences* (2009), which as a young graduate student served as a foundation text in making me feel that my 'queer mess' approach to research had a place

2   in the academy. The goal is not to tell the reader how to do 'queer conflict research' but to explain my own understanding of the concept through an exploration of different epistemic approaches.

2   I would be remiss not to note how research and advocacy on these topics have also been used as a justification for violent intervention in other countries deemed 'barbaric' or 'backwards' as well as within countries in an effort to securitize and consolidate power (Amar, 2013; Puar, 2018). As such, any form of advocacy needs to recognize neocolonial dynamics and topographies of power present in the international system.

3   Some organizations doing this work include international organizations such as Outright International, International Alert, Human Rights Watch, Rainbow Railroad, and MADRE; regional organizations such as CEJIL and ILGA Europe; and national organizations such as Caribe Afirmativo and Colombia Diversa. On 12 March 2023, representatives of the NGOs Afghan LGBT Organization and Colombia Diversa, along with the UN Independent Expert on Social Orientation and Gender Identity, participated in an Arria Formula Meeting on LGBTIQ inclusion in peace and security topics at the UN Security Council (see, for example, www.securitycouncilreport.org/whatsinblue/2023/03/arria-formula-meeting-on-integrating-the-human-rights-of-lgbti-persons-into-the-work-of-the-security-council.php).

4   Recognizing this concept of '*mainstream* political science' as problematic and normative, I use it here to highlight that, like it or not, there is a dominant or hegemonic approach to political science (based on positivism and causal inference). It has a lot of political and financial power in the academy and, as a result, gatekeeping is widespread, preventing scholars from accessing opportunities, particularly early career scholars. I put 'mainstream' in italics in order to destabilize its construction as the 'centre' of the discipline. In Chapter 2, José Fernando Serrano-Amaya delves into these topics further to reflect on how existing hierarchies of knowledge production impact the incorporation into the academy of certain forms of knowledge, particularly that produced by activists or produced in the Global South.

5   This chapter does not make the case for why the study of queer and trans lives is a question of political science or conflict studies. Phillip Ayoub (2022), in a recent piece in the *European Journal of Politics and Gender*, makes a particularly strong case for the unique potential that queer and trans studies bring to the field of political science. Additionally, my chapter does not detail the current challenges for queer and trans scholarship in the field, but interested readers should review pieces by Phillip Ayoub (2022), Marla Brettschneider (2011), Julie Novkov and Scott Barley (2010), Nicola Smith and Donna Lee (2015), and Laura Sjoberg (2014).

6   Regrettably, such dynamics exist for other marginalized groups too, particularly those interested in studying gender, race, disability, and class from the vantage point of politics (outside of comparativists studying electoral politics, where identity is a huge focus). Additionally, one's own positionality has a huge impact on how they are treated in the academy. In my own experience at the University of Oxford, the paradoxical support and alienation were a reaction to my education, class, professional experience, and race (all privileged in the academy) in contrast to my gender-expansive presentation and sexual orientation (not so much).

7   'Good research' in this case meant that regardless of my epistemological positioning and subject of focus, they were focused on making sure my research and argument were cogent, clear, and novel.

8   Most researchers of political violence, queer or not, are not necessarily interested in metaphysical considerations of ontology, but instead in political ontology. Hay (2011) defines 'political ontology … [as what] relates to *political being*, to what *is* political, to what *exists politically*, and to the units that comprise political reality'.

9   There is also, of course, abductive research, which is research that incorporates both theory testing and building in its design.
10 For each epistemological approach, I cite authors who undertake this approach in their research based on my understanding of epistemology and their research design. Sometimes authors explicitly cite their epistemological perspective (that is, Cai Wilkinson regularly positions their research as interpretive). Other times the epistemological position of the scholar might not be explicitly stated, but the approach itself lends itself to a specific epistemological tradition (that is, deconstruction as a more humanistic or postmodern approach).
11 Feminist standpoint theory can be considered just one intellectual antecedent among many; indeed, some may frame feminist standpoint theory itself as a product of Marxist theory. Heather Love (2021) argues that social theory on deviancy and stigma were core intellectual antecedents to queer theory, which would be interesting to further consider in relation to queer conflict research.
12 Chapter 3 (this volume) by Jamie Hagen, on the successful practices and current challenges to include the experiences and perspectives of lesbian, bisexual, and queer women in conflict research, furthers this dialogue on important questions regarding the importance of incorporating both gender and sexuality into queer epistemology. In recounting a workshop in Bogotá with queer and trans peace activists, Hagen details how monolithic analyses of war, those that only focus on sexuality or gender, risk ignoring how these two social structures intersect to impact queer women's lives.
13 This perceived familiarity does not necessarily mean that there will not be challenges to publish this research, or have it taught in the classroom, as our current political climate has highlighted how easily prejudice can be operationalized and prejudiced in the academy.
14 While all of these scholars demonstrate this approach in their research, Sarah Parkinson (2023) expands upon this methodologic approach and its benefits in detail in her book, *Beyond the Lines: Social Networks and Palestinian Militant Organizations in Wartime Lebanon*. Similarly, Milli Lake (2022) expands upon this approach and its benefits in a recent article in the *mainstream* disciplinary journal, *American Political Science Review*.
15 Though there are certainly some barriers that persist, personal anecdotes to me have revealed challenges in finding a receptive audience interested in acknowledging queer of colour critiques in this space as well as overcoming the concerns of ethical review boards who question whether queer and trans researchers can study anti-LGBTIQ violence in a safe and ethical approach.
16 As a queer conflict researcher, I have found warm and accepting communities within the International Studies Association (whose current president is, at the time of writing, Laura Shepherd) and the American Political Science Association (particularly the fabulous Interpretive Methodologies and Methods Group).

Acknowledgements

I would like to thank my co-editors, anonymous reviewer, Phillip Ayoub, and Alyson Price for feedback on this piece.

Bibliography

Amar, P. (2013) *The Security Archipelago*, Durham, NC: Duke University Press.
Ayoub, P. (2016) *When States Come Out*, Cambridge: Cambridge University Press.

Ayoub, P.M. (2022) 'Not that niche: making room for the study of LGBTIQ people in political science', *European Journal of Politics and Gender*, 5(2): 154–72. DOI: 10.1332/251510821X16345581767345

Bardall, G., Bjarnegård, E. and Piscopo, J.M. (2020) 'How is political violence gendered? Disentangling motives, forms, and impacts', *Political Studies*, 68 (4): 916–35.

Boellstorff, T. (2010) 'Queer techne: two theses on methodology and queer studies', in K. Browne and C. Nash (eds) *Queer Methods and Methodologies: Intersecting Queer Theories and Social Science Research*, London: Routledge, pp 215–30.

Boesten, J. (2014) *Sexual Violence during War and Peace: Gender, Power, and Post-Conflict Justice in Peru*, New York: Palgrave Macmillan.

Brettschneider, M. (2011) 'Heterosexual political science', *PS: Political Science & Politics*, 44(1): 23–6.

Brim, M. (2020) 'The house that queer theory built', *The Baffler*, [online] 12 February. Available from: https://thebaffler.com/salvos/the-house-that-queer-theory-built-brim

Browne, K. and Nash, C. (2010) *Queer Methods and Methodologies: Intersecting Queer Theories and Social Science Research*, London: Routledge.

Browne, K. and Nash, C. (eds) (2016) *Queer Methods and Methodologies: Intersecting Queer Theories and Social Science Research*, Abingdon: Routledge.

Cohen, D.K. (2016) *Rape during Civil War*, Ithaca, NY: Cornell University Press.

Collins, P.H. (2003) 'Toward an Afrocentric feminist epistemology', in Y.S. Lincoln and N.K. Denzin (eds) *Turning Points in Qualitative Research: Tying Knots in a Handkerchief*, Lanham, MD: Rowman Altamira, pp 47–73.

Corbetta, P. (2003) *Social Research: Theory, Methods and Techniques*, New York: Sage Publications.

Crenshaw, K. (1991) 'Mapping the margins: identity politics, intersectionality, and violence against women', *Stanford Law Review*, 43(6): 1241–99.

Della Porta, D. and Keating, M.J. (2008) 'How many approaches in the social sciences? An epistemological introduction', in D. Della Porta and M.J. Keating (eds) *Approaches and Methodologies in the Social Sciences: A Pluralist Perspective*, Cambridge: Cambridge University Press, pp 19–39.

Dotson, K. (2011) 'Tracking epistemic violence, tracking practices of silencing', *Hypatia*, 26(2): 236–57. DOI: 10.1111/j.1527-2001.2011.01177.x

Foucault, M. (1990) *The History of Sexuality: Volume 1: An Introduction*. New York: Vintage Books.

Foucault, M. (1995) *Discipline and Punish: The Birth of the Prison*, 2nd Vintage Books ed, New York: Vintage Books.

Foucault, M. (2003) *Society Must Be Defended: Lectures at the Collège de France, 1975-6*. 1st Picador pbk ed. New York: Picador.

Foucault, M. (2007) *The Order of Things: An Archaeology of the Human Sciences*, repr. ed, Routledge classics, Routledge, London.

Fricker, M. (2007) *Epistemic Injustice: Power and the Ethics of Knowing*, Oxford: Oxford University Press.

Fujii, L.A. (2009) *Killing Neighbors: Webs of Violence in Rwanda*, Ithaca, NY: Cornell University Press.

Fujii, L.A. (2021) *Show Time: The Logic and Power of Violent Display*, Ithaca, NY: Cornell University Press.

Hammers, C. and Brown III, A.D. (2004). 'Towards a feminist–queer alliance: a paradigmatic shift in the research process', *Social Epistemology*, 18(1): 85–101. DOI: doi.org/10.1080/0269172042000249408

Haraway, D. (1988) 'Situated knowledges: the science question in feminism and the privilege of partial perspective', *Feminist Studies*, 14(3): 575. DOI: 10.2307/3178066

Harding, S. (1986) *The Science Question in Feminism*, Ithaca, NY: Cornell University Press.

Harding, S. (1987) 'Is there a feminist method?', in *Social Research Methods: A Reader*, Bloomington, IN: Indiana University Press, 456–64.

Harding, S. (1991) *Whose Science? Whose Knowledge?: Thinking from Women's Lives*, Ithaca, NY: Cornell University Press.

Hartsock, N. (1983) 'The feminist standpoint: developing the ground for a specifically feminist historical materialism', in S. Harding and M.B. Hintikka (eds) *Discovering Reality: Feminist Perspectives on Epistemology, Metaphysics, Methodology, and Philosophy of Science*, Dordrecht, Holland: D. Reidel, p 284.

Hay, C. (2011) 'Political Ontology', in *The Oxford Handbook of Contextual Political Analysis*, Oxford: Oxford University Press, pp 78–96.

Hoover Green, A. (2018) *The Commander's Dilemma: Violence and Restraint in Wartime*, Ithaca, NY: Cornell University Press.

Lake, M. (2022) 'Policing insecurity', *American Political Science Review*, 116(3): 858–74.

Lorde, A. (1980) 'Age, race, class, and sex: women redefining difference', in A. Lorde (ed.) *Women in Culture: An Intersectional Anthology for Gender and Women's Studies*, Hoboken, NJ: Wiley-Blackwell, pp 16–22.

Love, H. (2021) *Underdogs: Social Deviance and Queer Theory*, Chicago, IL: University of Chicago Press.

Luker, K. (2009) *Salsa Dancing into the Social Sciences*, Cambridge, MA: Harvard University Press.

Majic, S. and Strolovitch, D.Z. (2020) 'Editors' introduction: mentoring and marginalization', *PS: Political Science & Politics*, 53(4): 763–9.

Mohanty, C. (1991) 'Under Western eyes: feminist scholarship and colonial discourses', in A. Russo, L. Torres, and C. Mohanty (eds) *Third World Women and the Politics of Feminism*, Indianapolis, IN: Indiana University Press, p 53.

Nagel, T. (1989) *The View from Nowhere*, Oxford: Oxford University Press.

Novkov, J. and Barclay, S. (2010) 'Lesbians, gays, bisexuals, and the transgendered in political science: report on a discipline-wide survey', *PS: Political Science & Politics*, 43(1): 95–106.

Parkinson, S.E. (2023) *Beyond the Lines: Social Networks and Palestinian Militant Organizations in Wartime Lebanon*, Ithaca, NY: Cornell University Press.

Puar, J.K. (2018) *Terrorist Assemblages*, Durham, NC: Duke University Press.

Rao, R. (2010) *Third World Protest: Between Home and the World*, Oxford: Oxford University Press.

Rao, R. (2020) *Out of time: The Queer Politics of Postcoloniality*, Oxford: Oxford University Press.

Ritholtz, S. (2022a) *Civil War & the Politics of Difference: Paramilitary Violence Against LGBT People in Colombia* (Ph. D. Dissertation, University of Oxford).

Ritholtz, S. (2022b) 'The ontology of cruelty in civil war: the analytical utility of characterizing violence in conflict studies', *Global Studies Quarterly*, 2(2).

Ritholtz, S. (2023) 'Is queer-and-trans youth homelessness a form of displacement? A queer epistemological review of refugee studies' theoretical borders', *Ethnic and Racial Studies*, 46(9): 1854–76.

Ritholtz, S. and Buxton, R. (2021) 'Queer kinship and the rights of refugee families', *Migration Studies* 9(3): 1075–95. DOI: 10.1093/migration/mnab007

Ritholtz, S. and Buxton, R. (2023) 'Sanctuary after asylum: addressing a gap in the political theory of refuge', *American Political Science Review*, 117(3): 1166–71.

Rolin, K. (2009) 'Standpoint theory as a methodology for the study of power relations', *Hypatia*, 24(4): 218–26. DOI: 10.1111/j.1527-2001.2009.01070.x

Sedgwick, E.K. (1990) *Epistemology of the Closet*, Los Angeles, CA: University of California Press.

Sedgwick, E.K. (2008) *Epistemology of the Closet. ACLS Humanities E-Book (Series)*, Berkeley, CA: University of California Press.

Shepherd, L. (2013) *Gender, Violence and Security: Discourse as Practice*, London: Zed Books.

Sjoberg, L. (2014) 'Queering the "territorial peace"? Queer theory conversing with mainstream international relations', *International Studies Review*, 16(4): 608–12.

Smith, N.J. and Lee, D. (2015) 'What's queer about political science?', *British Journal of Politics and International Relations*, 17(1): 49–63.

Spivak, G.C. (1985) 'Can the subaltern speak? Speculations on widow sacrifice', *Wedge*, 7–8 (winter/spring): 120–30.

Stanley, L. and Wise, S. (1990) 'Method, methodology and epistemology in feminist research processes', in L. Stanley (ed.) *Feminist Praxis: Research, Theory and Epistemology in Feminist Sociology*, Abingdon: Routledge, pp 20–60.

Sullivan, N. (2003) *A Critical Introduction to Queer Theory*, New York: NYU Press.

Tschantret, J. (2018) 'Cleansing the caliphate: insurgent violence against sexual minorities', *International Studies Quarterly*. DOI: 10.1093/isq/sqx074

Waites, M. (2018) 'Genocide and global queer politics', *Journal of Genocide Research*, 20(1): 44–67.

Weber, C. (2016) *Queer International Relations: Sovereignty, Sexuality and the Will to Knowledge*, Oxford: Oxford University Press.

Wedeen, L. (2015) *Ambiguities of Domination: Politics, Rhetoric, and Symbols in Contemporary Syria*, Chicago, IL: University of Chicago Press.

Wilcox, L.B. (2015) *Bodies of Violence: Theorizing Embodied Subjects in International Relations*, Oxford: Oxford University Press.

Wilkinson, C. (2014) 'Putting "traditional values" into practice: the rise and contestation of anti-homopropaganda laws in Russia', *Journal of Human Rights*, 13(3): 363–79.

Wittig, M. (1989) 'On the social contract', *Feminist Issues*, 9(1): 3–12.

Wood, E.J. (2006) 'Variation in sexual violence during war', *Politics & Society*, 34(3): 307–42. DOI: 10.1177/0032329206290426

Wood, E.J. (2009) 'Armed groups and sexual violence: when is wartime rape rare?', *Politics & Society*, 37(1): 131–61. DOI: 10.1177/0032329208329755

Wylie, A. (2003) 'Why standpoint matters', in R. Figueroa and S. Harding (eds) *Science and Other Cultures: Issues in Philosophies of Science and Technology*, New York: Routledge, pp 26–48.

Young, I.M. (1980) 'Socialist feminism and the limits of dual systems theory', *Socialist Review Oakland*, 10(2–3): 169–88.

Young, I.M. (1994) 'Gender as seriality: thinking about women as a social collective', *Signs: Journal of Women in Culture and Society*, 19(3): 713–38.

Young, I.M. (2011) *Justice and the Politics of Difference*, New York: Princeton University Press.

2

Queering the Politics of Knowledge in Conflict Research

José Fernando Serrano-Amaya

Introduction

Dealing with ethical and political dilemmas is at the core of conflict research. Long-term discussions about these dilemmas include scholarship about the rightfulness of interventions in global geopolitics (Trim and Simms, 2011), the challenges of conducting research on conflict areas (Nordstrom and Robben, 1995), and the impact of the risk of harm in peace and conflict practice (Anderson, 1999). Discussing the ethical and political implications of knowledge production is also necessary when exploring queer research practices in the broader context of conflict research. In specialized areas such as Conflict Resolution Studies, a core idea is the production of knowledge for analytical and normative purposes (Miall, Ramsbotham, and Woodhouse, 2003).

As much as it is important to produce knowledge useful to illustrate practice, the normative side of Conflict Resolution Studies raises concerns from a queer perspective (Warner, 1999). Suspicion arises from the logics of normality within conflict resolution theory and practice, which originated from dichotomist and categorical thinking intended to make clear divisions between peace and war. While these divisions are useful for directing practice, they become problematic in terms of the logic of linear paths that support them. The return to a 'normal' form of governance is implicit, even in more critical ideas and practices such as reparation, post-conflict reconstruction, or reconciliation. A queer epistemology is important to challenge regimes of normality implicit in conflict studies as well as the operationalization of analytical strategies and methods.[1]

The evolution of queer methods has led to the production of innovative knowledge and discussions on the limits of traditional methodologies in social sciences and humanities (Browne and Nash, 2010). As Cooper-Cunningham argues in this volume (Chapter 4), no method is 'innately' queer but methods can be used queerly to acknowledge violence without reducing (queer) people to victims, to make queer issues relevant in international relations and to call attention to the intersections between everyday and global politics. Such developments continue to have a limited presence in conflict research.

Building on these interventions and critiques, this chapter is an invitation to connect areas of knowledge and practice regarding queer conflict research that have been developed separately and are now converging. I make this connection discussing the politics of knowledge production in conflict research from a queer perspective. Such perspective comes from a focus on the contribution of queer organizations and queer researchers in the development of the field and from the study of the experiences of LGBTIQ[2] individuals and collectives to transform conflicts. I argue that queering the politics of knowledge in conflict research requires focusing analysis on the interactions between academia and activism—where the convergence between knowledge and practice is taking place—and understanding these interactions as fluid, heterogeneous, and overlapping. This departs from normative (heterosexed) epistemologies that seek to construct and understand relations as being neat, homogeneous, and separated areas for thinking and practice. As such, the field of queer conflict research has produced a type of knowledge that challenges standard divisions between areas of expertise and offers a unique opportunity to explore other paths for the development of queer research practices.

To develop this argument, I start with a discussion on my own positionality and approach to the topic. I then discuss three different aspects of the politics of knowledge drawing on my work in Colombia as it relates to the study of violence imposed on LGBTIQ individuals and collectives. While the three aspects differ in their focus (hierarchies; representations; visibilities and speech), I discuss them in relation to how they operate, including for whom they operate, by whom, and for which purposes.

On positionality, method, and theoretical conversations

I have participated for more than two decades in the production of knowledge for academic and activist purposes. Some of my work was written as an attempt to 'make visible' gender and sexual diversity in peacebuilding (Serrano-Amaya, 2004) in a moment in which those issues had limited attention in the specialized literature. Indeed, in the early 2000s, there was little documentation of the participation of gender and sexually diverse collectives in peacebuilding. Other parts of my work were influenced by working with public institutions and non-governmental organizations on gender-based violence, LGBTIQ rights, and civil society participation in peacebuilding. Such experience gave me the opportunity to learn the language of institutions and see how activist struggles were translated into public policies. It also produced within me a certain exhaustion with narratives of suffering and the counting of violence. This made me, at the same time, reluctant to continue the path of 'working with the victims' and motivated me to explore activism as the mechanism to understand sexual orientation and gender identity in relation to armed conflicts and political transitions (Serrano-Amaya, 2014).

Some use the term 'activist scholarship' to describe my work. As such, I find it useful to reflect on my experience as a scholar since it explores the interconnections between academia, activism, and knowledge production. Some feminist perspectives consider activist scholarship as the knowledge and pedagogical practices that result from the engagements of academic institutions in social change and at the service of progressive social movements (Sudbury and Okazawa-Rey, 2015; Dean, Johnson, and Luhmann, 2018). In sociology of law debates, activist scholarship can produce interesting approaches but may be challenged on the basis of what political commitment(s) the scholar brings forward in their work (Lempert, 2001). In some debates, academia and activism are pictured as separate, with activist scholars urging academics to integrate while warning them to make this integration carefully.

As much as I connect with those debates common in the Global North academia, I want to stress the specificities of writing mostly from a place in the Global South as I do in my work in Colombia. Debates on the need to connect academia and activism sound a bit awkward in Latin America given the long traditions of integrating the two as detailed in perspectives such as *Investigación Acción Participativa* (Fals-Borda, 1991). Discussions in the past decades in US-based academia about the tension over being an insider or outsider in research (Naples, 1997) are less significant when life and research are enmeshed. The latter is the reality faced by many Global South scholars due to the proximity of their research with struggles for social change.

Finding ways to survive in a permanently precarious job market with shifting work positions also impacts research practice. Navigating sometimes separated fields and other times hybrid spaces is not just the result of a particular life experience but also a characteristic of structural conditions affecting academia and activism. In the Global North, particularly in academia in the US, academic discussions on gender and sexualities have followed a path of increasingly specialized and institutionalized area studies. What I experience has been an intense production of knowledge on issues of socio-political conflict and queerness outside academia, in more interlinked areas of discussion often led by committed activism. As has been argued by Black feminists (hooks, 2000), this activist knowledge is no less rigorous, valid, or theoretically important.

The increasing interest in gender and sexualities in conflict research is also located in a critical political context. In Colombia, for at least the last decade, there has been a legal and political interest in the documented cases of homophobic violence in the context of political conflict. This is due to the implementation of legal frameworks such as *Ley de Víctimas* (The Victims Law, LAW 1448, 2011), in which recognition as a 'victim' was extended to the partners in a same-sex relationship. This development was accomplished by an alliance between committed lawyers and policy makers, alongside activists demanding more specialized and technical knowledge about LGBTIQ people as legal subjects.

Queering the politics of knowledge calls attention to interactions between academia and activism with theoretical, political, and ethical implications. These implications are important for students and researchers, as well as activists and policy makers. Centring the relationship between academia and activism is not just about finding connections, as has been explored and demanded for some time from activists and committed academics. Although important, the tendency has been to mainly look at the issue from one position: connecting academia with activism (Datta, 2017), rather than viewing the relationship as bidirectional.

In interactions between activists and academia the attention is still focused on what academic scholarship activists read and talk about as a site of knowledge. In this contribution, I would instead like to move the discussion one step further to consider how in queer conflict research both academia and activism are producers of expert knowledge in intermingling ways. This argument is in dialogue with existing interventions that critique who gets to be a knowledge producer, in what context, and for which reasons. As I will illustrate in the chapter, such intermingling happens in contradictory and conflicting ways that question any assumption of homogeneity or purity inside activism as well as academia.

Hierarchies: legitimate and subordinate knowledges

Cultural studies scholar Catherine Walsh (2003) argues that the politics of knowledge is the practice of making certain knowledge relevant and recognized as proper knowledge, while other knowledge is put aside and devalued. The result is not only the inclusion of some ideas, theories, or methodologies in the canon of disciplines, while others are ignored or marginalized, but also the making of certain issues of relevance for academic research agendas. Such practices of knowledge make some topics relevant for social and political attention at specific moments, even if the problem existed before. For a queer approach to conflict research, then, it is important to discuss why violence against LGBTIQ individuals and collectives is sometimes rendered invisible while at other times is made a matter of importance.

There is a risk in characterizing knowledge on queer lives during conflict, in Colombia and beyond, as a novel phenomenon. It would be incorrect to assume that it has only been due to recent institutional (both local and international) interest that knowledge on this topic has been produced. The documentation of how armed conflict affects LGBTIQ individuals and collectives can be traced to decades prior, mostly by activists with an interest in raising awareness on the impact of violence but also to document their participation in peacebuilding. Why did such previous knowledge not reach a relevant status to foster the kind of interest that has developed more recently? This is the result of a hierarchy of knowledge in which, while current knowledge production uses mainly an expert language of rights, legal and conflict research concepts, previous knowledge used mostly language of experience, emotions, and descriptions of events that was not always systematically written or theorized but nevertheless of value.

The increasing interest in including queer issues in scholarship on transitional justice and peacebuilding in Colombia can be seen as an activist and academic reaction against the 'politics of not-knowing' (Nordstrom, 1999). For decades what was happening with LGBTIQ individuals and collectives in relation with armed conflict and political violence was explicitly ignored. Despite the existing knowledge in these areas, there was a lack of attention paid by state institutions and, at least partially, by academia and peacebuilding organizations. This ignorance, or the 'politics of not-knowing' was a choice, especially since information on these areas was produced by activists. The passage from 'not-knowing' to making queer research a discrete area of analysis and intervention is less a movement from scattered to accumulated information but rather the result of a politics of knowledge mediated by an expert discourse that combines activist expertise with legal and historic memory knowledge.[3]

The interest of documenting the experiences of LGBTIQ individuals and collectives in relation to armed conflict in Colombia can be explained as a consequence of four key developments:

(i) international attention on the inclusion of peacebuilding and victimization in the agendas of informal and formalized LGBTIQ organizations since early 2000s;
(ii) legal changes that opened spaces for including same-sex couples, sexual orientation, gender identity, and diversity in legal frames related to victims of armed conflict such as *Ley de Víctimas* (The Victims Law, LAW 1448, 2011);
(iii) the development of state infrastructures specialized on memory work such as *Centro Nacional de Memoria Histórica*—National Centre for Historic Memory (2011) and its equivalents at regional or local level;
(iv) the creation of a transitional justice system as a result of the Peace Agreement (2016) and related with issues of truth making, legal

prosecution, and reparation of victims in which gender and LGBTIQ topics were included. In this process, a specialized knowledge makes LGBTIQ people visible in the eyes of transitional justice and peacebuilding.[4]

When looking at the results of such long processes in terms of production of specialized knowledge, the international interest in queer research in the case of Colombia and the broader inclusion of queer issues in transitional justice and peacebuilding is understandable. In fact, most of such production has been possible due to the support of international cooperation agencies, embassies, and international allies, as can be seen on the websites cited previously. International support has been pivotal for the making of this field of expertise due to the lack of action by state institutions. Given this rising interest, there is a resulting increase in the number of students, universities, and non-governmental organizations from the Global North arriving to the country to pursue their degree studies and to develop research. Colombia has become the new laboratory for testing perspectives on the inclusion of gender and sexualities in conflict research, transitional justice, and peacebuilding in general for gender identity and sexual orientation in particular.

Growing interest has also raised concerns among local organizations on the problems already identified in the critiques to colonial research (Dei and Jaimungal, 2018; Conversation with Mosaic, Chapter 9). This includes the instrumentalization of testimonies and documentation of events for theory building in the Global North or the disparities in access to publication (Connell, 2007). While most of local research is produced in Spanish, what gets published in academic journals, and therefore receives attention by international scholars, is in English. Prominent Colombian organizations are often saturated because of the need to attend to the requirements of international visitors and developing strategies to deal with the constant call to 'speak with a victim' or interview 'the experts'. Such international researchers then extract knowledge for self-serving purposes with little positive local impact.

When looking at the landscape of knowledge production in Colombia, activists and organizations have created archives on their experiences with violence and armed conflict that fill a gap in documentation and theory building. This occurred years before recent publications on the topic that have now gained international recognition and status as legitimate knowledge.[5]

Interestingly, even if there has been information about LGBTIQ experiences published as human rights reports, this type of publication may not obtain the status of legitimate knowledge. This may be because of resistance from state institutions who seek to censor these organizations and their publications. In the case of Colombia, in 1996 Juan Pablo Ordoñez wrote a report connecting socio-political violence with extra-judicial killings against *homosexuales*. This was done in a time before the current language that established a separation between sexual orientation and gender identity or homogenized subjects under the problematic LGBTIQ acronym (Ordoñez, 1996). The report was written originally in English and had a prologue by Noam Chomsky, who denounced the participation of the US in 'dirty war' strategies and called the attention of international organizations on the violence against gays and lesbians in Colombia.

The writing of the report can be seen as an example of the 'boomerang strategy' used by human rights activists to raise awareness on local issues by local authorities demanding attention of international third parties (Allendoerfer, Murdie, and Welch, 2020). Building on sociologist Matthew Waites' call to decolonize the 'boomerang strategy' concept (2019) by emphasizing local agency and the navigation of local actors in Global North/South power relations, it is important to discuss why this report had limited impact in launching a research, activist, and policy agenda on victimization of LGBTIQ in relation to socio-political violence in Colombia. Ordoñez's report articulated 'sexual orientation', 'human rights', and 'social cleansing' to reveal a hidden and denied dimension of socio-political violence in the country. This process would not have been possible without the platform provided by the US-based organizations that not only financed the writing of the report but that also offered support to Ordoñez, who had to leave the country as a result of threats about his work.

Ordoñez remembered how the report received attention from Colombian diplomatic authorities abroad who were concerned with the reputation of the country but received little attention from local authorities.[6] Amid the diverse activism of the moment, there was no political and collective subject who could receive the results of throwing the boomerang. The 'LGBTIQ victim of armed conflict' as a particular subject for policy and activism did not yet exist. Interestingly, as described above, the focus on LGBTIQ subjects as agents for peacebuilding anticipated the later and current focus on LGBTIQ victimization.

Representations: the regimes that allow a subject to exist

Debates on the regimes of representation play a central role in audio-visual production determining how issues of poverty, violence, and subordination do/do not deserve inclusion in a debate on queer conflict research. There is a long tradition of critique on the uses of misery, poverty, and violence to produce representations of Latin American countries. In 1978, Colombian filmmakers Luis Ospina and Carlos Mayolo wrote the manifesto *Pornomiseria*—Misery Porn, to denounce the conversion of poverty or social suffering into commodities for mainstream viewers of film production.

They read their manifesto in Paris, for the launching of the movie *Agarrando Pueblo*, as an act of confrontation of Global North audiences attracted by Global South suffering. Even without having a particular status in academic production, the term has been a permanent point of reference in local discussions within Colombia about violence.

Violence in Colombia, as elsewhere, is a topic that is highly gendered and sexualized. Yet, debates on the regimes of representation have had limited impact or presence in these specialized areas of conflict research. Nowadays, there is an accumulated knowledge in the emerging area of Critical Conflict and Peace Studies on the need for a deeper engagement with key debates in feminist scholarship (McLeod and O'Reilly, 2019) and on the importance of challenging the Eurocentric matrix of knowledge/power still embedded in Peace Studies (Parada, 2020). These developments open space for discussions about how regimes of representation and knowledge production affect the increasing interest by researchers in sexual orientation, gender identities, and queer issues in conflict research.

The queering of conflict research has fluctuated between an interest of including women and gender and sexual diverse subjectivities in the narration or reconstruction of what happened during conflicts, and the challenging of the assumptions underlying key concepts and practice in the area. The first interest is a direct reaction to a history of denial of how conflicts have a gendered and sexual order that distributes suffering disproportionately on those affected by patriarchy and hetero/cissexism. The second is a critique on how those hierarchies are embedded in the constitution of the fields of knowledge and expertise.

Considering the experiences of those in the margins of gender and sexual orders during conflict raises specific methodological and ethical questions. One of these challenges is the lack of documentation or the problems with obtaining adequate data. Documentation by international human rights organizations of abuses against gender or sexual minorities was still rare in the early 1990s, as mentioned in reports that attempted to engage with appropriate information to produce systematic analyses (Laviolette and Whitworth, 1994; Rosenbloom and IGLHRC, 1996). This does not directly imply that there was no information, as I illustrated in the previous section, but that this information tends to be in informal documents, comes from disparate sources, and faces the problems of documenting issues of gender and sexuality that tend to be of less interest or explicitly ignored.

Documenting violence against gender and sexual minorities during active conflict means facing additional challenges. Albarracín (2011), in an article written when there was still limited attention on the topic, identified three obstacles in the documentation of anti-homosexual violence in Colombian armed conflict. The first obstacle was the effects of fear, shame, or security risks on victims that may cause them to deny the reasons for their victimization. The second obstacle is that since homophobic violence can be justified culturally and socially, homophobic reasons for violence can be hidden. The third obstacle he observes is that socio-cultural conditions can affect forms of homophobic violence and therefore their expression and management. Similar challenges have been identified by international humanitarian organizations working on other contexts, including researching violence against men during conflicts (ICRC, 2021).

Methodological challenges in the documentation of violence against LGBTIQ subjects during conflicts or in political transition periods is an area in need of more development, especially with the increasing interest by state institutions and international organizations in the topic. Still, as much as it is important to produce more detailed and in-depth information on the situations faced by LGBTIQ individuals during conflicts and in political transitions, it is important to first call attention on the regimes of representation that make queer subjects a relevant matter for documentation of human rights violations, for academic purposes and for the implementation of transitional justice instruments. These regimes of representation include, for example, reparative measures, memory work, and truth telling.

This discussion on the politics of knowledge requires a deeper consideration of how representations of LGBTIQ people in conflict are produced, for whom, and for which purposes. In particular when documenting the impact of armed conflict on LGBTIQ persons, LGBTIQ organizations and their participation in peacebuilding has been mainly a matter of interest from activists. Still, as mentioned above for the case of Colombia, a state response to activism has also led to the production of some knowledge on the topic resulting in a hybrid knowledge on queer issues during and after conflict. Such hybrid knowledge combines, in disparate ways, key elements of the identity politics that are the core of activism and state understandings of harm and justice, such as human rights frames and the state's own explanations of the roots of violence.

Organizing around a supposed collective identity (Bernstein, 2002) helps to create a sense of political action and articulate activism. Identity politics of this kind also define, restrict, and limit action to what creates a sense of collectivity. The iteration of violence related to gender identity or sexual orientation, for example, is important in situations of impunity or when issues of the status of victims are being discussed, as is characteristic during conflicts or after them and when instruments of transitional justice are implemented. These collective memories of violence, which often situate violence within a broader paradigm of discrimination, serve as a kind of foundational myth for collective organization.

There are two effects of this association between collective memories, identity politics, and violence: (i) it became the standard frame for narrating collective memories of violence; and (ii) it makes invisible the narratives of those who are not part of groups defined by identity politics. One example of these logics is the growing body of literature on violence against LGBTIQ people produced by Colombian activists under the concept of prejudice (Colombia Diversa, 2020). In this case, prejudice acts as the connector of the disparate identities of those covered under the LGBTIQ acronym and refers to a permanent and constitutive experience resulting from the negative perception by a perpetrator of violence.

The interest in including LGBTIQ perspectives in the narration of conflicts can operate under other regimes of representation not directly linked with identity politics imposed by institutional historical memory. An interesting example of this combination of dissimilar politics of representation can be seen in *Aniquilar la Diferencia. Lesbianas, gays, bisexuales y transgeneristas en el marco del conflicto armado colombiano* (CNMH, 2015).[7] The report is one of the most detailed and systematic accounts of the suffering imposed on LGBTIQ individuals and collectives during the Colombian armed conflict. I identify three forms of representation in the report: (i) the need to produce state historical memory; (ii) a victim-centred perspective; and (iii) the language of poststructuralist gender and sexuality theories. The three forms intersect to create a system of expertise on violence, gender, and sexuality that constitute lesbian, gay, bisexual, and transgender persons as legitimate subjects of memory and victimhood.

In relation to the first form of representation, the report was produced by *Centro Nacional de Memoria Histórica*, a public institution created for the purpose of documenting and researching the violence that occurred during the conflict and to respond to the duty of a state memory. The report was a state response to a long history of denial and intentional public ignorance on the violence faced by LGBTIQ people with high value as a research product and tool for activism. A long process of lobbying from LGBTIQ organizations and academics was behind the production and publication of the report, which was financed by international cooperation agencies and national institutions. With the report, the memorialization of violence against LGBTIQ persons and collectives was included in an extensive field of official accounts of the different repertoires of violence used by armed actors in their struggles for power.

The second form of representation is explicitly mentioned in the report in its attempt to tell the memories of victims to dignify them (CNMH, 2015: 20). Almost three parts of the 471 pages of the report are dedicated to describe and explain the diverse forms of violence imposed on LGBTIQ people, their causes, and consequences. With extensive quotes from interviews, included in the title of the sections, the report focuses on the narratives of victims. The last part of the report is dedicated to practices of resistance, coping with suffering and the strategies for individual and collective action. The report can be read keeping in mind the dilemma suggested by Roxani Krystalli (2021) to explore victimhood without imposing the charge of narration on victims. This approach calls on readers to neither fetishize the narration of testimonies as inherently healing or dignifying, nor dismiss the value of victim-centred narrations. In this case, the expert voice of those trained and delegated with the duty of making memory, translated testimonies into historical memory. These memories in turn contribute to the production of LGBTIQ people as victims for historical accounts. These stories were rendered invisible under politics of not-knowing only a few decades ago, and through the report were then made visible under the bureaucratic logic of institutions and the language of memory and transitional justice.

The third form of representation, the language of norms associated with the concept of 'heteronormativity' (CNMH, 2015: 23), acts as the theoretical glue of the report. Heteronormativity, a concept gaining space in Anglophone literature, emphasizes the functioning of gender and sexuality as a regulatory system. It operates in the report as the explanatory terms to define LGBTIQ persons as those who step aside from traditional gender norms, binaries, and dichotomous orders. Interestingly, the report defines itself as a document of historical memory and not as a conceptual piece of work (CNMH, 2015: 24). Even if the report defines itself in such a way, it makes theoretical choices and uses an implicit theoretical frame to connect data with meaning. This frame focused on normative systems and less on practices, while at the same time a focus on victims' experiences was claimed.

These three forms of representation operate by blurring theory and putting victims' voices at the centre, suggesting that testimonies speak for themselves while failing to address the translation of experiences of violence by expert voices and their implicit conceptualizations. The result, however, is problematic. Which voices are included and which go unacknowledged, as well as what makes some experiences 'emblematic' or representative, is a matter that deserves further discussion.

Visibility and speech: discussing the purposes

Calls for visibility and speech play an important role in debates on gender, sexuality, and political power. The 1997 Amnesty International report *Breaking the Silence: Human Rights Violations Based on Sexual Orientation* (Amnesty International, 1997), for example, covered several of the topics discussed in queer conflict research, such as extrajudicial executions, arbitrary killings by armed actors, and asylum seeking. In recalling the report, I am not intending to locate it in some kind of genealogy of queer ethical dilemmas on approaches to conflict but to call attention to the metaphor it is based on. 'Breaking the silence' constitutes not only a way to name some knowledge production but also to state a research and political agenda. The name of the report suggests not only the importance of queer people talking but also an instance of being heard, as an outcome of writing a report about human rights abuses.

The parallel metaphor to speaking up and being heard is coming out and being seen. Denouncing the 'invisibility' of the human rights abuses suffered by lesbian women and gay men in international human rights instruments was at core of the pivotal work of Laviolette and Whitworth (1994). In the case of Colombia there has been an ongoing effort from LGBTIQ organizations to document violence through systematic reporting (Caribe Afirmativo, 2019; Colombia Diversa, 2005). In these cases, strategies for visibility focus on the production of statistical information to prove the magnitude and systemic patterning of such violence against LGBTIQ people, since quantitative data is still the 'hard data' useful for making an issue visible for public interest. Moving from invisibility to visibility and from silence to speech offers a path for the inclusion of queer analysis in conflict, especially when this inclusion is relevant for both activism and the implementation of transitional justice instruments.

Still, as has been extensively discussed in feminist (Casper and Moore, 2009), queer (Edward and Greenough, 2020), and decolonial (Dei and Jaimungal, 2018) scholarship, it is important, in the emerging field of queer conflict studies, to maintain a critical view on who produces visibility and for whose gaze. Even more importantly, since visibility has different meanings and implications for different collectives, problems arise from combining disparate political agendas under the LGBTIQ acronym. Additionally, it would be misleading to assume that violence against gender and sexually diverse collectives has always been under the regime of the 'invisible' or 'unspoken'. There has been certain visibility and audibility around events of trans/homophobic violence before our current translation of them into the expert language of peacebuilding and transitional justice. Against the call for 'visibility' expressed by activist and expert knowledge (Albarracín and Rincón, 2013), it can be argued that there has been a permanent spectacle of violence (Mason, 2002) in the victimhood of queer subjects.

In the case of Colombian scholarship, some research about the victimhood of LGBTIQ people results from reporting acts of 'social cleansing' violence and threats in newspapers (CINEP and Justicia-y-Paz, 1996). This reporting renders collectives of LGBTIQ people visible through 'spectacle', reproducing social stereotypes around victims while making them visible for primarily a certain and particular (heterosexual) public gaze. However, such visibility applies for some in the umbrella term while keeping others invisible.

In her study of 'social cleansing' in Cali, sociologist Gómez (2012) analysed headlines from the sensational press related to violence against *travestis*, concluding that they are pictured in very stereotypical ways, associated with marginality, crime, and threats to social order. She argues this visible spectacle reproduces social prejudices and justifies violence since the ways of speaking about them in the media makes them vulnerable to the same violence that is intended to be denounced by activists. Meanwhile, the research based on the currently highly used concept of 'prejudice' is founded on cases of violence against homosexual men (Gómez, 2007). Both examples show ways in which violence against members of the LGBTIQ community is brought to visibility and then translated to specific interests and understanding of victimization.

Acquiring visibility under certain understandings of violence gets more complicated when it is not an external representation made by others but a way of framing personal narratives and challenging research protocols. My PhD research protocol, for example, included some considerations for not requesting information on personal experiences of violence, to protect participants from feeling the need to speak about this with me. Despite the fact that participants were not requested to narrate personal experiences of violence, they did it several times, challenging my ethics protocols. With the intention of avoiding the already problematic over-interest on victims' narratives that I was witnessing, I imposed a silence on what was expected from the narratives that participants wanted to share with me. In sharing their experiences, they were reacting to my silence and demanding the chance to express what was relevant for them, even if it was painful. Switching off the recording was my immediate answer, but this dynamic demanded a further discussion about such narratives in my research and on what participants were doing in the sharing of such painful experiences.

Through the years in which LGBTIQ issues have acquired new visibility during the peace dialogues in Colombia, the role for LGBTIQ activists in the country has changed. Our involvement in lobbying and activism for making LGBTIQ issues relevant led to the 2016 Peace Agreement and its implementation in the current transitional justice system.[8] Informal conversations with colleagues in activism and my own participation in workshops and events to strengthen the participation of LGBTIQ people in peacebuilding are making evident some saturation among those who are constantly requested to give their testimonies and the instrumentalization of their narratives to create expert knowledge. Especially, when some voices are often presented as representative of LGBTIQ victimhood and suffering, where their testimonies are intended to illustrate a collective knowledge rather than reflect the individual experience. After decades of silence, we are now facing a moment in which academics, journalists, cooperative agents, or public employees want to talk to a 'real LGBTIQ victim'. As Krystalli (2021) found, this is already problematic for victims of conflict in general. It is even more problematic for a topic in which acquiring visibility as a victim brings issues of prejudice and exposure to violence or risks unleashing new forms of violence onto identified victims, as is the case with LGBTIQ people.

The path from invisibility to visibility and from silence to speech is indeed problematic, fractured, and uneven. It is even more problematic assuming there is a path facilitated by knowledge production focused on testimonies, victimhood, and orientation towards violence. Much of this rests on assumptions that visibility is a desired and neutral goal that will bring more safety and justice. However, Colombian LGBTIQ activists have long warned of the risk of visibility as a factor for more violence, not only for social leaders but also for those who are visible in their communities and neighbours as same-sex couples or transgender persons (Caribe Afirmativo and Colombia Diversa, 2018). Research on anti-gender politics in a global perspective shows that backlashes against LGBTIQ rights can occur in parallel with state-protection and increasing visibility of LGBTIQ issues in public debates (Lind and Keating, 2013; David and Roman, 2018; Corrêa and Kalil, 2020; Serrano-Amaya, 2021). The gains obtained by some from visibility may result in new dangers for others.

These issues raise important questions about the role of visibility and speech as core concepts in queer conflict studies. If visibility and speech are not problematized for their risk of having a progressive and linear path, these unexamined concepts risk continuing the view on non-normative gender and sexual experiences in need of normalization. If visibility is assumed as the answer to the denial of violence against queer subjects in conflicts without discussing the meanings of such visibility, or for whom it is relevant or not, it may bring more harm than justice. As discussed above for the case of Colombia, acquiring visibility in public policies or transitional justice instruments mainly as victims may result in taking agency from the subjects or looking at them just as resistance actors and not as creative protagonists of social change.

It is not my intention here to deny the importance of visibility and speech. The need for more documentation, research, and public discussion of the violence suffered by individuals and collectives due to gender identity and sexual orientation is still an urgent matter for activism, academia, and international alliances for producing knowledge with social impact. This is especially evident if we consider the lack of attention by governments on this violence and its marginal place in dealing with protracted conflicts. Acknowledging the importance of such demands for speech about and visibility of LGBTIQ communities should be considered alongside what and who resists being seen and what may not be translated into the gaze and speech of peacebuilding or conflict research. A discussion on queering conflict research needs to be aware of such problems and develop alternatives.

Conclusion

The paths of telling the stories of LGBTIQ experience, from not-knowing to knowing, from denial to visibility, are political. One of the problems faced with the development of the field of queer conflict research is the risk of normalizing violence when making it a matter of academic discussion, activist mobilization, and state intervention. The normalization of violence can occur when it is the common trope to include some collectives in official accounts of conflicts. An example of this is the association of all LGBTIQ individuals and collectives within a single community who all face the same prejudice violence. As much as this visibility is important in the accounts of conflict—for example, in transitional justice mechanisms and memory work—it also risks framing LGBTIQ experiences as a new category of victimhood for the treatment of experts' systems.

The development of the field of queer conflict research is facilitating the emergence of a new wave of professional activism with a literacy in the language of rights, gender, sexuality, peace, and conflict and a unique knowledge/power to navigate in between spaces and languages. As I illustrated with the case of Colombia, queer conflict studies is a hybrid field developing from academia in terms of the type of knowledge produced, as well as in activism, in terms of where it is emerging. This emergence affects the North/South relations already problematized in the sociology of knowledge that reflects structures of power across this divide. A primary aspect to this division is the value awarded to scholarship written in English and published in specialized journals in the Global North. These outputs also tend to veer towards colonial research practices that can be illustrated well with the colloquial term 'parachute research': when a researcher lands or 'parachutes' into a situation with little preparation or understanding, with the aim to collect 'data' and to subsequently leave, having extracted the required material without much concern for the subject of study. A practice sometimes justified by the novelty of the topic or by the 'need to do something for those suffering'.

Still, there are also hierarchies in activism. Those who can speak with state institutions, donors, and global human rights organizations have political and social capital that facilitate key actors engaging with their issues and understanding of queer conflict research more than others. They may be the ones setting the agenda. Problems arise when considering who lacks such levels of literacy. If not all can speak or want to speak the language of rights and of state policies, what languages can they use to express their grievances and struggles for dignity? How can a field that arises challenging power relationships transform those relationships created by its own emergence?

Finally, this queer conflict research can be a space for possibilities. North/South relationships are also heterogeneous. Academics, activists, and policy makers travel from places bringing with them knowledge and expertise and facilitating exchanges. Organizations in the Global South cooperate among themselves and sometimes in alliances with those in the Global North. Colombian LGBTIQ activists working on peacebuilding participate in global networks with other activists in countries facing or recovering from socio-political violence. Colombian activists have learned a lot from South African peers. The primacy of English can be challenged not only with more translations but also with publications in multiple languages. As mentioned above, international organizations play a key role as funders, providers of technical support, and lobbyists with homo/transphobic states. There is space to create more meaningful, equitable, and joyful peer partnerships in which new generations of young academics and activists trained in social media and new technologies play a key role.

Notes

1. See Samuel Ritholtz's explanation of queer epistemology in Chapter 1.
2. I use the acronym LGBTIQ as a descriptive term for disparate political agendas related to issues of gender, sexuality, and power hierarchies. The acronym is under permanent debate and must be used in a way that is mindful of the term's origin in the global politics of rights. Its uses are contested and heterogeneous in part for assuming some commonality and association among disparate political projects, identities, and social positions. In the case of Colombia, the most common use of the acronym is LGBT, which I use here when referring to local use of the term in the country.
3. As illustrated by Patricio Simonetto in this volume (Chapter 6) by considering the challenges of creating queer archives, the problem I am discussing here is not about making visible something that was apparently made invisible through certain operations. Instead, following Simonetto, I argue that it is the creating of a diversity of archives of documents, testimonies, and statistics that gives existence to queer subjects as a matter of interest in conflict studies. Some of these archives can be as ruthless as those described by Simonetto while others can embody a collection of very touching, empowering, and painful feelings.
4. Such knowledge is extensive and includes a variety of reports produced by LGBTIQ organizations (see, for example: https://caribeafirmativo.LGBTIQ/publicaciones/informes/; https://colombiadiversa.org/publicaciones/) and by state institutions (see, for example: https://centrodememoriahistorica.gov.co/aniquilar-la-diferencia/), plus areas specialized in gender and diversity that develop technical knowledge (see, for example: https://www.jep.gov.co/JEP/Paginas/uia/Grupos-misionales.aspx; https://comisiondelaverdad.co/en-los-territorios/enfoques/de-genero; https://ubpdbusquedadesaparecidos.co/actualidad/unidad-de-busqueda-y-caribe-afirmativo-agilizan-incorporacion-del-enfoque-de-genero-para-comunidad-LGBTIQi-en-el-proceso-de-busqueda-de-personas-desaparecidas/).
5. Organizations that have been carefully documenting, archiving, and providing information include an LGBTIQ initiative, *Planeta Paz*, who in the early 2000s created a listserv on Yahoo as a communication and information service. Unfortunately, the list was hacked years later, causing the loss of intense debates and information. There, informal reports were discussed and shared to create collective action and to provide information for lobbying and activism. Such initiatives were also developed by early networks, including Proyecto Agenda (2001). Additionally, in the early 2000s, *Mujeres al Borde*, a collective of queer and transfeminist women, created several short videos expressing their understanding of peace and conflict that were used in educational activities and knowledge exchanges with peacebuilding organizations. These were alternative sites for knowledge production that have not been recognized as legitimate as they do not follow the normative practice of writing and publication used in academia or mainstream activism.

6   For more information on this case and the frame in which such information was obtained, see: Serrano-Amaya (2014).
7   Ximena Chanaga (2020) also did a critical reading of the report. Her analysis focuses on how the politics of knowledge in reports like this produce epistemological injustices with a particular impact on transgender persons.
8   For a description of this process, see: José Fernando Serrano-Amaya (2017).

Acknowledgements

I would like to express my acknowledgement to the editors for their comments in the previous versions of this chapter. This contribution is based on results of the research *Políticas y pedagogías de la reconciliación* supported by the *Fondo de Apoyo a Profesores Asistentes FAPA*, Universidad de los Andes.

Bibliography

Albarracín, M. (2011) *Retos para la investigación de la violencia contra la población LGBTIQ en el marco del conflicto armado*, Bogotá: Universidad de los Andes.

Albarracín, M. and Rincón, J. (2013) 'De las víctimas invisibles a las víctimas dignificadas: los retos del enfoque diferencial para la población de lesbianas, gays, bisexuales, transgeneristas e intersexuales (LGBTIQI) en la Ley de Víctimas', *Revista de Derecho Público*, (31): 1–32.

Allendoerfer, M.G., Murdie, A., and Welch, R.M. (2020) 'The path of the boomerang: human rights campaigns, third-party pressure, and human rights', *International Studies Quarterly*, 64(1): 111–19. DOI: 10.1093/isq/sqz082

Amnesty International (1997) *Breaking the Silence: Human Rights Violations Based on Sexual Orientation*, London: Amnesty International.

Anderson, M.B. (1999) *Do No Harm: How Aid Can Support Peace or War*, Boulder, CO: Lynne Rienner.

Bernstein, M. (2002) 'Identities and politics: toward a historical understanding of the lesbian and gay movement', *Social Science History*, 26(3): 531–81.

Browne, K. and Nash, C.J. (2010) *Queer Methods and Methodologies: Intersecting Queer Theories and Social Science Research*, Burlington, VT: Ashgate.

Caribe Afirmativo (2019) *Nosotras resistimos. Informe sobre violencias contra personas LGBTIQ en el marco del conflicto armado en Colombia*, Barranquilla: Caribe Afirmativo.

Caribe Afirmativo and Colombia Diversa (2018) *La discriminación, una guerra que no termina. Informe de derechos humanos de personas lesbianas, gays, bisexuales y trans. Colombia 2017*, Bogotá: Caribe Afirmativo, Colombia Diversa.

Casper, M.J. and Moore, L.J. (2009) *Missing Bodies: The Politics of Visibility*, New York: New York University Press.

Chanaga, X. (2020) *Injusticias epistemológicas en las construcciones de memorias sobre las mujeres trans* en el marco del conflicto armado colombiano: una mirada desde los estudios culturales y las epistemologías trans**, Bogotá: Universidad de los Andes.

CINEP and Justicia-y-Paz (1996) *Noche y Niebla*, Bogotá: CINEP.

CNMH (2015) *Aniquilar la diferencia. Lesbianas, gays, bisexuales y transgeneristas en el marco del conflicto armado colombiano*, Bogotá: Centro Nacional de Memoria Histórica.

Colombia Diversa (2005) *Derechos humanos de lesbianas, gays, bisexuales y transgeneristas en Colombia*, Bogotá: Colombia Diversa.

Colombia Diversa (2020) *Los órdenes del prejuicio. Los crímenes cometidos sistemáticamente contra personas LGBTIQ en el conflicto armado colombiano*, Bogotá: Colombia Diversa.

Connell, R. (2007) *Southern Theory: The Global Dynamics of Knowledge in the Social Sciences*, Crows Nest: Allen & Unwin.

Corrêa, S. and Kalil, I. (2020) *Políticas antigénero en américa latina: Brasil – ¿la catástrofe perfecta?*, Rio de Janeiro: ABIA – Asociación Brasileña Interdisciplinar de SIDA.

Datta, A. (2017) 'Queering knowledge in West Bengal: academia in the hands of activists', *Anthropology Matters Journal*, 17(1): 1–28.

David, P. and Roman, K. (2018) 'Disentangling and locating the "global right": anti-gender campaigns in Europe', *Politics and Governance*, 6(3): 6–19. DOI:10.17645/pag.v6i3.1557

Dean, A., Johnson, J., and Luhmann, S. (2018) *Feminist Praxis Revisited: Critical Reflections on University–Community Engagement*, Ontario: Wilfrid Laurier University Press.

Dei, G.J.S. and Jaimungal, C. (2018) *Indigeneity and Decolonial Resistance: Alternatives to Colonial Thinking and Practice*, Bloomfield, NJ: Myers Education Press.

Edward, M. and Greenough, C. (2020) *Queer Literacy: Visibility, Representation, and LGBTIQ+ Research Ethics*, Cham: Springer.

Fals-Borda, O. (1991) *Acción y conocimiento: como romper el monopolio con investigación – acción participativa*, Bogotá: CINEP.

Gómez, M.C. (2012) 'Sexualidad y violencia. Crímenes por prejuicio sexual en Cali 1980–2000', *CS*, (10): 173–205.

Gómez, M.M. (2007) 'Violencia, homofobia y psicoanálisis: entre lo secreto y lo público', *Revista de Estudios Sociales*, (28): 72–85.

hooks, b. (2000) *Feminist Theory: From Margin to Center*, Boston, MA: South End Press.

ICRC (2021) '"That never happens here". Sexual and gender-based violence against men, boys and/including LGBTIQIQ+ persons in humanitarian settings', Norwegian Red Cross.

Krystalli, R.C. (2021) 'Narrating victimhood: dilemmas and (in)dignities', *International Feminist Journal of Politics*, 23(1): 125–46.

Laviolette, N. and Whitworth, S. (1994) 'No safe haven. Sexuality as a universal human right and gay and lesbian activism in international politics', *Millennium Journal of International Studies*, 23(3): 563–88.

Lempert, R.O. (2001) 'Activist scholarship', *Law & Society Review*, 35(1): 25–32.

Lind, A. and Keating, C. (2013) 'Navigating the left turn', *International Feminist Journal of Politics*, 15(4): 515–33.

Mason, G. (2002) *The Spectacle of Violence: Homophobia, Gender, and Knowledge*, New York: Routledge.

McLeod, L. and O'Reilly, M. (2019) 'Critical peace and conflict studies: feminist interventions', *Peacebuilding*, 7(2): 127–45. DOI:10.1080/21647259.2019.1588457

Miall, H., Ramsbotham, O., and Woodhouse, T. (2003) *Contemporary Conflict Resolution*, Cambridge: Polity.

Naples, N. (1997) 'A feminist revisiting of the insider/outsider debate: the "outsider phenomenon" in rural Iowa', in R. Hertz (eds) *Reflexivity and Voice*, Thousand Oaks, CA: Sage, pp 70–94.

Nordstrom, C. (1999) 'Wars and invisible girls, shadow industries, and the politics of not-knowing', *International Feminist Journal of Politics*, 1(1): 14–33.

Nordstrom, C. and Robben, A.C.G.M. (1995) *Fieldwork under Fire: Contemporary Studies of Violence and Survival*, Los Angeles, CA: University of California Press.

Ordoñez, J.P. (1996) *No Human Being Is Disposable: Social Cleansing, Human Rights and Sexual Orientation in Colombia*, Washington, DC: International Gay and Lesbian Human Rights Commission, Colombia Human Rights Committee, Proyecto Dignidad.

Parada, E. (2020) *Estudios críticos de paz. Perspectivas decoloniales*, Bogotá: CINEP.

Proyecto Agenda (2001) *Informe preliminar de derechos Humanos segundo semestre 2000 y primer semestre 2001*, Bogotá: Proyecto Agenda.

Rosenbloom, R. and IGLHRC (1996) *Unspoken Rules: Sexual Orientation and Women's Human Rights*, London: Cassell.

Serrano-Amaya, J.F. (2004) *Queering Conflict: The Invisibility of Gender and Sexual Diversity in Peace Building* (Master in Conflict Resolution), Bradford: University of Bradford.

Serrano-Amaya, J.F. (2014) *Chiaroscuro: The Uses of 'Homophobia' and Homophobic Violence in Armed Conflicts and Political Transitions* (PhD), Sydney: University of Sydney.

Serrano-Amaya, J.F. (2017) 'La tormenta perfecta: ideología de género y articulación de públicos', *Sexualidad, Salud y Sociedad*, (27): 149–71.

Serrano-Amaya, J.F. (2021) 'Políticas antigénero en América Latina: una mirada panorámica', in S. Corrêa (eds) *Políticas antigênero na América Latina: resumos dos estudos de casos nacionais*, Rio de Janeiro: Associação Brasileira Interdisciplinas de Aids, pp 21–43.

Sudbury, J. and Okazawa-Rey, M. (2015) *Activist Scholarship Antiracism, Feminism, and Social Change*, New York: Routledge.

Trim, D.J.B. and Simms, B. (2011) 'Humanitarian intervention: a history' [online]. Available from: http://search.ebscohost.com/login.aspx?direct=true&db=e000xww&AN=366189&site=eds-live

Waites, M. (2019) 'Decolonizing the boomerang effect in global queer politics: a new critical framework for sociological analysis of human rights contestation', *International Sociology*, 34(4): 382–401. DOI:10.1177/0268580919851425

Walsh, C. (2003) 'Las geopolíticas del conocimiento y colonialidad del poder. Entrevista a Walter Mignolo', *Polis, Revista de la Universidad Bolivariana*, 1(4): 1–26.

Warner, M. (1999) *The Trouble with Normal*, Cambridge, MA: Harvard University Press.

3

Workshop as Queer Feminist Praxis: Insights from Colombian Queer and Trans Women Organizing for Peace

Jamie J. Hagen

Introduction

Queer and trans women continue to be overlooked in research about women and LGBTQ (lesbian, gay, bisexual, transgender, and queer) people's experiences in conflict. Including these experiences of conflict in queer conflict research, and research about gender, peace, and security in general, begins with recognizing those who are most marginalized under hetero-/cisnormative patriarchal regimes are also agents of peacebuilding when implementing UN Security Council 1325 and the Women, Peace, and Security (WPS) agenda (S/RES/1325 2000). The WPS agenda was developed from a set of ten UN Security Council resolutions beginning with Security Council Resolution 1325 passed in 2000. These resolutions established the framework for the only UN Security Council agenda with a primary focus on women's experiences (Basu et al, 2020). However, none of the resolutions discuss sexuality, mention LGBTQ people, or discuss sexual orientation and gender identity (Hagen, 2016). Coalition building between LGBTQ organizations and feminist[1] peacebuilders can help address this exclusion (Nagarajan and Hagen, 2023).

This chapter takes a queer feminist approach to integrating LGBTQ women's voices in the WPS agenda. I show how a workshop organized using a queer feminist methodology can bring together individuals often excluded from discussions about queer conflict research. I then explain why a queer feminist workshop presents a valuable methodology for coalition building, highlighting the findings from a workshop of this kind in Bogotá, Colombia. The insights from this workshop show not only how this method can be effective, but also how this approach can create space for LBTQ women to inform next steps for implementing a more expansive gender perspective across all four pillars (participation, prevention, protection and relief and recovery) of the WPS agenda.

Workshop as queer feminist methodology

Cisheteronormative approaches to a gender analysis of women's experiences in global politics have historically failed to include queer and trans people (Shepherd and Sjoberg, 2012; Wilcox, 2017; Inton-Campbell and Inton-Campbell, 2022). Applying queer theory to gender, peace, and security work pushes a gender perspective beyond binary thinking about sex and gender by acknowledging that cisgender people have a gender identity too. The framing of white heterosexuality as the norm is actively upheld every day through the politics of racism, sexism, and patriarchy, which everyone is a part of, even members of LGBTQ communities (Rich, 1980; Ward, 2008).

A heteronormative understanding of both women and gender can have an exclusionary impact, not only failing to engage with LGBTQ communities, but also failing to understand the harms experienced by LGBTQ people in conflict (Hagen, 2016; Myrttinen and Daigle, 2017; Ashe, 2018; Bueno-Hansen, 2018).[2] This gap is in large part an issue of translation between siloed communities. In my queering WPS research, I ask that policy makers, researchers, and practitioners be wary of cissexism, or the assumption that only cisgender people are 'normal' and 'right' (Hagen, 2016). Focusing on how lesbian, bisexual, transgender, and queer women experience conflict reframes the default perspective of woman as a heterosexual-cisgender woman in conflict. Instead, a broader gender perspective in peace and transitional justice accounts for the full spectrum of women including LGBTQ people (Alvarado et al, 2018; Fobear and Baines, 2020).

Even given these limitations, the WPS agenda offers a framework for mobilizing funding, political commitments, and international collaboration necessary for ensuring a gender perspective in peacebuilding. However, WPS programming often continues to privilege heterosexual relationships, leaving aside women with diverse sexual orientations and gender identities. Addressing the gap in attention to LGBTQ experiences is not only a practice of theory building but also one where involving practitioners who engage in direct services can better inform gender, peace, and security practice. Local civil society organizations play a critical role as knowledge brokers, translating human rights concerns from the local to the national and international community (Merry, 2006; Thoreson, 2014). Queer feminist approaches to studying LGBTQ interventions in peace and security emphasize networking between queer women and feminists invested in WPS and in peacebuilding. My understanding of a queer feminist approach draws on work by transnational queer feminists who aim to shift power dynamics in knowledge production. Which people are viewed as experts on WPS, whether it be internationally, or locally, is not neutral. As Browne et al write, 'Developing within and (although only at times explicitly) from feminist questionings of objective knowledges and power relations in research processes, participatory research is inherently concerned with recognising and contesting hierarchies' (2017: 1379). A queer feminist workshop that is Global South-based and Global South-led centres the expertise of queer and trans women in peace and security.

Relationships matter when it comes to visibility, politics, and power. Though this varies by context, patriarchal gender norms and the legacy of exclusion of women's rights as a central tenet of LGBTQ rights movements has led to a segregation of feminist and women's movement organizing from other movements. Many conducting queer conflict research rely on working with community members who are easier to reach because of visibility around their queer identity. This approach often leaves out queer women who due to double marginalization under patriarchy and heterosexism may not be visible in the same way or have access to the same networks. Sometimes this exclusion of queer women as interview subjects or in survey data within queer conflict research is justified on the basis of a limited timeline for completing the research that does not allow time for finding women interviewees in addition to men, who may be easier to find. Researchers visiting a conflict context for only a short time may only speak to those who are most visible and vocal. As a result, non-governmental organizations or those conducting queer conflict research often focus on the experiences of cis gay men, failing to also speak with lesbian, bisexual, transgender, and queer women. Rather than accepting this exclusion, a queer feminist approach to researching experiences of gender in peace and conflict prioritizes LBTQ women's experiences.

Much of the focus on future directions for WPS, and feedback on ongoing WPS efforts, take place during consultations with academia, civil society, and policy makers during the drafting of WPS National Action Plans (NAPs). NAPs are documents indicating the steps states are taking (or planning to take) to implement WPS resolutions. There are now over 100 WPS NAPs with some countries having multiple NAPs, renewed every four or five years. As of early 2023, 13[3] of the 104 countries with NAPs currently mention LGBTQ people. Recognizing the relevance of LGBTQ experiences to the WPS agenda is on the rise as this is nearly double the number of NAPs mentioning the topic just one year before.[4]

A workshop offers one way to facilitate an intersectional discussion about centring queer and trans women in WPS policy, including NAPs. Workshops provide a space to bring communities and knowledges together in a non-hierarchical and non-extractive way, thus promoting a 'non-dominant' collaboration between and among Global North/Global South participants. The workshop allows for a dialogic, consultative process with elements of participant observation. Over the years gender, peace, and security work has professionalized, resulting in a hierarchical dynamic with a greater value of expertise of those based in or educated in the Global North versus those in the South. Workshops serve as a valuable site for qualitative studies that engage in ethnographic research with a group of people in focused dialogue (Haastrup and Hagen, 2021). A queer feminist workshop, where queer and trans women facilitate the discussion, creates a supportive space for LGBTQ people to share their experiences and perspectives as a form of expertise about WPS. This approach also avoids harmful practices of extraction and framing LGBTQ communities as simply victims, rather than also experts and peacebuilders.

More than simply adding LGBTQ people to the conversation, a workshop developed and facilitated with a queer feminist approach moves away from the colonial narratives of 'rescuing gays' by focusing on the more structural dilemmas in global politics that must be addressed for gender justice (Bracke, 2012). Asking queer questions (Rao, 2014) about security means not only having an awareness of the diversity of sexual orientations and gender identities, but also asking how queering challenges us to think beyond limiting binaries such as Global North/Global South; peace/conflict; activist/expert; and perpetrator/victim, to show how often rather than one or the other there is a grey area of both/and. A queering of security opens space for a transformative vision through challenges that have been hindering practitioners working on issues of peace and security (Amar, 2013; McEvoy, 2015; Wilkinson, 2017).

Queer feminist practice ensures diversity across multiple identities (race, gender, sexuality, class, ability). In practice, economic and organizational limitations can hinder the reality of this inclusiveness, determining who can be in the room, and who is not able to attend. As such, findings from workshops can provide very valuable insights but should not be presented as a stand-in for the views of everyone in the community. Nevertheless, this research methodology empowers the collaborative practice of queer feminist research where the community most impacted by the research topic at hand not only provides information but also analyses the research together with those conducting the workshop. Thus, organizing a workshop of this kind depends on funded organizers who have deep ties to the community to do the work, so there is trust with those invited to participate and those engaging in the research.

Even with unprecedented momentum in philanthropy toward creating resourcing pipelines for grassroots movements, funding for queer and trans women's organizing[5] and coalition building is inadequate (Astraea, 2020). Bringing together feminist peacebuilders with organizations focused on supporting queer women through a workshop is one way to address this gap. This became important in the drafting of Colombia's first WPS NAP beginning in 2022. It can be a place to have hard conversations, in private, between key stakeholders. Although these are not exclusive groups, there are many civil society organizations focusing on women's inclusion in peacebuilding that do not include LGBTQ rights or attention to sexuality as part of their work.

Queer and trans social justice organizers have long valued coalition building. The Combahee River Collective, a Black lesbian feminist group, released their groundbreaking statement in 1997 that began, 'our politics at the present time would be that we are actively committed to struggling against racial, sexual, heterosexual, and class oppression, and see as our particular task the development of integrated analysis and practice based upon the fact that the major systems of oppression are interlocking'.[6] Intersectional organizing of this kind recognizes that people carry multiple identities, and that achieving liberation requires uniting struggles. Working with feminist organizations is one of the best ways to help facilitate intersectional research about women inclusive of LGBTQ people within ongoing WPS projects,[7] with attention to their sexuality, race, class, ability, and gender (Davis and Stern, 2018; Outright Action International, 2020).

Methodology in practice: Colombian workshop on queering women, peace, and security

The lead-up to the first Colombian NAP offered an opportunity to again highlight LGBTQ expertise as a part of implementing the Colombia peace process. Colombian activists in Colombia Diversa, a Bogotá-based organization that promotes and defends LGBTQ rights in Colombia, have long pressured the Colombian government to acknowledge the violence faced by LGBTQ individuals in the country from armed conflict but also ongoing discrimination and prejudices in the country today (Colombia Diversa, 2020). Scholarship by María Mercedes Gómez argues that violence targeting LGBTQ people is a form of prejudice-based violence (Gómez, 2013).[8] Recognizing conflict-related violence that targets LGBTQ people as a form of gender-based violence is another way to queer gendered harms in peace and security (Loken and Hagen, 2022). Caribe Afirmativo,[9] an organization that has worked to provide direct services to LGBTQ people in Colombia for over 13 years, engaged in 'traveling forums and dialogues' in several Colombian cities in 2016 to mobilize LGBTI activists (Maier, 2020) as part of the peace process and continues to provide *Casas de Paz* (houses of peace) across Colombia. They have also published their own reports about the recognition of the rights of sexual diversity and gender identities in the country, including extensive national reporting about violence due to prejudice against LGBTQ people in the framework of the Colombian armed conflicts.[10] These organizations monitor the experiences of targeted violence, homo-, bi-, transphobic prejudice-based violence in the Colombian peace process, and report findings to the Special Jurisdiction for Peace (JEP).[11] Colombia's inclusion of violence against LGBTQ people as a dimension of the conflict has set a precedent for the importance of queer expertise in peace and security in future peace processes.

In the run up to the development of Colombia's first WPS NAP, Colombia Diversa saw an opportunity for consultation with women peacebuilders. The Peace and Transitional Justice Team, Camila Sánchez, María Susana Peralta Ramón, Valentina Parra, Laura Beltrán, and Camila García[12] organized a workshop[13] in October 2022 applying a queer feminist methodology, recognizing this as a valuable next step for meaningful consultation in the WPS NAP development process. The team[14] invited 12 participants active in women's peacebuilding work in Colombia, including four queer and trans women LGBTQ organizers from regions across the country. As such, the workshop was designed from a South-based country (Colombia) and informed by a conversation led by and for queer and trans communities (Colombia Diversa). Workshop participants joined from the Fundación Artemisas, Liga Internacional de Mujeres por la Paz y la Libertad – Colombia, Red Nacional de Mujeres, Corporación Humanas, DeJusticia, ForumCIV – Colombia, and Católicas por el Derecho a Decidir.[15] Several of the organizations who participated in the workshop do not primarily work on LGBTQ issues, offering an opportunity for movement building to integrate these issues into their feminist organizing agenda.

When queer experience of conflict is filtered through those working at the international level, and the UN is charged with advocacy, the complexities of queer experience of conflict as experienced nationally, regionally, or at the grassroots level is often lost. This approach also continues to prioritize the most privileged subjects: English speakers. Colombia Diversa's workshop was conducted in Spanish. The opening and closing discussions had simultaneous English and Spanish interpretation. The breakout groups were in Spanish, with two participants receiving whisper interpretation in English.

Laura Beltrán, a member of the Colombia Diversa team who works closely on implementing UN SCR 1325, explains that for her a central part of her work is 'to make people understand that LGBTQ issues are not accessories, but rather we need these rights to be a truly inclusive and a truly democratic society' (2020).[16] In workshop breakout discussions participants discussed not only ways to queer three of the four pillars of WPS—the protection pillar, prevention pillar, and participation pillar of WPS—but also some of the continuing challenges for bringing queer and trans voices into conversation with feminist women's peacebuilding leaders in the Colombian context. All of the participants spoke of the workshop as a valuable space for learning with and from each other, reflecting on their work across movements. The workshop facilitated three aspects of coalition building between LGBTQ organizers and women peacebuilders: (1) subverting the hierarchy of expertise in peacebuilding; (2) redefining concepts such as (in)security and justice; and (3) facilitating honest discussions, challenges, and opportunities in alliance building.

Subverting the hierarchy of expertise in peacebuilding

Everyone who participated in the workshop agreed that the LGBTQ community belongs in conversations about gender, peace, and security, however participants noted several challenges for this inclusion. While some lesbians were a part of the central organizing for women's peacebuilding in Colombia, these women have not made sexuality and queering a central component of their approach to feminist peacebuilding. The workshop presented an opportunity for shifting expertise, prioritizing insights from queer and trans organizers who do integrate sexuality and LGBTQ rights as a dimension of their organizing.

As Colombia Diversa's Peace and Transitional Justice Coordinator, María Susana Peralta Ramón, explains, 'the main challenge is that we're not taken seriously'. During the workshop, the need for intergenerational respect across movements was apparent, especially as many queer and trans advocates did not have access to the same economic, political, and social privilege experienced by some of the other women working in the women's peacebuilding sector. While the international community celebrates the inclusivity of the Colombian peace process, locally there is frustration about how this is playing out in practice. A workshop participant from Fundación Artemisas argued (Participant 1, 2022):

'We have made progress in advancing a differential and intersectional perspective, but this [peacebuilding] space continues to be quite closed. We're talking to each other. There is a lot of knowledge that has been accumulated but we continue to fall on the same mistakes with respect to the negotiation challenges because we keep seeing a lack of participation of women and LGBTI persons.'

These 'same mistakes' are not limited to the Colombian context, but instead reflect the continuing challenges for integrating a gender perspective in peacebuilding.

One participant with decades of experience in women's peacebuilding in Colombia discussed a lack of recognition of previous work to include an LGBT perspective in WPS. 'Sometimes I feel that young men and women feel this is the first time we're talking about the existence of trans women' (Participant 3, 2022). She also clarified sexuality was a part of the framework of liberty and equality sought for women within UN SCR 1325.

'I was very close to feminist women who worked in New York to try to get [UN Security Council Resolution] 1325 to be issued in 2000. We [Colombian women peacebuilders] worked with them, and we wrote letters to each other talking about what it entailed, to have this [resolution] for peacebuilding and for women to be given that importance under 1325. After 20 years of 1325 we have also identified the things it was missing.' (Participant 3, 2022)

She addressed not talking about youth or about LGBT women as two of these absences in UN SCR 1325.

A trans human rights organizer from Tumaco, in the Nariño department (country sub-division), reflected on her positionality as a Black trans woman (and the only Black person at the workshop) doing LGBTQ social justice work: 'My passion for this work and this leadership is to break the ice. I like to enter different spaces to state that we as trans women need and have the same rights' (Participant 12, 2022). She also spoke of the need for her advocacy in all communities, not just diverse populations. She emphasized, 'We can't just stay within the same circle'. Instead, she spoke of walking 'the meandering paths that we have ahead', emphasizing that this work can take us in unexpected directions. 'As a trans woman, I have fought hard for the recognition of LGBTI and cisgender women' (Participant 12, 2022). She explained that her work is not just for trans women, but all women, 'because I was born from a cisgender woman' (Participant 12, 2022). Making this connection between the fight for trans rights to the struggles at the core of the women's rights movements was highlighted throughout the workshop.

While organizing the workshop, the Colombia Diversa team made sure that the queer and trans leaders invited to speak were from outside Bogotá, to include voices from the territories. Other participants at the workshop also reflected on the need to hear from people from the regions outside the capital, given the capital is where most international actors focus time, funding, and analysis. Speaking about her work with the non-profit

DeJusticia, which focuses on public policy proposals, advocacy, strategic litigation, and training programmes focused on human rights in Colombia and the Southern Cone, one feminist peacebuilder explained: 'That is very important for us, those of us who continue working from Bogotá, to know about your experience about your work and to be able to discuss some of the issues that we discuss in the social networks or from the urban setting ... you live through them differently' (Participant 6, 2022).

Although the overlap of work by LGBTQ organizations and peacebuilding organizations is not formally recognized by women's peacebuilding organizations, workshop participants referred to collaborations they had already initiated. Beltrán of Colombia Diversa argues: 'We know women, feminists, and LGBT persons have always worked hand in hand with peacebuilding since Havana'[17] (Participant 6, 2022). She opened the workshop by asking, 'What are the practical challenges for these alliances to materialize in the territories [non-urban areas]?' (Participant 6, 2022). Two ongoing challenges are (1) whose voices are received as experts on women's experiences and (2) how to consider queer and trans experiences beyond victimhood. Additionally, the peace experienced in Bogotá, the site of our workshop, is not experienced equally across Colombia. Many people in other regions face displacement, poverty, and continuing threats of violence and insecurity. Beltrán continued:

'No one is better at that than the women leaders that we have invited to tell us about what experiences and challenges and opportunities for coordination have been between LGBT and women's organisations and movements in the territories. If we want implementation of differential measures for LGBT women, we need this feminist alliance to be solid in the territorial organisations and in the projects that we implement.' (Participant 6, 2022)

The queer feminist approach to the workshop allowed for revisiting women's participation in WPS in reframing not only which women are included by inviting queer and trans women, but also how these women are included, by platforming queer and trans organizers as experts.

Redefining concepts like (in)security and justice

Queer feminist analysis challenges who and what provides security for women in their everyday lives. Together, workshop participants looked more closely at specific security risks for LBTQ women, situating them within known security risks for all women in Colombia. One of the lesbian movement organizers shared how members within her communities face different levels of security threats with implications for who can lead social mobilizing for change (Participant 11, 2022): 'If it is true that violence for women and LGBT populations are similar, we have to be responsible and accountable for our [women and LGBT] spaces.' While others agreed, some note how complicated this can be for those in the LGBTQ community. For example, a trans organizer argued that it is not the police who provide protection for trans community members, but rather non-state armed actors. She explained, 'They always talk about peace, peace, peace, but what is peace for many people who live in the central regions? And what is peace for those people who live in the territories like us?' (Participant 12, 2022). This awareness led the participant to create an organization that provides a space for women who have children with diverse sexual orientation to find a place of acceptance. She argues providing security for LGBT community members is about much more than education:

> 'We think that creating awareness and education about the trans population and gay population is enough, but no it is not. We need to educate moms, brothers, uncles, nephews, all siblings, all core family, for us to start as a trans population to have inclusion in our lives and have acceptance. Otherwise, we will always live here, seeking rights in a constant struggle.'

Building on this discussion, workshop participants raised concerns about the limitations of the current security responses to address the danger faced by human rights defenders in the country targeted for challenging gender norms. Colombian security measures lack collective community-level care for LGBTQ people. Instead, all protection measures focus on individual human rights defenders. Initiatives such as Alianza Cinco Claves (5 Claves) between five feminist organizations—Women's Link, Colombia Diversa, Corporación Humanas, Red Nacional de Mujeres, and Corporación Sisma Mujer—are working to integrate this community-level understanding of care in organizing for women within a queer and trans approach.[18]

Participants also noted how the continuing hypermilitarization of security responses presents risks to those under the control of armed actors meant to be their protectors. Instead, participants argued for developing a feminist, non-reactive security that would allow queer women access to justice when responding to violence, including femicidal violence. Throughout the workshop, participants argued for the need for building a feminist, demilitarized approach to security that can confront the lack of access to justice, the continuing femicidal violence, and the limits of the patriarchal justice systems together. The queer and trans human rights defenders participating in the workshop spoke of the current security efforts relying on individual protection approaches that are costly and isolating.

A lesbian human rights defender attending the workshop from the Nariño department, talked about the security offered by the police in more detail. She spoke of her experiences as part of a group looking for missing LGBT people: 'For security they sent us a male policeman that just makes us sign an attendance sheet to prove that he was there. We feel unprotected and we have to go back to our territories that way.' In response to this lack of protection, she is part of a group of lesbian and trans women working to raise their voices. The group initially met secretly but have now been public about their activism: 'We decided it was not sufficient to meet in a secret setting. We decided to raise our voices' (Participant 10, 2022). She continued, 'We were tired of the violence of the prejudice and of all the violence against our sisters and all the killings against our sisters. We were at the frontline fighting for those who were there, those who had been there and those who could not be there' (Participant 10, 2022). Together with other queer women they met in the city of Pasto, the capital of Nariño, and formed a *batucada* group using drums to, 'scream and shout it out' (Participant 10, 2022). Even if this resistance in some ways made the women vulnerable to additional violence due to their protest, she said the experience was memorable and beautiful. 'We felt protected because it was a feminist women's group, but we had LGBT people next to us supporting' (Participant 10, 2022). She speaks about how Pasto served as, 'a soothing place where we came together to tell each other that we were not alone but rather that we could work together to heal all these wounds that were being inflicted on us' (Participant 10, 2022). She also noted that this is not a new struggle, but a long-time 'joint struggle in sisterhood' across movements.

Another lesbian organizer workshop participant from the Meta department insisted, 'We should erase from our vocabulary "tolerance". We need to talk about "respect"' (Participant 11, 2022). Her insistence on this comes from her experience of working with Colombia's *Búsqueda de Víctimas* (Search Unit for Missing Persons), looking for missing people displaced during the conflict. As other advocates have noted, trans people have taken it upon themselves to look for trans people who have been displaced during the conflict, as often families do not mourn the loss of their trans children (Hagen and Dupuis-Vargas Latorre, 2022). Given these dynamics, the idea that tolerance is enough to make LGBTQ communities safe has proven not only dangerous, but also deadly. Drawing on these insights during workshop discussions, the women also highlighted the role LGBTQ people can play in developing the processes of risk analysis, along with the initial construction of appropriate security measures. Finally, they argued that to take LGBT social leaders' experiences of risk and safety into account, protections designed with only cisgender and heterosexual women in mind must be redesigned.

In discussions of justice, workshop participants agreed that Colombia's queer feminist approach invites looking beyond what was offered within official truth commission process, a process that has left many LGBTQ survivors disappointed. Together they spoke of the limitations of approaches to justice that do not account for the discrimination faced by LBTQ women. Concrete recommendations to address this limitation include the establishment of protocols for the identification, study, and prosecution of cases of prejudiced-based violence targeting LGBTQ people, and staff training on protocols that include clear sanctions when violated. In addition, collective protection mechanisms instead of only individualized security responses are necessary to provide a more robust form of protection and security.

Another theme of the workshop was how important solidarity between movements is for protection and the overall security of queer lesbian, bisexual, and trans women. Many in the room emphasized their 'persistence and insistence' on keeping this issue of women's safety as a dimension of LGBT rights on the table in the contexts where they work. The possibilitites to improve these pathways for queer feminist solidarity were strengthened through the workshop.

Facilitating honest discussions about alliance building

Workshops provide a space to facilitate challenging discussions about sexuality and gender more safely, while building alliances among peacebuilding communities. Discussing identity-based language as it relates to organizing strategy can be especially challenging. The unique private setting among those known to be friendly to queer and trans communities allowed workshop participants to speak openly about their differing views on who to include in this work, and appropriate language to use related to gender and sexuality.

Agreeing on terminology for speaking about queer women and those with diverse sexual orientations and gender identities more broadly continues to be difficult. There is much debate about terminology for LGBTQ communities and the potential for this terminology to be colonial or otherwise contested. For example, Colombia Diversa used *mariconear* as a translation for 'to queer' for the workshop, which was especially unsettling for some of the women.[19] Whereas a direct translation of queering would be *cuirizar*, Colombia Diversa is committed to using what they view to be the more radical term *mariconear*, which translates as 'faggoting'. They view it as a queer feminist act of reclamation, like the use of the term 'dyke' by some protest groups such as the Dyke March[20] who use the word as an act of protest while organizing events to celebrate lesbian visibility. Queering itself is also a contested topic that has been discussed extensively among Latin American feminists, including among *lesbianas feministas* (Bueno-Hansen, 2014). Pascha Bueno-Hansen writes, 'combining queer women of color feminisms and Latin American lesbian feminisms under a queer unifying umbrella buttresses historical and structural inequalities' (2014: 325).

A Colombian feminist at the workshop explained why she still believed there were risks with the queering framework and why she was not convinced of the value of queering WPS (Participant 5, 2022). Her hesitancy stemmed from the concern about who else was then included in WPS spaces, and the potential for co-optation of the space by gay men. She elaborated, 'in its most liberal translation, *mariconear* ends up including men in translating this agenda'. A second participant agreed with this point, stating, 'I don't agree with *mariconear* as the translation of queering, I think it's too strong' (Participant 3, 2022). Despite her resistance to using the term *mariconear*, she did agree that confronting prejudice-based violence as defined throughout Colombia Diversa reports was a crucial next step for those working on gender, peace, and security.

Colombia Diversa's Peralta Ramón has thought about this challenge a lot. From her position as a queer feminist invested in alliance building, she argues:

> 'Queering around [UN Security Council Resolution] 1325 is not so much [about] the population to protect but the analysis category that it can offer to peacebuilding … Alliance between the feminist movement and LGBT communities offers greater protection for the members of both groups. It offers strength to move forward and to provide gains to both groups.' (Bogotá workshop, 15 October 2022)

She notes how this is especially important for taking seriously the experiences of trans men in conversations about gender, peace, and security. How and when to include men in queering peace and security work is a challenging issue. Historically, in Colombia as elsewhere, men have been granted greater access to political power in the form of access to resources, as well as political visibility. This has also proven to be the case within LGBTQ movements, where cisgender gay men continue to be the most visible. Fear of gay men taking over space that women peacebuilders have worked so hard to get is in part the reason why some feminists have reservations about inviting men from the LGBTQ movement to collaborate. In response to this fear, one of the two trans organizers in the room left participants with a question: 'how do we understand that gender and sexuality norms are oppressive against us all?' (Participant 12, 2022). Feminist- and trans-inclusive work for gender justice also includes men, gay and trans, while recognizing the existing privileges granted to cisgender men. Concluding the discussion, workshop participants reflected on the consolidation of a feminist intersectional political aim to confront this feeling of competition.

As the workshop ended, participants spoke of the future directions for integrating LGBTQ people's needs across peace and security efforts. Speaking to the network of feminists in the workshop, Camila Sánchez of Colombia Diversa argued:

> 'Although the gender perspective is an innovative thing in the Colombian peace process, to get it to materialize is the biggest challenge of this work. We need to make this real. People are saying that Colombia is doing innovative things and changing the field, but we need to make that real.'

Applying a queer feminist analysis to organizing the workshop meant that conversations that people may not have felt comfortable sharing before the workshop were openly discussed with those who disagreed. While these challenges were not resolved by the end of the day, the workshop offered a space for voicing them.

Conclusion

The workshop format incorporates more voices in queer conflict research. A queer feminist approach to this transnational research method offers a valuable tool for conducting this research in a way that serves everyone participating in the research project. Through the workshop, and continuing peacebuilding work led by Colombia Diversa, LGBTQ women in collaboration with feminist organizations have shown the new dimensions of peace and security that a queer feminist approach brings to WPS implementation. A Global South workshop led by queer feminists allowed queer and trans participants to subvert the hierarchy of expertise in peacebuilding. Participants were also able to have difficult discussions about redefining concepts such as (in)security and justice from the perspective of the LGBTQ community. Together, the workshop participants were able to have honest discussions about alliance building for queering the WPS agenda in Colombia.

In the workshop detailed in this chapter, Colombian LGBTQ human rights advocates working with the peace and justice team at Colombia Diversa evidenced the importance of prioritizing sites of participation from the perspective of queer and trans women. Together, these findings illustrate not only how queer and trans women's insights matter for the LGBTQ community in Colombia, but also how these insights make for a stronger approach to implementing WPS more broadly. This workshop approach can be applied elsewhere, as more researchers aim to include queer and trans organizers as gender experts in peace and security.

Notes

1. I recognize feminist as inherently trans-inclusive.
2. For an in-depth consideration of this, read the 2022 Peace and Security Report issued by the Independent Expert on protection against violence and discrimination based on sexual orientation and gender identity: www.ohchr.org/en/calls-for-input/2022/report-independent-expert-protection-against-violence-and-discrimination-based
3. There are at least 18 countries with present or previous NAPs with at least one reference to LGBT people or sexuality: Albania, Argentina, Croatia, France, Germany, Iraq, Ireland, Italy, Japan, Nepal, Norway, Paraguay, Sweden, Switzerland, South Africa, The Netherlands, the UK, and Uruguay. Women, Peace and Security NAPS are available to review via the WILPF Monitoring and Analysis of National Action Plans on Women, Peace and Security Database: https://1325naps.peacewomen.org/
4. Paul Kirby, Hannah Wright, and Aisling Swaine note in their analysis of the UK NAP, 'the extent of this inclusion can be overstated: there is one reference to "sexuality" in the third [UK] NAP and one to "sexual orientation" in the fourth' (2022). Inclusion of LGBTQ issues in one NAP does not mean inclusion in the next version of a country's NAP, with some countries writing new NAPs every four to five years. Furthermore, mentioning LGBTQ people does not mean the country has engaged with the queer and trans community during consultation of the NAP, or that a queer analysis was applied in writing the document.
5. Astraea's work and research focuses on trans-inclusive funds. The organization raises and distributes funds to programmes and initiatives led by and for diverse constituencies, prioritizing groups led by lesbians and queer women, trans and gender non-conforming people, intersex people, and people of colour.
6. https://web.archive.org/web/20170224021117/http://circuitous.org/scraps/combahee.html
7. Beyond their NAPs, some governments have publicly taken up the call to include attention to LGBTQ people in their gender, peace, and security work, with others making commitments to do so at the March 2023 UN Security Council Arria-formula meeting (UN Web TV 2023). Two years earlier in 2021 the UK government Gender, Peace and Security portfolio funded two projects focusing on 'LGBT+ inclusive approaches to conflict and the Women, Peace and Security agenda'. The first research project was conducted by the organization Protection Approaches and resulted in the publication *Queering Atrocity Prevention*, which examines the cis-heteronormative assumptions at the intersection of the WPS, responsibility to protect (R2P), and atrocity prevention (2021). International Alert conducted the second UK-funded project, focusing on opportunities for an LGBT+-inclusive approach to WPS in Nepal and Myanmar (Sow et al, 2022). International non-governmental organizations such as Outright International and the Centre for Feminist Foreign Policy have also begun doing work at the intersection of LGBT communities and WPS.
8. See also: Colombia Diversa (2020), *Orders of Prejudice. Systematic Crimes against LGBT People in the Colombian Conflict*, Bogotá; Colombia Diversa (2020), '¿Quién nos va a contar? Informe para la Comisión de la Verdad sobre experiencias de personas lesbianas, gays, bisexuales y trans en el conflicto armado colombiano', Bogotá.
9. https://caribeafirmativo.lgbt/
10. See publications at: https://caribeafirmativo.lgbt/publicaciones/investigaciones/
11. See: Caribe Afirmativo (2019), 'Nosotras Resistimos'; both organizations contributed to the truth commission report on gender and sexuality: Comisión de la Verdad (2022), 'Mi Cuerpo Es La Verdad', Bogotá.

12 Members of the Colombia Diversa team are included by name given their existing visibility as advocates of LGBTQ rights. Other participants in the workshop are anonymized given the sensitivity of the topics discussed.
13 In Autumn 2021, Anupama Ranawana, a UK academic colleague and researcher with Christian Aid UK, approached me about an opportunity to bridge research and policy in the intersection of WPS and LGBTQ human rights. On Ranawana's recommendation, together a team of four women— two openly queer—developed the research project 'Queering Women, Peace and Security (WPS): improving engagement with lesbian, bisexual, transgender, and queer (LBTQ) women in WPS programming'. The October 2022 workshop was organized to inform outputs from the project, including this chapter, a toolkit, and a policy brief.
14 Anupama Ranawana (of Christian Aid UK), Natalie Mercer (of Christian Aid Colombia), and I also attended and participated in the workshop discussions.
15 Full details for each organization, including websites, are provided at the end of the chapter.
16 Following additional funding from Outright International granted in early 2023, Colombia Diversa continues to engage in the observational process offering reflections and analysis of the ongoing negotiations and activities around developing Colombia's first WPS NAP.
17 Colombian peace talks for the 2016 peace deal took place in 2012 in Havana, Cuba.
18 See, for example, their appeal for a joint case on sexual and reproductive violence, and violence based on victims' sexual orientation and gender identity: www.sismamujer.org/wp-content/uploads/2021/10/The-opening-of-a-national-case-of-sexual-and-reproductive-violence.pdf
19 *Marica* or *maricón* is to faggot, as *cuir* is to queer. In Colombian youth slang, *marica* can also be used as 'dude' or 'babe' between heterosexual and homosexual people. For a longer discussion about the genealogy of the word *mariconear* and the possible historical erasures of its use, see Simonetto's Chapter 6, this volume.
20 The New York Lesbian Avengers organized the logistics of the first Dyke March in New York City, in 1993, creating a manifesto addressing the necessity of grassroots lesbian organizing, especially given the anti-gay bills being pushed by the right wing. There are now Dyke Marches all over the world. Read more here: www.nycdykemarch.com/herstory

Workshop participants
All quotes are from 15 October 2022

Individuals
- María Susana Peralta Ramón, Colombia Diversa
- Valentina Parra, Colombia Diversa
- Laura Beltrán, Colombia Diversa
- Camila García, Colombia Diversa
- Camila Sánchez, Colombia Diversa
- Anupama Ranawana, Researcher, Christian Aid, UK
- Nathalie Mercier, Christian Aid, Colombia
- Jamie Hagen, Queen's University Belfast, UK
- Participant 1, Fundación Artemisas
- Participant 2, Liga Internacional de Mujeres por la Paz y la Libertad (LIMPAL)
- Participant 3, Red Nacional de Mujeres
- Participant 4, Red Nacional de Mujeres
- Participant 5, Corporación Humanas

- Participant 6, DeJusticia
- Participant 7, ForumCIV – Colombia
- Participant 8, Católicas por el Derecho a Decidir
- Participant 9, Representative of LGBT people from Doncello, Caquetá
- Participant 10, Lesbian organizer from Nariño and expert in efforts for finding missing LGBT persons
- Participant 11, Lesbian organizer from Meta and expert in efforts for finding missing LGBT persons
- Participant 12, Trans organizer from Tumaco, Nariño

Organizations
- Colombia Diversa is a non-governmental organization that since 2004 has fought for the rights of those people who have been discriminated against for loving, being or appearing 'different'. In order to live in an equal society for all, Colombia Diversa carries out strategic litigation, advocacy and research on the human rights of lesbians, gays, bisexuals and trans people in Colombia.
- Fundación Artemisas (*Artemis Foundation*) is an organization focused on advocacy issues, mobilization, and feminist political participation, integrating the affective component for the construction of networks and the creation of audiences that contribute to the visibility, expansion, and emergence of feminist agendas. https://somosmuchas.org/quienes-somos
- Liga Internacional de Mujeres por la Paz y la Libertad (LIMPAL) (*Women's International League for Peace and Freedom – Colombia, WILPF*) is an intersectional feminist pacifist and anti-militarist organization focused on feminist peacebuilding and security. www.limpalcolombia.org/es/
- Red Nacional de Mujeres (*National Women's Organization*) is a diverse collective of social organizations, leaders, and independent women who, for 30 years, have been participating in processes for the guarantee, promotion, and defence of women's rights in Colombia. www.rednacionaldemujeres.org/
- Corporación Humanas (*Humans Corporation*) is a non-governmental organization focused on feminist studies and political action oriented towards the promotion and guarantee of human rights and gender justice from an intersectional approach at the national, regional, and international levels. www.humanas.org.co/
- DeJusticia (*Organization of Justice*) is a non-profit legal organization that, through action and research around legal and social studies, is committed to the promotion of human rights in Colombia and the Southern Cone. www.dejusticia.org
- ForumCIV is a Swedish organization that advocates for the strengthening of processes in defence of civil society in different countries around the world. www.forumciv.org/int/where-we-work/colombia/country-programme

- Católicas por el Derecho a Decidir (*Catholic Women for the Right to Decide*) is an organization that brings together the movement of Catholic feminist women in defence of women's rights for a life free of violence and discrimination, especially rights related to sexuality and reproduction. https://cddcolombia.org/

Bibliography

Alvarado Cóbar, J., Bjertén-Günther, E., and Jung, Y. (2018) 'Assessing gender perspectives in peace processes with application to the cases of Colombia and Mindanao', *SIPRI*. Available from: www.sipri.org/sites/default/files/2018-11/sipriinsight1806.pdf

Amar, P. (2013) *The Security Archipelago*, Durham, NC: Duke University Press.

Ashe, F. (2018) 'Reimaging inclusive security in peace processes: LGB&T perspectives (PSRP Report)', Global Justice Academy, University of Edinburgh.

Astraea Lesbian Foundation for Justice (2020) 'Vibrant yet under-resourced: the state of lesbian, bisexual and queer movements', *Astrea* [online]. Available from: https://fundlbq.org/wp-content/uploads/2020/06/Astraea_MamaCash_LBQ_Report_VDEF-v2-SPREADS.pdf

Basu, S., Kirby, P., and Shepherd, L. (eds) (2020) 'Women, peace and security: a critical cartography', in *New Directions in Women, Peace and Security*, Bristol: Bristol University Press.

Bracke, S. (2012) 'From "saving women" to "saving gays": rescue narratives and their dis/continuities', *European Journal of Women's Studies*, 19(2): 237–52. DOI: doi.org/10.1177/1350506811435032

Browne, K. et al (2017) 'Towards transnational feminist queer methodologies', *Gender, Place & Culture*, 24(10): 1376–97.

Bueno-Hansen, P. (2014). 'Queer/lesbiana dialogues among feminist movements in the Americas', in S.E. Alvarez et al (eds), *Translocalities/Translocalidades: Feminist Politics of Translation in the Latin/a Américas*, Durham, NC: Duke University Press, pp 321–39.

Bueno-Hansen, P. (2018) 'The emerging LGBTI rights challenge to transitional justice in Latin America', *International Journal of Transitional Justice*, 12(1): 126–45.

Colombia Diversa (2020) 'Orders of prejudice: systematic crimes committed against LGBT people in the Colombian armed conflict', *Colombia Diversa* [online]. Available from: https://colombiadiversa.org/colombiadiversa2016/wp-content/uploads/2020/07/english-version-Orders-Of-Prejudice.pdf

Davis, L. and Stern, J. (2018) 'WPS and LGBTI rights', in S.E. Davies and J. True (eds) *The Oxford Handbook of Women, Peace and Security*, London: Oxford University Press, pp 657–68.

Fobear, K. and Baines, E. (2020) 'Pushing the conversation forward: the intersections of sexuality and gender identity in transitional justice', *International Journal of Human Rights*, 24(4): 307–12.

Gómez, M.M. (2013) 'Prejudice-based violence', in C. Motta and M. Saez (eds) *Gender and Sexuality in Latin America: Cases and Decisions. Ius Gentium: Comparative Perspectives on Law and Justice 24*, Springer: Dordrecht.

Haastrup, T. and Hagen, J.J. (2021) 'Racial hierarchies of knowledge production in the Women, Peace and Security agenda', *Critical Studies on Security*, 9(1): 27–30.

Hagen, J. (2016) 'Queering women, peace and security', *International Affairs*, 92(2): 313–32.

Hagen, J. and Dupuis-Vargas Latorre, N.S. (2022) 'An interview with Nikita Simonne Dupuis-Vargas Latorre about trans men's rights in Colombia today', *Peace Review*, 34(4): 476–80. DOI: 10.1080/10402659.2022.2128737

Inton-Campbell, J.M. and Inton-Campbell, M.N. (2022) 'Trans-ing peace studies: an introduction', *Peace Review*, 34(4): 465–75.

Kirby, P., Wright, H., and Swaine, A. (2022) 'The future of the UK's Women, Peace and Security policy', LSE Centre for Women, Peace and Security Policy Brief 07/2022.

Loken, M. and Hagen, J.J. (2022) 'Queering gender-based violence scholarship: an integrated research agenda', *International Studies Review*, 24(4): 1–22.

Maier, N. (2020) 'Queering Colombia's peace process: a case study of LGBTI inclusion', *International Journal of Human Rights*, 24(4): 377–92.

McEvoy, S. (2015) 'Queering security studies in Northern Ireland', in M.L Picq and M. Thiel (eds) *Sexual Politics in World Politics: How LGBTQ Claims Shape International Relations*, London/New York: Routledge.

Merry, S.E. (2006) 'Transnational human rights and local activism: mapping the middle' *American Anthropologist*, 108(1): 38–51. www.jstor.org/stable/3804730

Myrttinen, H. and Daigle, M. (2017) 'When merely existing is a risk: sexual and gender minorities in conflict, displacement and peacebuilding', *International Alert*. Available from: www.international-alert.org/wp-content/uploads/2021/08/Gender-Sexual-And-Gender-Minorities-EN-2017.pdf

Nagarajan, C. and Hagen, J.J. (2023) 'Supporting queer feminist mobilisations for peace and security', Centre for Gender in Politics Policy Brief, [online] 29 March. Available from: www.qub.ac.uk/research-centres/centre-for-gender-in-politics/PolicyBriefs/PolicyBriefs/Filetoupload,1722887,en.pdf

Outright Action International (2020) 'The Women Peace and Security agenda and its implications for LGBTIQ people'. Available from: https://outrightinternational.org/sites/default/files/WomenPeaceSecurity2020.pdf

Protection Approaches (2021) 'Queering atrocity prevention'. Available from: https://img1.wsimg.com/blobby/go/131c96cc-7e6f-4c06-ae37-6550dbd85dde/Queering%20AP_nohyperlinks.pdf

Rao, R. (2014) 'Queer questions', *International Feminist Journal of Politics*, 16(2): 199–217.

Rich, A. (1980) 'Compulsory heterosexuality and lesbian existence', *Signs*, 5(4): 631–60. www.jstor.org/stable/3173834

Shepherd, L.J. and Sjoberg, L. (2012) 'Trans-bodies in/of war(s): cisprivilege and contemporary security strategy', *Feminist Review*, 101(1): 5–23. DOI: doi.org/10.1057/fr.2011.53

Sow, N., Onslow, C., Dahal, S., and Pemberton, A. (2022) 'Breaking the binary: LGBT+ inclusive approach to the Women, Peace And Security agenda in Nepal and Myanmar', *International Alert*. Available from: www.international-alert.org/wp-content/uploads/2022/11/LGBT-Breaking-Binary-WPS-Nepal-Myanmar-EN-2022.pdf

Thoreson, R.R. (2014) *Transnational LGBT Activism: Working for Sexual Rights Worldwide*, Minneapolis, MN: University of Minnesota Press.

United Nations Security Council (2000) Resolution 1325. S/RES/1325 (2000). Available from: https//undocs.org/S/RES/1325(2000)

UN Web TV (2023) United Nations Security Council Arria-formula Meeting: 'Integrating the Human Rights of LGBTI persons into the Council's Mandate for Maintaining International Peace and Security'. Available from: https://media.un.org/en/asset/k13/k133or09cy

Ward, J. (2008) *Respectability Queer: Diversity Culture in LGBT Activist Organisations*, Nashville, TN: Vanderbilt University Press.

Wilcox, L. (2017) 'Practising gender, queering theory', *Review of International Studies*, 43(5): 789–808. www.jstor.org/stable/26619165

Wilkinson, C. (2017) 'Introduction: queer/ing in/security', *Critical Studies on Security*, 5(1): 106–8. DOI: 10.1080/21624887.2017.1294830

PART II

Queer Methods of Conflict Research

4

The Visual as Queer Method

Dean Cooper-Cunningham

The *punctum* as entry point

In 2013, international news coverage started to emerge about a new Russian law that prohibited the positive depiction of non-traditional (meaning non-heteronormative) relations, lifestyles, and ideas. My first encounter with Russian state homophobia[1] was a news article that reported the passing of the so-called 'gay propaganda law'. The article was accompanied by a headline photograph of four individuals huddled together, one with blood streaming down their face, surrounded by police officers. I remember the moment I saw this photograph quite distinctly because it shocked me, left me feeling uncomfortable, and that image has stuck with me ever since.

Figure 4.1 is strikingly similar to the photographs accompanying those news articles. The moment I saw that photograph and read reports about the gay propaganda law, it wasn't immediately clear to me what its passing really boiled down to: arbitrary moralizing about the types of sex, bodily pleasures, and erotic desires one is allowed to have and legitimately pursue. I did not have the vocabulary to articulate what Russia's new law meant in terms of sex. I hadn't really considered that there might be a politics of sex. Nor was I able to put words around international dimensions of Russia's politicization of sex beyond pointing to 'the international community's' obligation to do something. That sex and homophobia might be part of a broader geopolitical strategy—what I have since conceptualized as 'heteronormative internationalism' (Cooper-Cunningham, 2021: 11, 46; Gifkins et al, 2022: 11)—was surprising when I first encountered that image and long after.

That is the power that an image holds. Power to inspire thought, exploration, reflection, inquisitiveness, and theoretical play. Seeing that image in 2013, I failed to think through the politics or the power of visual

Figure 4.1: Untitled photograph by Mads Nissen (2013)

Source: Panos Pictures, image no. MNN01245RUS.

representation, which is ironic given that it was a photograph of homophobic violence that provoked me; or to use Roland Barthes' terminology, it possessed the amorphous 'punctum', that which 'pricks me (but also bruises me, is poignant to me)' (1981: 27). An image can have an immediate affective and vividly experienced effect on an individual, but it can also take time for the political to surface and become clear. In my case, this happened over several years. Those years involved finding the tools, vocabulary, and knowledge of queer and visual politics to enable me to grasp what was going on in a meaningful way. This does not diminish the power of the visual—it demonstrates its complexity: it takes work to read images and, contrary to the idiom that images speak a thousand words, it might not always be clear what they 'say' at first.

The politics of sex and the visual aren't often considered core parts of how we think and teach International Relations (IR). The result is a reproduction of the powerful and ordering ideas that sex is a purely personal thing (thereby perpetuating the power of heteronormativity) and that photographs are mundane objects used merely to illustrate stories that capture the whole truth in a way that words cannot. Both sustain dominant understandings of sex and images as apolitical, making it difficult to see how a photograph representing a law that ultimately governs sex, bodily pleasure, and erotic desire could raise questions of importance for international politics. This is particularly acute in the scholarship on conflict and atrocity prevention (Hagen, 2016; Gifkins et al, 2022). In my research, the visual emerges as an important site of activism that reconfigures who and what we consider important for analysis in IR. This affects how we study and think about queer issues in international politics. In what follows, I provide some tools, vocabulary, and knowledge for thinking about the queer potential of visual methods for IR.

Queer-visual entanglement

Far from just calling attention to, and representing, homophobic violence through photojournalism, the visual, conceived broadly as including visual artefacts (that is, images, monuments, flags) and visibility (that is, what is allowed to appear and be seen), is a crucial part of queer politics. Visual artefacts are mobilized in a variety of ways, both oppressive and liberatory. For example, the pink triangle was attached to suspected homosexual bodies during the violent Nazi German campaign to 'cleanse' Europe of supposed societal threats. Turning to more liberatory examples: the rainbow flag was created by a collection of activists at the Gay Community Center in San Francisco in the 1970s and there was an outpouring of sex-positive imagery in response to the US government's homophobic public health campaigns, rooted in sexual shaming during the first years of the AIDS crisis. Today, the now iconic 'Gay Clown Putin' memes circulate as part of the international condemnation of Russia's 'gay propaganda law' that started in 2013.

In terms of visibility, queerness has always had a close and complex relationship with (in)visibility. Performing one's sexuality and/or gender in line with dominant cisheteronormative expectations is deeply intertwined with the (in)security one experiences in society. The ability of queer people to 'pass' as cisgender and/or heterosexual has for a long time been a strategy for seeking security, a way of navigating cisheteronormative sociality in which queerness is constituted as aberrant, in need of correction or punishment. This is captured by an individual at the 20th anniversary of the Stonewall Riots: "We are political people by the very nature of our being because our entire society is constructed to deny our existence" (DIVA TV 1989: 00:12:50). In a world ravaged by numerous overlapping, protracted moral conflicts about appropriate sexual desire, bodily pleasure, and gender expression, making one's queerness invisible can be a source of security by not marking oneself out as differing and instead as 'normal' and thus unthreatening to dominant sociality (Bersani, 1996; Warner, 2000).

As a source of security, however, invisibility only works because (the visibility of) queerness is, in the first instance, deemed abhorrent, abnormal, and non-heteronormative desires a moral flaw in need of erasure or control. Those bodies that do not fit cisheteronormative scripts and perform their gender and sexuality in ways that contradict dominant sociality put themselves at risk of violence, be that from the state or wider society. It is worth noting here that the body is 'informed by a visual, gendered logic' (Åhäll, 2018: 150). The body is as such also a visual thing that we see and then make assumptions about based on visual markers such as dress, body language, mannerisms, and so on. The body, therefore, performatively reproduces sex/gender by either conforming or flouting sex/gender norms. How bodies present and behave publicly as well as how they are disciplined is thus connected to the visual.

The social and political significance of the visual is by no means a new thing, particularly for movements organized around issues of gender and sexuality. AIDS activists harnessed the visual as a powerful political tool to call attention to government inaction and the state's wilful killing of queer people, and gay liberationists used the visual in campaign for sexual liberation free from practices of stigmatization and shaming. There are vast archives (for example, the New York Public Library's Gender and Sexuality Collection), social media accounts, and books dedicated to documenting this queer activism and they contain a significant amount of visual material (Finkelstein, 2018; Riemer and Brown, 2019; Cooper-Cunningham, 2021: ch. 5).

The above examples barely skim the surface of the ways the visual constitutes queer politics, cultures, and histories. However, they demonstrate the role that the visual has played in queer resistance *and* homophobic oppression from the visual symbols placed on queer bodies to the flags used to resist state and social homophobia to the cisheteronormative logics that make it possible to be securely visible in public. That the visual has been used as a mode of queer resistance and oppression is unsurprising given that: (a) those who are oppressed, sought silent, and/or ignored often use the visual as a means to make their voices heard, produce knowledge, document and share (counter-)cultures, and make critical interventions in politics (Campbell and Shapiro, 2007: 132; Bleiker, 2018a: 8; Cooper-Cunningham, 2019; McGarry et al, 2020); and (b) the state actively struggles to control what/who is made visible, given the possibility of appearing in public, and how it/they appear (see, inter alia, Foxall, 2013; Shim, 2017; Tsinovoi, 2018; Hansen and Spanner, 2021; Cooper-Cunningham, 2022).

The visual is a site of queer culture, activism, resistance, and contestation that is both representative and constitutive of the politics underpinning various queer projects globally through predominantly word-based artefacts (for example, news articles, zines, speeches, and pamphlets) and predominantly body-based actions (for example, in-the-street protest, Pride, and political funerals). The visual can also serve as a way of representing and, therefore, seeing queer (in)security and identity-based violence. As such visual representations of widespread homophobic violence might be considered an epistemic site to be included as a risk indicator in atrocity prevention frameworks. Scholars working on queer political issues, broadly understood, ought to be engaging with and developing visual methods to allow the complexities of queer subjectivity, political participation, insecurities, resistance, culture, and forms of sociality to emerge. Seeing homophobic/transphobic oppression and using the visual as an epistemic entry point to studying conflict is a growing necessity given that we know anti-queer politics so often precedes conflict escalation and genocidal campaigns (Gifkins et al, 2022) and that visual and bodily means of articulating (in)security are often resorted to by oppressed groups.

In my research on Russian state homophobia and international activism against it, the visual has played a critical role both in terms of Russia's gay propaganda law, which limits space for the public visibility of queer people and queerness, and in the use of images and the public visibility of queer bodies in activism against Russian state homophobia. This is indicative of the power and politicality of the visual, particularly with regards to the way images can highlight and bring international attention to queer security issues; as did the photograph opening this chapter. That photograph was my first encounter with Russian state homophobia. Initially, it represented violent state homophobia but it has subsequently, after much research and theoretical percolating, come to represent something much larger: Russia's geopolitics of the family (Abrahamsen, 2020) and its 'heteronormative internationalist' project (Cooper-Cunningham, 2021).

In this chapter, to connect visual methods with queer theorizing, I draw on IR's critical methods and visual literatures as well as my experience using visual empirical material in research about Russian state homophobia. I argue that visual theory and methods, while not innately queer, can be used in ways that: (a) bring our attention to the insecurities queer people face without always already reducing queer people to monolithic, eternally victimized subjects; (b) constitute queer issues, especially homophobic politics, as matters of international concern; and (c) can encourage us to see the connections between everyday security problems (that is, those caused by heteronormativity and patriarchy) and broader internationalist projects grounded in ideas of national security, progress/regress, and identity politics.[2] Drawing on my research about Russian homophobia, I will show how the use of visuals brings attention to and enables critical engagement with Russia's heteronormative geopolitical project by showcasing queer people's vulnerability to state oppression as well as their resistance to it (Cooper-Cunningham, 2021).

In terms of structure, I first outline how I understand queer before moving to a discussion of critical methods and theorizing. Then, I outline what I call a tripartite word–image–body model for studying the visual in terms of security. In this approach, I recognize the opportunity for words, images, and bodies to be analysed together. I apply this approach in an analysis of two images on international contestation of Russian state homophobia.

Queer

'Queer' has been conceptualized and mobilized in many different ways in the years since its first appearance as an activist project and then as a theoretical idea. Sometimes it is used as a reference to LGBT+ issues or an umbrella term for LGBT+ identities; sometimes it refers to the destabilization of hegemonic ideas about sexuality and gender; sometimes it references a political project grounded in antinormativity and antisociality[3] that emerged in the 1980s—the list is unending.[4] Given the manifold conceptualizations and uses of queer, it is important to be precise around its use here. In my work, I follow Lauren Berlant and Michael Warner's position that: 'Queer social theory is committed to sexuality as an inescapable category of analysis, agitation, and refunctioning' (1998: 564).

Like feminist and de-/post-colonial thinking, queer cannot be detached from its political roots, which are firmly embedded in early gay and lesbian liberation as well as AIDS activism.[5] Gay liberationists, lesbian feminists, and AIDS activists pointed out that homophobia and anti-queer projects are, fundamentally, grounded in sexism and moralizing about the types of sex, bodily pleasures, and erotic desires one is allowed to have and legitimately pursue (Warner, 1993a; Berlant and Warner, 1998; Warner, 2000). The hegemonic orders produced and sustained by this moralizing are not negligible: cisheteronormative understandings of gender and sexuality are core organizing principles of society that sustain hierarchies and dominant power relations that privilege the cisgendered and/or heterosexual subject (Foucault, 1978; Bersani, 1996; Warner, 2000). Through 'institutional carriers', such as schools, hospitals, scientific associations, and states' and international organizations' policies, 'oppressive identity models and social norms' are repeatedly (re)produced (Seidman, 1993: 109).

This all plays out on people's bodies by structuring how a specifically shaped body is understood in terms of its gender and then how that specifically gendered body is expected to desire other gendered bodies. This has been the target of much queer politicking, particularly that of the early gay and lesbian liberation movements. The simplification of gender into masculine/feminine and sexuality into heterosexual/homosexual dichotomies precludes any legitimate acknowledgement of the wayward workings of pleasure, desire, and individual subjectivity that works beyond those binaries.

In terms of international politics, we are now seeing sex play a key constitutive role in geopolitical projects as ever-increasing numbers of states implement moralistic positions on non-heteronormative sexuality and non-cisgender performances into their foreign policies. Today, Russia is spearheading an internationally appealing political project grounded in so-called 'traditional family values' that has facilitated similar homophobic projects across Europe (Holm and Tjalve, 2018; Abrahamsen, 2020; Gifkins et al, 2022). The entry of sex into international politics often includes stigmatizing/shaming of other states for their 'decadent' or 'uncivilized' stances on queerness and how they handle 'deviation' from the cishetero normal. This, in turn, starts to structure relations between states. As such, sex can be said to have an international politics (Peterson, 2014).

In the case of Russia this comes in the form of political homophobia[6] (for example, the censoring of queerness in public through the gay propaganda law in 2013 and constitutional amendments in 2020 enshrining marriage as between a man and woman), which has been consistently legitimized through a discourse of a foreign, un-Russian queer threat emanating from the West (Healey, 2018). This queer-friendly and threatening West is known in Russian foreign policy discourse as 'Gayropa' (Riabov and Riabova, 2014; Foxall, 2019). This discourse has morphed into an illiberal internationalist project grounded in heteronormativity that purports to save this Gayropean space of moral decadence and immorality from itself. A significant part of that project is an internationally appealing package of 'traditional family values' that works through a logic of shame and stigmatization of the non-cisheteronormative, which has been taken up by the Global Right (Mudde, 2019; Abrahamsen, 2020).

This discourse has also been used by Putin to justify the war in Ukraine. Since announcing a 'special military operation' in 2022, he has consistently referred to Western sexual degeneracy to justify the invasion. Declaring the annexation of Luhansk, Donetsk, Zaporizhzhia, and Kherson in September 2022 and in his State of the Union address in February 2023, Putin invoked Western immorality and rejection of 'traditional' sexuality/gender norms and 'family values' as evidence of the threat that the 'uncivilized', 'degenerate' West poses to Russia. Since at least 2014, Putin has consistently discursively constituted Ukraine as part of Russia and Ukrainians and Russians as one people (Düben, 2020). Following the Kremlin's discursive constitution of Ukraine as Russian, Western sexual decadence thereby also threatens Ukraine. Moralism around appropriate sexuality and gender play a key justificatory role in this conflict; Russian national security is entangled with sexuality and gender.

Keeping Berlant and Warner's emphasis on sexuality as a category of analysis and agitation, the focus of my queer analytic always sits squarely on *the politics of sexual shame and stigma*. My analysis also accounts for the power structures and normative organizations of society that flow from what is, at a meta level, arbitrary moralizing about sex, pleasure, and desire.[7] Focusing on the politics of sexual shame and stigma means paying attention to how stigmatizing and shaming practices about so-called 'deviant' sexuality and gender are mobilized for violently hierarchical, exclusionary, and disciplinary social and political projects. Given that I am using queer within an IR context, I pay particular attention to how such projects of sexual moralism go international and get organized into a sexualized geopolitics, as we see in the case of Russia.

Recognizing the importance of queer's genealogy, both at the conceptual and political level, my use of queer draws on the politics of gay liberation and AIDS activism. In particular, I draw on a queer politics that is radically antinormative and antisocial, which has at its core a commitment to ceaselessly questioning relations of power and refusing to moralize about consensual sex, pleasure, and desire (Cohen, 1997; Warner, 1999, 2000; Gould, 2009).

While the destabilization and the deconstruction of binaries is one way to show the arbitrariness of cisheteronormative ideas, norms, and disciplining (Wilcox, 2014; Weber, 2016; Leigh, 2017; Richter-Montpetit, 2018), queer can be more than plurality and the complicating of binaries:

> Destroying deeply entrenched and resilient systems of oppression such as patriarchal gender and heteronormativity is not as simple as pointing to their discursive, socially (re)produced, contingent nature. Destabilizing powerful discourses and showing their reliance on obedience, repetition and fear of transgression is only one step … Queer is more than resistance to heteronormativity by showing how it works. It is more than mimicry, parody, troubling or a camp reworking of hegemonic forms of the social – the compulsory practice of heterosexuality – and is instead 'a potentially revolutionary inaptitude … for sociality as it is known'. (Bersani, 1996: 75)

Positioning queer as a method of destabilization, or as having an ontology of multiplicity, is to constitute queer praxis as a fight for plurality and undecidability. While an important aspect of the queer project, I understand queer as a political project that goes beyond a plural logic and is not detachable from questions of sexuality and its gendered nature.

Queer can and should be used to understand and deconstruct social and political projects that deploy racist, sexist, misogynistic, ableist, classist identity constructs and work through binary Self/Other, normal/abnormal, safe/dangerous logics to justify highly politicized actions, but it is more than exploding binaries and cultivating a sociality of pluralism. It is a perpetual struggle against oppression and hierarchies (Cohen, 1997). Queer also embraces positive conceptualizations of alterity, differing, and deviance in a way that refuses to empower some over others through dichotomously constituted hierarchies and refuses to 'sanitize or morally legitimize sexual difference and instead takes delight in shame' (Cooper-Cunningham, 2022: 313).

Keeping all of this in mind, my use of queer draws on the activist and antagonistic politics of queer as well as its focus on sex, bodily pleasure, and erotic desire. Queer refuses normativity, is anti-assimilationist, is oppositional, is non-proscriptive, and rejects cisheteronormative sociality. Queer is 'fierce pride in bucking political, emotional, and sexual norms' (Gould, 2009: 264). Used as such, and in keeping with Cohen's formulation, queer is attentive to all those who are penalized for their divergence from cisheteronormative culture.

Queer methods

Nothing is inherently 'queer' (Berlant and Warner, 1995). Likewise, no method is an inherently *queer* method. Researchers working on queer issues are often reticent about methods and methodologies, leaving the 'how' of queer research swept under the carpet (Browne and Nash, 2016: 1, 7). How, then, can we talk about queer methodologies and the visual as a way of doing queer research?[8]

Many queer theorists use 'discourse and textual analyses to consider how power relations are constituted and maintained in the production of social and political meanings' (Browne and Nash, 2016: 6). Queer academic scholarship, particularly as it has come into IR, has a close connection to poststructuralism and many adopt a discursive epistemology, ontology, and, therefore, methodology. Beyond academe, queer thought and activism that sought to shift debates and political projects beyond exclusive and problematic identity politics also have a close link to postmodernism/poststructuralism; particularly that of liberation activists and those advancing an antinormative, antisocial, and antiauthoritarian agendas (Seidman, 1993; Warner, 1993b: xi).

My theorization of queer, outlined above, is grounded in a poststructuralist understanding of the social and political as constituted in discourse but it is also deeply connected to liberationist, antinormative, and antisocial queer thought that commits to a perpetual interrogation of all relations to power (Bersani, 1996; Cohen, 1997; Edelman, 2004). Coming from a poststructuralist epistemological and ontological perspective, the main thrust of my methodological approach to studying queer issues in international politics comes from discourse analysis.

Starting from a discursive epistemology and ontology, and building on Lene Hansen's work (2000, 2006, 2011), I have previously advocated for extending the parameters of discourse analysis that are found in most discourse analysis in IR to include the visual and body as foci in research on gender- and sexuality-based insecurity (Cooper-Cunningham, 2019). Recognizing the vital importance of the visual and the body as epistemological sites through which we can gain and produce new knowledge—and consequently challenge powerful ordering ideas around sexuality, insecurity, and agency—I have developed what I call a tripartite word-image-body model for studying security issues and conflict-related vulnerabilities that builds on Hansen's (2000) work on silence (Cooper-Cunningham, 2019, 2020). I outline this model in the next section and demonstrate how it can be used analytically in the next again.

Claudia Aradau and Jef Huysmans (2014) argue that the methods we use are a critical part of theorizing. How we study the world and its issues are a crucial and inseparable part of the type of knowledge we produce about the world. In contrast to dominant understandings of 'scientific' research, theory, empirical data, and methods/methodologies are fundamentally inseparable. They all come together to create research 'results' and, thus, structure the (types of) knowledge produced (Aradau and Huysmans, 2014; Browne and Nash, 2016: 2). Acknowledging the deep connection between the constituent parts of all research projects is important for recognizing the power that methods possess in *creating* knowledge in specific and limited ways. To date, most knowledge (created) about 'queer' issues has been epistemologically limited to written/spoken words—at least in work considered academic.

Taking seriously the argument that methods are not separate from but embedded in the theories and knowledge we produce, the methods we use to *do* research deemed queer inevitably shape and are shaped by our conceptualization and understanding of what 'queer' is. In visual research, this is particularly pronounced because all images are open to multiple possible interpretations depending on the knowledge one brings to an image in reading it. Seeing queerly, therefore, comes from the knowledge—our theorizations of the social and political—that we bring to bear on an image and any subsequent analysis.

This leads to my answer to the following question about the 'queer' of queer methods:

> If methodologies are meant to coherently link ontological and epistemological positions to our choice of methods, are methodologies automatically queer if queer conceptualisations are used? Can we have queer knowledges if our methodologies are not queer? Is there such a thing as queer method/methodology/research? (Browne and Nash, 2016: 2).

Since our methodologies are invariably inflected by our queer theorizing and thinking, our ontologies and epistemologies, they become queer the moment they are put in service of queer research or political projects. This is not to say that a method is and forever will be queer because methods can be used for different projects with different politics. It is, rather, to say that methods, as our research tools, become (temporarily, transiently) queered when we use them to ask queer questions and to pursue a 'queer intellectual curiosity' (Weber, 2015) that probes around questions of sexuality and the politics of sexual shame and stigma.

Given that queer is such a contested concept and that its critical potential is often said to come from being unstable, slippery, and flexible as an approach (Butler, 1993; Browne and Nash, 2016), I find it pertinent and most productive to define a method(ology) as queer by the political and theoretical commitments underpinning the research undertaken. While somewhat sympathetic to the argument that queer's potential lies in its malleability, concepts need to be clearly delineated and theorized to be analytically useful—at least in their immediate usage. In this sense, there also has to be some unifying 'core', which, of course, can change and evolve over time. When it comes to 'queer', the important genealogical and political points I made above must be kept in mind when using—or for that matter developing—a queer approach to research. The core of queer as I use it is a focus on the politics of sex and the power structures that flow from normative, moralistic, formulations of appropriate/deviant sexuality and gender.

Keeping this in mind, I hold that a method can only ever be queer temporarily and it should enable researchers to: (a) understand, locate, challenge, make visible, study queer (in)security; and/or (b) delineate, uncover, locate, and thereby enable challenges to, cisheteronormative sociality and its attendant power structures. Methods are the tools we use to conduct research and, just as a house can be built, renovated, and/or torn down using hammers, drills, and the like, methods (our academic tools) can be used to do all different kinds of research, queer or not. As such, I take seriously Browne and Nash's point on 'queer' methods being those that 'let us speak to or interact with people, usually on the basis of sexual/gender identities and within anti-normative frameworks' (2016: 1). Building on Cohen's (1997) work, I would add that queer methods are the tools we use to interrogate and identify relations to power with a view to (proposing strategies for) their elimination. My tripartite word-image-body approach, discussed below, opens up the epistemological sites we turn to and therefore enables scholars to see and challenge heteronormative power structures as well as the way that conflict and atrocity, as is the case with Russia's current geopolitical campaigns, can be so deeply connected to moralizing politics around sexuality and gender.

The visual

Over the last decade, the visual has gained increasing prominence as a site for theorizing international politics and as a source of data in IR scholarship, yet remains in the periphery of what is often considered central to IR (Bleiker, 2018a; Cooper-Cunningham, 2020; Loken, 2021). Acknowledging that we live in the 'age of the image' (Williams, 2018), IR scholars have drawn on the visual in various, innovative ways such that visual research has become an established and ever-growing area of study in IR that is brimming with epistemological, ontological, and methodological debate (Williams, 2003; Hansen, 2011; Andersen, Vuori, and Mutlu, 2015; Bleiker, 2015, 2018b; Adler-Nissen, Andersen, and Hansen, 2019; Callahan, 2020). This effervescent body of work—known as Visual IR—provides an excellent starting point for thinking through the visual as queer method, particularly as it relates to queer people's (in)security.

Images 'surround everything we do' and as such 'shape international events and our understanding of them' (Bleiker, 2018a: 1). The visual can therefore be said to affect how we interact with, understand, interpret, and are affected by political events (Williams, 2018; Callahan, 2020). Rune Saugmann Andersen and Juha Vuori (2018) argue that critical security scholars have been at the forefront of developing visual methods and theory in IR and they show that the visual comes into critical security studies in three ways: visuality as modality (images represent and signal security); as practice (images construct (in)security); and as method (images are a research tool used to make security visible). The first two, as I have noted previously (Cooper-Cunningham, 2017), are the most common way of engaging images in IR: treating images as artefacts through which we come to know, make sense of, and act in the world. That is to say, people see, feel, do, and make international politics visually.

There are wide-ranging and long-standing epistemological, ontological, and methodological debates about the visual in IR. Like many Visual IR scholars, though, I understand images as polysemous, which is to say that their meaning cannot be pinned down definitively, that they do not have a single, universally received, message, and that an image does not tell a whole and truthful story in and of itself. Instead, following Barthes (1977) images are 'multivocal with audiences determining what they say through their interpretation(s)' (Cooper-Cunningham, 2019: 390).

This means that different individuals potentially interpret the same image differently because they draw on different personal experiences and knowledge to read it (Barthes, 1977: 46–7; Hansen, 2011: 58). People interact with, read, and experience images in context and read them through different intertexts. As such, an image and its meaning can be said only to come 'into existence through constitutive interactions with audiences and producers' (Cooper-Cunningham, 2019: 390). We, therefore, need to include various other texts and images in a visual analysis because these attribute meaning to the image(s) under study; they are the 'stock' that we draw on to interpret images.

Based on an understanding of images as polysemous, Hansen (2011) sets out four key dimensions in the study of images of security. First, an image and its constitution, which means looking at an image's content and the strategies of depiction its creator uses. Second, analysing an image's immediate intertext/intervisuality, which means looking at the text and images on or around the specific image(s) under study. Third, analysing wider policy discourses, which means analysing the policy discourses an image is speaking to or connected with. For instance, the many images printed in 2013 of Russian homophobia almost always refer to the gay propaganda law, so this would be brought into the analysis. Fourth, analysing other texts that ascribe meaning to the image in question, which means turning to debates about what an image is said to mean.

In addition to this, how an image is circulated, how it is used, and how it is spoken about are also important: does it cross borders, get used in protests, or capture widespread attention? All of these factors affect the arguments one can make about an image, how they are read, and what political status they are attributed. For example, when a particular visual motif (for example, the rainbow flag) is used in protest marches it acquires a different status than if it were not.

Building on this and feminist work on silence, I propose a tripartite approach to studying (in)security that recognizes: (1) words, (2) images, and (3) the body as epistemic sites. Analysing these three sites of analysis together we can see and understand security problems specifically and international politics more broadly. If one proceeds with a sole focus on discourse as written or spoken, other ways of speaking and intervening in international politics, and consequently queer politics, get disregarded and left out. The visual and/or bodily, in conjunction with and/or separately from words, show and tell stories (Cooper-Cunningham, 2019: 401) and the tripartite approach allows scholars to 'see' (in)security in sites that extend beyond written/spoken words thereby enabling a better engagement with, in this case, queer (in)security problems as announced by those who are targeted by the state for annihilation and erasure from public space as well as their experiences of conflict.

Many sexuality-based movements and queer activists have acknowledged the importance of the body (hunger-striking, street protest) and the visual (posters, memes) in resistance projects against the state and heteronormative society. This is evident in ACT UP New York's use visual and bodily activism during their campaign against the US government's AIDS policies: they combined posters, buttons, stickers, flags, and other visual artefacts with marches, protests outside pharmaceutical company offices, political funerals, and the scattering of the dead bodies' ashes on the lawn of the White House (Gould, 2009; Finkelstein, 2018).

The use of the body and the visual in addition to written and spoken words indicates that a theorization of discourse 'as something more expansive and complex, enacted through and exceeding words' is required in order to understand how images and (representations of) embodied practices combine to constitute (in)security (Cooper-Cunningham, 2019: 387). Understanding the body and the visual as ways of announcing (in)security is to epistemologically expand the sites we draw on to study (in)security. We must look beyond written/spoken words (for example, government documents, news media) about political issues (for example, state homophobia, conflict) because sometimes there are none or they are not the primary way of announcing (in)security. Including the body and the visual in our analyses allows for a better exploration of the complicated ways that (in)security is articulated and the way it is negotiated by those put in threatening circumstances. Just because there are no words articulating the vulnerabilities and insecurities a group faces does not mean there are no images articulating (in)security.

Words, images, bodies are inextricably linked not just in the way that they connect to announce (in)security but also in the sense that written/spoken forms of discourse, particularly those about gender and sexuality, get attached to bodies because of their visual appearance. Whether the body complies or submits to those written/spoken forms of discourse is another matter: as a visual thing, the body can become a site through which textual/vocally produced and coded norms are contested. They can, therefore, be used to resist or enforce norms, dominant power structures, and orderings of society.

Bringing the visual and the body in as epistemological sites in conflict and security-related research, we must proceed carefully so as not to reproduce epistemological hierarchies. Words, images, and bodies must have equal analytic footing; none should have primacy. In queer research, where there is often an imposed silence on individuals and communities, scholars must think about other epistemological sites through which to understand and explore international political phenomena. When we are speaking of issues with such high stakes as conflict and insecurity, it is important to look at a broad range of materials.

Seeing queer (in)security

Traditionally, conflict is associated with and conceptualized as physical violence occurring at multiple scales but most obviously in war. In my use of 'conflict' here, I include a broader range of 'conflicts' such as societal conflicts over values, norms, and rights. These structural conflicts still involve violence, albeit not necessarily physical, and (historically) underpin and create conditions for mass violence by enabling the creation of enemy Others and bogeymen at domestic and international levels. All of this relates directly to the issue of security—the concept I have structured my discussion around—which for most queer people involves the ability to exist without (fear of) persecution, oppression, and discrimination on the basis of sexual behaviours and/or gender performance. In this sense, 'security' extends beyond physical violence to include social and welfare issues.

Returning to the Russian context, Putin created a scapegoat in queer people, particularly gay men, in passing the gay propaganda law (Wilkinson, 2018). It was in the midst of economic turmoil, allegations of corruption, and popular domestic resistance to the incumbent regime that the 'Gayropean' threat was cooked up and queer people demonized in Russia (Healey, 2018). Successfully cultivating an existential societal conflict over Russian national identity and values created the necessary conditions for the likes of Chechnya's near genocidal 'gay purge', the drafting of a list of queer organizations and individuals to be targeted during the invasion of Ukraine (Crocker, 2022), and the cultivation of a global homophobic and transphobic network composed of states, politicians, government officials, and civil society actors.

Taking the visual seriously as an epistemological terrain upon which to understand international politics and queer security problems means that we are able to *see* queer issues in a new light. The visual has consistently been a part of queer politics, both as a tool of resistance and of oppression. This means that the visual is an important source of knowledge about queer (in)security that enables us to rethink and complicate our understanding of security, agency, vulnerability, and power.

I have primarily used the visual as a means of understanding and analysing the (international) politics of sex and resistance to a Russian geopolitical project rooted in heteronormative sexual politics, which I call Russian *heteronormative internationalism* (Cooper-Cunningham, 2021). To demonstrate how word, image, and body come together I want to return to the image that opened this chapter (Figure 4.1). This photograph was taken at a protest in St Petersburg in June 2013 and shows four people huddled together, one with a bloodied face, surrounded by riot police officers who are identifiable from their uniforms (see Guillaume, Vuori, and Andersen, 2018 on uniforms). But how exactly does this image signify *queer* (in)security?

It is not immediately clear from the photograph who the beaten individuals are, what their politics is, why they have been beaten, what the intentions of the riot police are, whether these individuals are aggressors, or whether they are vulnerable individuals in need of protection. There is also nothing in that image that suggests the people photographed are queer or that the image was taken in Russia. This could be a photograph of any group of people who had been beaten up and surrounded by some sort of militarized group. It is only through the immediate intertext of the image's publication in news media and the captions in the Panos Pictures image database that the interpretation gap is narrowed and the audience gets the information that it is about Russian LGBT politics and state homophobia.

Like all images, this photograph requires interpretation. Answering the above question about whether these four are victims of violence in need of protection or are perpetrators being detained for a crime depends on your politics that then inform the perspective from which you understand these individuals and approach the image. As per the gay propaganda law, these four could be considered criminals in their public support and display of queerness, but I only know that they were protesting the state's homophobic policies at a Pride march alongside other activists waving rainbow flags earlier in the day because I have looked at a whole series of other images from this event where protesters confronted homophobic activists and police officers. They might, however, also be considered victims of state-sanctioned homophobic violence that is the result of the propaganda law. Again, one needs to bring prior knowledge to this photograph when reading and trying to unpack its politics.

Both of these interpretations, while oppositional, are linked to discourses about security: one of a queer threat to Russian national security pedalled by the Russian government, another of queer insecurity at the hands of that same government represented by photographs of homophobic violence such as Mads Nissen's image (Figure 4.1) and activist dissemination of stories and other images (for example, Gay Clown Putin memes) that bring attention to the government's aggressive campaign of homophobia that is rooted in an illiberal and anti-Western ideology.

The polysemy and possibility of different readings of an image is usually narrowed by text on or near the image, by other text(s) that discuss the image, and by other images that anchor its meaning and the tools we use to interpret it. That I interpreted Figure 4.1 as representing Russian state homophobia and queer insecurity is primarily due to its use in Western media to visually represent news stories about Russia's gay propaganda law and from a familiarity of the visual vernacular of representations of state violence and resistance. In terms of the tripartite model, Figure 4.1 is obviously the image part of the tripartite approach. The words element comes from bringing into the analysis Russian domestic and foreign policy from the gay propaganda law to the speeches and documents that constitute its heteronormative internationalist project rooted in an active campaign about 'traditional' heteronormative, patriarchal family values.

In terms of the body, by showing the bleeding and vulnerable queer body this image has a particular power. Bringing Fierke's (2013: 79) work on the body into connection with the visual, images of violence paired with the reality of the 'injured or dying body' communicate 'a larger experience of social suffering' and thereby make queer insecurity and homophobic violence more tangible, creating conditions for challenging heteronormative power. The visual power of four activists surrounded by police officers, fighting against the propaganda law for the right to appear in public evokes 'emotions that go beyond words' (Fierke, 2013: 11–12), reminding us all that the state can withdraw its support for marginalized groups at any moment, thereby drawing attention to the vulnerability of all bodies to the powerful coercive state apparatuses.

Not only does that photograph show how the queer body is vulnerable to state-sanctioned violence and disciplining, it highlights how *all* bodies are policed and disciplined. That image evokes the politics of the body and its targeting by heteronormative structures. Bringing this to our attention through affective registers that prompt us to consider how far the Putin regime is willing to go to persecute queer people at home and abroad, that image also highlights how vulnerable we all are to persecution for simply seeking out bodily pleasure and following our desires. The visual representation of suffering and vulnerability make the body a site of resistance through and upon which homophobic politics plays out. Its representation is an important political expression for those stigmatized by the Russian government and marked as dangerous, foreign threats. It forces the spectator to confront power head on, which in this case is cisheteronormativity, and to question one's own relation to it.

This is an important point about images: they have an affective quality that provokes different reactions in different individuals (Adler-Nissen, Andersen, and Hansen, 2019; Callahan, 2020). Recognizing that queer scholars, like their feminist counterparts, often follow an intellectual curiosity in conducting research, the image can be a vital starting point that enables theorizing about international politics. In my case that meant tracing the links between the threat of state and social homophobia to queer individuals in Russia/Russian geopolitics, with a focus on how this then challenges the liberal international order (Holm and Tjalve, 2018). That image set off my own investigation into practices of media representation of queer (in)security that led me to another of Nissen's images that complicates ideas of victimhood and turns our attention explicitly to sex and to the queer politics of joy: 'Jon and Alex', a World Press Photo award-winning photograph (Figure 4.2).

In this regard, the visual does much more than simply show queer (in) securities in monolithic terms of queer victimhood. It also shows moments of queer joy and rupture, moments where insecurity is not all encompassing, not the entire essence of one's being, but one part of a person's existence; a part that is repeatedly negotiated and experienced. This is not to diminish the threat that many queer people face but instead to complicate that story and to demonstrate that queer insecurity is not reducible to an unliveable life of all-consuming victimhood. There is agency in being insecure and there are opportunities for resistance and reconfiguring one's relations to power. Figure 4.1 and the images captured at the same event show one of those instances.

'Jon and Alex' (Figure 4.2) brings our attention, in a very confronting manner, to the exact object of queer politics: sex. This photograph captures two men having sex and sharing an intimate moment. What makes this image powerful, in a queer way, is its confrontation of heteronormativity and sexual stigma. This more intimate image, shot in the home of the two men, has a softer edge to Figure 4.1, which appeared in initial coverage of the gay propaganda law. That it is shot in the home of the two men highlights the pervasiveness of the insecurity queer people in Russia face: domestic laws such as the propaganda law, anti-Western foreign policy, the Russia versus

Figure 4.2: Jon and Alex by Mads Nissen (2014)

Source: Panos Pictures, image no. MNN01651RUS.

Gayropa sexual geopolitics, and these two men's personal lives collide in the very moment they have sex. The embodied act of seeking sexual pleasure and its dissemination through a photograph highlights how the act taking place in their private space makes them vulnerable to the type of violence we see in Figure 4.1. Not only does a queer analysis of this photograph serve to show how the personal is international, it shows how the state is founded on and persists through the perpetuation of heteronormative structures that work upon all bodies.

'Jon and Alex' destabilizes the image of queer Russians as purely passive victims. It shows how queer life finds a way, how queer people persist despite facing everyday insecurities, and how not even the threat of violent homophobia and state-sanctioned persecution is enough to force every body into compliance with the state's heteronormative project. The image does not upend the discourse of queer insecurity but instead complicates it: these photographs are a means through which these two queer Russians carve out their own space and resist the gay propaganda law and the state's desire to get into their bedroom. The intimacy and closeness Nissen achieves in this photograph shows the complexity of insecurity and how it is not always experienced as brutal and physically violent: this photograph shows humanity in all its vulnerability which is a powerful and ethical means of representing queer (in)security that calls attention to the very real threat of arbitrary moralizing about sex, pleasure, and desire. A threat that has unfortunately followed previous patterns and ended in massive violence and war.

Conclusion

In this chapter, I argued that no method is inherently queer. Those that we choose to use in our research are only ever temporarily queer and to be considered queer they should enable researchers to: (a) understand, locate, challenge, make visible, study queer (in)security; and/or (b) delineate, uncover, locate, and thereby enable challenges to, cisheteronormative sociality and its attendant power structures. Introducing my tripartite approach to studying international politics, I showed how those who are oppressed, silenced, and/or ignored often use the visual and the body as means to make their voices heard, produce knowledge, articulate insecurity, and make critical interventions in politics. In the case of Russian politicized homophobia, such interventions challenge the state's active struggle to control what/who is made visible, given the possibility of appearing in public, and how it/they appear.

The tripartite word-image-body approach highlights the importance of looking beyond text/word and expanding discourse to include the complex interaction between words, images and bodies. Images of resistance and body-based activism such as a street protest or simply flouting gendered ideals can take the place of and/or complement speech. This means that 'saying nothing can be doing something and doing something can be saying something' (Cooper-Cunningham, 2019: 389). Bringing the body and the visual in as additional epistemological sites in research on queer issues and conflict not only calls attention to the body as a site of disciplining but also shows how particular bodies become the targets for evisceration and annihilation in conflict.

The two images studied above highlight the prevalence of identity-based violence and make this more tangible for spectators in a way that words cannot capture. More than that, they might also be considered a risk indicator for propensity for atrocity crime and escalation to more intense conflict. Photographs of homophobic violence and the less public parts of queer life, hence, become demonstrative of the fact that the body is the primary battleground through and upon which international politics plays out. This is the case whether it be in war and conflict or as part of a much larger geopolitical project, such as Russia's effort to balance against the West that is legitimized with discourse about a morally corrupt and regressive 'Gayropa'. The visual is a vital part of how international politics is experienced and performed. Queer IR will be better equipped to identify challenges to the cisheteronormative order and announcements of queer (in)security by taking this seriously moving forward.

The visual can be brought into the study of international politics and used to ask queer questions in so many different ways. This chapter pointed only to the way that I have brought the visual into queer research. My aim here was to take the mystery out of doing visual scholarship and to encourage methodological play by those interested in using visual data. It should, therefore, not be taken as a manifesto outlining what visual politics ought to be. A pluralist approach is key to understanding the complexity of the visual and how queer security issues are announced and represented. I encourage researchers to take seriously the connections between words, images, and the body going forward: they come together to communicate in incredibly powerful ways and are equal parts of discourse that require our attention for their ability to comply with or resist cisheteronormative sociality.

Notes

[1] I understand homophobia as 'arbitrary moralising about sex, desire, and bodily pleasure that produces, sustains, and secures heteronormativity as the norm and that which should be universally shared' (Cooper-Cunningham, 2021: 3) where heteronormativity is 'the institutions, structures of understanding, and practical orientations that make heterosexuality seem not only coherent—that is, organized as a sexuality—but also privileged' (Berlant and Warner, 1998: 548, fn 2).

[2] While beyond the scope of this chapter, state-directed homophobia exposes a connection between social and societal security. Social security, held by the Copenhagen School to encompass individual issues such as access to welfare and social justice, is generally separated out from societal security. Where the former includes threats *in* society, the latter includes threats *to* society and its collective survival. State-sponsored homophobia, however, exposes how discourses of societal insecurity (for example, Russia's discourse about the foreign 'Gayropean' threat to Russian society and national security) impact individuals who are constituted as threatening, thereby rendering them insecure *in* society. The separation between social and societal/national security, as Hansen (2000) points out, is not see neat: discourse of a threat to Russian security (queerness) plays out on individuals as they become targets of social homophobia (for example, vigilante groups luring gay men to fake dates on Grindr only to beat and torture them).

[3] 'Antisociality' means the refusal to be subsumed into the norm or folded into the neat and tidy organizations of society demanded by heteronormative sociality. Queer antisociality is contempt for dominant heteronormative organizations of society (Bersani, 1987, 1996; Edelman, 2004). Thus, it is also antinormative in its resistance to powerful moral discourses about 'normal' sexuality and gender performances (Warner, 1999, 2000).

[4] An excellent resource for a genealogy of queer political writings is *The Routledge Queer Studies Reader* (Jagose and Hall, 2013).

[5] I am cognizant of the Anglo-American roots of the queer political project I take inspiration from. This is not without issues and comes with silences and hierarchies of knowledge built into it. However, inspired by Cathy Cohen's (1997) work, I take the queer project to be ever shifting but committed to a perpetual interrogation of all relations to power. In this sense, the queer project I advocate, while inspired by queer activists and thinkers of the Euro-Atlantic, questions *all* moralistic and normative projects tied to sexuality and gender. With this as its driving force, such a model can be deployed reflexively and with due attention to power in various contexts beyond that of its emergence.

[6] I use the term 'political homophobia' to mean 'state-directed hostility towards, stigmatisation of and persecution of individuals who deviate from cisheteronormative demands; essentially, it is fear of the queer, that which is at odds with straight culture and crosses the line between good and bad sexual practices and gender performances (see Warner, 2000)' (Cooper-Cunningham, 2022: fn 1).

7   When I say arbitrary moralizing about sexual pleasure and desire, I refer to the meta argument that any attempt to police the wayward workings of desire is futile and therefore all normative constitutions of moral/appropriate sexuality are arbitrarily drawn lines in the sand. As Warner writes: 'Sex has a politics of its own. Hierarchies of sex sometimes serve no real purpose except to prevent sexual variance. They create victimless crimes, imaginary threats, and moralities of cruelty' (2000: 25). This does not mean that the lived experience of sexual norms and the political context in which heteronormativity governs is negligible and without adversity.
8   Methodology being the 'organising principles that link our ontological and epistemological perspectives with the actual methods we use to gather data' (Browne and Nash, 2016: 2).

Bibliography

Abrahamsen, R. (2020) 'The right family: the personal is geopolitical', *Centre for International Policy Studies*, [online] 14 December. Available from: www.cips-cepi.ca/2020/12/14/the-right-family-the-personal-is-geopolitical/

Adler-Nissen, R., Andersen, K.E., and Hansen, L. (2019) 'Images, emotions, and international politics: the death of Alan Kurdi', *Review of International Studies*, 46(1): 75–95.

Åhäll, L. (2018) 'Gender', in R. Bleiker (ed.) *Visual Global Politics*, New York: Routledge.

Andersen, R.S., and Vuori, J.A. (eds) (2018) *Visual Security Studies: Sights and Spectacles of Insecurity and War*, London: Routledge.

Andersen, R.S., Vuori, J.A. and Mutlu, C.E. (2015) 'Visuality', in C. Aradau, J. Huysmans, A. Neal, and N. Voelkner (eds) *Critical Security Methods: New Frameworks for Analysis*, Abingdon: Routledge, pp 85–117.

Aradau, C. and Huysmans, J. (2014) 'Critical methods in International Relations: the politics of techniques, devices and acts', *European Journal of International Relations*, 20(3): 596–619.

Barthes, R. (1977) *Image, Music, Text*, translated by S. Heath, New York: Hill and Wang.

Barthes, R. (1981) *Camera Lucida: Reflections on Photography*, New York: Hill and Wang.

Berlant, L. and Warner, M. (1995) 'What does queer theory teach us about X?', *PMLA*, 110(3): 343–9.

Berlant, L. and Warner, M. (1996) *Homos*, Cambridge, MA: Harvard University Press.

Berlant, L. and Warner, M. (1998) 'Sex in public', *Critical Inquiry*, 24(2): 547–66.

Bersani, L. (1987) 'Is the rectum a grave?', *October*, 43(Winter): 197–222.

Bleiker, R. (2015) 'Pluralist methods for visual global politics', *Millennium Journal of International Studies*, 43(3): 872–90.

Bleiker, R. (2018a) 'Mapping visual global politics', in R. Bleiker (ed.) *Visual global Politics*, New York: Routledge, pp 1–29.

Bleiker, R. (ed.) (2018b) *Visual Global Politics*, New York: Routledge.

Browne, K. and Nash, C.J. (2016) 'Queer methods and methodologies: an introduction', in K. Browne and C.J. Nash (eds) *Queer Methods and Methodologies: Intersecting Queer Theories and Social Science Research*, London: Routledge, pp 1–23.

Butler, J. (1993) 'Critically queer', *GLQ: A Journal of Lesbian and Gay Studies*, 1(1): 17–32.

Callahan, W. (2020) *Sensible Politics: Visualizing International Relations*, Oxford: Oxford University Press.

Campbell, D. and Shapiro, M.J. (2007) 'Guest editors' introduction', *Security Dialogue*, 38(2): 131–7.

Cohen, C. (1997) 'Punks, bulldaggers, and welfare queens: the radical potential of queer politics', *GLQ: A Journal of Lesbian and Gay Studies*, 3(4): 437–65.

Cooper-Cunningham, D. (2017) 'Analysing but not seeing: what's missing when we forget images in IR', *E-International Relations*, [online] 6 March. Available from: www.e-ir.info/2017/03/06/analysing-but-not-seeing-whats-missing-when-we-forget-images-in-ir/

Cooper-Cunningham, D. (2019) 'Seeing (in)security, gender and silencing: posters in and about the British women's suffrage movement', *International Feminist Journal of Politics*, 21(3): 383–408.

Cooper-Cunningham, D. (2020) 'Visual methods and international security studies', *E-International Relations*, [online] 12 June. Available from: www.e-ir.info/2020/06/12/visual-methods-and-international-security-studies/

Cooper-Cunningham, D. (2021) 'The international politics of sex: visual activism in response to Russian state homophobia', *PhD Political Science*, University of Copenhagen.

Cooper-Cunningham, D. (2022) 'Security, sexuality, and the Gay Clown Putin meme: the queer politics of play in international responses to Russian state-directed homophobia', *Security Dialogue*, 53(4): 302–23.

Crocker, B. .(2022) 'U.S. letter to the U.N. alleging Russia is planning human rights abuses in Ukraine', in United States State Department (eds), Washington: Washington Post.

DIVA TV (1989) 'Pride 69–89 (VHS #01066)', 00:26:30, New York, DIVA TV. VHS.

Düben, B.A. (2020) '"There is no Ukraine": fact-checking the Kremlin's version of Ukrainian history', *LSE Blogs*, [online] 1 July 2020. Available from: https://blogs.lse.ac.uk/lseih/2020/07/01/there-is-no-ukraine-fact-checking-the-kremlins-version-of-ukrainian-history/

Edelman, L. (2004) *No Future: Queer Theory and the Death Drive*, Durham, NC: Duke University Press.

Fierke, K.M. (2013) *Political Self-sacrifice: Agency, Body and Emotion in International Relations*, Cambridge: Cambridge University Press.

Finkelstein, A. (2018) *After Silence: A History of AIDS through its Images*, California: University of California Press.

Foucault, M. (1978) *The History of Sexuality, Vol. 1: An Introduction*, translated by R. Hurley, New York: Pantheon.

Foxall, A. (2013) 'Photographing Vladimir Putin: masculinity, nationalism and visuality in Russian political culture', *Geopolitics*, 18(1): 132–56.

Foxall, A. (2019) 'From Evropa to Gayropa: a critical geopolitics of the European Union as seen from Russia', *Geopolitics*, 24(1): 174–93.

Gifkins, J. et al (2022) *Queering Atrocity Prevention*, London: Protection Approaches. Available from: https://protectionapproaches.org/queeringap

Gould, D. (2009) *Moving Politics: Emotion and ACT UP's Fight Against AIDS*, Chicago, IL: University of Chicago Press.

Guillaume, X., Vuori, J.A., and Andersen, R.S. (2018) 'Making security visible: police uniforms and the social meaning of policing', in J.A. Vuori and R.S. Andersen (eds) *Visual Security Studies: Sights and Spectacles of Insecurity and War*, London: Routledge, pp 114–30.

Hagen, J. (2016) 'Queering women, peace and security', *International Affairs*, 92(2): 313–32.

Hansen, L. (2000) 'The Little Mermaid's silent security dilemma and the absence of gender in the Copenhagen School', *Millennium Journal of International Studies*, 29(2): 285–306.

Hansen, L. (2006) *Security as Practice: Discourse Analysis and the Bosnian War*, New York: Routledge.

Hansen, L. (2011) 'Theorizing the image for security studies: visual securitization and the Muhammad cartoon crisis', *European Journal of International Relations*, 17(1): 51–74.

Hansen, L. and Spanner, J. (2021) 'National and post-national performances at the Venice Biennale: site-specific seeing through the photo essay', *Millennium: Journal of International Studies*, 49(2): 305–36.

Healey, D. (2018) *Russian Homophobia from Stalin to Sochi* (1st edn), New York: Bloomsbury Academic.

Holm, M, and Tjalve, V.S. (2018) *Visions of an Illiberal World Order?*, NUPI.

Jagose, A. and Hall, D. (2013) *The Routledge Queer Studies Reader*, London: Routledge.

Leigh, D. (2017) 'Queer feminist international relations: uneasy alliances, productive tensions', *Alternatif Politika*, 9(3): 343–60.

Loken, M. (2021) 'Using images as data in political violence research', *Journal of Human Rights*, 20(3): 373–9.

McGarry, A. et al (2020) *Aesthetics of Global Protest*, Amsterdam: Amsterdam University Press.

Mudde, C. (2019) *The Far Right Today*, Cambridge: Polity.

Peterson, V.S. (2014) 'Sex matters', *International Feminist Journal of Politics*, 16(3): 389–409.

Riabov, O. and Riabova, T. (2014) 'The decline of Gayropa? How Russia intended to save the world', *Eurozine*.

Richter-Montpetit, M. (2018) 'Everything you always wanted to know about sex (in IR) but were afraid to ask: the "queer turn" in international relations', *Millennium: Journal of International Studies*, 46(2): 220–40.

Riemer, M. and Brown, L. (2019) *We Are Everywhere: Protest, Power, and Pride in the History of Queer Liberation*, New York: Ten Speed Press.

Seidman, S. (1993) 'Identity and politics in a "postmodern" gay culture', in M. Warner (ed) *Fear of a Queer Planet*, Minneapolis, MN: University of Minnesota Press, pp 105–42.

Shim, D. (2017) 'Sketching geopolitics: comics and the case of the Cheonan sinking', *International Political Sociology*, 11(4): 398–417.

Tsinovoi, A. (2018) 'Social media and the remediation of diplomacy: images and international politics in the digital age', *PhD Department of Political Science*, University of Copenhagen.

Warner, M. (1993a) *Fear of a Queer Planet: Queer Politics and Social Theory*, Minneapolis, MN: University of Minnesota Press.

Warner, M. (1993b) 'Introduction', in M. Warner (ed) *Fear of a Queer Planet: Queer Politics and Social Theory*, Minneapolis, MN: University of Minnesota Press.

Warner, M. (1999) 'Normal and normaller: beyond gay marriage', *GLQ: A Journal of Lesbian and Gay Studies*, 5(2): 119–71.

Warner, M. (2000) *The Trouble with Normal: Sex, Politics, and the Ethics of Queer Life*, Cambridge, MA: Harvard University Press.

Weber, C. (2015) 'Queer intellectual curiosity as international relations method: developing queer international relations theoretical and methodological frameworks', *International Studies Quarterly*, 60(1): 11–23.

Weber, C. (2016) *Queer International Relations: Sovereignty, Sexuality and the Will to Knowledge*, New York: Oxford University Press.

Wilkinson, C. (2018) 'Mother Russia in queer peril: the gender logic of the hypermasculine state', in S. Parashar, J.A. Tickner, and J. True (eds) *Revisiting Gendered States: Feminist Imaginings of the State in International Relations*, Oxford: Oxford Studies in Gender and International Relations.

Wilcox, L. (2014) 'Queer theory and the "proper objects" of international relations', *International Studies Review*, 16(4): 612–15.

Williams, M. (2003) 'Words, images, enemies: securitization and international politics', *International Studies Quarterly*, 47(4): 511–31.

Williams, M. (2018) 'International Relations in the age of images', *International Studies Quarterly*, 62: 880–91.

5

Poetry as a Queer Epistemological Method: Disrupting Knowledge of the Lebanese Civil War with Etel Adnan's *The Arab Apocalypse*

Andrew Delatolla

Introduction

Poetry, and literature more generally, is increasingly used in the disciplines of International Relations and Political Science as a subject of study to understand political and social issues (Dorfman and Mattelart, 1975; Hunt and Sands, 2000; Bleiker, 2001; Doucet, 2005; Grayson, 2013). As discussed in this chapter, poetry and literature can also act as a queer methodological tool to intervene, question, reinterpret, and transform how we think about issues and, in particular, conflict and war. In doing so, poetry can be destabilizing for established social scientific categories, long-held assumptions about conflict, war, and even political violence. In this chapter, I use Etel Adnan's *The Arab Apocalypse*,[1] an epic poem written about the Lebanese Civil War (1975–90), as a queer epistemological method to disrupt our understanding of the war. This poem was chosen due to its explicit discussion of the Lebanese Civil War, and its importance in the vast oeuvre of literature on the specific conflict. *The Arab Apocalypse* provides a queer epistemologically derived critique and disruption of general and normative assumptions of the Lebanese Civil War—putting forward a critique of how we *know* conflict, war, and political violence and how we study it.

Arts and literature, and in the case of this chapter, poetry, capture a more complete narrative of the Lebanese Civil War, in a manner that can more successfully explore its contradictions, revealing queer logics of conflict. Adnan's poem, *The Arab Apocalypse*, with its complex and tangled explanations of the conflict, its evolution and development, and its conclusion, avoids the traps of orientalist and romanticized narratives and categories that facilitate much of the academic research on the Lebanese Civil War. That being said, the analysis of *The Arab Apocalypse* that is developed in this chapter is not an inalienable truth. Instead, as Thom Donovan (2010) argues: 'any hopes one might have of achieving mastery over the language of [*The Arab Apocalypse*] is completely challenged. One can only fail and produce the best possible outcome in this failure. Interpretation is not enough. No explanation either.' While the academic scholarship on the Lebanese Civil War has covered different and compelling explanations for its outbreak, prolongation, and conclusion, these different accounts have been produced within standard or normative (White [Western] hetero-masculinist) epistemic methodological practices in the social sciences and humanities. In other words, and as Charles Tilly notes, 'social science's strongest insights do not take the form of stories and often undermine the stories people tell' (2002: 26).

Building on feminist scholarship that unsettles what counts as 'real' knowledge,[2] I argue that the use of arts and literature, and specifically affective poetry, can provide the enduring first-hand accounts that not only challenge, but also *queer*, the foundations of social scientific methods, methodology, and knowledge. Here, queering is disruptive of White (Western) hetero-masculinist linear logics of temporality, cause, and effect, and is generative of novel ways of thinking. Art and literature often do not function within the bounded categories and classifications that the social sciences rely on to make sense of the world. Instead, they are reflective and reflexive, expounded from experience that provides insight into a particular positionality. By reading *The Arab Apocalypse* as a method, I argue that Adnan's queer feminist epistemic engagement with the Lebanese Civil War provides a unique positionality that disrupts linearity, temporality,[3] and draws attention to trauma[4] as a way to understand conflict.

The aim of this chapter is to show how literature and the arts can be used as source material for social science research, how it can expose queer logics that disrupt existing narratives of conflict, and how this can help formulate new ways of understanding conflict and political violence. The following section introduces *The Arab Apocalypse* in relation to the Lebanese Civil War. Here, I provide a guide to how I have read, understood, and unpacked the poem. What follows is a queer reading of the poem, where I focus on the problems of linearity and temporality in discussions of conflict and how understanding trauma can serve as a framing mechanism to better understand conflict. First, it considers the contradictions of reality—the normality of daily life and the abnormality of conflict which blend to produce new realities that quickly become the new familiar. In doing so, it questions the temporal rationalization of peace and conflict: when does peace conclude and war begin and end? The following section examines how trauma is a motivating and mobilizing force that provides insight into decision making and also challenges long-held assumptions about the Lebanese Civil War and Lebanese society.

Disrupting knowledge: a guide to how I have read *The Arab Apocalypse*

This chapter builds on existing critiques of knowledge production and our 'will to knowledge'. It begins from critiques of common methods used in the social sciences and how they are, in the first instance, epistemologically produced in relation to Whiteness, masculinity, and heterosexuality (Weber, 2016: 18–71). And, relatedly, have their origins in imperialism and colonialism (Quijano 2000; Grosfoguel 2010, 2013). The knowledge generated from these positions is produced in relation to epistemic methodological traditions considered to be 'normal' or 'standard' in the social sciences; reflecting the 'normal' or 'standard' bodies of those engaged in knowledge production. In other words, this knowledge is generated by White (Western) and hetero-masculine bodies, traditionally for White (Western) and hetero-masculine bodies. Although we can argue that academic knowledge production has become more diverse since the mid-20th century, the *disciplining* nature of academic knowledge production asks diverse bodies with diverse experiences, from which their knowledge of the world is produced, to abandon or suspend these epistemic logics in order to orientate themselves towards 'normal' or 'standard' positions.

The critique of 'normal' or 'standard' positions of knowledge production builds on the arguments made by Cynthia Weber's intervention in *Queer International Relations*. As such, this chapter follows from existing arguments that the logical form of enquiry generally applied to the social world, in an effort to create a better understanding, is embedded in historic structures of White (Western) hetero-masculinity (Escobar, 2007; Mignolo, 2007; Quijano, 2007; Schiwy, 2007; Morgan, 2018). Although the social sciences have consistently attempted to position social scientific inquiry and study as objective (Code, 1991, 2013), this sense of objectivity, as argued here, is, first, epistemic of a particular (White) hetero-male positionality and therefore not objective at all. Second, and following from the first point, it has produced limitations on our understanding of the social world and politics, war, and conflict, specifically. With regards to the first point, it can be argued that the positionality of the researcher (race, gender, sexuality, class, education, and so on), mobilizes their preferences on how to engage in social scientific enquiry, and the kinds of puzzles, problems, or questions that they find of interest. By following the logics of normative social scientific methodology and training, there exists a coloniality of knowledge that sways between romanticization and orientalism (Hoagland, 2020). In the case of Lebanon, from the romanticized evocation of Beirut as the 'Paris of the Middle East' to the orientalist gaze that views the country as 'Hezbollahstan' (Stephens, 2008), both are drawn from a coloniality of knowledge with its histories located in Western imperialism and colonialism.[5] This history has methodological foundations in logics of Whiteness and hetero-masculinity: where knowledge is held and created by the White/Western-educated researcher who engages in an intellectual paternalism; shaping the kinds of knowledge and logics that are considered acceptable. Third, and of particular interest to this chapter, the normative standard and accepted methods and methodologies in the social sciences produce limitations by attempting to weed out the messiness of reality in an aim to rationalize the irrationality of politics.

Where rationality maps onto the bifurcated knowledge systems of the masculine and feminine (that is, binary hierarchical assumptions, such as the strong and the weak) as well as the homosexual and the heterosexual (the perverse and the normal), a queer episteme is one that accepts the possibilities of the 'and/or': the multiple categorizations and characterizations of existence that are not necessarily mutually exclusive (Weber, 2016: 41). Adnan's positionality concerning sexuality, as a feminist queer author and artist, is reflected in her work, where—as discussed in the sections below— the queerness of reality is prioritized over simplified 'objective truths'. To better understand Adnan's positionality, I have engaged with her other writing and interviews. This has helped me understand her politics, her relationship to the world, and the logic it produces.

Highlighting her attention to sexuality and gender as organizing social structures, what can be called her queer and feminist sensibilities, Adnan, in an interview with Kathleen Weaver for *Poetry Flash* (1986), notes how 'men identify themselves through their sexuality. They identify someone else through their sexuality.'[6] For the male heterosexual, understanding the self and the world is productive of binary genders (masculine and feminine: the strong and the weak; the public and the private) and sexualities (heterosexual and homosexual: the normal and the perverse; the (re)production of social power structures and the threat to those structures). From this position, sexuality is an episteme that helps us understand ourselves and the world.

Notably, throughout the conversation with Weaver, Adnan critiques male heterosexuality as the standard of normality, and highlights how masculinist sexual virility is concerned with power. Here, Adnan reflects on the writing of French author, André Gide, known as a symbolist, for his critiques of empire, and his writing on sexuality. According to Adnan, Gide's 'in praise of sensuality' was a symbol of anti-masculine decadence that was evidence, as argued by to right-wing Catholics, for why France lost World War II. A decadence that was considered *irrational*[7] and embodied by Gide's progressive, as well as problematic, position on sexuality and sensuality. According to the right-wing Catholic French logic, Gide's decadence was a failure of male heterosexuality, which was evident of an effeminacy that did not match his biological sex. Although not completely in the category of 'perversion', Gide did not wholly occupy the category of 'normal' either. Rather, his position can be understood as 'queer'.

Analysing and referencing Gide's story, Adnan argues that the logic behind French conservative Catholic positions meant that the masculinist failure caused by decadence could be avoided with the repression of human expression, the latter being a basis for masculinity and masculine sexual virility. The repression of human expression, as foundational to masculinist sexual virility, results in an untethered violence characterized by power and domination (Weaver, 1986). Here, two aspects become evident. First, that masculine positionalities reinforce a linear and binary logic to understand the world; one that perpetuates power dynamics, domination, and hierarchies. Second, despite the thrust of conflict, war, and violence being associated with masculinist positions, a queer feminist episteme allows us to understand how conflict produces knowledge that exists in contradicting and multiple realities. That *irrational* realities do not have to be *rationalized*. Adnan gets to this position, arguably, from her own experience of failure: failure to embody the socio-cultural variant of hetero-femininity that engages in the normative heterosexed world and its embedded logics. Here, I use Adnan's poetry to expose the queer logics that emerge from her positionality.

Adnan's engagement and writing on the Civil War, particularly in reference to her understanding of *apocalypses*, discussed below, reflects the experiential subjugation of violence, its production in relation to daily life.[8] However, her writing does not exist in a space of pacifist ideological framings. Rather, it offers a critique to the dominant narratives of this specific conflict, especially those which are uncontroversially reproduced in the scholarship on the Lebanese Civil War. These dominant narratives speak of sectarianism, third-party involvement, and of hetero-masculinist desire, which mobilize actors towards power. At times, these histories refer to the Civil War as being a conflict of 'outsiders' (Tuéni, 1982), absolving Lebanese nationals involved in bringing the country to 15 years of violent conflict. These narratives often blame the Palestinians for their reckless behaviour as refugees, the Syrians and Israelis for their physical occupation of the country (Badran, 2009), the French for establishing a flawed system of governance, and the Arab and Syrian nationalists for wanting to absorb Lebanon into a greater Syrian state—dissolving Lebanon of its distinct (Christian) character (Zamir, 1978).[9] In parallel, the Lebanese Civil War is also discussed as a conflict made entirely by its own population, a war of Muslims against Christians (O'Ballance, 1998: 12)—the modern continuation of the Muslim conquests and Christian crusades, a conflict over the national identity of the state, and a power grab when the state was at its weakest. The extremities of these narratives are dubious, serving political and ideological trends and offering simplified versions of history that dominate the realities of those who have lived through the conflict. In common with one another, the conclusions drawn are often developed from a normal epistemic position that is methodologically White (Western) and masculine; overshadowing the diverse experience of conflict or harnessing that experience for a specific end.

This begs the question, although beyond the scope of the chapter, what does *queer desire* motivate individuals towards, if not power? Arguably, queer desire disrupts patterns of 'normal' and 'universal' relations as an emancipatory practice from the repressive practices of masculinist sexual virility, but to what end? Here, thinking through the notion of queer desire requires analysis that moves away from a masculinist epistemic framing of politics and conflict, understood as a desire for power, and towards a queer epistemic project, one that possibly does not have a goal.

Engaging this queer epistemic project and reflecting on the lived realities and politics of the Lebanese Civil War (1975–90), *The Arab Apocalypse* offers a reflexive engagement. Adnan does not rehearse the standard, often depersonalized, framings and linear narratives of conflict and power. Instead, Adnan reflects on her experience of living the conflict, positioning the reader of the poem in the streets of Beirut where daily life became enmeshed in the violence of gunfights and shelling. By reading and re-reading the poem in this way, Adnan's positionality, how she experienced the conflict, and her understanding of the conflict become increasingly evident. In this retelling of the Lebanese Civil War, Adnan does not play on long-held tropes of resilience; she encapsulates feelings of alienation experienced by conflict and the continuation and banality of everyday life that has been pockmarked by the decisions of others. In using this epic poem as a means to understand the Lebanese Civil War, an alternative space of knowledge is provided—one that challenges accepted methods and methodologies, providing a queer feminist epistemological methodology that dispels the necessity of linearity and objectivity to reveal another kind of truth.

The Arab Apocalypse not only avoids the extractive, generalized, romanticized, and orientalist constructions of Lebanon and the Lebanese Civil War, but also, crucially, brings the story of the Civil War back to an epistemological position that is personal. To read *The Arab Apocalypse* is like being transported to Adnan's positionality. Whether intentional or not, her relationship to the environment of conflict is a feminist position that is reflective and reflexive (England, 1994; Rose, 1997; Hemmings, 2012). Here, the epistemological position of White (Western) hetero-masculinity that emphasizes 'objectivity' and depersonalization is not accentuated. Instead, Adnan holds the proverbial hand of the reader, inviting them to a specific place and time—one that existed in her memory.

Etel Adnan's *The Arab Apocalypse* offers a queer feminist understanding of conflict, and specifically the Lebanese Civil War by disrupting the linearity and causality imposed by 'scientific' thinking. There are no dates, no time stamps, and the 'events' that are discussed are entangled with one another, creating a temporal elasticity where the days blur together during conflict. While the logic of time is transformed, the conflict is marked by trauma and what Adnan refers to as 'apocalypses'. This acts to reinforce the positionality of the storyteller—in this case, Adnan—one that is reflexive and does not emphasize temporal linearity as equivalent to truth by its objective measurement. By forcing the reader to consider the affective positionality of the individual who has experienced the conflict, the corrective lens that is normatively asked for in the social sciences is abandoned. Instead, a reflexive immersion into an individual's memory and experience of conflict, unmediated by methodological purity, reveals the distortions of time, the blurring and obscuring of party divisions, the feeling of loss through destruction, and a helplessness to control one's own mortality. In doing so, the reader embodies Adnan's positionality; a practice that is foreign to the social scientific researcher who seeks objective truth when such objectivity can only be found by tallying the names of the dead, the missing, and the disappeared. Even when engaging in such practices of quantification, these truths are always incomplete.

By reading *The Arab Apocalypse* as a method to derive alternative epistemic knowledge, as well as a critique of normal and standard social scientific methodology, new avenues towards comprehension are produced. This is not necessarily a knowledge-generating programme, as the knowledge already always exists in documentary forms such as *The Arab Apocalypse*. It is, however, a way to engage in research that does not attempt to separate trauma from experience and extract 'facts' in the pursuit of knowledge. Explored in the below sections of this chapter is an analysis of how Adnan provides a layered narrative of conflict—one that is an epistemically queer feminist method to understand conflict and, specifically, the Lebanese Civil War.

Adnan layers the narrative of conflict, reflecting a lived experience that embeds her positionality and trauma into the events by using different methods. First by tying the experience of conflict into daily life, exposing its emergence from the positionality of an individual bystander of the politics, militias that engulfed her life. Her submergence into the conflict, however, transformed her from bystander to witness, shrouded with guilt for being unable to stop the actions of others, producing feelings of culpability—what some may call 'survivor's guilt'. Here, she is not a researcher writing history, reading history, or trying to find answers in a conclusion. Adnan traces the forceful continuity of daily life as well as its changes, the interruptions, and the events that cannot be disrupted. Second, Adnan punctuates her writing with signs and symbols—what she has described as 'excess of emotions … I wrote by hand, and here and there, I put a word, and I made instinctively a little drawing, a sign … Maybe it is because I see these apocalypses …

because my first thought is always explosive. It is not cumulative' (Obrist, 2014). This relationship between memory, experience, and emotion in relation to the conflict, and the inability to engage in cumulation, arguably, speaks to a kind of queer methodology to conflict that allows blind spots, wilfully created or subconsciously developed, to exist without correction and without reference to a historical timeline, causality, or rationality. In doing so, it understands conflict as irrational and contradictory, thereby as an event that cannot be rationalized by a will to knowledge or methodological engagement.

Queering linearity and temporality: tensions between war and peace

The social sciences emphasize the importance of linearity and temporality to discuss events, case studies, and attempt to evidence causation. While I do not argue that this is necessarily a problem, the significance of linearity and temporality in social science methodology emerges from a need for objectivity and the reliance on fact to help fill gaps in knowledge. Yet, in the case of conflict, war, and political violence, the experience of linearity and temporality is often subjective and the gaps in knowledge are filled with emotional responses. Here, knowledge is produced from the non-linear experience, what can be understood as a queer epistemology. Discussed in this section is an intervention in temporal linearity and its abstracted reality in the context of conflict and war.

Adnan begins *The Arab Apocalypse* with what reads as the banal passing of the day. In a style and manner reflective of the works of Gertrude Stein, the repetition, or what Stein refers to as 'beginning again and again' (Springer, 1991: 193), of the sun and the ordinary scenes of life in Beirut fill the first four pages. Here, Adnan sets the scene, a day goes by, and another day, the sun rises, it takes on different hues, it produces different light, it is yellow, green, red, and blue; each repetition is a new 'beginning again and again'. The division of daily life, marked by the sun's appearance, references a division of time that later wanes as the conflict unfolds.

As the first four pages end, the reader begins to understand the universality of the sun, of daily life under the sun, regardless of traditions and culture. While the sun is universal, it is not experienced in a uniform manner. It appears everywhere but is not the same everywhere that it appears. Yet, the sun always marks a new day; it sees off the moon; it oversees the heat it produces, the life it gives, and takes away; and it is a reminder that the days continue. Here, a linear experience of time can be traced, where the days are similar but distinct, there is a new different beginning.

Unlike Stein's poetry, however, Adnan's use of punctuations, small drawings, that interrupt her writing, cause literal pause. It can be imagined

Figure 5.1: Etel Adnan, from *The Arab Apocalypse*, p 7

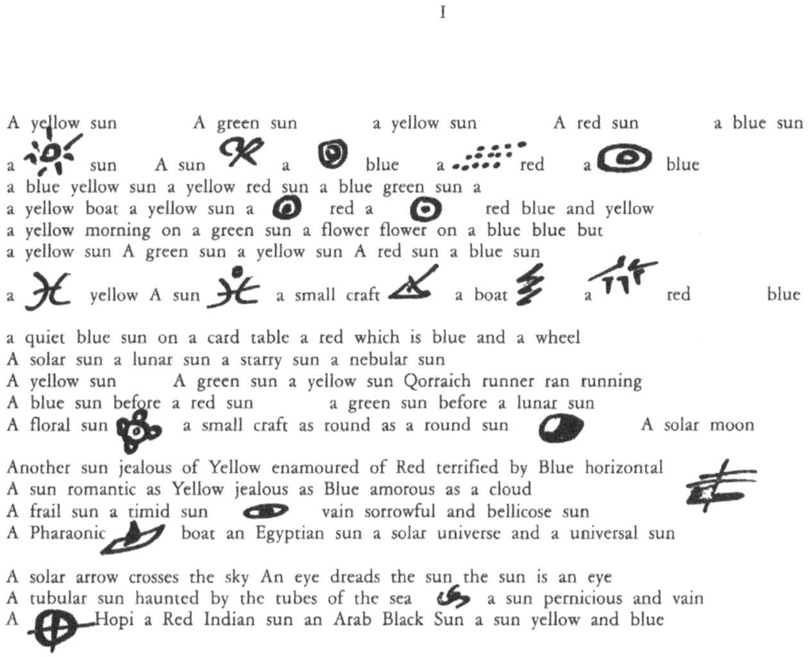

I

A yellow sun   A green sun   a yellow sun   A red sun   a blue sun
a 🌣 sun   A sun ✱ a ◉ blue   a ⋰⋰ red   a ◉ blue
a blue yellow sun a yellow red sun a blue green sun a
a yellow boat a yellow sun a ◉ red a ◉ red blue and yellow
a yellow morning on a green sun a flower flower on a blue blue but
a yellow sun A green sun a yellow sun A red sun a blue sun
a ⚥ yellow A sun ⚥ a small craft ⛵ a boat ⚡ a 🔥 red   blue
a quiet blue sun on a card table a red which is blue and a wheel
A solar sun a lunar sun a starry sun a nebular sun
A yellow sun   A green sun a yellow sun Qorraich runner ran running
A blue sun before a red sun   a green sun before a lunar sun
A floral sun ✿   a small craft as round as a round sun ◉   A solar moon

Another sun jealous of Yellow enamoured of Red terrified by Blue horizontal
A sun romantic as Yellow jealous as Blue amorous as a cloud   ≢
A frail sun a timid sun   ⊙ vain sorrowful and bellicose sun
A Pharaonic ⛵ boat an Egyptian sun a solar universe and a universal sun

A solar arrow crosses the sky An eye dreads the sun the sun is an eye
A tubular sun haunted by the tubes of the sea ໒ a sun pernicious and vain
A ⊕ Hopi a Red Indian sun an Arab Black Sun a sun yellow and blue

Source: The Post-Apollo Press, 1989. Reprinted with permission of The Estate of Etel Adnan and The Post-Apollo Press.

that these apocalypses, as Adnan describes them, bring her world to a stop. Here, in reference to the sun, it is evocative of a moment of pause, perhaps emerging from a dimly lit interior to the raucous city streets, looking up at the sky and allowing for a moment for the body and mind to adjust to the new environment. A small explosion of bliss and exaltation before the day continues. While the effect that these pages serve to remind the reader of the everyday lives that were lived before the conflict, allowing the reader to position themselves in relation to Adnan, almost as if the reader can occupy the same experience, they also provide a reminder of the elasticity of time, the gaps that are naturally produced throughout and the day, and the not always linear experience of life.

While the focus on the sun in the first pages of *The Arab Apocalypse* represents the banality of everyday life prior to conflict, the importance of the sun is not to be diminished. Referencing *The Epic of Gilgamesh*, the sun-god, Shamash, has given people the 'power ... to bind and to loose, to be the darkness and light of mankind' (Sandars, 1964: 115). It is accepted that Shamash, the sun, sees it all, allowing humans to make decisions, even those that the sun does not like. In the case of Adnan's writing, the Arab is no more and no less than a subject of the sun, much like Gilgamesh understood his inferior position in relation to Shamash, whose power was all encompassing. Similar to how the sun follows Adnan through her daily routines before the eruption of conflict, it continues to do so during the conflict. However, with the conflict, her relationship to the sun changes. Where the banality of the everyday disappears, the sun, much like everything else, becomes an active participant in the conflict, as Shamash does in the *Epic of Gilgamesh*. Following from this position, Adnan writes, 'O sun which tortures the Arab's eye in the Enemy's prison!' and continues by highlighting how the passing of time and trauma are held together, with trauma obscuring temporality.

A simple reading of these pages in relation to the rest of the poem is that the repetition of daily life evokes a sense that life goes on. Yet, this sentiment is limited by questioning whose life goes on and the kinds of traumas that occur that disable a sense of daily life, provoking an experience where time expands and contracts, the days become blurred, and, in the moment of these apocalypses, stops altogether. Adnan's reflection on her reality provokes a contradiction to how we discuss conflict, where the experience of conflict can diverge from exact timelines. This is evident later in her writing when the appearance of the sun, its announcement as a prelude to the new day, is staggered by the events being described.

As the tone is initially set in the first pages of *The Arab Apocalypse*, it quickly begins to explore the unfolding of the conflict. Often discussed as the trigger of the Civil War, the 1975 Bus Massacre is referred to as 'the non-event'. Here, Adnan is referring to Phalangist[10] gunmen who killed 27 Palestinian refugees in the Ayn al-Rummunah district of Beirut. The event is often viewed as a consequence of an attack on a church congregation in East Beirut where Phalangist party members Joseph Abu Assi, Antoine Husseini, Dib Assaf, and Selman Ibrahim Abou were killed. Yet, by referring to this as 'The night of the non-event' (Adnan, 1989: III, 11), Adnan provides an antithesis of how the outbreak of the Lebanese Civil War is normally described.

Adnan's positioning of these developments as a non-event also forces the reader to consider other events, possibly more important events over a longer timeline, that have contributed to the development of the Lebanese Civil War. In other words, by discussing it as a non-event Adnan's perspective challenges the periodization of the conflict. In the first instance, from Adnan's position, the event did not present itself as an environmental shift in the country. In the second instance, she implicitly references the longer history of Lebanese, Levantine, and Arab politics and society, requiring the reader to re-engage with the political and social context and history. For example, revisiting this history of conflict can reference forms of state making and nation building by the French throughout the 19th and 20th centuries; the establishment of the state of Israel and the Palestinian Nakba in 1948; the

POETRY AS A QUEER EPISTEMOLOGICAL METHOD

Figure 5.2: Etel Adnan, from *The Arab Apocalypse*, p 10

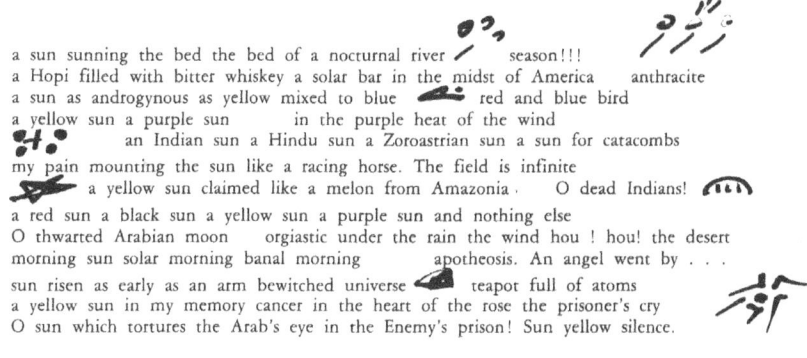

10

Source: The Post-Apollo Press, 1989. Reprinted with permission of The Estate of Etel Adnan and The Post-Apollo Press.

1958 crisis; and the politics concerning the collapse of Intra Bank in 1966, without ever mentioning these events. This disrupts the 'starting point' of the Lebanese Civil War as a rational periodization of the start of the conflict, often discussed as 13 April 1975.

By challenging the starting point of the Lebanese Civil War, Adnan presents a conundrum for researchers engaged in normative methodological practices. Specifically, she presents a narrative where the accepted *cause* of the Lebanese Civil War is much more complex, historically produced, and filled with contradictions. By understanding the production of conflict in this manner, the linear relationship between cause and effect is problematized, as is the dichotomy between peace and conflict. In other words, the means to understand how the social world functions according to 'normal' social scientific methods and methodology is disrupted. Adnan forces the reader to consider the longer scale of history, with multiple overlapping, contradicting variables and asks the researcher to question: when does peace end and war begin?

The non-event, according to Adnan, was like previous events: disturbances. Yet, the accumulation of disturbances, the pinnacle being the night of the non-event, was there: 'War in the vacant sky' (Adnan, 1989: III, 11).

The environmental shift is detailed by the sun's absence in that moment, where previously the sun's omnipresence was the only object worthy of note; however, war overshadowed all else. As daily life came to a standstill following that night, the sun is referenced as rising in the East 'from the mosque' to the West, or 'the vacant Place'. Unlike the first pages when there was a pause to admire the sun, there was nowhere to escape: no shade, an allegory for the coming apocalypse.

Figure 5.3: Etel Adnan, from *The Arab Apocalypse*, p 11

III

The night of the non-event. War in the vacant sky. The Phantom's absence.
Funerals. Coffin not covered with roses. Unarmed population. Long.
The yellow sun's procession from the mosque to the vacant Place. Mute taxis.
Plainclothed army. Silent hearse. Silenced music. Palestinians with no Palestine.

The night of the Great Inca did not happen. Engineless planes. Extinguished sun.
Fishermen with no fleet fish with no sea fleet with no fish sea without fishermen
Guns with faded flowers Che Guevara reduced to ashes. No shade.
The wind neither rose nor subsided. The Jews are absent. Flat tires.
The little lights are not lit. No child has died. No rain
I did not say that spring was breathing. The dead did not return.

The mosque has launched its unheeded prayer. Lost in the waves.
The street lost its stones. Brilliant asphalt. Useless roads. Dead Army.
Snuffed is the street. To shut off the gas. Refugees with no refuge no candle.
The procession hasn't been scared. Time went by.   Silent Phantom.

11

Source: The Post-Apollo Press, 1989. Reprinted with permission of The Estate of Etel Adnan and The Post-Apollo Press.

Similarly, in the final pages of *The Arab Apocalypse*, Adnan describes the political realities of the conclusion of the Civil War and the material and immaterial realities as the environment shifts once again. The post-war environment is often discussed as a period of development, retrospection, and reconciliation. It is thought to be a period of unease, with conflict always being around the corner, yet marked by declarations of pacific agreements between elites. Although Adnan does not describe the political agreements, policies, government making in the immediate post-war period, she reflects on her surroundings, presenting a queer reality where conflict is said to have concluded but the new 'post-conflict' environment is assembled on the foundations of violent conflict. This, again, blurs the categories of peace and conflict, prompting the question—when does conflict finish and peace begin?

As fighting between the Lebanese factions came to an end, Adnan references the Syrian occupation of Lebanon: 'There are more Syrian kings in the ant-hills than ants STOP THEM!' (Adnan, 1989: XLVI, 65). The vision of a post-conflict environment held by many is one of a new pacific environment, a sense of return to the sun-pocked days, yet the Syrian army officers, referred to as Syrian kings, continued to occupy Lebanon following the Ta'if Agreement,[11] became the rulers, law bearers, and judges who dictated the lives of the population. Although the Syrian occupation was meant to maintain order and a pacific environment, they were not innocent of crimes or neutral purveyors: 'They drank drops of sweat and infants' blood' (Adnan, 1989: XLVI, 65). The Syrian presence as a continued marker of coercion blurred the boundary between war and peace.

Adnan's writings on the emergence of the Lebanese Civil War reflects a dynamic of contradiction and complexity that is rarely captured in the academic writing on conflict. The outbreak of war, as Adnan describes it, does not occur overnight, but is reflective of a process that alters the background to which we live and experience life. In this process, the familiar is changed, absences and vacancies appear, and the voids are not filled; a new familiar is created. This is not necessarily captured by scholarship that is engaged in hetero-masculine logics which places events in binary categories, describing events as linear; that seeks to understand why or how the war started by tracing a political desire for power; and which presents the post-conflict situation as one of divergence from conflict (Chamie, 1976; Haugbolle, 2005). In Adnan's writing, the categories—temporality of war and peace—are queered. Here, Adnan highlights the ongoing particularities of war for which a new reality is once again developed.

Trauma as queering: understanding the Lebanese Civil War

By engaging with *The Arab Apocalypse* as a queer feminist epistemological method, we are able to gain insight into Adnan's experience and positionality, our understanding of the Lebanese Civil War, and, more generally, of conflict. The knowledge that emerges from this engagement reveals multiplicities and disrupts linear logics of conflict that are normally based in White (Western) hetero-masculine logics. Here, the chapter explores how trauma is *queering*. In other words, trauma disrupts previously held logics and sensibilities. In the case of the Lebanese Civil War, we can understand how trauma informs sectarianism. Although many of the existing analyses and arguments that are concerned with sectarianism in Lebanon are problematic, viewing sectarianism as an inherent or biological force, by examining sectarianism through the spectrum of trauma it is possible to disrupt long-held assumptions of the Lebanese Civil War.

As the conflict, as told in the poem, unfolds and the violence of each event begins to surpass the previous, the apocalypses, 'explosive' first thoughts, while not cumulative, reference ongoing incomprehensible traumas. The tragedies mount, from the Sabra and Shatila massacre, the use of chemical weapons, to the massacre at Quarantina. It provokes Adnan to command 'STOP'. 'STOP' becomes an echo, a word that lingers in the air as it bounces off events. It acts as a circuit breaker, a plea for pause, with the brutality of the conflict transforming the banality of everyday life. Notably, despite the long process of conflict development—discussed in the previous section—the experience of conflict produces an anxious temporality that is difficult to measure. It is an apocalypse that appears without much warning as the deteriorating environment occurs in a manner that individuals and society acclimatize to. Although, by definition, an apocalypse presupposes a conclusion for everyone, the conclusion is experienced differently by different people. These apocalypses take on a similar dynamic as the sun; they are universal but not uniform. For those who are dead, the violence draws their worlds to a decisive end. For those who survive, despite physical continuity they become ensnared by a psychological process. This is an apocalypse as trauma alters every aspect of life.

Throughout the poem Adnan generously offers her own experience of trauma to make sense of conflict. Trauma acts as a motivating factor that shapes a desire for salvation and survival, possibly as a way out. This is dissimilar to the masculinist desire for power, although it could produce similar violent results. However, unlike masculine desires for power leading to untethered violence, trauma is tethered—it is a link to the subject that cannot be broken. Discussing how trauma shapes desire, however, Adnan writes that 'a sun-ambulance carries Christ to the insane asylum ... Close to the monkeys' (Adnan, 1989: X, 25). Here, the stability found in religion is altered through trauma; it becomes the factor that makes us ill and irrational. This critique serves a dual purpose. First, it disrupts how the Lebanese Civil War is often framed as motivated by sectarianism and thus needs to be understood as a sectarian conflict. Second, it exposes the traumas—the depths of deprivation and loss caused by conflict—that is fertile ground for religion to root itself in society in a novel fashion.

In the first instance, the emphasis on sectarian conflict found in much of the scholarship limits our comprehension of the real political and social complexities of the conflict. A focus on sectarianism constrains the narrative to one that is focused on the discourses of the militia-leadership; treating the 'other' as an existential threat. In the context of the Lebanese Civil War, sectarian discourses served a propagandic and mobilizing purpose. Sectarian discourses helped construct the self and the other, where the self was always in existential danger and the other was always dangerous. Dangerous to the community and nation that the self belongs to and inherently represents.[12] These narratives are, effectively, an elite desire for political power which play on the population's desires for salvation and survival but does not explain the desires or the role of the population. Where attempts have been made to explain the desires of the population, there is often a discussion of *inherent* or *embedded* sectarianism, an argument laced with biological determinism that is deeply problematic. For example, the assertion that the Christian Orthodox community were the *Muslims of the Christians*, reducing the entire Christian Orthodox community to a sectarian trope and painting them as *traitors* to the ultra-nationalist Christian right.[13]

Second, the traumas of conflict provide opportunities for sectarianism to become rooted in society, a response to the apocalypse, and fulfilling the purpose of propaganda by transforming society.[14] In trying to make sense of these dynamics, Adnan is engaged in a critique of the illogical conclusions which portray the conflict as a matter of inherent sectarianism; by using Adnan's writing as that of a witnessed account of the conflict, it is possible to work through the prevalent sectarian narratives to highlight the contradictions and understand the function of trauma in producing a *fait accompli* (see Figure 5.4).

For the mother in the poem, who 'was beating raw meat', the mix of psychological and physical manifestations of conflict, the traumas, on the individual are apparent. The mother evokes hunger and desperation, where 'she ate with cannibal eagerness'. The *icons*, in this passage, represent the psychological and the bread represents the physical. They are a trauma-initiated desire for salvation and survival with direct reference to the Church. After which, she 'sang a solar litany on Resurrection Sunday', the Muslim equivalent of Friday morning prayers.

In moments of enduring suffering and trauma, religious differences helped mobilize animosity and conflict, because, in these moments, salvation and survival were finite. However, as Adnan notes, these witnesses, across religious divisions, are otherwise the same. They exist in the same sphere of trauma and are moving towards the same goal. The perceived and real threat to their survival provokes the same response: 'the mother and the recitant met in the fire / I saw them throw their cut-up fingers on the Church's platter'. And, as in their mutual hungers, desire for survival and salvation, 'the saint did not come to their rescue the Companions neither'. Adnan evokes an important feeling of dismay, of being let down by the religious beliefs that, in their desperation, they held on to. These beliefs structured their eagerness to fight, to turn their backs on their neighbours, justified by a sense of righteousness. They could no longer blame the politicians, militia leaders, or religious leadership for the violence, becoming the 'thing' that they feared in the *other*. And when the promised salvation and holy intervention did not occur on their behalf, they continued to fight. Here, Adnan notes that 'the sun's pain rose on the thermometer', a reference to Gilgamesh, and despite lack of salvation and holy intervention, the 'muezzins and priests posted bulletins of victory', claiming that the deaths were not in vain.

Adnan's writing draws out the political positionalities inhabited by individuals, politicians, and religious leaders, and in doing so shows how the opposing factions are mere reflections of each other; how distinctions between good and bad, leader and follower are not clear. Adnan blurs these boundaries, where responsibility becomes queered. For example, both mother and recitant are victims of conflict and responsible for conflict, for their own and each other's trauma. What Adnan highlights in this passage is the complexity of conflict, where everyone holds responsibility and everyone holds trauma, where the beginning and end points are no longer distinguishable, and victory is empty in meaning.

Figure 5.4: Etel Adnan, from *The Arab Apocalypse*, p 48

XXIX

the sun is unsettled dissident eruptive in anarchy
I forbade the sky to traverse my eyes   STOP   Running
They came with yellow ears and drained nostrils
I saw cross-bearers with   death in their sockets
the boys cried STOP the girls didn't spread the linen
the father died of a heart-attack on a boat named Cyprus
the mother was beating raw meat   the enemy surged from the stone mill
She ate with cannibal eagerness the icons and the bread
Then sang a solar litany on Resurrection Sunday
the sun-muezzin intonated prayers till the evening of palms
the mother and the recitant met in the fire
I saw them throw their cut-up fingers on the Church's platter
The saints did not come to their rescue   the Companions neither
between two epic pauses they fought   believe it!
the sun's pain rose on the thermometer
muezzins and priests posted bulletins of victory
the combatants remained horizontal on the horizontal line of the sea

48

Source: The Post-Apollo Press, 1989. Reprinted with permission of The Estate of Etel Adnan and The Post-Apollo Press.

In the final lines of this page, Adnan writes: 'the combatants remained horizontal on the horizontal line of the sea'. While Adnan refers to the bodies as combatants rather than the 'dead', she is illustrating the likely inevitability of their fate: death. Here, it is a death whose commemoration is swept out to the sea, remaining distant, much like the horizon line, but never raised towards the heavens. This is in contention with the 'posted bulletins of victory' because, if there was indeed victory, the dead would be celebrated, remembered, and cared for.

This section has explored Adnan's experience of trauma from the Lebanese Civil War and the impact of trauma on conflict perpetuity. Challenging long-held assumptions concerning the Lebanese Civil War, the question *why* individuals fight is drawn out, with no definitive answer or explanation. But, do we need an answer? By exploring these dynamics without searching for a causal relationship, we *know* conflict changes. We can abandon White (Western) hetero-masculine knowledge systems that continuously colonize and speak for subjects being 'researched'. It encourages the researcher interested in conflict to alter how they engage with a subject, to take an expansive position on what forms of knowledge are worthy of engagement, such as poetry, literature, art, music, and film. By beginning here, we can abandon extractive practices that seek ownership of knowledge. We can, instead, seek to understand the positions, experiences, and responses of individuals. After all, how can we claim to know a conflict, a society, a community, without paying attention to how they choose to talk about their experience?

Conclusion

The Arab Apocalypse by Etel Adnan, like other works of art and literature, offers an affective and reflexive communication regarding conflict that is not always grasped in academic scholarship on conflict, war, and political violence. Adnan's positionality and episteme that pervade the pages of the epic poem is one that is feminist and queer. In doing so, and as Cynthia Weber argues, this episteme, her feminist and queer way of knowing, 'ignite[s] in modern surveyors … a frustration with the impossibility of knowing [the conflict] for sure' (Weber, 2016: 3).

While this intervention is primarily and specifically concerned with the Lebanese Civil War, general arguments can be made about research in the social sciences. This includes understanding the White (Western) and heteromasculine dynamics of knowledge production in the social sciences and questioning how knowledge is attained, what counts as 'real knowledge', and whose knowledge matters. As explored in this chapter, this can mean turning to other kinds of documents, including art and literature, to gain novel understandings of a particular problem, challenging long-held narratives, and disrupting the binary categories deployed in academic scholarship. In doing so, however, it is not enough to engage with poetry and literature, but seek out an understanding of the author's oeuvre, experience, and politics—their positionality. Here, we can understand poetry and literature, and other art forms, as knowledge producing.

Within the epic poem, Adnan explores the competing realities of the Civil War, but in doing so positions herself as a witness, living with the consequences of elite desires and politics, and the overarching structures of empire. As a witness, Adnan problematizes many of the enduring 'facts' of the conflict, including its linearity, temporality, and causes and consequences. Discussed in this chapter is the disruption of knowledge regarding when conflict starts and ends, altering the timelines, and putting forward a more complex argument that queers the categories of peace and war and our will to knowledge. Similarly, Adnan problematizes the logics of empire by making an intervention in the narration of sectarianism. Building on feminist reflexivity, she disrupts a long-held 'truth' of the Lebanese Civil War and Lebanese society by arguing, as others have done in different circumstances (Aldoughli, 2021), that sectarianism is not inherent, but a resulting mobilizing force of trauma.

Notes

1. Etel Adnan (1925–2021) was an activist, writer, poet, and artist who identified as a lesbian. Etel Adnan's biography, written by Kaelen Wilson-Goldie, was published in 2018. The poem was largely a response to the Tel al-Zataar siege and massacre, home to around 30,000 Palestinian refugees and committed by Christian forces, lasting 59 days and subsequently mimicked by Adnan in the structure of the poem into 59 stanzas (Adnan in *Middle East Report*, 1989; Plum, 2020: 2–3).
2. Simone de Beauvoir argued that the 'representation of the world as the world itself is the work of men; they describe it from their own point of view that is their own and that they confound with the absolute truth' (2010: 166).
3. Linearity is questioned and explored by scholars including Kimberly Hutchings (2008), who discusses how ideas of time are based in Western political thought, which determines what we can and cannot know about politics. Siba Grovogui (2016) argues that temporal linearity is a product of empire. Grovogui's argument highlights the Western centric framing of temporality and Adnan's obfuscation of temporal linearity.
4. Borrowing from Karin Fierke (2004), trauma is understood as 'a "dislocation" accompanied by an inability to mourn or speak of the trauma' where trauma in relation to conflict is 'more difficult to come to terms with because the pain is a byproduct of intentional action', at which point trauma becomes isolated 'to another level of experience [...] the political, where [it becomes] part of the mobilisation of group solipsism' (472, 476, 490).
5. The politics of citation are important here: on the one hand these critiques require citation. However, citing scholarship that is extractive and engaged in racist tropes only advances the professional visibility of those authors by, first, encouraging them to continue on this research track and, second, providing them with favourable data that will help them win research funding, grants, and academic positions.
6. An argument that comes through clearly in Patricio Simonetto's chapter in this volume.
7. Irrational is italicized because it is only irrational so far as we hold hetero-masculine epistemes to be rational.
8. Other poets who have engaged in a similar fashion include Warsan Shire and her poem 'Home'; Maram al-Masri's collection of poems, *Liberty Walks Naked*.
9. Meir Zamir writes that Emile Eddé wanted to secure Lebanon's distinct Christian character, an ideological and imperial racist construction of Lebanon that has persisted from 1860 until the contemporary period (see Delatolla, 2021).
10. The Phalange (Kataeb) are an ultra-nationalist Christian Lebanese political party and were a prominent paramilitary organization.
11. The Ta'if Agreement, or the National Reconciliation Accord, sought to formally put an end to the conflict with the principle of 'mutual coexistence'.
12. Zeina Maasri (2009) explores these dynamics by analysing political and propaganda posters from the Lebanese Civil War.
13. The trope developed because many prominent Christian Orthodox figures had aligned themselves with leftist and Arabist political parties.
14. Similarly, Rahaf Aldoughli (2021) argues that sectarianism in Syria has become embedded through issues of ontological security.

Bibliography

Adnan, E. (1989) 'Arab Apocalypse', *Middle East Report*, [online], 160 (September/October). Available from: https://merip.org/1989/09/arab-apocalypse/

Adnan, E. (1989) *The Arab Apocalypse*, Sausalito: The Post-Apollo Press.

Aldoughli, R. (2021) 'Collectivizing trauma and narrative in the Syrian War: sectarianization and ontological security', *SEPAD Discussions: The Middle East in 2050* [online]. Available from: www.sepad.org.uk/announcement/collectivizing-trauma-and-narrative-in-the-syrian-war-sectarianization-and-ontological-security

Badran, T. (2009) 'Lebanon's militia wars', in B. Rubin (ed), *Lebanon: Liberation, Conflict, and Crisis*, New York: Palgrave Macmillan, pp 35–62.

Bleiker, R. (2001) 'The aesthetic turn in international theory', *Millennium*, 30(2): 509–33.

Brett, S. (2008) 'From Lebanon to Hezbollahstan', *The Wall Street Journal*, [online] 13 May. Available from: www.wsj.com/articles/SB121063617750986741

Chamie, J. (1976) 'The Lebanese Civil War: an investigation into the causes', *World Affairs*, 139(3): 171–88.

Code, L. (1991) *What Can She Know?: Feminist Theory and the Construction of Knowledge*, Ithaca, NY: Cornell University Press.

Code, L. (2013) 'Taking subjectivity into account,' in L. Alcoff and E. Potter (eds), *Feminist Epistemologies*, New York: Routledge, pp 15–48.

De Beauvoir, S. (2010) *The Second Sex*, London: Vintage.

Donovan, T. (2010) 'Teaching Etel Adnan's *The Arab Apocalypse*', *Poetry Foundation*, [online] 10 February. Available from: www.poetryfoundation.org/harriet-books/2010/02/teaching-etel-adnans-the-arab-apocalypse

Dorfman, A. and Mattelart, A. (1975) *How to Read Donald Duck: Imperialist Ideology in the Disney Comic*, New York: International General.

Doucet, M.G. (2005) 'Child's play: the political imaginary of international relations and contemporary popular children's films', *Global Society*, 19(3): 289–306.

England, K. (1994) 'Getting personal: reflexivity, positionality, and feminist research,' *The Professional Geographer*, 46(1): 80–9.

Escobar, A. (2007) 'Worlds and knowledges otherwise', *Cultural Studies*, 21(2–3): 179–210.

Fierke, K. (2004) 'Whereof we can speak, thereof we must not be silent: trauma, political solipsism and war', *Review of International Studies*, 30(4): 471–91.

Ghassan, T. (1982) 'Lebanon: a new republic', *Foreign Affairs*, 61(1): 84–99.

Grayson, K. (2013) 'How to read Paddington Bear: liberalism and the foreign subject in *A Bear Called Paddington*', *BJPIR*, 15(3): 378–93.

Grosfoguel, R. (2010) 'Epistemic Islamophobia and colonial social sciences', *Human Architecture: Journal of the Sociology of Self-Knowledge*, 8(2): 29–38.

Grosfoguel, R. (2013) 'The structure of knowledge in Westernised universities: epistemic racism/sexism and the four genocides/epistemicides', *Human Architecture: Journal of the Sociology of Self-Knowledge*, 1(1): 73–90.

Grovogui, S. (2016) 'Time, technology, and the imperial eye: perdition on the road to redemption in international relations theory', in A. Agathangelou and K. Killian (eds), *Time, Temporality and Violence in International Relations*, London: Routledge, pp 45–60.

Haugbolle, S. (2005) 'Public and private memory of the Lebanese Civil War', *Comparative Studies of South Asia, Africa and the Middle East*, 25(1): 191–203.

Hemmings, C. (2012) 'Affective solidarity: feminist reflexivity and political transformation', *Feminist Theory*, 13(2): 147–61.

Hoagland, S.L. (2020) 'Aspects of the coloniality of knowledge', *Critical Philosophy of Race*, 8(1–2): 48–60.

Hunt, P. and Sands, K. (2000) 'British Empire and post-empire children's literature', in R. McGillis (ed) *Voices of the Other: Children's Literature and the Postcolonial Context*, New York: Garland Publishing, pp 39–54.

Hutchings, K. (2008) *Time and World Politics: Thinking the Present*, Manchester: Manchester University Press.

Maasri, Z. (2009) *Off the Wall: Political Posters of the Lebanese Civil War*, London: IB Tauris.

Mignolo, W.D. (2007) 'Delinking', *Cultural Studies*, 21(2–3): 449–514.

Ndlovu, M. (2018) 'Coloniality of knowledge and the challenge of creating African futures', *Ufahamu: A Journal of African Studies*, 40(2): 95–112.

O'Ballance, E. (1998) *Civil War in Lebanon, 1975–92*, New York: Springer.

Obrist, H.U. (2014) *Etel Adnan in All her Dimensions*, Milan: Skira.

Plum, H. (2020) '"I planted the sun in the middle of the sky like a flag": in and of Etel Adnan's Arab apocalypse', *College Literature*, 47(3): 1–31.

Quijano, A. (2000) 'Coloniality of power and Eurocentrism in Latin America', *International Sociology*, 15(2): 215–32.

Quijano, A. (2007) 'Coloniality and modernity/rationality', *Cultural Studies*, 21(2–3): 168–78.

Rose, G. (1997) 'Situating knowledges: positionality, reflexivities and other tactics', *Progress in Human Geography*, 21(3): 305–20.

Sandars, N.K. (trans.) (1964) *The Epic of Gilgamesh*, Baltimore, MD: Penguin Classics.

Schiwy, F. (2007) 'Decolonization and the question of subjectivity', *Cultural Studies*, 21(2–3): 271–94.

Springer, M.D. (1991) 'Repetition and 'going round' with Wallace Stevens', *The Wallace Stevens Journal*, 15(2): 191–208.

Stephens, B. (2008) 'From Lebanon to Hezbollahstan', *Wall Street Journal*, May 13. Available from: www.wsj.com/articles/SB121063617750986741

Tilly, C. (2002) *Stories, Identities, and Political Change*, London: Rowman and Littlefield.

Weaver, K. (1986) 'The non worldly world: conversations with Etel Adnan', *Poetry Flash*, 158. Available from: www.eteladnan.com/reviews/interview_poetryflash.pdf

Weber, C. (2016) *Queer International Relations: Sovereignty, Sexuality and the Will to Knowledge*, Oxford: Oxford University Press.

Zamir, M. (1978) 'Emile Eddé and the territorial integrity of Lebanon,' *Middle Eastern Studies*, 14(2): 232–5.

6

Queer Tools for the Ruthless Archive: Methodological Notes on Trans and Queer Exploration in Argentinean Archives

Patricio Simonetto

Introduction

There is a widespread belief that queer history works against invisibility. As researchers, we usually start with the illusion that our work consists of going to the archive to illuminate secret stories of people that have transgressed gender and sexual rules. We usually start our research projects convinced that we will shed light on the lives erased by the heterosexual gaze. However, while visiting archives, many researchers find, with surprise, that at least since the 19th century, societies have been obsessively talking and producing knowledge about the shifting human sexual experience in general and with particular emphasis on those lives considered 'deviated' by doctors, bureaucrats, and policy makers. Historians then discover that rather than a treasure chest full of secrets, archives are challenging spaces to find the traces of changing sexual practices and imaginaries. The archival documents present pieces of complicated puzzles with which we attempt to formulate histories of sexuality.

From a queer perspective, finding documents is easier than analysing them. Researchers usually feel first a quick excitement when they find hundreds of pages of, for example, doctors writing about sexual lives that they considered abnormal or police reports about men looking for sexual encounters with other men in cities. Nevertheless, after reading the material, historians often feel frustrated about the challenges of working with fragmented material about how political elites and medical professionals imagined sexuality with little attention to the experiences of those people transgressing the rules. Queer and trans lives—I use these identifiers to define the lives of those crossing what were considered the gender and/or sexual rules of their time—are usually described by others in fragmented documents such as newspaper articles, police reports, or court records. However, as discussed below, the use of contemporary identifiers can be problematic for historical research; creating a temporal colonization. As such, we cannot access queer lives directly. We go to the archive to fish for events that can illuminate their life: an unfortunate encounter with a police officer or the morbid interest of a tabloid journalist (Farge, 2013). Therefore, it is almost impossible to find any trace of their life experiences on their own terms, or the terms that we understand today, which forces us to deal with categories produced in unequal power conditions. While moving from one document to another, the illusion of the transparency of the documents' fades: How can a perspective focused on fluidity and the distrust of fixed categories help us build a stable historical narrative? How can queer historiography approach these experiences that we usually know through the words of powerful others? How can we ethically work with these materials?[1]

This chapter explores some notes about queer and trans methodology and archival research based on my experience working on the Latin American history of sexuality. This chapter does not propose a monolithic understanding of how to do archival research. Instead, it explores the potential of a paradoxical perspective that usually offers more challenges than solutions. The text explores how queer historians have contributed to developing a sensibility that helps us know the risks of the demand for stability in historical writing (Amin, 2017). In recent years, the so-called archival turn expanded the interdisciplinary definition of the notion of the archive by examining the practices and theories of recollection and curation—and their social and political impact (Marshall and Tortorici, 2022). The theorization of expansive and sometimes uncontrollable archives, usually referred to with capitals: 'The Archive' needs to be explored to understand this logic of knowledge production and preservation beyond assuming an always universal machinery of archival practices.

The main contribution of this chapter is to bring forward a queer sensibility in the archives, the uncomfortable feeling that boosts the formulation of questions to distrust stable and teleological narratives. Here I ask questions that any historian of sexuality faces while navigating archives: How should we approach archives? How can we build historical narratives with fragmentary documents? What are the limits and potentialities of working with documents produced in frameworks of intense social hierarchies? What can we know about those subjects who left no traces of their own experiences? What is our link as researchers to the archive? More concretely, in this chapter, these questions relate to documents that I found while researching the history of male homosexuality, trans embodiment, and histories of sex work in Argentina. Addressed in this chapter are two intimate stories of Marina and Arturo that highlight the violence of the archive.

Archival research allows us to rethink violence and conflict from a queer historical perspective. As the editors of this volume argue in the Introduction,[2] turning to queer stories of conflict expands the notion of political violence beyond circumscription to classic scenes of political conflict (between states or social groups). Instead, I want to call our attention to how the documented encounters of sex workers, male homosexuals, and trans people with agents of the state destabilize the mainstream heteronormative periodization of conflict and violence. Here, I mean that the prolonged practices of state and community violence against gender and sexual transgressions redefine the margins of what is violence and what is conflict, while inviting new questions about which violence was accepted, the intensity of this violence, in which contexts it occurred, and against whom this violence was committed. For example, the histories of violence against people who we would now define as the LGBTIQ+[3] community in Latin America problematize the mainstream circumscription of political violence to periods of military dictatorships, raising questions about the heteronormativity of our accepted periodizations. At the same time, I draw attention to how archives have much more than histories of violence to offer. I also reflect on the challenges of building conjectural stories based on fragments to bring back the joy and resistance of those who, between doctors' examinations and police officers' harassment, forged joyful lives beyond sexual and gender norms.

This chapter explores three main issues while navigating archives with a queer sensibility. First, I explore archives as spaces of power and how historians negotiate with the conditions of production of archival documents. Second, I examine the challenges of studying gender and sexual experiences as represented in archives going beyond our modern language and labels for understanding sexuality. Finally, I emphasize the power of disidentification in historical heterosexual practices. Disidentification is the important practice of identifying conceptual and practical differences associated with identifiers throughout history, recognizing gender and sexual identities are not historically stable and constant.

Dealing with ruthless archives

There are many types of archives, understood as collections that document history, including private and public collections, those held by grassroots organizations and those held by businesses. Newer archives are emerging, focusing on LGBTIQ+ histories, in an attempt to foment queer historical narratives. Some of these archives are accessible, such as national archives, and other collections are legally restricted by the state; including documents that expose state violence in instances of war and genocide. Archives are dynamic spaces in which researchers must negotiate with the institutional history, regulations, and archivists when accessing the material. Archives are not passive and transparent reservoirs. They are institutional projects through which multiple social groups, and usually the state, have built their authority over the past (Stoler, 2010).

Even if archives can sometimes be ruthless spaces of knowledge production, they are also scenes of conflict. While revisiting the images of famous La Princesa de Borbón (The Bourbon Princess), who would be recognized as a trans woman today, allocated to the National Archive of Argentina, I noticed that an archivist wrote ~~puto (faggot)~~ behind the princess' beautiful portraits, refuting the alleged neutrality of the archives. I cannot know who wrote these words on the photograph, maybe it was written by the journalists that used the photographs for the multiple stories that they published about her in the early 20th century. Regardless, the fact is that someone tried to scratch out that inscription and replace it with the famous name that made her a noticeable character in many South American cities in the early 20th century. The act of crossing out that derogatory words defining the possible readings leaves a mark on the historical imaginations that characterizes our treading of these characters. Yet, a queer methodology in the archives shows us there is always the open potential of formulating other readings against those demeaning words.

In the last decade, historians and literary critics have challenged the alleged neutrality of archives. There has been an increased theorization on the challenges of working with 'traditional archives'—where documents are stored and organized (Arondekar et al 2015; Caimari, 2020). Scholars such as Elena Martínez and Diana Taylor emphasized the strong relation between institutional archives and state projects and the power dynamics involved in producing a collection—for example, in reproducing the dominance of certain voices over others (for example, doctors over patients, policemen over prisoners, and so on). These scholars call our attention to the predominance of written documents and how they construct memory at the expense of oral knowledge (Taylor, 2003; Martínez, 2014). Traditional archives usually preserve more documents about the physicians' point of view of those considered 'sexually deviated' than the words of LGBTIQ+ people.

Foundational works about historiography by Michel Foucault and Jacques Derrida raise questions about the archives as spaces of power, drawing attention to the historical perspective they present: Which documents are preserved or discarded and why? What does the condition of production of those documents tell us about that time in history and how can we deal with it? Inspired by this work, queer historian of colonization Zeb Tortorici (2018) brings to our attention how traditional historiography usually takes for granted the truth of documents and lacks perspective about their history.

Contrasting colonial sodomy (a condition defined by a sexual practice) with modern homosexuality (an identity) in New Spain, Tortorici questions how this 'sin against nature' was materially recollected. He shows the role of the production of material evidence in New Spain in supporting discourse with which the colonial authorities made sense of sexual practices. In doing so, he also engages with afterlives of these cases; namely, how they were preserved and survived through the archive. Questioning how 'silences' have been produced in the archive calls our attention to how certain perspectives are preserved and materialized in the archives over others. Rather than reducing these silences to the expression of practices of power, we can also explore them as a result of multiple practices with which people avoided the agencies of power that produced documents (for example, when queer people take measures to avoid police imprisonment or medical examination).

In this text, I use the concept of 'ruthless archives' to define the process with which traditional archives reproduce unequal power dynamics in the making of documents and how historians deal with these power dynamics (Simonetto, 2021). Even if researchers usually project human rationality on the archive in informal conversation, talking about it as if it were a living being, understanding archives as ruthless institutions can help us make sense of more complex dynamics at play. Archives can reproduce hierarchical and unequal power dynamics depending on how the materials are organized, and what language is used in the documents and by the archivist. Archives produce a language through which the words of doctors, police officers, and bureaucrats persist over sex workers, trans people, or homosexuals' voices. Archiving queer and trans lives is done by reproducing a logic that generally does not consider how LGBTIQ+ people would want to be remembered. Even more problematic, these archives preserve people in ways that they might not want to be remembered publicly. An excellent example of this is the thousands of police records of men having sex with other men that did not always define themselves publicly as homosexuals or the records of trans people in which police officers usually misgendered them (Ryan, 2017, 2022; Hulme, 2021).

The archive is ruthless because it works without questioning intimate personal desires. To rescue LGBTIQ+ stories from these derogatory classifications, historians need to examine their relationship with how they tell stories about LGBTIQ+ lives. An understanding of how the archive is organized provides us with the ability to navigate it. Understanding the historical conditions of production of documents provides us with the tools to track the slight traces of those subaltern lives apparently silenced in the archive.

Telling Marina's story through the archives

A good example of archival production about queer experience historically is the library of the Medicine College of the University of Buenos Aires.

The archive is organized by a system of cards which reproduce the categories doctors used to define 'sexual abnormalities' (for example, 'homosexuality' or 'sexual inversion'). The cards make it possible to find all the publications on the topic, some of which, beyond the doctors' intentions, resulted in rich chronicles recording brief statements or photographs of their subjects. Since the late 19th century, Argentine physicians have played a crucial role in defining the gendered, sexual, and racial limits of citizenship. Members of powerful families and the local elites, first hygienists and eugenist doctors, colonized state agencies and shaped normalized standards of sex that they understood vital for national development (Rodriguez, 2006). While reading their collections of chronicles, studies, and photographs of alleged homosexuals and prostitutes—a very vague category in which they aggregated all those they understood as sexually deviated—I found the case of Marina, whose own story reveals the complex challenges of writing queer and trans history.

In 1944, Doctor José Belbey published Marina's photograph in multiple medical journals (Belbey, 1944, 1955). Marina was a 20-year-old transgender woman[4] imprisoned for 'dressing as the opposite sex'. Belbey's articles were foundational to the modern medical category of *travestismo* in Argentina (Belbey, 1944). Belbey took the concept from the influential German psychiatrist Richard Von Krafft-Ebing.[5] A few years later, mainstream handbooks used by psychiatric institutions employed the concept of *travestismo* as a regular and defined type of sexual deviation. *Travestismo* was a word for doctors to label one kind of sexual dissidence on what they understood as the homosexual spectrum that went beyond (or *traversed*) a person's 'sexual orientation' and instead embraced gender identity which was recognized as dressing as the 'opposite sex'. It is impossible to know if *travestismo* meant anything to Marina. The concept was not used as a community identity until the late 1960s. However, the word allowed me to understand how doctors were imagining Marina, and even more importantly, the words preserved by the archive helped me to identify other cases of people crossing the frontier of what was understood as gender in their time.

Marina was born in Buenos Aires City in 1924. She was an orphan abandoned by her parents at an early age. Like other children of poor working-class families, she worked in the domestic service of a wealthy house. Beginning in 1919 the state developed charities and public organizations to look for jobs for children who were considered in need. This practice was promoted by social reformers to produce what they considered productive citizens (Guy, 2009). Marina ran away from many workhouses, a regular occurrence among children forced to work under these conditions who often tried to escape from an extreme hierarchical relationship with adults that sometimes included physical abuse. At 14, Marina claimed legal independence from her tutor (her legal guardian) and looked for a domestic service job. She explained to Belbey that it was better to be considered a woman to get a good position as a housemaid. However, she felt her transformation to living as a woman progressively took control over her whole life. Nonetheless, maybe her claim of autonomy was more than just looking for a proper job and instead a desperate search for freedom. Marina explained that living with other female workers allowed her to learn about female expressions, clothing, and make-up. She described paying attention to tips that her colleagues gave her. She told doctors how she discovered all the details that composed her femininity until 'she did not need to lie anymore', which shows the role of sociability in producing embodied knowledge and technologies (Belbey, 1944).

In 1941, Marina abandoned her work in the domestic service and moved to a home with her friends. She started working as a sex worker in the streets and brothels of Buenos Aires. Marina worked as a dancer in a working-class pub where men drank and purchased sexual services. During the 1940s and 1950s, some homosexuals, usually referred to as *transformistas*, offered sexual favours in brothels or private parties (Malva, 2011). She was a *copera*, a lady that offered company and alcoholic drinks to their clients to get commissions. When asked to have penetrative sexual encounters, she refused, saying that she had her 'period' in an attempt to protect her identity (Belbey, 1944).

The legal and medical context, specifically the role of doctors, is useful for understanding the material conditions that produced Marina's photograph and testimony that was then mediated by Belbey's words. It is important to be aware of the power of policemen and doctors in forcing Marina to narrate her life, and how alternatively queer historical insights can create a counternarrative centred on Marina's actions to deal with the state and medical violence in her everyday life (Sears, 2015). Marina—like many other people selling sex—was submitted to the constant policing of policemen and doctors.

The history of criminalization and policing of sexual practices in Argentina is also a history of the documentary production of queer, trans, and sex workers' lives. For example, the global abolition of the regulated systems of prostitution displaced the documents from the local records to the trial courts and police offices. Something similar happened with the criminalization of homosexual practices: under the law criminalizing homosexual sex between men, state actors began to collect details of the lives of homosexual men. In Argentina—like other Latin American countries—the impact of liberalism led to the decriminalization of all private sexual practices between consenting adults (Ben, 2010).

Although liberal laws failed to stop the policing of sexuality, the lack of a legal ground for the persecution of men who had sex with men granted them a higher degree of freedom than what had been experienced previously. Since the 1930s, the convergence between the cultural, economic, and political liberal crisis and the local elites' growing fears about urban modernity's effects led to a more active state intervention to construct a 'public morality' (Simonetto, 2016). The global debate about 'public morality' boosted the creation of legislation that likened sexuality and politics as complementary components of social order (Fuechtner, Haynes, and Jones, 2017). Local and regional governments passed legal mechanisms that repressed young people, the urban poor, sex workers, and sexual dissidents. Military and civil governments passed morality laws to police public life. In 1933, the city of Buenos Aires penalized those who 'appear on the public streets dressed or disguised in clothes of the opposite sex', those who 'incite or publicly offer a carnal act, without distinction of sex', and those who present as 'subjects recognized as perverts in the company of minors under 18 years' (Gentili, 1995). The Province of Buenos Aires took similar restrictions in 1955 condemning the sale of sex in public spaces, and in 1966 began punishing those who 'in everyday life dress and pass themselves as a person of the opposite sex'. Along the same lines, Argentina abolished the system of regulated brothels in 1936. Even if someone was legally capable of selling sex independently, police officers practised a punitive interpretation of the law in which they imprisoned sex workers for short but repeated times (Guy, 1991; Simonetto, 2019).

Through Belbey's chronicle, we know that Marina and other trans people were aware of the power of documents for the state. Marina did not have any legal identity documents as a man or woman; being invisible before the state was her way of building a shield to protect herself. In making herself otherwise invisible to state surveillance, she only left traces as a woman on state medical records. Her lack of legal identity documents may have been a strategy to avoid gender classification by the state. When Marina was imprisoned in 1939, they sent her to the San Miguel Asylum, a prison for women administered by a religious order. What is evident in the archives is that Marina was initially able to negotiate the way the state recorded her life: policemen did not question Marina's female identity, so she was imprisoned in a women's jail seven times, where she was educated in house chores by religious women to recover her femininity (Belbey, 1944). It was only later, when the police detained her for a short period, they decided that she was lying about her female identity, despite her performance, and sent her to the Institute of Legal Medicine to study her trans experience. Belbey found Marina's experience of having her gender scrutinized in this way surprising and unique.

In documents retrieved from the *Archivos de Criminología, Medicina Legal y Psiquiatría*, which acted as a platform for sexual normalization since the beginning of the century (Belbey, 1944, 1955), a medical committee claimed that Marina avoided doing mandatory military service, a requirement for any man to access Argentinian citizenship. Nevertheless, the committee suggested not to send her to the barracks: 'This person should not be considered for conscription that all citizens must attend for moral reasons, because of his true sex [...]. A good job, a good example, and the strict vigilance of his impressions will lead to a better result [than military service] because they are the source values of dignity' (Belbey, 1944). During these years, the army's hierarchies were concerned about the potential extension of 'sexual deviations' among soldiers since the government abolished regulated prostitution (Simonetto, 2019). Belbey's medical team also produced photographs to serve as a type of testimony to Marina's female performance. The photographs help us to understand the violent condition in which the testimony was produced, and reflect a transphobic practice that sought to publicly portray Marina as an example of an alleged fake gender performance; what doctors defined as *invertidos sexuales* or *travestis*.[6] According to a wider scientific photographic genre, Belbey compiled examples of how sex could be 'falsified'. He edited cases defined as *invertidos* in previous journals' issues and reinterpreted them under the new lens of *travestissement* (Figure 6.1) (Belbey, 1944, 1955).

Doctors like Belbey used photographs of trans people to present gender as a binary with only two real genders (women/men), arguing that people have a 'real nature' contrary to their claimed gender identity. This transphobic visual genre of medical gender identity documentation acted as a counter-gender technology in which physicians tried to re-inscribe their patients' bodies, and in turn their patients, with what they considered their true gender (Scheiwiller, 2016). Belbey published four photographs to define Marina. The two images at the top show Marina's everyday self-presentation. The two at the bottom show her without any make-up and with a short haircut (Figure 6.2). If photography is a space of encounter between expectations and desires, these images underscore the struggles between two points of view of Marina's gender embodiment (Edwards, 2009). Marina's expression between sadness and motionlessness, illustrating her unhappiness with the process of being gendered by the state, seems to perturb the narrative of the doctors about her gender identity (Cho, 2014).

These photographs look like a photo for an identity card or legal document, a place where the state denied her identity as a trans woman. The picture is a result of state and medical policing, including detention by police officers, doctors' interrogation, and newspapers discussing her personal life. It is also a material dispossession of the goods that defined her self-perception: her make-up and long hair. The doctors submitted Marina's body to a violent gender re-inscription. The haircut or hairstyle they forcibly gave her to make her look like a 'male' is part of a long tradition of physical violence. Hair, in particular, is a distinctive element of gender which can make LGBTIQ+ people vulnerable to policing as well as physical violence. As illustrated here, hair is personal property that state forces and other violent actors cut

Figure 6.1: Image of Marina standing[7]

DISFRAZADO DE MUJER (TRAVESTISSEMENT)
Durante seis años vistió y vivió como mujer

Source: José Belbey, 'Sobre *travestissement*', Archivo de medicina legal, IV, 1944, 120.

to humiliate or mark their sovereignty over the imprisoned queer or trans body. For example, in 1923, the ultra-right-wing nationalist group, the Patriotic League, conducted street arrests of men considered disorderly, removing their moustaches. It was a popular tactic among soldiers and police officers when targeting beggars, bandits, and Indigenous people. Decades later, during the 1960s and 1970s, the police morality department would use forced shaving to condemn young hippies, homosexuals, and *travestis*. Likewise, police officers banned *travestis* from shaving their body hair and forced them to grow a beard as a practice of humiliation. Together these

Figure 6.2: Images of Marina[8]

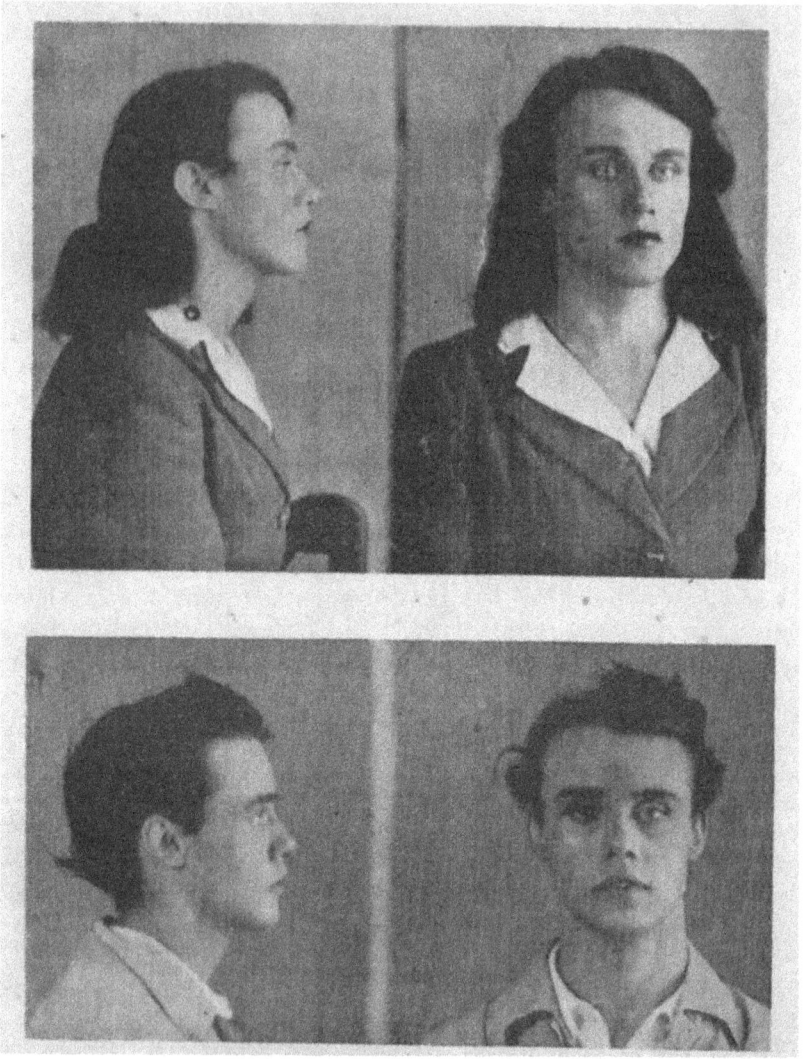

Source: José Belbey, 'Sobre *travestissement*', Archivo de medicina legal, IV, 1944, 124.

acts highlight a long genealogy of violent state practices that police how people embody gender.

Queer historians—as do many historians of subaltern groups—debate the responsible use of photographs like these of Marina. Elena Martínez questions how 'all historical representations carry the responsibility of thinking not just about how they are coloured by present categories, memories, and political concerns but about how they can avoid enacting or re-re-enacting forms of historical violence' (Martínez, 2014). In reality many of the documents we work with in the archives are the product of medical or police violence. As researchers retrieving queer and trans stories, we have the challenge of producing a narrative that neutralizes the primary intentions of their authors. Even if there is no formula, I think that analysing these images is useful on at least two levels. First, as Kevin Coleman (2015a) shows in his analysis of the photographic archives of the United Fruit Company in Central America, sometimes these photographs allow us to think about all the images the archives do not want us to see. Along with the pictures in which Belbey tried to destroy Marina's female embodiment, he published a personal portrait which allows us to imagine the multiple pictures that have not been preserved, the moments of joy in which Marina could build the image of how she wanted to be seen by others. Marina's personal portrait also allows us to reconstruct the power relationship that shaped that image. We must remember that photography is always a space of conflict between what the producer wants to show and what the portrayed can negotiate. Additionally, at present, and with contemporary research practices, the right to see, to uncover, or make visible, has become a mandate beyond individual rights that is sometimes at the expense of individual agency (Coleman, 2015b). Exploring these aspects of contention and conflict, Ariella Azoulay (2015) argues that if we imagine citizenship as a shield that protects certain subjects, there are moments in which photographers can expose bodies without protection, portraying them in an abusive and violent situation.

In his study of trans-visual archives during the Franco era in Spain, Javier Galeano (2022) explores how historical writing might work with materials usually produced for medical pathologization or social control. While the 'ethics of turning away' from police and forensic documents on trans experiences could help us avoid enacting the violent institutional portrayal of trans bodies as sexual monstrosities, avoiding them could also erase trans people from the historical narrative. Fernández Galeano engages with trans activists and scholars' statement that 'visibility means existence' to explore how historical writing can produce a narrative focused on the trans agency of self-representation through medical or criminal photography. In his own words, he proposes that 'visual materials created by trans women, even when archived as part of their prosecution, provide a means to reach beyond a forensic analysis and toward transhermeneutics, namely, trans women's reading of their own self.'

While it is valid to formulate a question about whether we should use these images, I propose here to invert the question to ask how we can use these images to avoid re-enacting the medical violence against Marina's body. In this sense, the question is not only if we should show this image or not, but instead, if we can formulate a historical narrative that inverses the intentions of this picture. In contrast with Belbey's intention of seeing this picture as proof of Marina's portrayal as a male citizen, the role of queer historians is to distrust doctor's categorization and to formulate a narrative focused on how Marina was undeniably a woman, and how she used this photo to reaffirm her femininity beyond medical power.

Marina's story connects multiple violent practices that together build the archives about her experience as a trans woman in Argentina in the 1920s. The police violence promoted by the Argentine state and other cases of violence experienced by the LGBTIQ+ community in which civil society attacked people for transgressing gender norms are the basis of archival production: doctors' pictures, police reports, and news articles. Registers were then classified in state archives using the language of doctors, in Marina's case, in the Medicine College of the University of Buenos Aires library under the label 'Homosexual'. However, these documentary sources were not simply testimonies of passive subjects' violent victimization by state authorities. Marina's picture and story survive in these polyphonic documents.[9] Even if her voice is historically denied in Belbey's writing, it is a clue with which, after identifying the conditions of violence, we can recognize traces of her life: how she survived and embodied her fabulous femininity.

Bodies and archives: photographies, language, and historical narrative

Doing archival research demands patience to navigate the ruthless dynamics of traditional archives. Beyond the bundle of institutional regulations, every archive has a language that organizes it, and researchers must learn this language to find material. Usually, researchers formulate questions with a language that does not match the archive. The archive is often using a language of homogeneous categories to define individuals considered sexually 'abnormal'; a language derived from state agents or physicians, that do not reflect the trans experience (Stryker, 2008). Learning the archive's language takes time, but acquiring this knowledge is worthwhile because it helps us as researchers ask the right questions when engaging with the archivist or when reading archive catalogues as maps to trace the sexual nomads crossing gender and sexual frontiers. Queer history provides us with tools to produce narratives for understanding trans lives historically, while also expanding historical imagination to avoid reproducing the power relationships that dominate traditional archival production.

Amin Ghaziani and Matt Brim (2019) point out the difficulties of defining what queer methodology is because it is a theory that emphasizes the fluid nature of social reality. Researchers must consider that as sexuality changes over time, so has the language used to describe and construct our experiences of sexuality. Researchers must be careful regarding how to navigate archives in which some concepts about gender can seem transparent, but hide complex historical dynamics. For example, how homosexuality was understood began to transform during the 20th century. When it comes to working with archives, I propose bringing a sense of distrust to the categories with which individuals in positions of power (for example, doctors, lawyers, or police officers) try to make sense of gender. Here I want to address the need to understand how language evident in the archive worked in its time. David Halperin (2000) points out that historians of sexuality need a 'strategy for accommodating the aspects of sexual life that seem to persist through time and the dramatic differences between historically documented forms of sexual experience'. This starts with a methodological suspension of current categories of identity. Moreover, it is important to create a distance between those categories and rationalities about gender in the present from those of the past.

Elena Martínez (2014) emphasizes the need to explore the links between classification and power in both past and present that are embedded in archival documents given the possible implications these links have in our understandings of sexuality and subjectivities. She applies this analysis in her groundbreaking study on the case of the 'hermaphrodite' Juana la Larga in New Spain. Martínez asks whether trans and queer history can help us to abandon the idea that categories such as 'man', 'woman', or 'homosexual' are transparent and transhistorical. The field of trans history has developed rich scholarship to help us think about how the previous history of sexuality usually reproduced the power contained in specific categories reducing different trans subjects in the figures of gay and lesbian history (Stryker, 2008; Heyam, 2022).

One of the main challenges of archival research is how historical narratives deal with the opacity of the documents' language. How do we reconstruct the multiplicity of gendered and erotic experiences usually reduced to the limited medical or state-bureaucratic vocabulary? Queer and trans history emphasizing fluidity can help us avoid structured and fixed sexual identities. Queer and trans historiography considers the history of concepts such as 'homosexuality' and 'sexual inversion' to understand how these terms worked differently for physicians and patients while exploring how the intersections of race, gender, and class shaped diverse historical experiences. Sometimes, however, researchers uncritically use modern understandings of sexual identities to discuss the past. The challenge is how to make sense of these histories and their contemporary relevance. There is not necessarily a straightforward connection between contemporary understanding and frameworks of being queer and histories of sex and gender difference.

Since the 1990s, Latin American gay historians have worked to understand the difference between how local sexual dissident categories are discussed in our modern understanding of sexuality and how these categories were understood in the early 20th century. In their studies of *maricas*—usually related to effeminate men looking for sex with manly men—historians found an incommensurable experience for the late 20th-century notion of gender and sexuality structured over the division between homosexuality/ heterosexuality. Gay history showed that *maricas* participated in hierarchical sexual relationships with male partners who understood themselves as heterosexual following the social belief among the popular classes that sexual deviation was related to being the person penetrated during sex (Salessi, 1995; Ben, 2010; Peralta, 2017). This literature was inspired by George Chauncey's book *Gay New York* (Chauncey, 2019), which helped to explain the binary-gendered working-class culture before the emergence of the binary homo/heterosexuality sexual relationships. While this reading was useful for understanding queer visibility in pre-war New York as well as how the intersections of race and social class diversified an alleged homogeneous queer experience, Latin American readings of this analysis build a different teleological narrative. This alternative narrative focuses on sexual experiences over bodily ones, transforming the heterogeneous field of sexual deviation to one focused on a history of modern male homosexuality.

The main problem of this approach is that it often places diverse identities in a genealogy of male homosexuality. This potentially makes distinct trans histories invisible, especially when considering the historical differentiation between *maricas*[10] and *invertidos sexuales*, the latter being a concept used by doctors to define those people dressing occasionally or permanently with 'clothes of the opposite sex' (Bao, 1993; Salessi, 1995; Ben, 2009; Inausti, 2011). In recent years, trans history challenged this understanding. In his study on famous cases of *invertidos sexuales*, Mir Yarfitz (2023) uses the concept of 'anal overdetermination' to point out the need to expand historical imagination and language to understand gender embodiment experience beyond erotic-oriented practices. This means expanding historical imagination to avoid restricting our understanding of these subjects only through their sexual encounters and to produce narratives that, for example, focus on their gender embodiment. In fact, Chauncey's (2019) recent revision of his study inspired by trans history about fairies in New York offers a good starting point to refresh our reading about 'sexual inversion'. He points out that even if he explored fairies' femininity to understand the gender topographies of working-class culture, he still assumed this in the spectrum of homosexuality. He did not consider what it could mean that some people defined themselves by their gender identity and expressions, not only sexuality. While this does not mean that we should reduce these early experiences to other modern categories such as transgender, he points out how exploring the sexual inversion embodiment and its complex dialogue with sexual desire could open new paths for queer history.

The question behind this debate is how queer and trans history can help us to distrust and distance ourselves from both the language of the archive and our own vocabulary as researchers. This new reading turns against problematic past approaches overfocused on people's sexual behaviour and with an understanding of gender diverse performance as a strategic parody. While doctors underlined the alleged artificiality of *invertidos*' gender experience, some studies built a reading against the grain, transforming their performance into a parody that undermined the binary medical notions of gender (Salessi, 1995). Even if this perspective was helpful to show how physicians socially constructed their analysis of gender diversity, it also became a double-edged sword that projected an over-rationality to the past and overlooked the material gendered experience of sexual inversion. Queer tools can help us to pursue a reading of LGBTIQ+ lives that maps the genealogy of archival categories of gender and sexuality while engaging with the fact that gender encompasses far more than sexual desire. Importantly, work by trans scholars helps us understand that 'sexuality' and sexual desire do not always align in conventional ways with gender identity (Stryker, 2008).

This approach to the archive could be properly expanded by analysing the case of *Mujeres-hombres* (Women-men) in Argentina, a concept used by doctors and journalists to define *invertidos sexuales*, people we would understand today as trans men. I found this photographic collection by learning the language of the Argentine National Archive (*Archivo General de la Nación*). It was a journalists' collection from *Caras y Caretas*, a popular magazine in Buenos Aires in the early 20th century. The folder promised to bring together female figures from Buenos Aires. However, the title was sarcastic: it was a collection of personal portraits of *Mujeres-hombres*. The language of the archive worked by relocating these lives to what the archivist considers their true nature: one reduced to their genitalia. A trans reading of these stories challenges gay dominance over historical narrative and allows us to formulate an understanding of stories of LGBTIQ+ lives like Arturo, which I explore below, focusing on his joy of embodying masculinity.

Arturo, who was given the name Dafne at birth, took several portraits: walking in the street with friends, painting, or posing as thinking. In every photograph, he embodied what was popularly understood as a male attitude. His chosen name was Arturo de Aragón. He seems proud and happy, as shown in the pictures taken in 1905 as part of a series of private photographs of *Mujeres-hombres*. However, the circle cut from this original portrait was then used to design a tabloid article in the popular urban magazine *Caras y Caretas* where a journalist wrote:

> Here are photographs of an interesting subject that in the view of readers will appear as a fresh fifteen-year-old adolescent, but in fact, she is just a young lady, whose neatness, along with one of those resolutions that only women, friends of extremes by temperament, know how to

adapt, has led her to conceal herself with such admirable perfection that she has been a man for ten consecutive years.[11]

With this circulation of his personal archive through the newsroom, journalists re-classified him as *Mujeres-hombres*, underscoring the alleged artificiality of Arturo's gender embodiment.

According to the journalist, Arturo was born in 1882 in Sorbolo (Italy) and named after his mother, Dafne Vaccari. Being part of a family with a prominent social position, he travelled around Europe until he settled in South America. He was 24 years old when he was photographed with his friends, wearing male clothes and embodying a masculine attitude in public spaces. The journalist explained his transformation by saying that when Arturo was 14 years old, a man sexually attacked him. There is no way to fact-check this claim, but it is possible that Arturo decided to report this story to the journalist as a way to validate his gender.

Arturo started moving at a young age. In his late teenage years he performed as a male comic actor. He then became involved in political activities as an agitator and moved through French cities such as Paris, Lyon, and Marseille to participate in public conferences. In 1900, he enlisted as a sailor and

Figure 6.3: Image of Arturo

Source: Archivo General de la Nación (Argentina). Photography department. Code: AR-AGN-CYC01-sff-405346. Serie: Ladies figures.

moved to Argentina. In Buenos Aires, he worked as a longshoreman in the barracks[12] before moving to London to work on a boat for meat exportation. Following his time in London he decided to come back to Argentina, like other immigrants travelling through the country performing different jobs, first harvesting cornfields and then working as a construction worker. Back in Buenos Aires, Arturo climbed the social ladder. He found employment in retail, but the company fired him after he contracted smallpox. Broke and without a source of income, he decided to work as a policeman, which explains how, like other immigrant *Mujeres-hombres*, he could get his legal documents identifying him as a man. Arturo was well known as a good lover, he flirted with several women, and then he became the regular lover of an Italian merchant's wife. After their romance was exposed, the Italian merchant took his wife back to Italy. Arturo, now alone, decided to return to his old life as Dafne. This was a possible reaction to the threat of social exclusion or simply because their boundaries between masculinity and femininity were flexible.[13]

Arturo's photograph is an excellent example of the archival research of multiple paradoxes. Every document is an archive because it recollects the numerous practices and movements involved in its production: from taking the image to its preservation. Every detail in this picture is a trace of the battle for gender embodiment. On the one hand, Arturo's portrait underscores his male embodiment, especially when paying attention to the pose and clothing. On the other hand, the fact that the archivist classified Arturo as a woman shows the multiple struggles to define his gender legacy, and how he should be remembered.

The portrait was a popular genre in Buenos Aires in the early 20th century (Torricellas, 2009). Recent studies show how ordinary people's photographs shaped modern ideas of gender, class, and race (Grandin, 2004; Coleman, 2016; Coronado, 2018). These studies analyse self-fashioning practices people use to negotiate how they want to be seen by others. Arturo's portrait contrasts with doctors' practices to disembody gender affirmation practices of patients like him. The photography instead affirms his gender: clothes, posing, and space to encode a persistent self-image to negotiate their portrayal over time.

These photographs circulated in private circles and then in publications. The images are examples of self-fashioning practices with which people transitioning codified their gender and interpretation of gendered performances. The gestures, clothing, and objects were part of an agential cultural practice to negotiate the violent trans/homophobic conditions of production of those photographs with which they reinforced their male embodiment. The pictures produced a visual culture of belonging that inscribed themselves in the male cultural universe. While in private or in restricted circles, these portraits could work as technologies of embodiment.

At the same time, their public circulation was a tool of journalists and doctors to reaffirm restrictive notions of sex by destroying trans experience. Even under these challenging conditions, it is possible that the circulation of these images was also open to interpretation and stimulated new ideas about gender, especially by LGBTIQ+ people looking to affirm their gender.

Arturo's general classification as a *Mujer-hombre* was the first step in a long process of classification and archival. Like others grouped in this photography collection, the photographs were catalogued as a 'female figure'. This represents a move by the state to enforce violent sovereignty over Arturo's gender embodiment. Although it is easy to locate Arturo in contemporary discussions and classifications of trans identity, as is done throughout this chapter, we must also be wary of applying contemporary identity classifications onto historical figures. As much as possible, we need to explore how individuals, such as Arturo, may have experienced their gender identity and how they explored gendered embodiment. If archival practices work to destroy Arturo's embodiment, then we must also be aware of how even with the best intention, our historical narratives could produce new forms of harm.[14] While working with these photographs and trying to reconstruct their circuits—from the personal production, to the public life in magazine pages, to the newspaper room archive, to a national public collection—I struggle to understand how we should narrate these lives. Every trace of Arturo's life archives under a certain logic, an accumulation of time and knowledge to shape the legitimate limits of sexual embodiment. Trans history helps us move beyond previous approaches to modern sexual identities to explore the diverse experiences of crossing gender frontiers.

Lost in translation: queer (dis)identification and heterosexual history

In this section, I focus on what happens when the researcher exercises the queer sensibility to understand heterosexual experiences historically. I want to be emphatic with this: it is essential to work on this disidentification with the past. When a gay, lesbian, or trans historian is exploring the archive, it is easy to feel tempted to build a monolithic bridge between ourselves and past experiences. Even if many of those experiences and stories speak to our present story, assuming them as a prehistorical dimension of our present can lead to a homogeneous understanding. The most challenging part of the disidentification with the queer past is to be able to understand, for example, that being a homosexual in Argentina in the 1970s conjured a totally different understanding of sexuality than being a gay person in Argentina today. Similarly, an understanding of the identity of *invertido sexual* cannot be equivalent to our modern understanding of what being trans is today. We need to complicate our understandings of gender and sexuality to be able to respect and understand our subjects' experiences on their own terms and to avoid projecting the present over the past.

There are also physical feelings we face as researchers while navigating the archive. Researchers cannot be surprised if they feel a deep sadness after hours of reading police reports. I was often devastated by hours of reading reports of arbitrary arrests of sex workers who spent their days in prison and were often victims of terrible police punishments.[15] With this, I do not mean that researchers have to abandon these feelings to be able to analyse these histories. Instead, as Ivan Jablonka recently proposed, it is more about being able to be honest with oneself to be able to counterbalance those feelings in our analysis (Jablonka, 2020). But beyond rage and sadness, there is an emotional experience, which can be best described as *transversal* to anyone navigating the archives: decades of challenging the positivist views of documentary sources could not erase my feeling of finding a 'goldmine' of evidence in the archive. It is an immediate physical feeling, something that made me shake with excitement, knowing this evidence will change the total previous understanding of gender and sexuality in my field.

I have seen several archival 'goldmines'. In 2016, I was reading an extensive box of boring medical reports about venereal disease in the 1920s and 1930s when I found a letter signed by a young general who became the most famous Argentine president: Juan Domingo Perón. His letter was just the first in a big box of documents in which the military requested the state provide sex workers to soldiers, arguing access to sex with sex workers would deter homosexual deviation among those soldiers conducting missions in Patagonia.[16] The document proved something I found in many theoretical texts about sexuality and the state: sexuality had a central role in shaping ideas of social order in Argentina. Like Perón's military colleagues, he believed that without access to sexual services, homosexuality and masturbation would rise among soldiers. These were not isolated statements or beliefs. Working-class leaders, policy makers, doctors, and military officers imagined male heterosexual desire as ungovernable, viewing this an especially concerning issue in the case of workers who, guided by their 'physiological desire', could be vulnerable to venereal diseases and sexual deviations. Likewise, these commentators placed male sexuality at the core of national development, insisting on men's role in populating a country.

Finding the letter changed my dissertation project, which previously focused on women sex workers, and the role of men in the sexual market. I instead began to ask myself why I had formulated my questions about those with alleged deviated sexualities rather than about those who embodied heterosexual and cisgender norms? Guided by this preoccupation, I returned to my archive of hundreds of trial records in which women accused of selling sex defended themselves, and noticed the role of police officers. I noticed how police usually called the men who had allegedly purchased the sex to be witnesses of the alleged crime. I also noticed their use of racist and sexist forms of working-class slang to exalt their masculinity.

There was a dominant language and knowledge reproduced in documents in the archive. A traversal language of male embodiment: a code with which men have been imagining and talking about their sexuality and their bodies through time. My complicated relationship with the heterosexual model of masculinity as a gay man helped me to identify what many heterosexual historians ignored. Cisgender heterosexual men also deployed technologies, knowledge, and techniques to embody masculinity: performing rituals like going in groups to a brothel. I found myself reading several testimonies of working-class men, mostly from small towns and rural areas where purchasing sex was part of everyday entertainment. I found references to men buying sex in trade union documents,[17] doctors' reports, trial records, and military letters. I could not avoid the surprise that male discourses about buying sex were so transparent, and how many historians have omitted these stories, failing to recognize it as part of everyday male leisure.[18] My queer distance from the hetero-masculine world presented in the archive helped me see something perhaps oblivious to others: the important political and social role paying for sex plays in how men perform cisgender heterosexual masculinity.

The language used by heterosexual men across the documents was based in an androcentral sexual imaginary using metaphors about their body parts, while talking openly about their genitals and sexual acts to reaffirm themselves as men.[19] These metaphors were used to describe their genitals, portraying their appendages as violent and savage instruments. The men usually described themselves as beasts without control, imagining their bodies moved by an uncontrollable sexual drive. At times they would reference their 'creole nature', which is associated with a closeness to the 'natural' world. They repeated that they did not use condoms because they understood that protection was part of the female nature, arguing that this was a female duty that men could not control. Skin-to-skin contact reinforced a violent male imagination and placed it in the core of sexual pleasure.

A vital dimension of archival research is related to establishing a relationship with documentary sources. I could not find myself in the testimonies by these men. In addition to being gay, I am not entirely part of that working-class male culture. Identification in the archive often creates problems because of obscure concepts related to gender and sexuality. We as queer researchers try to analyse queer lives being similar to ours despite the different identities and material experiences that mediate them. It is not easy to find a base of shared understanding about sexuality, and I found this is even more complicated when reading stories of heterosexual cisgender men. However, this feeling of being lost in translation, yet making an effort to understand what the concepts of certain archival representations of cis-heterosexuality meant to the people speaking about them, illustrates the power of queer disidentification.

As queer researchers, we can see what is presented as 'unnatural' about sexuality and gender that, maybe, a cisgender heterosexual researcher cannot. This queer distance from the documents could help us read these testimonies and formulate an interpretation about gender and sexuality that breaks the order that the police archive created. We can point out that just as queer identities, heterosexuality changed through time and space. By revisiting these archives about sex work in 1920s and 1930s Argentina it becomes evident that heterosexuality is as socially constructed as other sexual experiences. In illustrating this through police records, archival news coverage, and courtroom testimony I was able to undermine any distinction between alleged natural and unnatural sexualities represented by the archive.

Conclusion

This chapter explores questions about doing archival research as a part of uncovering queer histories while drawing on my experience navigating traditional archives researching queer topics of sexual commerce, masculinity, femininity, homosexuality, and gender embodiment. Once we recognize the inequalities that produced those documents, we can explore questions that create alternative historical narratives of those lives. Every document is a space of conflict: Arturo choosing his poses and Marina staying motionless but still showing her emotions. These documents offer guidance and clues of potential queer readings.

To support new politics of belonging, LGBTIQ+ communities are creating archival collections governed by queer and feminist logics. In the past two decades the 'archival turn' in feminist and LGBTIQ+ activism has led to the creation of many grassroots-based archives. These feminist and queer archives include more intimate documents that challenge the cisgender-heterosexual logic predominance in traditional public archives. Recognizing the importance of this shifting in how we frame LGBTIQ+ experiences, some traditional archives are rethinking their previous catalogues, and in different countries there is a progressive emergence of collections curated under queer or trans parameters.[20]

Queer history helps us place ourselves in our documents, challenging us to reflect on how we feel when we read them. Yet, doing queer archival research means living with conflict and we must also identify our own relationship with them. When we as researchers applying a queer methodology face words that are challenging to translate there is a possibility of decoding meanings that other researchers usually consider natural. There is nothing better than getting lost in the archives. Queer sensibility in the archives helps us to know when to distrust words of power and create other narratives of the past beyond those told explicitly in the archival documents. While making queer and trans narratives of the past more visible and accessible, we can in turn imagine more habitable futures for LGBTIQ+ communities.

Notes

1. There is also notable difficulty with trying to find and trace the lives of women and lesbians in the archives.
2. See the Introduction of this volume.
3. Lesbian, Gay, Bisexual, Trans, Intersex, Queer, and other.
4. Marina probably would not have used this term to describe herself. However, we would now understand her experience as trans/transgender.
5. Richard Von Krafft-Ebing (1840–1902) is considered one of the founders of 'sexual science'. His book *Psychopathia Sexualis* (1886) was one of the first compendiums of alleged sexual perversions which included his concept of *travestiment* as a 'metamorphosis sexualis paranoia'. Sometimes he describes it as similar to what is later called the theory of the 'wrong body'; that is to say, people that understood that they were trapped in the wrong gendered body (Bullough, 1975).
6. The reproduction of these photographs raises a number of ethical issues. This includes the reproduction of medical violence on the subject. The use of these images in this chapter is intended to honour Marina.
7. The reproduction of these photographs raises a number of ethical issues. This includes the reproduction of medical violence on the subject. The use of these images in this chapter is intended to honour Marina.
8. The reproduction of these photographs raises a number of ethical issues. This includes the reproduction of medical violence on the subject. The use of these images in this chapter is intended to honour Marina.
9. For related analysis about applying a polyphonic approach to reading photos, see Dean Cooper-Cunningham's writing (Chapter 4, this volume) about photos of Russian LGBTIQ+ activists.
10. See also Hagen's discussion of this term as it relates to organizing by the LGBTQ organization Colombia Diversa in Colombia in Chapter 3, this volume.
11. *Caras y Caretas*, 21 July 1906, 407, p 63.
12. *Caras y Caretas*, 21 July 1906, 407, p 63.
13. *Caras y Caretas*, 31 May 1930, 1.652, p 76.
14. For example, in her work on the trans male general of the Mexican Revolution, Amelio Robles, Gabriela Cano criticizes how women's history reduced him to his genitalia in order to point out 'women participation' in the revolution (Cano, 2009).
15. See Resource Guide II for details: queer trauma resource.
16. Perón, Juan Domingo. War Department. Min. Secreto; caja 3, n. 31 (Archivo General de la Nación, Buenos Aires). 3 March 1944.
17. For example, in 1917, the Candy Workers Union's magazine asked its readers: 'Where are your most sacred interests? In the cafe, in the brothels, in public amusements or the union?'
18. Feminist scholarship offers many notable exceptions, including Cynthia Enloe's (2014) *Bananas, Beaches, and Bases: Making Feminist Sense of International Politics*.
19. In 1954, Luis, a young rural worker from the northern rural area of the Buenos Aires Province, attended the police station to accuse women of giving him venereal disease. Article 202c of the Argentine Penal Code punished the transmission of infections as a violation of public health, under which police imprisoned women who sold sex. Luis went with his father and other workers on the farm. He stated that he was feeling 'severe swelling and pimples on the head of the bug'. He explained to the police that they did

not use a condom: they did it 'a la Criolla' (as creoles, a racist reference to the bestiality associated with rural culture) and that he 'only fucked her once'. The oldest friend of the group stated that he used 'no lining with the rifle'.

20. P. Simonetto and M. Butierrez, 'The archival riot: travesti/trans* audiovisual memory politics in twenty-first-century Argentina', *Memory Studies*, [online] 8 February 2022, 17506980211073100. Available from: https://doi.org/10.1177/17506980211073099

Acknowledgements

This research is funded by a Marie Skłodowska-Curie project entitled 'Was sex inflexible?' (project number 886496). I am thankful for the multiple conversations with Mir Yarfitz for our debates about the challenges of writing trans and queer history. I developed a broader explanation of my approach to trans history and the study of some of the cases named in this chapter in: P. Simonetto (2024), *A Body of One's Own: A Trans History of Argentina*, Austin, TX: University of Texas Press.

Bibliography

Amin, K. (2017) *Disturbing Attachments: Genet, Modern Pederasty, and Queer History*, Durham, NC: Duke University Press.

Arondekar, A. et al (2015) 'Queering archives: a roundtable discussion', *Radical History Review*, 122: 211–31.

Azoulay, A. (2015) *Civil Imagination: A Political Ontology of Photography*, London/New York: Verso Books.

Bao, D. (1993) 'Invertidos sexuales, tortilleras, and maricas machos: the construction of homosexuality in Buenos Aires, Argentina, 1900–1950', *Journal of Homosexuality*, 24(3–4): 183–220.

Belbey, J. (1944) 'Sobre *travestissement*', *Archivo de medicina legal*, IV: 103–35.

Belbey, J. (1955) 'La medicina legal sobre travestissement', *La semana médica*, 23: 123–44.

Ben, P. (2009) *Male Sexuality, the Popular Classes and the State: Buenos Aires, 1880–1955*, Chicago, IL: University of Chicago Press.

Ben, P. (2010) 'Male same-sex sexuality and the Argentine state, 1880–1930', in J. Corrales and M. Pecheny (eds) *The Politics of Sexuality in Latin America: A Reader on Lesbian, Gay, Bisexual and Transgender Rights*, Pittsburgh, PA: University of Pittsburgh Press, pp 33–43.

Bullough, V.L. (1975) 'Transsexualism in history', *Archives of Sexual Behavior*, 4(5): 561–71.

Caimari, L.M. (2020) 'El momento archivos', *Población & sociedad*, 27(2): 222–33.

Cano, G. (2009) 'Amelio Robles, andar de soldado viejo. Masculinidad (trangénero) en la Revolución Mexicana', *Debate feminist*, 39: 14–39.

Chauncey, G. (2019) *Gay New York. Gender, Urban Culture, and the Making of the Gay Male World, 1890–1940*, New York: Basic Books.

Cho, L. (2014) 'Anticipating citizenship: Chinese head tax photographs', in E.H. Brown and T. Phu (eds) *Feeling Photography*, Durham, NC: Duke University Press, pp 158–80.

Coleman, K. (2015a) 'The photos that we don't get to see: sovereignties, archives, and the 1928 massacre of banana workers in Colombia', in D.E. Bender and J.K. Lipman (eds) *Making the Empire Work: Labor and United States Imperialism*, New York: New York University Press, pp 104–33.

Coleman, K. (2015b) 'The right not to be looked at', *Estudios Interdisciplinarios de América Latina y el Caribe*, 26(2): 43–63.

Coleman, K. (2016) *A Camera in the Garden of Eden: The Self-Forging of a Banana Republic*, Austin, TX: University of Texas Press.

Coronado, J. (2018) *Portraits in the Andes: Photography and Agency, 1900–1950*, Pittsburgh, PA: University of Pittsburgh Press.

Edwards, E. (2009) 'Photography and the material performance of the past', *History and Theory*, 48(4): 130–50.

Farge, A. (2013) *The Allure of the Archives*, New Haven, CT: Yale University Press.

Fuechtner, V., Haynes, D.E., and Jones, R.M. (2017) *A Global History of Sexual Science, 1880–1960*, Los Angeles, CA: University of California Press.

Galeano, J.F. (2022) 'Running mascara: the hermeneutics of trans visual archives in late Franco-era Spain', *Radical History Review*, 142: 72–92.

Gentili, R.A. (1995) *Me va a tener que acompañar: una visión crítica sobre los edictos policiales*, El Naranjo.

Ghaziani, A. and Brim, M. (2019) *Imagining Queer Methods*, New York: New York University Press.

Grandin, G. (2004) 'Can the subaltern be seen? Photography and the affects of nationalism', *Hispanic American Historical Review*, 84(1): 83–111.

Guy, D.J. (1991) *Sex & Danger in Buenos Aires: Prostitution, Family, and Nation in Argentina*, Lincoln, NE: University of Nebraska Press.

Guy, D.J. (2009) *Women Build the Welfare State: Performing Charity and Creating Rights in Argentina, 1880–1955*, Durham, NC: Duke University Press.

Halperin, D.M. (2000) 'How to do the history of male homosexuality', *GLQ: A Journal of Lesbian and Gay Studies*, 6(1): 87–123.

Heyam, K. (2022) *Before We Were Trans: A New History of Gender*, New York: Hachette/Seal Press.

Hulme, T. (2021) 'Queer Belfast during the First World War: masculinity and same-sex desire in the Irish city', *Irish Historical Studies*, 45(168): 239–61.

Insausti, S.J. (2011) 'Selva, plumas y desconche: un análisis de las performances masculinas de la feminidad entre las locas del Tigre durante la década del ochenta', *Revista Latinoamericana de Estudios sobre Cuerpos, Emociones y Sociedad*, 3(7): 29–42.

Jablonka, I. (2020) *A History of the Grandparents I Never Had*, Redwood City, CA: Stanford University Press.

Malva (2011) *Mi recordatorio: autobiografía de Malva*, Buenos Aires: Universidad de Buenos Aires.

Marshall, D. and Tortorici, Z. (2022) *Turning Archival: The Life of the Historical in Queer Studies*, Durham, NC: Duke University Press.

Martínez, M.E. (2014) 'Archives, bodies, and imagination: the case of Juana Aguilar and queer approaches to history, sexuality, and politics', *Radical History Review*, 120: 159–82.

Peralta, J.L. (2017) *Paisajes de varones: genealogías del homoerotismo en la literatura argentina*, Barcelona: Icaria.

Rodriguez, J. (2006) *Civilizing Argentina: Science, Medicine, and the Modern State*, Chapel Hill, NC: University of North Carolina Press.

Ryan, H. (2017) 'Inventing, and policing, the homosexual in early 20th c. NYC' [online]. Available from: www.hughryan.org/recent-work/2017/9/7/inventing-and-policing-the-homosexual-in-early-20th-c-nyc

Ryan, H. (2022) *The Women's House of Detention: A Queer History of a Forgotten Prison*, New York: Hachette/Bold Type Books.

Salessi, J. (1995) *Médicos, maleantes y maricas: higiene, criminología y homosexualidad en la construcción de la nación argentina (Buenos Aires 1871–1914)*, Rosario: Beatriz Viterbo.

Scheiwiller, S.G. (2016) *Liminalities of Gender and Sexuality in Nineteenth-Century Iranian Photography: Desirous Bodies*, London: Routledge.

Sears, C. (2015) *Arresting Dress: Cross-Dressing, Law, and Fascination in Nineteenth-Century San Francisco*, Durham, NC: Duke University Press.

Simonetto, P. (2016) 'La moral institucionalizada. Reflexiones sobre el Estado, las sexualidades y la violencia en la Argentina del siglo XX', *El@tina. Revista electrónica de estudios latinoamericanos*, 14(55): 1–22.

Simonetto, P. (2019) *El dinero no es todo: compra y venta de sexo en la Argentina del siglo XX*, Buenos Aires: Biblos.

Simonetto, P. (2021) 'Raúl Luis Suarez's smile and the ruthless archive', *NOTCHES*, [online] 2 May. Available from: https://notchesblog.com/2021/03/09/raul-luis-suarez-smile-and-the-ruthless-archive/

Stoler, A.L. (2010) *Along the Archival Grain*, Princeton, NJ: Princeton University Press.

Stryker, S. (2008) *Transgender History*, New York: Hachette/Seal Press.

Taylor, D. (2003) *The Archive and the Repertoire*, Durham, NC: Duke University Press.

Torricellas, A. (2009) 'Sensibilidades e imágenes generizadas del 'yo' en la década del 40: lo visual y el dispositivo fotográfico en la construcción de la masculinidad', *Cadernos Pagu*, 199–234.

Tortorici, X. (2018) *Sins Against Nature: Sex and Archives in Colonial New Spain*, Durham, NC: Duke University Press.

Yarfitz, M. (2023) 'La Bella Otero's overdetermined anality: tales of sexual inversion in early twentieth-century Buenos Aires', *Journal of Latin American Cultural Studies*, 70.

PART III

Queer Experiences of Conflict Research

7

Researching Queer Lives in the Shadow of North-East Nigeria's Conflict

Chitra Nagarajan

Introduction

Over a decade after the conflict in north-east Nigeria erupted into violence, killing 41,596 people (Council on Foreign Relations, 2021), displacing 1.7 million, contributing to 5.1 million at risk of being critically food insecure, and putting 8.7 million in need of urgent assistance (United Nations Office for the Coordination of Humanitarian Affairs, 2021), the profoundly gendered effects of insecurity and their interaction with gender power relations have been documented to some extent. While men are more likely to be arbitrarily arrested, subjected to prolonged detention without trial, and extrajudicially killed (Amnesty, 2016), women tend to be forced to navigate the safety and well-being of themselves, their children, and elders with armed opposition groups (AOGs), commonly known as Boko Haram, security forces, and community militias as well as to strategize how to keep families secure, fed, and sheltered (Matfess, 2017; Nagarajan, 2019). Even the explicit inclusion of gender into security policy can produce specific gendered security harms as a simplistic approach to 'women', rather than gendered power relations, which leaves the Nigerian government ill-equipped to respond to the complex gendered dynamics of conflict while a neglect of human rights and the role of state actors in abuses actively enables gendered security harms (Pearson and Nagarajan, 2020). Moreover, the experiences of people with non-normative sexual orientations, gender identities, gender expressions, and/or sex characteristics (SOGIESC) remains as a major gap in knowledge.

This chapter recounts my experiences of, and reflections on, conducting a study (Nagarajan, 2022) examining the impacts of violent conflict on people of diverse SOGIESC in north-east Nigeria—the only analysis of such that exists to date. I led the study, designing research methodology, conducting interviews, analysing data, and writing up findings and recommendations. In this work, I was assisted by Bala Mohammed, who found respondents to interview and provided interpretation, and Xeenarh Mohammed, whose organization The Initiative for Equal Rights (TIERs)[1] was a recipient of funds and provided research assistance. Their roles will be further discussed below.

This is an area that proved challenging to research, for a range of reasons ranging from risks linked to the conflict to legal and societal vulnerabilities. While researching queer lives is not explicitly banned in Nigeria, LGBTQI rights activism and support for this activism is criminalized in Nigeria. To date, however, nobody engaged in such activities has been arrested. The chapter starts by providing background and context of both the violent conflict between governments of the region and AOGs, and the legal and social context for queer people in Nigeria. It then presents an overview of study methodology, focusing on sampling, the challenges we faced and limitations stemming from these challenges, and key findings. It looks at how people of diverse SOGIESC experience the similar (gendered) harms as others but see the discrimination and stigma they face reducing their abilities to cope and adapt. It also examines the additional specific harms they face, from barriers to accessing education, healthcare, livelihoods, and humanitarian aid to brutality and violence from AOGs and state actors alike. It shows how space for non-conformity has reduced as a result of the conflict. The chapter continues on to describe key ethical considerations around access, knowledge, extraction, and learning. It does so by presenting research design and realities around: first addressing power, in particular who controls the production and sharing of knowledge; next, ensuring safeguarding, safety, security, and well-being of respondents, researcher, and queer communities at large; and finally, maximizing benefit to queer people as integral to the research process. It ends with my reflections and conclusions.

It is important to note here difficulties around the use of language. There are some terms, such as yan daudu[2], that are used in north-east Nigeria to describe certain groups that fall within the umbrella of people of diverse SOGIESC, but many sexual orientations, gender identities, gender expressions, and sex characteristics do not find expression in local languages. Moreover, there is a lack of common terminology used across the different languages and ethnic groups of the region. Indeed, people often refer to actions (using verbs) rather than identities (using nouns); for example, 'I like women' rather than 'I am a lesbian' (or equivalent term in their language). Although the terminology of LGBTQI, queer, and/ or SOGIESC that first developed or became known in Western contexts is increasingly known and adopted in Nigeria, there are class, education, language, and regional dynamics at play around who uses these terms. In the absence of a clear set of words or phrases that can be used, I will instead use the terms people of diverse/non-normative SOGIESC, queer, and LGBTQI interchangeably with this fluidity in usage across the chapter aimed at emphasizing to the reader that none of these terms are ideal.

Context

North-east Nigeria and the wider Lake Chad Region have been embroiled in violent conflict for almost 15 years that has had profoundly differential impacts based on age, class, disability, and gender. Concurrently, Nigeria sees contestation around LGBTQI rights. While same-sex relations as well as the registration, operation of, participation in, and support for gay clubs, societies, and organizations is criminalized and significant levels of violence are perpetrated against queer people, there are indications, at the time of writing this chapter, that attitudes are starting to change. This section will present a short overview of the history of the conflict in the region and realities for queer people in Nigeria.

The 'Boko Haram-related'[3] conflict in the region affects the Far North region of Cameroon, the Region du Lac of Chad, the Diffa region of Niger, and the north-east of Nigeria, most significantly the states of Adamawa, Borno, and Yobe. Its root causes are varied and it is beyond the scope of the chapter to cover them in detail.[4] In brief, north-east Nigeria saw a reduction in economic prospects, living standards, and growth in wages from the 1970s onwards. This worsened in the 1980s against a backdrop of reforms required by the International Monetary Fund and World Bank, which led to a contraction of the state and the public services it provided (Vivekananda et al, 2019). In the 1990s and the first decade of the 21st century, Nigeria saw political transition, with the re-establishment of democratic forms of governance in 1999. However, this period also witnessed often violent and unethical political contestation, particularly around elections (Hoffmann, 2014; Mustapha and Meager, 2020), and, from the 1970s onwards, the country saw rising inequality, corruption, religious intolerance, and fundamentalism[5] (Mustapha and Bunza, 2015). This combination of factors led to the adoption of sharia codes across northern Nigeria states in 2000 and 2001, which drew upon the most patriarchal interpretations of Islam; erasing the diversity and pluralism of northern Nigerian Islamic thought and intellectual traditions (Uwais, 2004). The adoption of sharia codes was thus linked to the narrowing of permissible behaviour and restrictions on the rights and freedoms of women and people of diverse SOGIESC (Pereira, 2005; Gaudio, 2009; Last, 2015).

Those who advocated in favour of sharia codes had expected that a turn towards Islamic values and governance would counteract rising corruption, inequality, and injustice. However, these hopes proved to be short-lived (Eltantawi, 2017; Thurston, 2017; Hansen, 2020). Mohammed Yusuf, an

Islamic scholar who preached against social immorality and the corruption and inequality of 'Western' democracy and linked institutions (Thurston, 2016; Kassim and Nwankpa, 2018) in Maiduguri, the capital of Borno State, gained power against resulting widespread disillusionment by building on popular public narratives and critiques of the state. His mosque became a principal site of state critique, and his followers, known as the yan yusufiyya, included people of all social classes and backgrounds. The Borno State government attempted to co-opt this influence, but relations broke down (Thurston, 2017). In July 2019, yan yusufiyya members accompanying the body of a fellow member to a funeral were shot at by police who were enforcing a regulation that required motorcycle riders to wear helmets. The group subsequently launched attacks against churches, Christians, and police stations. The state responded with force, leading to the injuring and killing of hundreds of yan yusufiyya and the extrajudicial killing of Yusuf himself by security agents (Thurston, 2017).

This incident led Yusuf's remaining followers to go underground. They strategized and returned, calling themselves Jama'atu Ahl al-Sunna li-l-Da'wa wa-l-Jihad (JASDJ), translated as People Committed to the Propagation of the Prophet's Teachings and Jihad, often referred to by the media as Boko Haram, led by Abubakar Shekau (Thurston, 2016). While JASDJ became increasingly violent, security agencies undertook collective punishment of communities for not identifying JASDJ members (Amnesty, 2015). In 2013, the yan gora (also known as the Civilian Joint Task Force), a community militia, emerged to work together with security agencies to push JASDJ out of Maidurguri (Nagarajan, 2020a). Consequently, JASDJ spread its influence outside state capitals in north-east Nigeria's Adamawa, Borno, and Yobe states and over the border into Cameroon, Chad, and Niger, and attracted increased national and international attention in the wake of bomb blasts across Nigeria and the abduction of schoolgirls from Chibok in April 2014 (Parkinson and Hinshaw, 2021). Subsequently, countries in the region formed the Multi-National Joint Task Force which recovered some territory, working with community militias.

In 2016, JASDJ allied with Islamic State and, due to disagreements around the targeting of Muslim civilians and harshness of punishment of members for breaking group rules, split into two distinct groups with the objective of the new Wilayat al Islamiyya Gharb Afriqiyyah, translated as Islamic State West African Province (ISWAP), to focus on security agents, government officials, and their supporters rather than civilians indiscriminately (Mahmood and Ani, 2018). After the killing of Shekau by ISWAP fighters in June 2021, many JASDJ fighters surrendered to government authorities or joined ISWAP, which gained in territorial influence (Maclean and Alfa, 2021; Samuel, 2021).

Even prior to the conflict, north-east Nigeria was underdeveloped, with inadequate public service provision, weak governance (particularly in rural areas), and some of the worst social development indicators in the country (Nagarajan, 2019). The past decade of violence has made matters worse in much of the region, negatively affecting the provision of education, healthcare, and other services, particularly outside major towns (Segun, 2016). At the same time, in other areas, some internally displaced people have been able to better attend schools and receive free or lower-cost healthcare as a result of increased funding and attention, and the interventions of humanitarian and development actors (Nagarajan, 2019). Nevertheless, high levels of displacement, insecurity, and violence continue, cause deaths, disabilities, displacement, injuries, and human rights violations, and have destructive impacts on food security, incomes, and livelihoods, mental health and well-being, and family and social networks (Vivekananda et al, 2019).

Meanwhile, the situation of people of diverse SOGIESC in the Lake Chad Basin conflict is under-documented. Humanitarian, development, and peacebuilding actors navigate ways to interview and work with people formerly linked to AOGs listed as proscribed terrorist organizations but do not prioritize gaining any understanding of queer realities. However, the realities of people of diverse SOGIESC in other parts of Nigeria have received some attention. In Nigeria, same-sex sexual relations have been criminalized for decades with the Criminal Code Act (CCA) 1990 stating that any person who 'has carnal knowledge of any person against the order of nature' or permits a man to 'have carnal knowledge of him or her against the order of nature' is guilty of a felony and liable to 14 years' imprisonment (Criminal Code Act 1990, s. 214). It also declared that any male person who commits 'any act of gross indecency with another male person' in public or in private is guilty of a felony and liable to imprisonment for three years (Criminal Code Act 1990, s. 217). The sharia codes adopted in the 12 northern states also criminalized this behaviour (Gaudio, 2009). More recently, the Same Sex Marriage (Prohibition) Act (SSMPA) 2014 criminalized: the registration, operation of, participation in, and support for gay clubs, societies, and organizations (SSMPA, s. 5(2)); the public show of same-sex amorous relationships directly or indirectly (SSMPA, s. 5(2)); people of the same sex who enter a civil union or marriage contract (SSMPA, s. 5(1)); and those who witness or aid a same-sex marriage or civil union (SSMPA, s. 5(3)). Punishments provided in the SSMPA range from 10 to 14 years' imprisonment and, in April 2022, the National House of Representatives proposed an amendment to the SSMPA to criminalize 'cross-dressing' with associated punishment proposed to be six months' imprisonment or a fine of N500,000. There has been a significant spike in cases of illegal stop-and-search operations, unlawful detention, extortion, and targeted abuse and arrest based on perceived SOGIESC since the SSMPA was passed, particularly between 2019 and 2022, with location and socio-economic class of individuals targeted significantly impacting the severity of associated human rights violations (TIERs, 2022).

Moreover, state and non-state actors incite and carry out violence against people of diverse SOGIESC with state actors most likely to perpetrate invasion of privacy, arbitrary arrests, and unlawful detention, and members of the general public rather engaging in blackmail, extortion, assault and battery, and entrapment (kito) (TIERs, 2020). However, public attitudes are changing. Surveys carried out in 2015, 2017, and 2019 found that the number of people unwilling to accept homosexual family members had fallen from 87 per cent in 2015 to 60 per cent in 2019 (the question was not asked in 2017) while those who believed people should be jailed for 14 years for same-sex relationships dropped from 91 per cent in 2017 to 74 per cent (TIERs et al, 2015; TIERs and NOI Polls, 2017; TIERs and Vivid Rain, 2019). Although common perceptions are that northern Nigeria is more conservative than the south, this 2019 survey found that 30 per cent of north-east respondents said they would accept a homosexual family member and only 70 per cent of respondents either supported or strongly supported the SSMPA, the highest and lowest figures across all geopolitical zones respectively (TIERs, 2019). While these data show promising progress, public narratives continue to be largely inaccurate and stigmatizing, collapsing sexual orientation, gender identity and gender expression, and conflating homosexuality with paedophilia (Mohammed et al, 2018). Furthermore, discrimination, exclusion, violence, and linked vulnerabilities have increased during the COVID-19 pandemic (Nagarajan, 2020b).

Overview of the study

The chapter now continues to provide an overview of the study. It starts with an examination of the methodology used including our sampling decisions, the substantial challenges we faced, and research limitations. It next presents a summary of key findings of the research, looking at how harms faced by people of diverse SOGIESC are similar to, and different from, those experienced by others as well as how attitudes, narratives, and realities have changed over time.

Funded by the Canadian High Commission through a grant to TIERs in 2019–21, the study aimed to deepen understanding and analysis of the realities, challenges, and resilience as pertains to people of diverse SOGIESC in conflict-affected north-east Nigeria and to identify opportunities for intervention. Given the paucity of research in this arena, I took a broad approach and addressed the following three research questions:

1. What are the present realities for people of diverse SOGIESC?
2. How has space for people of diverse SOGIESC changed over time?
3. How do people of diverse SOGIESC protect themselves and support others?

We took explicitly intersectional feminist approaches and followed key principles of conflict sensitivity, gender transformation, and social inclusion (Nagarajan and Toogood, 2017). Using qualitative methods, we interviewed 22 queer people and 5 representatives of non-governmental organizations (NGOs) and United Nations (UN) agencies (some of whom were queer) in Hausa and/ or English in Maiduguri, the capital of Borno state in December 2020. I used a grounded-theory approach to code and analyse data gathered in order to document and acknowledge the contexts and situatedness of research participants' lives and the research context (Morse et al, 2021).

We had aimed for diversity in research participants; however, in practice, as will be discussed below, it proved challenging to find people willing to participate, not surprising given the context and subject matter. As a result, we used snowball-sampling techniques and, despite substantial efforts, were unable to ensure a range of ages (no respondent was older than 40 years), include meaningful numbers of people with disabilities (only one participant had a disability), or ensure gender balance (only 7 out of 22 queer respondents identified as women) among our participants. However, our respondents did span an array of sexual orientations, ethnicities (Babur, Fulani, Guduf, Hausa, Igbo, Kanuri, Margi, Michika, and Shuwa), and occupations (civil society, farmers, entertainers, journalists, sex workers, students, tailors, traders, and the food industry). They comprised Christians, Muslims, and people of no faith but did not include professed followers of Indigenous religions. This, however, is not surprising given such beliefs and practices can be marginalized and stigmatized. Moreover, while our participants included some diversity in gender identities and expressions, specifically when it came to yan daudu[6] and feminized men, we could not speak with masculine-identified women. Given the severe constraints under which this study was conducted, we were also not able to directly interview intersex people and, although I drew on previous conversations with NGO respondents in 2017–19 to inform the report, this limitation meant the significant gap in knowledge on the realities of people with variation in sex characteristics remains.

We faced other substantial challenges in conducting the study, most significantly the COVID-19 pandemic and risks associated with the subject matter. The two-year project was designed prior to the pandemic, taking freedom of movement and travel for granted. Funding started in late 2019; however, personnel changes at TIERs with a new incoming Director of Research and difficulties in finding researchers from the context led to a slight delay in project kick-off of a few months, which proved to be significant. By the time we developed an operational research approach, it was February 2020, and, in March 2020, the Nigerian government closed international borders, instituted a ban on inter-state travel, and announced other restrictions intended to curtail the spread of infection. We discussed the possibility of moving data collection online but, given the sensitive, precarious, and risky nature of the subject matter, decided we would be unable to monitor and mitigate any danger. We agreed that the safety and security of research participants was paramount; certainly more important than any commitment to a donor. As a result, we started data collection almost a year later than originally envisaged. Due to a shortened time frame, as well as heightened levels of insecurity that meant road travel around north-east Nigeria was no longer possible, scuppering our plans to conduct interviews in multiple locations, we restricted data collection to Maiduguri, the capital of Borno State. Other implications of these limitations will be described further below as they gravely affected our ability to conduct the study as imagined.

Despite these limitations, the study remains the only examination of queer lives in the north-east Nigeria conflict and contains many important insights that we hope will offer a foundation for future research as well as programming. It found that people of diverse SOGIESC face similar (gendered) harms to other conflict-affected people in north-east Nigeria. They are subjected to injuries, are left with lifelong disabilities, are displaced, often multiple times, face profound impacts of conflict on livelihoods, and are traumatized by having experienced and witnessed violence. Their abilities to cope with and adapt to the significant changes in their lives are determined by their socio-economic class and social networks, which can be negatively affected by the discrimination and stigma they face due to their SOGIESC. Moreover, queer women in particular have even lesser access to power and resources as a result of the interplay between their gender, SOGIESC, and poverty.

In addition, people of diverse SOGIESC that we interviewed spoke of how they face specific harms ranging from personal struggles due to internalized discrimination, fear, and lesser access to education and healthcare to additional livelihood barriers and increased difficulties accessing humanitarian aid. They are less able to report gender-based violence (GBV) compared with cisgender and heterosexual women when perpetrators are of the same gender, due to stigma and fears around criminalization. This dynamic has also been found in other contexts such as Syria and Turkey (Kiss et al, 2020). They experience family and societal marginalization, rejection, and violence. Lesbian and bisexual women can experience less suspicion than gay and bisexual men and yan daudu, yet face difficulties in attracting suitors if their sexual orientation is known, while being subjected to scrutiny if they remain unmarried. Given the extent to which women's material realities and social status depend on marriage and the challenges and risks unmarried women face, this reality is particularly critical. While some queer people have strong allies and relationships, people of diverse SOGIESC are also subjected to entrapment, extortion, and violence, and forced to leave communities with community militia members playing significant roles in policing morality, including through violence.

Furthermore, state actors and AOGs engage in significant brutality and violence. Police officers carry out mass arrests, beatings, and extortion of men who have sex with men and use informants within the queer community in order to do so. Those with money, power, and connections can often escape relatively unharmed, while others spend prolonged periods in police detention and face significant social isolation after release. Meanwhile, subsequent AOG leaders have preached against homosexuality, tying it to general societal decadence and degeneration. AOG members have warned, targeted, and chased people seen as 'immoral' out of areas and enforced strict gender binaries. Despite this ideology, AOG fighters have also sexually enslaved and raped men and yan daudu.

Current realities are not reflective of the situation in earlier times. In decades past, there was relative freedom and negative public discourse and violence against people of diverse SOGIESC was less common. However, freedom restricted considerably in recent decades, first with discourse around sharia and the institution of sharia codes in 2000, then with actions of AOGs having chilling effects from around 2011 onwards, and finally with the passage of the SSMPA 2014; intensifying public discourse and normalizing negative attitudes around homosexuality. Additionally, there is general moral panic around the changes brought about by the conflict, fuelled by boredom and crowded conditions that lead to more rumours and surveillance. While focus in political and community discussions in north-east Nigeria tends to be on women's bodies and behaviour, narratives also exist that displacement and poverty have led to more homosexual practices as a result of desperation and a belief that such sexual acts will confer wealth. Rumours of 'rampant lesbianism' are used to discredit women and girls who resist marriage or who are viewed as outspoken, independent, and not reliant on men. Although many respondents expressed desire to be in community, attempts among people of diverse SOGIESC to build networks and solidarity are affected by fear of police informants or stopped by others.

Despite the barriers to service provision and protection risks to which people of diverse SOGIESC are subjected, development, humanitarian, and peacebuilding organizations do not consider SOGIESC when it comes to their policy influencing, programmes, or even staff well-being. They provide little support to their LGBTQI staff with many entities unaware of the strong likelihood that some staff members are queer let alone responsive to the challenges and risks they face. Most analysis conducted by actors, whether this be protection assessments, water, sanitation and health surveys, or food security and livelihoods studies, do not consider or include queer people, leaving programmes to operate in cisnormative, endosexist, and heteronormative ways as a result.

The next three sections will examine, in turn, the mechanisms the study put in place to address power, ensure safeguarding, security, safety, and well-being, and maximize benefit to queer people, and how they worked in practice.

Addressing power

My discussion on ethical considerations at play during the research starts with examining issues of power. Who decides which areas will be studied and the funding available to do so? What are the barriers that exist to proper integration of SOGIESC dynamics into surveys, assessments, analyses, and other forms of knowledge production? In addition to addressing these questions, I will also reflect on my own positionality, our plans to conduct participatory research, and the barriers we faced to doing so in practice, as well as considering power dynamics between researchers and participants.

There were significant barriers in place to conducting research on SOGIESC in north-east Nigeria, raising questions around who has power to determine areas considered worthy of study and how SOGIESC can be integrated into research and analysis given endemic discrimination, stigmatization, and violence against queer people. The genesis for this study came from my experiences living and working in north-east Nigeria, where my work focused on civilian protection, conflict analysis, human rights, and peacebuilding. Over the years, I had come across stories of mob action against men suspected of engaging in sexual activity with other men, rumours around 'lesbianism' in camps for internally displaced people, and a case of surgery on a child to bring genitalia in line with binaristic norms, among other narratives and incidents. I was unable to fully investigate further, largely due to constrained time and limited resources, as well as the risks involved and my inability to mitigate them. This latter factor was particularly critical as I was working for organizations that were wary of upsetting their relationships with government, local communities, and colleagues, many of whom held discriminatory attitudes themselves. In one case, a text I had written in a draft report on gender relations which discussed the GBV was edited and sentences deleted where there was reference to people of diverse SOGIESC. This was the only substantial change made.

Consequently, although I was aware that a significant gap in knowledge existed and informed a lack of SOGIESC inclusion in development, human rights, humanitarian, and peacebuilding interventions, it was difficult to strategize a way forward. Integrating SOGIESC into my ongoing research by asking respondents related questions risked causing harm, either by having people talking about their anti-LGBTQI perceptions and inflaming these dynamics further or directly to queer people themselves. I did not want to put them in a situation where they were unable to talk openly, faced risk through their disclosures, or felt judged by fellow researchers and interpreters in my team (whose attitudes towards SOGIESC were not always clear). My dilemmas of working on conflict, gender, and human rights in north-east Nigeria but not examining SOGIESC were compounded by the lack of queer associations and organizations in the conflict-affected north-east that were visible even to local human rights organizations or LGBTQI activists in other parts of the country and prevalent social norms that made it challenging for people who were allies to express these thoughts openly.

Moreover, when I talked about the need for interventions to be inclusive of SOGIESC to people working in development, human rights, humanitarian, or peacebuilding, I was often dismissed. People worried about the potential impacts of doing so on government and community acceptance for their organizations, concerns particularly acute in the context of closing civic space, and backlash against changes in gender power relations brought about by the conflict. Others highlighted the existing proliferation of rumours circulating concerning NGOs and UN agencies that sought to discredit their work. I was also told that SOGIESC was not important given the scale of the crisis and number of other, more critical issues, with one (White, queer, European) woman telling me, "We can't be looking at this when people don't have food to eat". Among many foreign-aid workers to whom I spoke, there was a sense of SOGIESC being a luxury that we could focus on only when basic needs had been met and a complete lack of understanding both of the importance of acceptance, belonging, connection, and love by oneself, one's family, and one's society and that stigma and discrimination affect access to basic services, livelihoods, and humanitarian assistance. Even when talking with researchers who worked on queerness in other conflict-affected societies, I was told that north-east Nigeria was just too difficult and we should start with 'easier' contexts. I found it hard to believe that we could interview and work with people who had been part of AOGs which were listed and proscribed as terrorist organizations, developing strategies to deal with potential backlash, resistance, and stigma from government and community actors, but could not take the time to develop safe and ethical approaches to examine LGBTQI rights.

As a result, it was not with much hope that, at a meeting with a representative of the Canadian High Commission on north-east Nigeria's gender dynamics, I raised SOGIESC as one of the major gaps in the north-east Nigeria humanitarian response. I spoke of the need for research in this area to inform both mainstream humanitarian programming and specific interventions to support LGBTQI people and their organizations. I was encouraged by our subsequent conversation and even more so by a follow-up email asking me to contact the Canadian High Commission before any other donors with any research proposal I developed in this area.

While thinking through the approach to take, I was deliberate in reflections around who controls the production and sharing of knowledge, my own positionality,[7] and resulting implications for design. The obvious way forward would have been to discuss and partner with a LGBTQI rights association in the region. However, in all my years working there and asking LGBTQI people locally and activists in other parts of the country, I had yet to find such an association active in Adamwa, Borno, or Yobe states. Given many human rights activists I knew in these states were antithetical to LGBTQI rights and/or reluctant to be seen as openly supportive of them, I spoke with Xeenarh Mohammed, the Executive Director of TIERs, one of the more established LGBTQI rights organizations in Nigeria, about applying for funding. Although TIERs is based in Lagos, it has networks around the country and, importantly, would not dilute the research approach or findings to de-centre LGBTQI rights in any way.

Xeenarh Mohammed and I designed a participatory research study which involved training and providing ongoing support to LGBTQI people from different locations in north-east Nigeria to conduct research themselves. We saw working in this manner as critical to devolving power, recognizing the expertise people already had, and strengthening their capacities to conduct research. Our plan was for this project to not be a one-off research intervention but the start of supporting LGBTQI people in north-east Nigeria to undertake and lead this work. Indeed, the primary purpose of the programme was to ensure benefit to LGBTQI people and we saw expanding those involved in and controlling the means of production of knowledge as integral to doing so.

However, our research design had to be changed in practice. Despite our efforts, very few queer people in north-east Nigeria whom we contacted were willing and able to be involved. Many people had internalized stigma, were not fully open with themselves about the non-normative nature of their SOGIESC, and hoped it would change with time. They were reluctant to put themselves in a position where, as researchers in this study, they would be met with this reality and be in contact with other similar people. People also, understandably, had fears around discovery. They worried that government, security, or community actors would find out about the study, or that our respondents could include police informants who would report them. It proved challenging to find people willing to participate as respondents, particularly those from certain groups including women, older people, and people with disabilities, let alone people willing to be part of the research team. With time, we would have been able to build up the levels of trust and confidence required to discuss mitigation of risks and allay fears but, due to delays caused by the COVID-19 pandemic as described above, we were faced with time constraints and pressure to deliver, particularly given the difficulties of finding funding for this work in the first place.

We adapted to our new realities and I worked with Bala Mohammed, the Executive Director of Hope Alive Health Awareness Initiative (HAHAI) in neighbouring Bauchi state, to collect data. Although Bauchi state has been less affected by violent conflict, Xeenarh Mohammed and I felt it important to have someone who worked in the north-east on the team, particularly given the similarities between Bauchi and Borno state and the need for knowledge of cultural dynamics. Bala Mohammed also had a wealth of experience working with LGBTQI people in the north-east and contacts and networks which he mobilized to find respondents.

We considered power dynamics with respondents, particularly given these dynamics would be different from our intended participatory design. Bala Mohammed spent significant time with individuals and groups, over the telephone and in person, telling them about the research and its purpose, answering questions, and allaying fears in order to maximize participation in the study. We used networks and snowball-sampling techniques so people vouched for us and our study to their friends and acquaintances, and assured them of our intentions. At the start of interviews, we spent considerable time putting people at ease, providing clarity around the research, and ensuring informed consent. We gave people the option of not answering certain questions, stopping the interview as they wished, and the opportunity to choose their own pseudonyms. We revealed our own personal sexual orientations and answered any related questions people had. In order to address power imbalances to some extent, this was of particular importance, considering the issues we were asking them to discuss and fears around doing so in such a hostile environment.

Although we were unable to carry out the research study as designed, we hope that subsequent funding will enable us to continue to build relationships and networks and support mobilization and community building. In the future, we would like to carry out a truly participatory study based on a research agenda chosen by participants themselves and, with time, have strengthened capacities to the extent that they can undertake research themselves.

Ensuring safeguarding, safety, security, and well-being

The next area for ethical consideration this chapter examines is the steps we put in place to ensure safeguarding, safety, security, and well-being of research participants, researchers, and the LGBTQI community at large. It outlines our strategies and thought processes to understand the risks involved and mitigate them. We were particularly conscious of the need to take a holistic understanding of risk—one that went beyond physical violence to include mental health and well-being impacts, as well as potential consequences in terms of the perpetuation of damaging anti-queer narratives through our work.

The security and safety of respondents, researchers, and queer communities at large were paramount to our research design. Although we did not have a thorough understanding of security threats that queer people face in Maiduguri, we were able to extrapolate from our knowledge of violations against LGBTQI people in the rest of the country as well as of dynamics, narratives, and trends in the north-east. We discussed risk, strategized actions in mitigation, and put mechanisms and referral systems in place. We were conscious that dangers arose along a number of different lines, including the conflict dynamics in the area at large, attitudes around SOGIESC held by many government officials and security agents, gendered vulnerabilities, and other aspects of intersectional realities. We were also clear in our approach to the research that we wished to go beyond direct physical threats to take more holistic approaches that included impacts of our study on respondents' well-being and societal narratives around queerness.

With regards to the risk of direct violence, we restricted the number of people who knew about the study. Apart from myself, Bala Mohammed, colleagues at TIERs, and people working for the Canadian High Commission, the only people aware of the focus of our work were less than a handful of trusted individuals who helped us to find respondents, and with whom we discussed referrals if needed. Having lived in Maiduguri for years and given the nature of the city, we were guaranteed to come across people I knew and had to develop a way of responding to their questions. We planned data collection for a time when I was collecting data for another research project which I did during the working day, leaving evenings, weekends, and other 'free time' for this study. As I was no longer living in Maiduguri by this time, this arrangement meant I could answer any questions from acquaintances, colleagues, friends, and others as to my purpose in the city by reference to this other study. When we encountered others, I introduced Bala Mohammed as a friend who worked in sexual health who was currently in Maiduguri for meetings.

Moreover, we chose to stay in a hotel considered relatively safe by queer people in the city, with staff who did not ask questions, and held our interviews in one of our hotel rooms. Respondents were asked to choose their own pseudonyms which we used to refer to them during the interview, in our notes, and in the report. Interviews were recorded on my mobile telephone and tablet, with the consent of respondents, and these recordings were transferred to my laptop and deleted on the other devices during breaks in between interviews and at the end of each day. We took minimal written notes and I used an encrypted file storage system to store my notes and recordings of interviews. We also only interviewed people known to us and our respondents, or with whom Bala Mohammed had already spoken with in detail. In some cases, we chose not to interview some people who we judged might potentially be indiscreet or otherwise pose risks.

In these ways, we mitigated dangers linked to people, including state actors, becoming aware of our work, including through police informants.

We reduced the risk of police raids happening in the first place through our choice of interview venue and vetting of potential respondents and diminished any potential consequences through deletion of recordings and encryption. Despite these measures, we experienced some apprehension during data collection, partly in consequence of the anxiety expressed by our respondents. In contrast to other research projects on which I had worked, including those on sensitive topics such as human rights violations committed by state actors and community militias or with people formerly associated with AOGs, I was conscious that there would likely be few allies in Maiduguri, even among close friends and colleagues with whom I had worked for years, in the eventuality of a police raid or other forms of discovery and that actors who would help were in other parts of the country. We were relieved to finish data collection without any such event happening.

We were also conscious of the impacts of data collection on the emotional and mental health and well-being of respondents, many who lived in fear of discovery and resulting consequences. For example, on arrival into the interview room, many respondents sought assurance they would not be filmed or their faces otherwise captured. Some of them, in response to our guarantees around anonymity and confidentiality, shared that they had automatically looked around the room for hidden cameras at the start of the interview. In response, we reassured them there were no cameras present, undertook not to do anything without their express and informed consent, and outlined the measures we had taken to mitigate risk.

Furthermore, we were conscious that we would be discussing sensitive and potentially painful topics. We wished to mitigate the extent participation could contribute to re-victimization and re-traumatization. We purposefully did not seek to interview rape survivors about the violence to which they had been subjected but rather those who could tell us about GBV dynamics as they affect people of diverse SOGIESC. We believed that doing so would give us the information we sought. Through my friendships with people working on GBV, we had contacts with Hausa and Kanuri-speaking counsellors to whom we could refer if necessary and who would provide high-quality, confidential, and non-judgemental services. We offered to refer survivors of violence to them, whether or not they were research participants. One respondent, a young man who had disclosed his experiences of abduction by AOG fighters and sexual enslavement by a commander, was referred, with his consent. When I spoke with the counsellor to make the referral, I gave brief details of his case and we discussed its particularly sensitive nature and resulting measures that needed to be put in place. However, when I followed up with the counsellor concerned after a few weeks, I learned that they had spoken over the telephone and a counselling appointment had been made but that he had failed to show up as agreed. Her assessment was that he continued to be nervous and hesitant, despite her assurances. When Bala

Mohammed subsequently spoke with him, they discussed his concerns and ended the telephone call with him agreeing to make another appointment.

Another area which prompted thinking around referrals was dynamics around sexual exploitation and abuse, in the form of sex for jobs in the humanitarian sector. A respondent disclosed his experiences in this regard, sharing he had come to know someone working for a humanitarian agency who indicated to him that he could get him a temporary role with a stipend in exchange for sex and that he had received several such roles as a result. He said he knew others who had made similar trades. He did not want to report the person who had sexually exploited him but rather wished for this arrangement to continue as he saw this as his only hope of income, given his lack of contacts, networks, and other resources. When I discussed this case with a sexual exploitation and abuse focal point in the humanitarian response, I was told that, even if he did not want to make a report, I could make one without identifying him. We agreed that it would be difficult to investigate such a report given I had few details that could be used to identify the man concerned and that, in cases such as these, the wishes of the survivor were paramount, even if it meant that a case was not reported.

Finally, we did not want our study to inadvertently lead to the perpetuation of damaging anti-queer narratives in the community at large or trigger anti-LGBTQI action in any way. As a result, most of our respondents were queer themselves and the only non-LGBTQI people with whom we spoke were those working for INGOs who were trusted.

Maximizing benefit to queer people

After having examined issues of power and safety, this chapter will now turn to measures we planned to put in place to ensure benefit to queer people running alongside our study. In contrast to research processes that were extractive in nature, we wished to identify and provide areas of support required. This chapter will outline the areas of intervention that we identified were required before explaining the reasons why we have not, as of the time of writing, been able to pursue them.

While designing the proposal, Xeenarh Mohammed of TIERs and I were clear that we wanted interventions that provided benefit to queer people running alongside the research study. We were both only too aware of extractive research efforts that spoke with vulnerable and marginalized people on the basis that findings would inform programmatic interventions, only for such support to either never materialize or come to fruition only years later. We were determined to take a different approach. One of the main aims of the research study was to identify areas of support required, including through asking respondents directly, and for this analysis to inform interventions straight away. Although the complete budget for doing so was not covered by funding received by the Canada High Commission, TIERs provided co-financing of the project with this in mind.

As a result, we noted the contact details of respondents during data collection so they could benefit from forthcoming interventions themselves and connect us with other LGBTQI people in Maiduguri for outreach. I communicated with TIERs about potential interventions we could put in place, in general terms before the period of data collection and more concretely in catch-up conversations during and after data collection. We also offered services and referrals to those not involved in research; for example, to friends of respondents who had been subjected to sexual violence.

During data collection, we identified five initial areas of intervention required. First, we found a strong need for holistic security training in response to the blackmail, extortion, and entrapment to which LGBTQI people were subjected by state and non-state actors alike. This training would help people develop personal and collective safety plans, become aware of good digital security practices, and address aspects of well-being as a critical part of security and safety. The next area of intervention was around improving knowledge of human rights among LGBTQI people and communities in the north-east so that they became more aware of their rights under the Nigerian constitution, national law, and avenues of recourse if they were violated. We also believed that, through human rights and holistic security training, we could support community building, mobilization, and solidarity attempts. Third, we wanted improvement in access to healthcare through identification of allies who were healthcare workers to whom LGBTQI people could go for care and training of healthcare workers specifically in difference in sex characteristics and on the need for professional and non-judgemental services in general. Fourth, we wanted to start a programme of advocacy to civil society, international NGOs, and UN agencies in the north-east so they could make the changes necessary to organizational culture so workplaces were safe and nurturing for their LGBTQI staff; develop strategies for better SOGIESC inclusion into programming over time, including through training of staff and integration into conflict analyses, baseline studies, and humanitarian assessments; and train GBV case workers and members of the protection sector on the violence and protection risks people of diverse SOGIESC experience and develop referral pathways to provide effective and non-judgemental services. Finally, we wanted to institute information sharing and solidarity between people of diverse SOGIESC in the north-east and other parts of the community, including through engagement in joint investigations of violations and their reflection in monitoring and human rights reporting to national, regional, and international mechanisms.

Unfortunately, pandemic-related delays as well as staff turnover at TIERs meant the study was completed just before the end of the relevant grants and there were no resources to pay for the interventions envisaged. As matters stand, we are looking for funding to finalize the design of the research report to share the study's findings and to engage in the interventions it identifies.

Conclusion

This research was one of the most challenging and complex studies I have undertaken. Seeking to uncover the realities of a stigmatized and marginalized group in an area of 'live' conflict, in a context where there were no visible and outspoken representatives of this group, raised a plethora of ethical and practical questions. This chapter has provided an overview of the steps we put in place when it came to addressing these questions as well as our difficulties in taking forward our plans, leading to three overarching conclusions.

First, even in the most challenging circumstances, it is possible to conduct research on the impacts of conflict and violence on people of diverse SOGIESC but not possible for everyone to do so. Certain elements need to be in place beforehand. The only reason we were able to conduct these interviews was because I knew the region intimately, having lived in Maiduguri for many years, during which time I had conducted in-depth research on conflict, human rights, and security dynamics. Additionally, Bala Mohammed, my co-researcher, had the needed contacts and networks. This long-term embeddedness in, and relationship with, the context—and the security planning it enables—is a prerequisite to conducting this kind of research.

Second, enough flexibility, most notably in time, space, and funds, to enable adjustment to changing dynamics is key. Our initial funding application had been for a one-year period but the donor considered the project to be high risk and (serendipitously) decided to extend the grant to two years. While a global pandemic is an exceptional case, this research study experienced many other challenges in the face of which we were forced to adapt our planned approach. While our perfect research study on paper faced several barriers, which meant it was not implemented as envisaged, we were still able to deliver research findings within the (longer) grant period specified. Many gaps remain (most notably with our time and other constraints affecting the diversity of respondents we were able to interview) but our work provides a good foundation for us and others to build on in the future.

Third, engagement needs to go beyond a one-off (extractive) research project to be a longer-term programme of action-oriented research married with ongoing interventions that are of benefit to research respondents and queer communities at large, including through supporting community and movement building. This was where our study, due to pandemic-related delays and finite grant periods, had the largest gap between our plans and our practice. Yet, our experience offers a key area of reflection and learning. That the study was done via TIERs, a Nigerian human rights organization, provides more opportunities for finding additional funds to enable this work compared with an equivalent project implemented by external actors. Our experience clearly highlights the need for more action-oriented and participatory research, by and for queer people living in conflict-affected areas, and the need to strengthen research capacities and support movement building through long-term flexible funding for LGBTQI rights organizations.

Notes

1. I joined the Board of TIERs in 2022.
2. In this chapter, I will not be italicizing any words, given the reality that a diverse range of languages historically contributed to the development of English and continue to do so, that only words from certain countries tend to be italicized, and that many of these words are used freely in the English-speaking world. Highlighting them in this way exoticizes terms and concepts from areas subjected to colonial domination, resource extraction, slavery, and other forms of historical and contemporary injustice. My decision stands alongside the choices of other scholars and writers to resist the linguistic gatekeeping and unequal race and geopolitical dynamics that italicization represents, as part of our anti-racist, decolonial, and feminist praxis.
3. Please note that in the interests of conflict sensitivity and accuracy, this chapter will use the exact names of the groups involved where relevant and the term 'armed opposition groups' to refer to all those active in the region, as opposed to using the blanket term 'Boko Haram' which, rather than being the name of the groups themselves, is one given to them by the media, serves to simplify their message and aims, and falsely assumes there is one cohesive group rather than the number of groups and factions in existence.
4. For more, see Mustapha (2015) and Thurston (2017) for more background information.
5. The term religious fundamentalism is used here as distinct from religious conservatism and to signify the project whereby those engaged in it construct tradition in a way that is highly selective, at the same time dogmatically insisting that their reconstructions of text are sacred and therefore cannot be questioned (Cowden and Sahgal, 2017). They deny 'the possibility of interpretation and reinterpretation even while its adherents engage in both and note the importance of control over women's bodies, sexuality and rigid gender norms' (Bennoune, 2013: 16).
6. A Hausa term for those assigned male gender who express themselves in ways and engage in activities socially coded 'feminine'. They are often described as 'men who act like women' and many marry women and have families. Historically, yan daudu have played important roles in northern life but are now increasingly seen as immoral and persecuted (Sinikangas, 2004; Gaudio, 2009).
7. I was born in Maiduguri and have spent a significant part of my adult life working on the conflict in north-east Nigeria and the Lake Chad Basin region, including years living in Maiduguri, but am not Nigerian (I had Indian citizenship at birth and became a citizen of the UK as an adult). I have been part of LGBTQI rights movements in Nigeria since 2014 and am a co-editor of *She Called Me Woman: Nigeria's Queer Women Speak*, which aims to highlight queer women's realities, shift attitudes, and encourage allies to speak out, part of the first wave of cultural activism on LGBTQI rights through storytelling in Nigeria.

Bibliography

Amnesty International (2015) '"Our job is to shoot, slaughter and kill": Boko Haram's reign of terror', AFR 44/1360/2015, London: Amnesty International.

Amnesty International (2016) '"If you see it, you will cry": life and death in Giwa Barracks', AFR 44/3998/2016, London: Amnesty International.

Bennoune, K. (2013) *Your Fatwa Does Not Apply Here: Untold Stories from the Fight against Muslim Fundamentalism*, New York: Norton Books.

Council on Foreign Relations (2021) 'Nigeria Security Tracker', *CFR*, [online]. Available from: www.cfr.org/nigeria/nigeria-security-tracker/p29483

Cowden, S. and Sahgal, G. (2017) 'Why Fundamentalism?', *Feminist Dissent*, 2:7–39.

Eltantawi, S. (2017) *Shari'ah on Trial: Northern Nigeria's Islamic Revolution*, Oakland, CA: University of California Press.

Gaudio, R.P. (2009) *Allah Made Us: Sexual Outlaws in an Islamic African City*, Oxford: Wiley-Blackwell.

Hansen, W. (2020) 'The ugly face of the state: Nigerian security forces, human rights and the search for Boko Haram', *Canadian Journal of African Studies*, 54(1): 299–317.

Hoffmann, L. (2014) *Who Speaks for the North? Politics and Influence in Northern Nigeria*, London: Chatham House.

Kassim, A. and Nwankpa, M. (2018) *The Boko Haram Reader: From Nigerian Preachers to the Islamic State*, London: Hurst.

Kiss, L. et al (2020) 'Male and LGBT survivors of sexual violence in conflict situations: a realist review of health interventions in low- and middle-income countries', *Conflict and Health*, 14(11).

Last, M. (2015) 'From dissent to dissidence: the genesis and development of reformist Islamist groups in Northern Nigeria', in A.R. Mustapha (ed) *Sects and Social Disorder: Muslim Identities and Conflict in Northern Nigeria*, Suffolk: James Currey.

Maclean, R. and Alfa, I. (2021) 'Thousands of Boko Haram members surrendered. They moved in next door', *New York Times*, [online] 23 September. Available from: www.nytimes.com/2021/09/23/world/africa/boko-haram-surrender.html

Mahmood, O. and Ani, N.C. (2018) *Factional Dynamics Within Boko Haram*, Addis Ababa: Institute for Security Studies.

Matfess, H. (2017) *Women and the War on Boko Haram: Wives, Weapons, Witnesses*, London: Zed Books.

Mohammed, X., Nagarajan, C., and Aliyu, R. (2018) *She Called Me Woman: Nigeria's Queer Women Speak*, Abuja: Cassava Republic Press.

Morse, J.M. et al (2021) 'The maturation of grounded theory,' in J.M. Morse et al (eds) *Developing Grounded Theory: The Second Generation Revisited* (2nd edn), New York: Routledge, pp 3–22.

Mustapha, A.R. and Bunza, M. (2015) 'Understanding Boko Haram', in A.R. Mustapha (ed) *Sects and Social Disorder: Muslim Identities and Conflict in Northern Nigeria*, Suffolk: James Currey.

Mustapha, A.R. and Meagher, K. (eds) (2020) *Overcoming Boko Haram: Faith, Society and Islamic Radicalization in Northern Nigeria*, Suffolk: James Currey.

Nagarajan, C. (2019) *Gender Relations in Borno*, Abuja: British Council.

Nagarajan, C. (2020a) *To Defend or Harm: Community Militias in Borno State, Nigeria*, Abuja: Center for Civilians in Conflict.

Nagarajan, C. (2020b) *Gender and COVID-19 in Nigeria: Impacts on LGBTQI People*, Abuja: EVA and TIERs.

Nagarajan, C. (2022) *Lesbian, Gay, Bisexual, Trans, Queer and Intersex Realities in Northeast Nigeria*, Lagos: The Initiative for Equal Rights.

Nagarajan, C. and Toogood, K. (2017) *Guidance on Mainstreaming Conflict Sensitivity, Gender and Social Inclusion in Research*, Abuja: British Council.

Nigeria (1990) Criminal Code Act 1990.

Nigeria (2014) Same Sex Marriage (Prohibition) Act 2014.

Parkinson, J. and Hinshaw, D. (2021) *Bring Back Our Girls: The Untold Story of the Global Search for Nigeria's Missing Schoolgirls*, London: Swift Press.

Pearson, E. and Nagarajan, C. (2020) 'Gendered security harms: state policy and the counterinsurgency against Boko Haram', *African Conflict and Peacebuilding Review*, 10(2): 108–40.

Pereira, C. (2005) 'Zina and transgressive heterosexuality in northern Nigeria', *Feminist Africa*, 5: 52–79.

Samuel, M. (2021) 'Islamic State's determined expansion into Lake Chad Basin', *ISS Today*, [online] 21 August. Available from: https://issafrica.org/iss-today/islamic-states-determined-expansion-into-lake-chad-basin

Segun, M. (2016) '"They set our classrooms on fire": attacks on education in northeast Nigeria', New York: Human Rights Watch.

Sinikangas, M. (2004) 'Yan Daudu: a study of transgendering men in Hausaland West Africa', masters thesis. Department of Cultural Anthropology and Ethnology, Uppsala University.

The Initiative for Equal Rights (2020) *Human Rights Violations Report, 2020*, Lagos: TIERs.

The Initiative for Equal Rights and NOI Polls (2017) *Social Perception Survey on Lesbian, Gay, Bisexual and Transgender Persons Rights in Nigeria*, Lagos: TIERs.

The Initiative for Equal Rights and NOI Polls (2022) *2022 Human Rights Violations Report Based on Real or Perceived Sexual Orientation, Gender Identity/Expression and Sex Characteristics (SOGIESC)*, Lagos: TIERs.

The Initiative for Equal Rights and Vivid Rain (2019) *Social Perception Survey on Lesbian, Gay, Bisexual and Transgender Persons Rights in Nigeria*, Lagos: TIERs.

The Initiative for Equal Rights, the Bisi Alimi Foundation, and NOI Polls (2015) *Perceptions of Nigerians on LGB Rights: Poll Report*, Lagos: TIERs.

Thurston, A. (2016) *'The Disease Is Unbelief': Boko Haram's Religious and Political Worldview*, Washington, DC: Brookings Institute.

Thurston, A. (2017) *Boko Haram: History of an African Jihadist Movement*, Princeton, NJ: Princeton University Press.

United Nations Office for the Coordination of Humanitarian Affairs (2021) 'Nigeria Situation Report', *OHCHR* [online]. Available from: https://reports.unocha.org/en/country/nigeria

Uwais, M. (2004) 'Diversity of thought in the development of Sharia', in J. Ibrahim (ed) *Sharia Penal and Family Laws in Nigeria and in the Muslim World: Rights Based Approach*, Zaria: Ahmadu Bello University Press.

Vivekananda, J. et al (2019), *Shoring Up Stability*, Berlin: Adelphi.

8

Entangled Intimacies, Queer Attachments: Reflections on Fieldwork with a Diaspora of War

Ahmad Qais Munhazim

Trusting and distrusting while being Muslim

One Friday morning in August 2017, a recurring nightmare of headless men chasing me as houses were burning all over the city left me drenched in sweat in bed. I could see neighbours, cousins, and aunts getting on buses. I was running around looking for my family. I was awakened by a loud call from home, Kabul. I panicked as I answered. Random calls from home are never good news for those of us living in-between wars and displacements. My mother felt my panic on the phone and tried to calm me down. She said: "Everything is okay here. Don't panic. I just called because we are making *bolani* and I thought of you. Can you find a place near you to get some *bolani* or else we will not be able to enjoy it without you." Luckily, I was doing my fieldwork in California where it is not a major struggle to find good Afghan food. That afternoon I made my way to an Afghan restaurant in the East Bay to get some *bolani*, as I promised my mother. The tiny hole-in-the-wall restaurant was my usual Afghan food spot. This time I did not order my usual *Qabeli* plate. Rasool, the guy at the counter who spoke merely a few words to me despite my several attempts to talk to him, asked why I did not order my usual. I told him about my mother's call. That conversation broke the tension between us. Rasool started to talk about his mother and how concerned she gets about him despite her living in Kabul. After an hour of our chat and talking about our similar hang-out spots in Kabul, Rasool laughed and said he did not want to talk to me previously as he thought I was some sort of spy. Rasool added:

'You know it is hard to trust anyone in this country, especially when someone new all of a sudden appears in the Afghan community. I saw you at the mosque and a few times here, so I was thinking another spy is here to gather information about Muslims. Now that we talked, I feel like you are just like us. I hope you are not offended by my assumptions about you. This country makes you distrust your own blood.'

As a Muslim researcher, it was challenging to engage in ethnographic research with Muslims in the US at times of rising Islamophobia and racism. The challenge was not only my own positionality and proximity to the issues I was studying, but also building trust diligently and ensuring my community is cared for in the process. Research with Muslims at a time of enhanced securitization is complicated by several dilemmas (Milad, 2019). Academics have cooperated with the state in gathering information about Muslims with the intention to contribute to further policing and surveillance of Muslim communities and nations in the Global North and the Global South. The so-called 'War on Terror' provided a market for writing about Muslims and a moment of excitement for academics to 'cover Islam', as Edward Said argues. Said states that 'the market for representations of a monolithic, enraged, threatening, and conspiratorially spreading Islam is much greater, more useful, and capable of generating more excitement' (1997: xxviii).

As a result, there is a distrust of researchers living among Muslims and writing for and about them. This has extended to the Afghan diaspora; a community that has been under continuous state surveillance since 11 September 2001. Rasool's distrust of anyone new in the community is a product of 9/11 surveillance. The years of state-sponsored surveillance of the Afghan community and the current political climate impacting Muslims around the world have made Afghans suspicious of researchers. Afghans' distrust is also informed by the war in Afghanistan and the loss they all have made. Thousands of people disappeared in the dark during the Soviet occupation of Afghanistan (Maley, 2020). I was not only aware of these painful realities, but I also lived and continue to live them. Therefore, I understood Afghans' suspicion, their distrust in authority and researchers, and empathized with them. Valerie J. Smith, who has conducted in-depth qualitative research including ethnography, interviews, and focus groups with the Afghan diaspora in Fremont, CA, states that Afghans do not easily trust people (2009). They have every reason not to trust, bearing in mind the current political climate, as one of my comrades said, "*margazeeda aina az raispan maitarsa*" (the one who has been stung by a snake is scared of even rope). To gain trust, a researcher has to build relationships with the community leaders and respected individuals in the community. To this end, I volunteered with the Afghan organizations and established contacts with the scholars in the community and other well-respected and networked individuals in California, Washington, Maryland, and Virginia.

I lived among Afghan communities and attended gatherings and mosques regularly. From attending community events, such as poetry nights and funerals to weddings, I became an accepted part of the community in a short period of time. When I moved to Fremont, CA, to start my fieldwork and live among Afghans in 2017, part of me went with the assumption that I would immediately find a community, be welcomed, and connect with fellow Afghans right away. Another part of me, however, was terrified to enter the community with a queer identity and body. Throughout my time living in Minneapolis for undergraduate and graduate school, I had become too queer to hide or perform masculinity anymore. It was all a delusion that ended the first day I arrived in the field.

As an Afghan myself, I believed it would be easy to establish trust and start my work right away. However, I was not aware of how much Afghan diasporas in these concentrated communities have been affected by regimes of state security and surveillance that have shaken their sense of trust. With the increased state-sponsored surveillance of the Muslim communities, particularly Afghan diasporic communities, they have become cautious and suspicious when a newcomer joins their community and appears in social gatherings, participates in community activities, and lives in the neighbourhood, as Rasool put it. As my ethical and moral responsibility, I let the community know I was a researcher and that I was attending the events and gatherings as part of my research. I was, however, finding safety in secrecy around my own personal life. The researcher identity in many ways distanced me initially from the community. The community did not have a good perception of researchers. Rahila, an Afghan woman in her 50s who I contacted on Airbnb, was hesitant to rent me her room in San Francisco. She eventually did and I stayed with her for a week. As we sat down for tea on the first day I arrived, she asked me right away if I was queer. I responded with a "yes" and she laughed and said "I knew it". She then added that she was hesitant to rent me her room because she had a hard time trusting journalists and researchers coming to the community. Rahila said:

> 'I had to look you up to make sure you are legit and not a *jasos,* spy. Empires, states, and those with access to power have tried to fool us [Afghans] for centuries. Remember that one time Imam of Eid Gah masjid in Kabul who led prayers for 40 years turned out to be a British spy? Maybe you should tell people you are queer. They might trust you more like I did when I found that online.'

I went to the field with a sense of entitlement: "This is *my* community and they should be happy that finally one of their own kind is researching and writing about them." This sort of attitude, which is ingrained in many researchers' minds going to the field, created the initial barriers between the community and me. Part of this was also my attempt to downplay my other identities and present myself as an objective researcher. I realized I was doing interviews but they were quite rigid and structured in their forms and discussions that felt empty. I realized people were giving me answers that they assumed I wanted to hear. I was in search of a turn, an entanglement that would bring me closer to my comrades in the field.

The more time I spent in the field, the more people connected with me based on my identities and experiences other than that of a researcher. The conversations became more organic, vulnerable, and real. I utilized my life experiences, identities, and my positionality to more sensitively navigate the interviews and conversations, with the aim of cultivating a respectful and attentive research programme. I approached each person I met in the field as an individual with a unique experience and connected with them at different levels, honouring their experiences, while knowing that each person has a different way of responding to questions and processing the emotions that may accompany discussing war, displacement, homeland, surveillance, and sexuality. I was also fully aware that I was a researcher who is familiar with the cultural, historical, social, and political phenomena impacting Afghans in the US, so I remained attentive to their feelings, frustrations, vulnerabilities, respect, and safety throughout my research study. The shared sense of pain, vulnerability, displacement, and (in)security connected me with the Afghan community across different generations. From Afghans refusing to talk with me, I ended up officiating a queer Afghan wedding, led the weekly discussions with the elderly Afghan women in Freemont on gender, sexuality, and war, and made friendships that would later become a community. Fieldwork became a site of intimacy that brought me closer not only to my community but also to my own self, my queer self. This queer attachment to my own body and the moving beyond the shame, as Sally R. Munt (2017) urges us to do, allowed me to forgive, understand, and heal.

Entangled intimacies, shared war, and loss

"Alamganj burnt down. Its burning smoke is everywhere. Dad, let's leave. I can hear the tank engine outside, getting closer to our house. Let's leave Alamganj." One late Friday afternoon in September 2018, as I sat down for a conversation with Asad, a 30-year-old, newly arrived Afghan refugee in the US, and who came through the Special Immigration Visa programme having served the US military as a translator for five years in eastern Afghanistan, this popular song, written by Farhad Darya in the middle of the Soviet War in Afghanistan, played in the background at De Afghanan restaurant in Fremont, CA. Fremont became home to thousands of Afghans who first arrived in the US escaping the Soviet occupation in the 1980s. It soon came to be known as Little Kabul (Bailey, 2005). The very strong sense of Afghan community in Fremont continues to pull Afghans in even to this day, including Asad.

I met Asad for the first time in a Lyft ride when he picked me up from Abu Bakr Siddiq mosque in Hayward, CA, where I was attending a young Afghan-American man's *fatiha* (funeral ceremony). The man's sudden death was a mystery for almost everyone in the room, except for his family. During the Lyft ride, Asad and I connected warmly over our shared nostalgia of home and longing for our elderly mothers who lived in Kabul. We also found out that we grew up five blocks away from each other in the northern part of Kabul. Asad lost his oldest brother in a suicide bombing in Kabul in 2016 and his father went missing right after Asad was born during the Soviet military invasion of Afghanistan. He has one other brother in one of the refugee camps in Greece waiting for an unknown future for the past three years. He told me he could not bring his mother with him at the time of this departure but hopes that one day he can bring her to the US from where she now lives with his uncle's family in the outskirts of Kabul.

After the ten-minute Lyft ride, Asad dropped me off closer to downtown Hayward where I was meeting with a young Afghan-American woman activist, Aryana, who lost her mother in the early 1990s' war in Afghanistan. Following her mother's passing, Aryana moved to the US after receiving refugee status together with her father and sister. She later lost her father in gang violence two years after settling in Fremont.

Aryana and her sister grew up in the foster care system until they were adopted by an Afghan family as teenagers. Aryana advocates for social justice and gender equity, and she fights to address and end domestic violence in Afghan-American families, which she believes is rampant across all generations among the Afghan diaspora communities in the Bay Area. She also carries out aid projects in Afghanistan. Once a year, she collects financial donations and warm winter clothes from Afghan Americans all over the US and travels to Afghanistan where she volunteers with local and international NGOs that support Afghan war widows.

Aryana and I met a few times over tea, Afghan food, and hookah. During these hang-outs, we were remembering and re-remembering the war and how as kids we both lived it, survived it, and are still carrying it inside our bodies into the future. We laughed how we both were around the same age and as kids considering war normal, as something happening everywhere around the world. Some days we would sneak out from the bomb shelters and play with other rebellious kids outside on the streets. In some very weird and twisted ways, we both talked about those days of war as something to be missed. We possibly missed our childhood, the friends we made, but war? Why would anyone miss war? Is missing war part of PTSD? At times,

Aryana and I would cry together and share how war had messed us up in so many ways.

Aryana then introduced me to an elder in the Afghan community, Kaka Usman, uncle Usman who was well read and quite interested in young Afghans' education. When I met Kaka Usman, he immediately reminded me of my uncles—no wonder he was called uncle by other Afghans. He was caring, kind, attentive yet, at times, tough and authoritative. In his 60s, he held his posture better than I ever could and he would tell me "you seem to carry a lot of stress on your shoulders. Relax them, else you will get old before time. We Afghans carry war all over our bodies and it shrinks us like cotton." He always wore dark-coloured suits with white-chequered shirts and colourful ties.

When Kaka Usman came to know I was very new in the community and I did not have any family members around, he invited me over to his house for an Afghan dinner. After dinner he treated me with tea and some sweets from my childhood that I did not know still existed. I was told that Afghans who fled the war in the 1980s brought the recipes with them and now they make those sweets in the Bay Area. Kaka Usman and I listened to some old Afghan music and talked about home, Afghanistan, while his son and two daughters feeling bored would ask us to switch to English so that they could understand us fully. I felt a sense of home around them yet also nervous that Kaka Usman's son and daughters might pick up on my queerness and tell their father. I did not want to lose the sense of home Kaka Usman provided me so I did not disclose much about my personal life. I even found myself surveilling my own gender performances, concealing my queerness as much as I could. As I came to know Kaka Usman more closely, I let my guard down and began to be more myself, not the version I assumed he would like.

The time I spent with people like Asad, Aryana, and Kaka Usman in the field were intimate moments that were entangled with our shared trauma and loss, struggles in exile and nostalgia for home—for Afghanistan. These intimacies came as a surprise to me. Going into the field, I was trained in an academy and in a society to make assumptions about my own people. I was to assume they were homophobes who would never accept me. Partly, it was a survival mechanism. To survive as a genderqueer, Brown, Muslim, Afghan asylum seeker, I was to lose parts of me, to unlearn and distance myself from a queerness embedded within my displaced body, native language, and my ancestors' philosophies of love and intimacy. I questioned whether all I knew and all I was, was authentically queer. As Sonali Patel, in reference to Brown queer women in Canada, argues, 'while assimilation to Western culture is not often preferred, it is required in order to be recognized as authentically queer' (2019: 4). I believed I refused to assimilate within White Western queerness but parts of me knew I was changing. I wanted to be authentically and unapologetically queer so bad. Therefore, I distanced myself from Afghans and immersed myself into the Western queer world. I wanted to taste the rainbow on a tongue that still remembers how the empire's war tastes. I bought my first rainbow t-shirt from Target. I engaged in street activism and chanted along with other LGBTQ+ folks "we are here, we are queer" while the majority of them didn't acknowledge my existence as a human let alone a queer one. I went to Pride parades waving rainbow flags behind fancy corporation floats while they continued to bomb and drone my home and people in Afghanistan. I knocked on doors for same-sex marriage legalization all over Minneapolis, where I lived at that time, without questioning how heterosexual and White the institution of marriage is. I went to Sunday brunch with local gay liberal politicians flirting queerly and hoping for them to validate my queerness.

With all these queer assimilations, I started to think queerness was alien to Afghanness. Why was I able to talk about my sexual encounters so openly to my queer American friends but never to my friends back in Afghanistan? Were they too conservative? Was sex being a private matter oppressive? I questioned it all while trying to survive in a society that assumed my culture as 'conservative' and 'traditional' (Jones, 2016). It was later that I returned to seeing and believing queerness as embedded within every fabric of Afghan identity and experiences from war to displacement and beyond. It was when I returned to my people, my Afghan communities in California, Virginia, Washington, and Maryland where I conducted my fieldwork. When we allow ourselves to see queerness beyond the sexual identity and gender, we experience intimacy in complicated ways.

The past decades have witnessed emergence of research on intimate encounters and sexual attachments of queer ethnographers while doing fieldwork (Newtown, 1993; Lewin and Leaps, 1996; Rooke, 2009; Di Feliciantonio, Kaciano, and DasGupta, 2017; Langarita Adiego, 2019). Intimacies beyond sexual and romantic desires in the field—diasporic intimacies that intertwine nostalgia for home and struggles in exile of the researcher and interlocutors are yet to be explored attentively.

Using this space to think and reflect, I argue that departing from the sexual and romantic encounters in the field allows us to decolonize intimacies and queerly re-imagine relationships, attachments, friendships, and chosen kinships that are formed as a result of shared experiences of violence and surveillance, displacement, and war. In distancing from sexual intimacies, I draw from Lauren Berlant's framework of intimacy where they argue that intimacy is about 'something shared, a story about both oneself and others, that will turn out in a particular way. Usually, this story is set within zones of familiarity and comfort' (1998: 281). Here, I build on the work of Svetlana Boym (1998) who complicates the notion of intimacy, pushing beyond the boundaries of sexuality into intimacy as closeness, familiarity, de-familiarity, and shared secrets. Boym conceptualizing the phrase 'diasporic intimacy' argues that intimacy is intertwined with the concept of home. Here, home is the home left behind and the home made in exile. Diasporic intimacy 'reflects collective frameworks of memory that encapsulate even the most personal dreams. It is haunted by images of home and homeland, yet it also discloses some of the furtive pleasures of exile' (1998: 500).

To the Afghan diaspora, intimacy is about a shared space of comfort, secrets, and familiarity with homeland—its languages, stories, nostalgia, and violence. It was in the field where I encountered the depth of intimacy with people who I assumed would not accept my queerness. Our intimate ties with the war in Afghanistan, shared experiences of violence in leaving home, and navigating life under state surveillance at the airports, mosques, and public spaces and loss of home, family members and cultural communities allowed us to move past our differences. I am not here to argue that our gendered and sexed experiences of war, surveillance, and loss were insignificant. However, we connected at a much more intimate level, leaving the gendered and sexed differences as being understood and acknowledged through silent acknowledgements, care, and love. They did not parade around me with a rainbow flag flaunting their support for my queerness. However, they fed me homemade Afghan food, prepared cardamom tea, invited me into their homes, read poems about love, longing, homeland and escape with me in my mother tongue, and told me I am no longer alone but I have them. There were also times when we explicitly talked about sexuality and its complexities in Afghanistan but only once we built a deep trust. We moved beyond the limits of intimacy as sexual into intimacy as radical solidarities based on our race, national identity, immigration status, and homeland. This is what Christina Sharpe calls 'configuration of relations'" (2010: 190). Our relations to the systems and an empire that 'other' us brought us closer similarly to the experiences of Muslims in general in the US. In ethnographic study of Muslim youth in the US post 9/11, Sunaina Maira argues that Muslim youth connect with other youth of colour based on their 'distance from normative Americanness' (2005: 70). Their shared experience here is informed by race, class, ethnicity, and citizenship.

What my comrades in the field and I shared were war and loss, surveillance and Islamophobia, nostalgia, and yearning for the homeland. I found a home in each one of my comrades away from Afghanistan. They found the same in me. I realized for some of these Afghans, I was more than the queerness they would possibly see in me. I was, as Kaka Usman told me, "a piece of home". To my surprise, I felt no pressure to come out—expose my sexuality to people I met. It was understood, acknowledged subtly, and respected as something private. For instance, right before starting a focus group discussion with elderly Afghan men in Fremont, an Afghan elder, Haji Halim, asked me to sit next to him. As we started to chat, he said:

'You remind me of when I was young and had just moved to the US. It was in the 1980s. I had dreams and I was so excited for new beginnings, but I was married with three kids. All I could do was work all day and night to support my family. Marriage traps you. You are lucky that you aren't married or have kids. Don't let anyone pressure you into getting married. Find yourself a *ma'shoq* [lover] instead.'

Haji Halim's use of the word *ma'shoq*, a male lover instead of *ma'shoqa*, a female lover, was intentional. His critique of the institution of marriage and his encouragement for me to never get married was a queer affirmation and a very delicate acknowledgement of my queerness. As Haji Halim and I got to know each other more intimately over pots of tea, walks in a park near his house, and listening to classic Afghan music, he started to introduce me as his nephew to people. He would tell me that I could come to him if anyone bothered me or if I needed something. This sort of ethnographic encounter that Margot Weiss (2020) theorizes as 'queer entanglements' allows us to experience intimacy in a decolonial sense. As much as the Western queerness had told me that my people would never accept me, Haji Halim's gentle care for my queerness was a reminder that my ancestors and elders have been queer all along.

Haji Halim's encouragement of me to find a *ma'shoq* challenges the 'conservative' and homophobic discourse the West would like to force upon my people and home. Homophobic discourses are forced upon us to distance us from ourselves, our bodies, families, and nations. If I were to believe that my people are homophobic, I would not have experienced the queer care and love among my own people. To that, I also had to engage in what Gayatri Chakravorty Spivak calls 'critical intimacy' (Paulson, 2018)—a passion from inside to understand them and rationalize from a critical distance why people like Kaka Usman and Haji Halim were subtle not blatant in their support of my queerness. I had to learn what they had gone through as they were forced out of their homeland through wars and military invasions. I had to become an empathetic listener in hearing their stories of survival in a state that criminalizes their Muslim, Afghan, immigrant, and Brown existences. In doing so, I came to learn I had more in common with Kaka Usman and Haji Halim than I would ever have with a Western White queer.

Conclusion

The process of planning and beginning fieldwork is filled with 'conflicting emotions' (La Pastina, 2006: 724). On the one hand, there is a thrill about going to the field, meeting new people, and starting new relations and friendships. On the other hand, there are always uncertainties and hesitations. No matter how many times one goes to the field, there is always a slight fear around the unknown and the unexpected. When I chose to conduct ethnographic research with the Afghan diaspora in the US, it was already complicated for several reasons. I was not allowed to travel to Afghanistan for my fieldwork as I was living as an asylum seeker unable to travel outside the country. Trump's presidency had shaken the country and Muslim bans were in place. There was a continued rise around racist attacks and Islamophobia. It was also a post-Orlando shooting time when Muslims and Afghans had become yet again targets of enhanced surveillance and suspicion.

Despite these complications, my encounters in the field with Afghans were filled with moments of critical intimacies and feminist care that brought me closer to Afghans I once avoided. Our shared experiences around war, loss, death, surveillance, displacement, and homebondedness entangled us intimately. I delicately claimed my queer space within the Afghan community, but a queerness informed by Afghanness—embedded within the socio-cultural fabrics of Afghan society at home and in its diasporas. For those of us invaded, surveilled, and forced to flee, it is our decolonial attempt to form intimacies among ourselves in order to live, survive, and dream.

Bibliography

Baily, J. (2005) 'So near, so far: Kabul's music in exile', *Ethnomusicology Forum*, 14(2): 213–33.

Berlant, L. (1998) 'Intimacy: a special issue', *Critical Inquiry*, 24(2): 281–8.

Boym, S. (1998) 'On diasporic intimacy: Ilya Kabakov's installations and immigrant homes', *Critical Inquiry*, 24(2): 498–524.

Di Feliciantonio, C., Gadelha, K.B., and DasGupta, D. (2017) 'Queer (y) ing methodologies: doing fieldwork and becoming queer', *Gender, Place & Culture*, 24(3): 403–12.

Jones, L. (2016) '"If a Muslim says 'homo nothing gets done'": racist discourse and ingroup identity construction in an LGBT youth group', *Language in Society*, 45: 113–33.

La Pastina, A.C. (2006) 'The implications of an ethnographer's sexuality', *Qualitative Inquiry*, 12(4): 724–35.

Langarita Adiego, J.A. (2019) 'On sex in fieldwork: notes on the methodology involved in the ethnographic study of anonymous sex', *Sexualities*, 22(7–8): 1253–67.

Lewin, E., Leap, W.L., and Leap, W. (eds) (1996) *Out in the Field: Reflections of Lesbian and Gay Anthropologists*, Boston, MA: University of Illinois Press.

Maira, S. (2005) 'The intimate and the imperial: South Asian Muslim immigrant youth after 9/11', in S. Maira and E. Soep (eds) *Youthscapes: The Popular, the National, the Global*, pp 64–84.

Maley, W. (2020) *The Afghanistan Wars*, United Kingdom: Bloomsbury.

Miled, N. (2019) 'Muslim researcher researching Muslim youth: reflexive notes on critical ethnography, positionality and representation', *Ethnography and Education*, 14(1): 1–15.

Munt, S.R. (2017) *Queer Attachments: The Cultural Politics of Shame*, New York: Routledge.

Newton, E. (1993) 'My best informant's dress: the erotic equation in fieldwork', *Cultural Anthropology*, 8(1): 3–23.

Patel, S. (2019) '"Brown girls can't be gay": racism experienced by queer South Asian women in the Toronto LGBTQ community', *Journal of Lesbian Studies*, 23(3): 410–23.

Paulson, S. (2018) 'Critical intimacy: an interview with Gayatri Chakravorty Spivak', *Qualitative Research Journal*, 18(2): 89–93.

Rooke, A. (2009) 'Queer in the field: on emotions, temporality, and performativity in ethnography', *Journal of Lesbian Studies*, 13(2): 149–60.

Said, E.W. (1997) *Covering Islam: How the Media and the Experts Determine How We See the Rest of the World*, New York: Vintage Books.

Sharpe, C. (2010) *Monstrous intimacies: Making post-slavery subjects*. Durham, NC: Duke University Press.

Smith, V.J. (2009) 'Ethical and effective ethnographic research methods: a case study with Afghan refugees in California', *Journal of Empirical Research on Human Research Ethics*, 4(3): 59–72.

Weiss, M. (2020) 'Intimate encounters: queer entanglements in ethnographic fieldwork', *Anthropological Quarterly*, 93(1): 1355–86.

9

Doing NGO Research with Diverse SOGIESC Refugees in Lebanon, Syria, and Turkey: A Conversation

Zeynep Pınar Erdem, Charbel Maydaa,
Henri Myrttinen and Helena Berchtold

Introduction

Academic interest in the impact of political violence on persons of diverse sexual orientations, gender identities and expressions, and sex characteristics (SOGIESC)[1] has grown over the course of the past decade in political science, international relations (IR), and conflict studies. In addition to research conducted by academics, a large part of the on-the-ground research is done by staff of local and international non-governmental organizations (NGOs), especially in conflict-affected settings.[2] This is due to multiple reasons, among them the greater ease and speed at which NGOs, especially local NGOs, can conduct research with conflict-affected populations when compared with academic institutions, and the fact that these organizations in many cases already have pre-existing contacts to often hard-to-reach individuals and groups (on NGO research, see also Myrttinen and Mastonshoeva, 2019). For most NGOs, however, research is only one of the many activities, alongside service provision, policy formulation, and advocacy. This means that resources, including time, for research and analysis are limited and less of a priority.

Conducting research in conflict-affected and displacement settings entails a wide range of risks and challenges, both to researchers and research participants. This research also raises ethical concerns (see, for example, the edited volumes by Wibben, 2016; Åhäll and Gregory, 2017; Rivas and Browne, 2018 for discussions of these and the Resource Guide I in this volume). Many of these risks, challenges, and ethical concerns can be heightened when working with persons of diverse SOGIESC in contexts where these individuals face widespread discrimination and violence, such as in our three case-study countries here: Lebanon, Syria, and Turkey.

In this chapter, we, the authors, discuss and reflect on our experiences and the tensions of doing NGO research with diverse SOGIESC refugees, of engaging with local power-holders and international actors, including donor governments and UN agencies, and balancing the needs of research with the needs and concerns of research participants. All of us authors have been working on diverse SOGIESC research through MOSAIC,[3] a Lebanese NGO founded by activists and legal and health experts in September 2014. MOSAIC is committed to improving the health and well-being of vulnerable and marginalized groups in Lebanon and the broader Middle East and North Africa (MENA) region. In addition to research, MOSAIC provides legal and mental health services to persons of diverse SOGIESC and conducts advocacy work. Many of the beneficiaries of MOSAIC's work are Syrian refugees, but also Lebanese, Palestinians, as well as migrants from other MENA countries.

This chapter is structured mainly as a discussion between three of MOSAIC MENA's researchers, Zeynep Pınar Erdem, Charbel Maydaa, and Henri Myrttinen, written with the invaluable help of our fourth team member, Helena Berchtold. Pınar is an Istanbul-based researcher who, in addition to her work with MOSAIC, has been conducting research with diverse SOGIESC populations in Turkey and Lebanon, including Syrian refugees, for international organizations, including Human Rights Watch (2020). Charbel is one of the founders of MOSAIC MENA and has also been working on diverse SOGIESC rights through their position as co-chair of ILGA Asia. Henri has been working with MOSAIC MENA on a number of research projects since 2016, and has also worked on these issues outside the MENA region. Helena joined the MOSAIC team in 2020 as a research assistant.

Our reflections here draw both on past research as well as our experiences with two current research projects, one examining the impacts of the Syrian Civil War on persons of diverse SOGIESC as part of the UKRI-funded Gender, Justice and Security Hub coordinated by the London School of Economics and Political Science (LSE),[4] and the other, funded by the Sexual Violence Research Initiative, focusing on the experiences of lesbian, bisexual, and trans women in Lebanon and Turkey. Before we come to the conversation section, however, we will first give some background to diverse SOGIESC in Lebanon, Syria, and Turkey, with a special focus on refugees.

Background: diverse SOGIESC in Lebanon, Syria, Turkey

Since the outbreak of the Syrian Civil War in 2011, Lebanon and Turkey have been hosting large numbers of Syrian refugees, reaching an estimated

1.5 million in Lebanon as of 2020 and 3.6 million Syrian refugees in Turkey, as of September 2021. These figures, especially in the case of Lebanon, may in reality be higher (International Crisis Group, 2020; UNHCR, 2021). The vulnerabilities of the general Syrian refugee population are shared by Syrian refugees of diverse SOGIESC in Lebanon and Turkey (WFP, UNHCR, and UNICEF 2020). However, the latter often face additional vulnerabilities, or an exacerbation of existing vulnerabilities, due to individual and structural discrimination based on sexual orientation and gender identity (Kıvılcım, 2017; MOSAIC, 2020; Salem and Shaaban, 2020).

While parts of Turkey and Lebanon, especially Istanbul and Beirut, are often regarded as comparatively LGBTIQ+-friendly as opposed to other areas in the region, persons of diverse SOGIESC nonetheless face massive legal, social, economic, and political hurdles in their lives, imaginaries, and realities (Moussawi, 2020). That being said, migrants and refugees of diverse SOGIESC are not a homogeneous group but are affected by intersecting spheres of discrimination differently, depending on their age, socio-economic status, dis-/ability, and how they are 'read' by others, along with other factors (Human Rights Watch, 2020; Myrttinen et al, 2017; MOSAIC, 2020; UNHCR, 2017). For example, many refugees of diverse SOGIESC face xenophobic discrimination in addition to homophobia and transphobia; lesbian, bisexual, and trans women are systematically discriminated not only for their SOGIESC but also for being women in a heavily patriarchal society; and class-based discrimination is as widespread in the LGBTIQ+ community as elsewhere in society in Lebanon, Syria, and Turkey (Moussawi, 2020, Reid and Ritholtz, 2020).

In addition to general anti-LGBTIQ+ discrimination, refugees and forced migrants of diverse SOGIESC are under additional threat of harassment at the hands of authorities, security forces, as well as individuals from both the host community as well as other refugees for not performing according to dominant gender norms. In our interviews, Syrian refugees of diverse SOGIESC described their experiences of widespread discrimination. Interviewees detailed physical, emotional, and sexual abuse, including harassment as well as sexual exploitation in the work place and on the housing market. While refugees, in general, are at risk of blackmail due to their 'illegal' residency, refugees of diverse SOGIESC might be blackmailed under the threat of 'outing' them (MOSAIC, 2020). Mental and emotional health issues among persons of diverse SOGIESC are of immense concern, both for refugees and those from the host community (Kaplan et al, 2016; MOSAIC, 2020).

In both Lebanon and Turkey, the already-difficult situation of people of diverse SOGIESC, and in particular of refugees, has been further exacerbated by the combined impacts of the COVID-19 pandemic, major economic crises, political instability, and the mobilization of anti-LGBTIQ+ and anti-refugee sentiments for political reasons (MOSAIC, 2020). In a 2021 survey conducted by Oxfam with persons of diverse SOGIESC in Lebanon, 70 per cent of the participants reported having lost their jobs during the past year (Oxfam, 2021). The situation for non-Lebanese LGBTQI+ persons in Lebanon is particularly dire because of fewer job opportunities, fewer avenues for support, discrimination based on nationality, and the inability to return to their home countries (Oxfam, 2021).[5] For Syrian refugees, their lack of documentation has also negatively impacted access to COVID-19 vaccines, leading to a hesitancy to get vaccinated out of fear of being detained and/or deported in the process (Human Rights Watch, 2021a). People of diverse SOGIESC have told MOSAIC that they refrain from going to hospitals out of fear of being discriminated against, especially if their gender identity and appearance doesn't match the gender assigned to them on their passports. Furthermore, in Lebanon, the economic crisis has led to massive electricity and fuel shortages, affecting not only everyday lives but also service provision by NGOs and the healthcare system.

Additionally, in Beirut, the massive explosion in August 2020 had a major impact on the lives of LGBTIQ+ persons. Apart from deaths, injuries, and health and economic impacts, it profoundly shook the already-shaky sense of physical and emotional security of many (Assi et al, 2020; MOSAIC, 2020). The most heavily impacted parts of Beirut—Gemmayze, Mar Mikhael, and Geitawi—were not only home to many people of diverse SOGIESC, but also housed LGBTIQ+-friendly venues which were safe spaces but also provided many with jobs. Moreover, NGOs providing support for people of diverse SOGIESC are located in Beirut (Oxfam, 2021).

Drawing on an analytical concept developed in feminist IR research critiquing dominant binary notions of war and peace, persons of diverse SOGIESC often face 'continuums of violence' (Cockburn, 2004). The violence and discrimination do not begin with the outbreak of a conflict. While armed conflict often exacerbates harms against persons of diverse SOGIESC, it would unfortunately be wrong to assume that these harms end with a ceasefire or peace agreement. Through our research, we hope to contribute to a better understanding of the drivers of this violence and its impacts on persons of diverse SOGIESC. Importantly, however, we also want to go beyond the research aspect of our work, as important as it is, to also effect positive change for these populations. In the following discussion, we elaborate on our experiences to date.

Doing diverse SOGIESC research as an NGO

What are your experiences of doing research as an NGO? What are the advantages and disadvantages?

Charbel: The first thing that comes to mind is that working as an NGO led by LGBTIQ+ individuals, we get directly in contact with people from within the LGBTIQ+ community, involve them in our research, support them, lead by example, and study their personal and social context. This gives NGOs who work directly with and within the community a definite unique advantage. Moreover, we are able to build bridges and trust between academics and activists as well as with the community. Another important advantage for us especially as MOSAIC is being able to produce policy papers, academic articles, and research reports in Arabic, which in our region is still quite rare, as there is often little engagement by NGOs with academic research. Most academic institutions in the MENA region do not or are not able to work on SOGIESC issues. Furthermore, our work relies heavily on evidence-based knowledge. This knowledge then guides us to formulate practices and projects when planning future work that can be carefully designed to meet the needs identified by the research, advancing the community's current situation. Having this research and evidence makes it harder for state and non-state service providers opposed or reluctant to engage on SOGIESC issues to ignore it.

Henri: Having conducted research both in NGOs and academic institutions, both settings have their benefits and drawbacks. There are three main advantages of conducting research through an NGO: first, there is much greater flexibility amongst NGOs compared with academia in terms of being able to do research on much shorter notice. Second, the best local NGOs have built contacts and relations of trust with the research participants through service provision and outreach. Third, NGOs often have greater possibilities of 'giving back' something to research participants as compared with approaches which might prioritize academically valued outputs such as peer-reviewed articles. Such outputs are important academically, but are mostly of little tangible value to the research participants, especially as they are often inaccessible, being written in a foreign language, and hidden behind a paywall. That is not to deny that many academics in a personal capacity do 'give back' and engage themselves socially, politically, and otherwise, but academia as an institution often does not do so or encourage this. This is different for those NGOs that work directly with the communities, where there is more of a possibility to provide direct support, such as legal aid, referral to services, or the like.

There are, however, also downsides to NGO research. One of these is a trend towards the outsourcing of sensitive and potentially risky research to NGOs, especially locally based, Global South organizations, which do not have the safety nets of Global North institutions, such as insurance policies, the possibility of evacuating staff, or financial reserves that they can draw on. Second, while NGOs are more flexible in doing research, the time and resources are generally minimal compared with academia, and often the donors of NGOs do not care as much about research as they do about project implementation. Academia is also able to draw on a great array of theoretical and methodological frameworks, tools, approaches, and debates that may not be accessible to NGOs.

I think with MOSAIC we have also been very fortunate in being able to engage fruitfully with academia, such as in our collaboration with LSE, as well as with civil society, bridging some of the gaps between the two. This has allowed us on the one hand to build our research capacities and skills, and also use the possibilities and connections we have as an NGO to support our research participants more concretely through support services or other means, such as documenting their experiences through short films.[6]

Pınar: For me, one of the main purposes of our research is to raise the voice of LGBTIQ+ people and to help improve the lives they live by using our findings for advocacy both at the international and local level. Many research participants I interviewed told me that as LGBTIQ+ refugees who have been subjected to violence and discrimination in Syria, Lebanon, and Turkey, they needed to talk about their experience and they needed to be heard, despite how hard it is for them to talk about it. I heard many of them saying: "I am telling my story so that it does not happen to anyone else again." I believe that NGOs play a key role in raising the research participants' voices.

NGOs are able to make an impact through direct contact with research participants and the community as well as through service provision. Specific impacts might include creating awareness through advocacy meetings conducted with local and international institutions, training to local actors (such as healthcare workers, security forces, legal practitioners), enhancing existing services in referred institutions, and preventing discrimination against the research participants and the broader community.

What are your experiences of doing research on diverse SOGIESC? What have been your greatest insights from the research?

Charbel: Our research aims to benefit the LGBTIQ+ community, in particular those members who face increased risks. This includes, for example, those who are undocumented, are from less privileged socio-economic backgrounds, or have had less opportunities to get an education. For our research design, we usually start with focus group discussions with these people. We then let their concerns, input, and feedback guide us in designing our research. Therefore, a good amount of our projects stem from their needs that they highlight to us in an organized, studied manner. As a result, our participants' feedback has so far been positive in the sense that they see their realities reflected appropriately throughout our work. We seek to do justice to their everyday lived realities taking details and nuances into account. The positive feedback we have received for doing this really validates our work.

There are a lot of obstacles when it comes to working in research, whether it is from the political, the safety, or the socio-economic side. COVID-19 was definitely among the biggest challenges, hampering our research given the day-to-day difficulties the pandemic has created, including the limitations on the ability to do in-person interviews or focus group discussions. This has, for example, delayed our research on LBT women refugees' experiences in Lebanon and Turkey, as we were not able to have in-person meetings or travel outside our places of residence.

Research for me is about having focused awareness. Given that a lot of NGOs and other actors (for example, UN agencies) rely on our data, we need to make sure to reflect the real needs of the community as accurately as possible. Moreover, our research gives extra visibility to the community in general, and shines a light on the needs of those among us who are facing more difficulties.

Pınar: Research for me is the starting point of establishing evidence-based programmes tailored for refugees of diverse SOGIESC. In order to assess their needs and the gaps in specialized service provision or awareness-raising activities, service providers and humanitarian organizations need reliable research findings and data analysis. Research is not only useful while building and shaping the content of programmes tailored for persons of diverse SOGIESC, but also to access funding required to establish such programmes. Basically, whether an NGO or humanitarian organization receives the support of international donors depends on how convincing the research findings are.

One of the key research gaps is the explicit focus on the impact of sexual orientation and gender identity and its intersectionality with gender. Another one is the gap regarding research on violence and discrimination against women of diverse SOGIESC. A further gap that I would see is in the lack of research on bisexuals, which leads to bisexual erasure. All of these gaps in existing research reinforce the approach of seeing gender through a binary lens and obscure the experiences and intersectional vulnerabilities of women of diverse SOGIESC. This may result in overlooking the effects of sexual orientation and gender identity in the root cause of certain forms of violence (for example, so-called 'correctional rape', enforced marriages, marital rape) and discrimination, which therefore creates a barrier in establishing prevention and response mechanisms tailored for the needs of persons of diverse SOGIESC.

One of my greatest insights from conducting research with an international NGO (Human Rights Watch, 2020) was to see how central local partner organizations are for external researchers to be able to reach research participants. These local partners are essential conduits and potential gatekeepers, and it is essential that the relations between research participants, local partners, and external researchers are all based on trust and ethical research principles. Reaching out to a variety of organizations in the initial scoping phase is crucial to ensuring this, and avoiding selection bias or worse, such as research participants being put at risk or research being exploitative. Initial scoping and engaging with local partners is also crucial for understanding the context and identifying safe spaces to conduct your interviews in.

Henri: For me, there is still a very strong tendency, especially in the policy world, to homogenize the different people who are subsumed under the labels 'LGBTIQ+' or 'persons diverse SOGIESC' rather than really thinking through what role gender and its expressions, age, class, disability, and so on, play. I feel that there has often been more of a focus on gay (often urban, middle-class) men's experiences, as they have had the comparative space, privilege, and social capital to be heard and engage with researchers more than others, including especially women of diverse SOGIESC as well as those in rural or socio-economically disadvantaged locations (see also Moussawi, 2020). That is not to discount the very real vulnerabilities and needs of gay men, but rather a call to expand and nuance our scope of inquiry. This is why we as MOSAIC have sought, to the degree possible, to question ourselves and see if we are missing out on particular groups or individuals, and what we could do to address those gaps.

One of the greatest insights from the research for me has been realising the immense emotional and psychological costs of constant, everyday xenophobic, classist, sexist, misogynist, homophobic, and/or transphobic microaggressions refugees of diverse SOGIESC face. As a researcher, I have often focused more on 'big ticket' issues such as war, conflict-related sexual violence, transitional justice, and so on, but what really struck me was the toll that these seemingly smaller violences have on people's lives—the incessant drip-drip of disparaging comments, of disapproving looks, of hurtful 'jokes' at one's expense, and the need for constant vigilance (see also MOSAIC, 2020).

In terms of obstacles and overcoming them, I am simply amazed by how my colleagues, especially in Lebanon and Turkey, are able to keep on navigating and negotiating the ever-growing list of challenges over the past few years. The growing difficulties do, however, take a toll on everyone in society, and we need to also take self-care seriously as researchers and activists (see Resource Guide II, this volume).

What for you have been the biggest frustrations in doing research on diverse SOGIESC?

Charbel: My biggest frustrations thus far have been the limitations in funding which have forced us to cut down a lot of plans and tasks that would have really benefited the community. Allocation of resources has not always been taken seriously, and there have also been cases of fraud and deception from people falsely claiming to undertake projects related to the LGBTIQ+ community, flying under the radar.

Throughout the last couple of years, we have been unable to affect change at the local and national level, as our policies and concerns are not being taken into consideration by policy makers in Lebanon and other countries in the region. This has been really frustrating as well. This is due to the dominance of socially conservative, strongly heteronormative and patriarchal norms across the region, which are maintained by often illiberal political systems.

Another frustration has been the gap between words and deeds of Western governments when it comes to refugees of diverse SOGIESC. Even though there is a lot of talk about supporting SOGIESC rights in the Global South, when people actually have to flee oppression and try to seek asylum, there is little openness and all kinds of barriers are erected. Only a few allies are willing to support the refugees. I experienced this when trying to get Western countries to accept LGBTIQ+ activists from Afghanistan after the Taliban took power in 2021. I was also surprised by how many people assumed that there are no SOGIESC rights activists in Afghanistan!

Pınar: One of the biggest frustrations in doing research on persons of diverse SOGIESC in countries such as Lebanon and Turkey is knowing that the dissemination of research findings at the local level (that is, media, governmental institutions) will be challenging and maybe almost impossible. This is due to various reasons, such as the hostile socio-political environment towards persons of diverse SOGIESC in both countries. The constant political and economic instability also means that there are always other, seemingly more pressing issues that people have to focus on. This makes it challenging to achieve uptake locally to allow for positive change from our research. Another frustration linked to this same matter is the difficulty in convincing Global North INGOs to conduct research related to SOGIESC in these countries, since they are seen as a 'lost cause'. Since it seems very unlikely for this research to have a short-term impact in these countries when it comes to LGBTIQ+ rights, especially due to the impossibility of advocacy at the governmental level, the Global North INGOs might prefer not to invest time and money on research and reporting in these countries.

Henri: I think one of my main frustrations has been the mismatch between the massive needs and concerns that we see coming out of our research data, and how little we can do to address them. This is a frustration we also hear from our respondents—what good does another research report or policy paper do? I think there is a risk sometimes of research fatigue, especially among refugees and forced migrants whose needs are 'assessed' regularly by NGOs and UN agencies, but their fundamental situation often does not change as a result. I am also often disheartened by how much standing power patriarchy and other systems based on exploitation and inequality have. But as never-ending as the struggle feels (and most likely is), not doing it is also not an alternative for me.

Another frustration is the co-optation of SOGIESC rights as an issue to try and underscore supposed 'Western superiority' vis-à-vis societies and cultures constructed as being more 'backward', and Ghassan Moussawi (2020) has written about this insightfully in the Lebanese context. I think the risks of 'homonationalism' and the abuse of SOGIESC rights for essentially racist and xenophobic purposes are real, especially in the Global North.

Do you feel the research has any impact? On whom? And why/why not? How could the research be of more benefit to the research participants?

Pınar: I think the kind of applied research we do has an impact on multiple parties, such as the intended beneficiaries, NGOs, and humanitarian organizations providing services and support to the LGBTIQ+ community (for example, Human Rights Watch, 2020, 2021a, and 2021b; MOSAIC, 2020). Research enables LGBTIQ+ communities to be visible in policy discussions, service provision, humanitarian aid, and within the eyes of donors.

I believe that it is more beneficial to the research participants when they, along with local rights activists and NGOs, are consulted from the start and play a role in shaping the research, as they know what's happening on the ground and are best placed to identify their needs. They are also in direct contact with the community, local and governmental institutions on a daily basis, which I believe is key to making an impact and pushing forward. Participatory approaches also give participants more of a sense of agency, which can be very important for people whose needs, insights, and concerns have historically not been heard or taken seriously. That said, we also have to be careful not to overburden research participants with our demands on their time.

Henri: I do feel that the research we are doing has an impact, though not as much and as quickly as we would wish. Unfortunately, as Charbel and Pınar pointed out, there is often little openness among national or local state actors for our research, but over the years I have seen a lot of new interest and engagement from international actors such as INGOs, some donors, and UN agencies, which is encouraging. Even more importantly, while governments may be reluctant or unwilling to engage and socially conservative forces are on the rise, there is also simultaneously an increased acceptance in civil society more broadly for SOGIESC rights being a central cause. What I also find encouraging, exciting, and inspiring is traversing the divide between NGO work and academia through the research that we do. Although NGO research is by its nature often more utilitarian than academic research, it is always good to also step back and reflect critically on what it is we are doing with the help of the kinds of critical tools that more academic research gives us.

Notes

[1] We have chosen to mostly use the term diverse SOGIESC, but also use the term LGBTIQ+ (lesbian, gay, bisexual, trans, intersex, queer, and other) interchangeably. Please note that the examples we refer to here in our conversation will not cover all identities and aspects of diverse SOGIESC and LGBTIQ+, which we in no way mean as exclusionary but is rather a reflection of how our research participants self-identified.

2   This is not to say that academia as a whole has not engaged with LGBTIQ+ and diverse SOGIESC issues in the past. On the contrary, there is a wide and vibrant debate on these issues in many disciplines, but mainstream studies of political science, IR, conflict, peace, and displacement continue to remain largely un-gendered, let alone take diverse SOGIESC perspectives into account.
3   https://mosaic-mena.org/
4   https://thegenderhub.com/projects/changing-sogie-in-conflict-peace-and-displacement-in-the-mena/
5   This has been compounded by economic crises in Lebanon and Turkey, and the scapegoating of refugees for the economic situation and political corruption.
6   See, for example, www.youtube.com/watch?v=uC9URXBqLIs and https://youtu.be/wRq67sr5lic

Bibliography

Åhäll, L. and Gregory, T. (eds) (2017) *Emotions, Politics and War*, Abingdon: Routledge.

Assi, Y., et al (2020) 'A rapid gender analysis of the August 2020 Beirut Port explosion: an intersectional examination', *UN Women, CARE, UN ESCWA, ABAAD, UNFPA*, [online]. Available from: https://reliefweb.int/sites/reliefweb.int/files/resources/Rapid%20Gender%20Analysis_August%202020%20Beirut%20Port%20Explosion_October2020.pdf

Cockburn, C. (2004) 'The continuum of violence: a gender perspective on war and peace', in W. Giles and J. Hyndman (eds) *Sites of Violence: Gender and Conflict Zones*, Oakland: University of California Press, pp 24–44.

Human Rights Watch (2020) '"They treated us in monstrous ways": sexual violence against men, boys, and transgender women in the Syrian conflict', *Human Rights Watch*, [online] 29 July. Available from: www.hrw.org/report/2020/07/29/they-treated-us-monstrous-ways/sexual-violence-against-men-boys-and-transgender

Human Rights Watch (2021a) 'Lebanon: refugees, migrants left behind in vaccine rollout', *Human Rights Watch*, [online] 6 April. Available from: www.hrw.org/news/2021/04/06/lebanon-refugees-migrants-left-behind-vaccine-rollout

Human Rights Watch (2021b) '"They killed us from the inside": an investigation into the August 4 Beirut blast', *Human Rights Watch*, [online] 3 August. Available from: www.hrw.org/report/2021/08/03/they-killed-us-inside/investigation-august-4-beirut-blast

International Crisis Group (2020) 'Easing Syrian refugees' plight in Lebanon', *International Crisis Group*, [online]. Available from: www.crisisgroup.org/middle-east-north-africa/eastern-mediterranean/lebanon/211-easing-syrian-refugees-plight-lebanon

Kaplan, R.L. et al (2016) 'Suicide risk factors among trans feminine individuals in Lebanon', *International Journal of Transgenderism*, 17(1): 23–30.

Kıvılcım, Z. (2017) 'Lesbian, gay, bisexual and transsexual (LGBT) Syrian refugees in Turkey', in J. Freedman, Z. Kıvılcım, and N. Baklacioglu (eds) *A Gendered Approach to the Syrian Refugee Crisis*, Routledge: London.

MOSAIC (2020) *Impacts of the Syrian Civil War and Displacement on SOGIESC Populations*, Lebanon: MOSAIC.

Moussawi, G. (2020) *Disruptive Situations: Fractal Orientalism and Queer Strategies in Beirut*, Chicago, IL: Temple University Press.

Myrttinen, H. and Mastonshoeva, S. (2019) 'From remote control to collaboration: conducting NGO research at a distance in Tajikistan', *Civil Wars*, 21(2): 228–48.

Myrttinen, H., Khattab, L., and Maydaa, C. (2017) '"Trust no one, beware of everyone": vulnerabilities of LGBTI refugees in Lebanon', in J. Freedman, Z. Kıvılcım, and N.Ö. Baklacıoğlu (eds) *A Gendered Approach to the Syrian Refugee Crisis*, London: Routledge, pp 61–76.

Oxfam (2021) *Queer Community in Crisis. Trauma Inequality & Vulnerability. An Assessment of the Impact of the Economic Crisis, Pandemic and Beirut Blast on Queer Individuals Living in Lebanon*, Beirut: Oxfam.

Reid, G. and Ritholtz, S. (2020) 'A queer approach to understanding LGBT vulnerability during the COVID-19 pandemic', *Politics & Gender*, 16(4): 1101–9.

Rivas, A.M. and Browne, B.C. (eds) (2018) *Experiences in Researching Conflict and Violence: Fieldwork Interrupted*, Bristol: Policy Press.

Salem, M. and Shaaban, Z. (2020) 'Queers in quarantine: between pandemics and social violence in Lebanon', *Fes-Lebanon.Org*, [online]. Available from: www.fes-lebanon.org/fileadmin/user_upload/documents/-covid-19/Queers_in_Quarantine___Between_Pandemics_and_Social_Violence_in_Lebanon.pdf

UNHCR (2017) '"We keep it in our heart": sexual violence against men and boys in the Syria crisis', Geneva: UN High Commissioner for Refugees.

UNHCR (2021) 'Turkey fact sheet', *UNHCR*, [online]. Available from: https://reliefweb.int/report/turkey/unhcr-turkey-fact-sheet-september-2021-entr

WFP, UNHCR, and UNICEF (2020) '2020 vulnerability assessment of Syrian refugees in Lebanon', *WFP, UNHCR and UNICEF*, [online]. Available from: https://reliefweb.int/sites/reliefweb.int/files/resources/VASyR%202020.pdf

Wibben, A. (2016) *Researching War: Feminist Methods, Ethics and Politics*, Abingdon: Routledge.

Conclusion: Thinking (of) Queer Conflict Research

Laura Sjoberg

Most of 'conflict research' in the fields of politics and International Relations (IR) has, for decades, treated questions about sexes, genders, sexualities, and race as irrelevant to how conflict is conceptualized, understood, and discussed. When these issues are discussed in conflict research, they are often treated as variables which can be analysed without fundamentally changing either the substance or the methodology of conflict research as is traditionally understood. Early feminist scholars derided this approach to gender as 'add women and stir'—suggesting that the idea that scholarly work can incorporate gender without *thinking differently* is both intellectually and normatively problematic. Cynthia Enloe (1989) illustrated this point very well in a discussion of the US military—Enloe suggests that the increasing presence of women in the US military will not *automatically* change the military into a less masculinist institution. Instead, Enloe (2000) points out that, without other intentional substantive change, a US military organization with an increased number of women in it would be a masculinist institution with more women in it. It would take rethinking what the US military is, what it does, and how it works to change the gender dynamics in it—not just changing the sex balance of its soldiers.

An analogy to conflict research shows the importance of books like this one. Certainly, it is important for the field of conflict research to become welcoming or inclusive of those who have previously been excluded from its ranks, independent of any effect that it may or may not have on the substance of the field. But the inclusion of more diverse researchers in the field does not automatically change how research in the field works. A number of scholars have written about interacting with a field which imposes traditional understandings of the appropriate subject of research, appropriate definitions of what knowledge is, appropriate research methodologies and methods, and how to account for the results of completed research. These interactions can stifle creativity, restrict the substance of research, and maintain boundaries even when they appear to have been made permeable or even lifted. Cynthia Weber (2015: 29) argues that the imposition of the traditional standards of the field plays an intentional role in rendering invisible Queer IR as such, through homologization, figuration, and gentrification. As such, narrow views on what research is and how it is done staying a part of a presumed-inclusive field means that the field continues to be shaped by old (White, Western, masculinist, cisheteronormative) questions and old (White, Western, masculinist, cisheteronormative) ways of addressing those questions. Starting at feminist, queer, and decolonial questions necessarily looks different than starting at the traditional parameters of conflict research, as the authors across this book demonstrate convincingly.

Mimicking a key insight from Carol Cohn (2011) about feminist security studies,[1] thinking about queer conflict research has often been, for me, a question of how to relate to the 'conflict research' as such. Particularly, thinking about both representing queerness in the field and transforming inquiry inspired by queer concerns, I am interested in how much queer conflict research is to be shaped by ontological, epistemological, methodological, and political commitments of feminisms and queer theorizing and how much the research is to be shaped by the (often conflicting) inherited practices of the field. To the extent that queer conflict research is to be shaped by the former, how does one determine and navigate those commitments? I had always assumed that some balance of compromise was in order, perhaps even tilting towards catering to the inherited practices of the field in order to slowly move the parameters of the field of inquiry by incremental change. Others, like many of the contributors to this volume, envision queer conflict research *led by* 'telling queer stories of confronting political violence' (Hagen, Ritholtz, Delatolla), think about how to do that research, and provide examples of its commitments.

This volume largely starts at those questions and looks to map conflict research from queer. As Jamie Hagen, Samuel Ritholtz, and Andrew Delatolla note in the Introduction to this book, 'queering conflict studies extends beyond the study of LGBTQ people's experiences of political violence during conflict', including but not limited to having important implications for what the research is, how it is conducted, and how it is presented. Addressing what queer conflict studies research looks like is the key work of this book. Envisioning a future for queer conflict studies that complicates and even transforms how conflict research is performed, what it examines, and what it means, the authors across this volume consider seriously the theory and practice of 'queer conflict research'—in particular, exploring 'new approaches to the study of political violence'. These 'new approaches' consider how methods and methodology can be queered, and what that means for conversations between queer conflict research, feminist security studies, Queer IR, and critical work in security and transitional justice. It does so in three parts dealing with different dimensions of what queer conflict research is and how it works: queer approaches to conflict research, queer methods in the practice of conflict research, and addressing queer experiences of conflict research. Across these parts, this book provides key insights into what it looks like to do queer research in conflict studies, and what queer conflict research's political and epistemological commitments might be. This Conclusion looks at lessons learned across the book part by part, and makes some observations about potential futures for queer conflict research.

Queer approaches to conflict research

One of the key questions inherent in thinking about doing queer conflict research is what it means to approach conflict research from queer perspectives. A multi-layered approach to the question of what 'queer conflict' research and queer 'conflict research' might look like underlies several of the chapters in this book in different ways. The part on queer approaches to conflict research deals with how to navigate a field of 'conflict research' which at best ignores and at worst trivializes 'queer' as such (especially Chapter 4), how to define knowledge for queer conflict research (especially Chapter 5), and the ways that looking at different parts of queer views and queer experiences show different things (especially Chapter 6). All of these are important theoretical and practical questions for what queer conflict research is and can be.

In the first chapter, Samuel Ritholtz's 'The "queer" in conflict research as subject, structure, and method' confronts the difficulties of doing research in a field where many of the scholars make assumptions that make invisible queer research. When Ritholtz and other Queer IR scholars say that many scholars make assumptions that make invisible queer research, it might seem like a complex claim, but it is really one that is quite intuitive if we think about it. When the parameters of a conversation are set in a way that implicitly excludes alternatives, then it is uncomfortable to try to find the alternative, and it becomes somewhat invisible. Consider this frequent conversation-starter in circles where I grew up: "When are you going to get married?" While the question is innocent enough, and unproblematic to many who make the same assumptions about social and sexual life as the person asking the question, it does make several assumptions that make invisible alternatives. Those assumptions include (but are not limited to): that the person being asked the question is interested in a lifelong relationship with one other person (of the opposite sex), that the person being asked the question is interested in the institution of marriage, that heteronormative views of how relationships work apply to the person being asked the question, that someone is (or may at some point be) interested in marrying the person being asked the question, that getting married is itself a normative good, and so on. Being at the receiving end of this question seems simple and straightforward if you are say, cisgender, straight, in a heteronormative relationship, interested in making that heteronormative relationship into a marriage, and interested in sharing your relationship 'progression' with those around them. But being queer in a heteronormative space and being at the receiving end of this question can evoke a variety of emotions from awkward humour to genuine trauma. The very possibility of many non-heteronormative life choices is made invisible by the assumptions in the question.

In some ways, such is also the case with research on conflict. While the metaphor does not correspond one-to-one on an affective level (at least for me), sometimes the questions IR scholars ask and consider relevant already preclude the subjects, objects, and theories of interest to queer conflict research. For example, early in my IR education, I was taught that it was quite important to be able to account for 'the causes of World War I'—which would be a test of the viability of any theory of security. Putting aside the specific concerns of queer conflict research, I can now articulate my discomfort with that question on myriad levels: assumptions about the definition of what counts as the world for the purposes of 'world war'; assumptions about what counts as war and what counts as not-war; assumptions about the primacy of war in theorizing security; assumptions about the possibility, nature, and determinacy of cause; assumptions about the reliability of narrative information about the past; and assumptions about what is relevant information and what is not to determining 'a' 'cause' of 'war', to name a few. At the time, these were just parameters to a field that made me feel strange, and that was that. Now, in addition to articulating some of those general concerns, I can also ask questions inspired by my interests in feminist and queer questions, including but not limited to what assumptions about sex, gender, and sexualities are necessary to make the figurations of states and war possible; how those figurations change over time and space; how to best understand LGBTQ+ experiences in/of conflicts; what is learned from thinking about LGBTQ+ lives in relation to conceptualizing and understanding what conflict is, and so on. Those questions, though, were made invisible by the question of 'the causes of World War I' as phrased, even when they were seen as important in other disciplinary contexts and conversations.

My experiences as an undergraduate student in the 1990s do not seem that different from Ritholtz's experiences as a graduate student decades later in the 2010s. Ritholtz explains that, as a graduate student, they encountered a situation where 'the scholars of political violence at my university did not focus on queer-and-trans lives' and those who did queer work were largely in humanities departments. As such, support for doing queer conflict research was necessarily going to come from non-traditional places, and charting a path to do that work would necessarily be more complex than doing research for which there were more traditional structures of institutional support.

This story is an important one told by many scholars of queer (as well as feminist and decolonial) IR, where figuring out some of the ontological, epistemological, methodological, and normative dimensions of the research required a combination of intellectual entrepreneurship (for lack of a better term) and non-traditionally formed networks. That said, Ritholtz's chapter shows an impressive result of a non-traditional path of academic inquiry in two forms: the relatable narrative of looking for research support, and a set of important and clear insights into what queer conflict research is and how it works and/or might work. Ritholtz usefully suggests that there are three key ways to think about 'queer' in 'queer conflict research': 'queer as a subject, queer as a structure, queer as a method'. All three of these approaches have something, but something slightly different, to contribute to thinking about and doing queer conflict studies. Queer conflict studies can think about queer lives and queer subjects; queer social and political structures; and/ or queer ways of thinking about 'the world' as such. Some work that sees itself in the research programme does one of these things; some work does all of these things. Some scholars who set the boundaries of the field would be inclusive of minimalist approaches; others would suggest that all three are necessary. This becomes what Ritholtz calls an 'ontological tension in queer conflict studies'—is it about studying orientations or is there a certain epistemological approach, or both?

Ultimately, this is a key question for scholars of queer conflict studies, and maybe for the field as such (or maybe not, as striving for coherence may be one of those assumptions that the discipline as such always makes but may not be justified in making). Either way, the question of what the contours of the field are and what maps work for research in the field is one that researchers must confront. Ritholtz's chapter provides a suggested answer (in an 'intersectional approach to recognize how sexuality and gender as organizing principles of society that preserve hegemonic orders, among other exclusionary social structures, impact the research process'), but its key contribution is much greater than that very useful answer. Its key contribution, like one of the key contributions of this volume, is in providing future and developing members of the research programme with a vocabulary, a guide, and an example of how to navigate these issues in designing a research project—towards an end that (perhaps) most of queer conflict studies *can* agree on—looking to 'challenge hegemonic forms of knowledge'.

José Fernando Serrano-Amaya's Chapter 2, 'Queering the politics of knowledge in conflict research', focuses directly on the question of what knowledge is for queer scholarship and how to conceptualize it in terms of other views of knowledge in the field of conflict research. Particularly,

Serrano-Amaya is interested in yet another boundary that academia sets that does not make sense when thought about in terms of lived experiences. For as long as there has been work in conflict studies, researchers have looked to claim objectivity or disinterest in the result of their research, and a related divide between academic and political/activist work. I remember one of the early things I read in the field of conflict studies was Stephen Walt's (1991) post-Cold War 'The renaissance of security studies', where Walt, whose research to that point had largely focused on nuclear deterrence, argued that it is important to be detached from the results of one's research rather than personally or emotionally invested. My first reaction to reading that was how much sense it makes: research *must* be better if one is not invested in the result. A second reaction came soon thereafter, however: is it not impossible to be *disinvested* in the result of nuclear deterrence? Would that not mean one would, by extension, be *disinvested* in whether or not there was a nuclear war? Of course, years earlier, Carol Cohn (1987) had made a similar point much more clearly that I possibly could either then or now—as have a number of feminist, queer, and decolonial philosophers of science over the years: *people* are in the research in a wide variety of ways, and denying that is just another form of making invisible.

The recurrence of this point in feminist and queer research is a starting point for Serrano-Amaya, who proposes seeing 'interactions between academia and activism as fluid, heterogeneous, and in constant intersections' rather than as separate or separable. What happens next in the research process, though, is as important to Serrano-Amaya as starting with that set of assumptions. Focusing on the multiple and complex intersections between the world 'out there' and academia as such allows Serrano-Amaya to bring attention to the knowledge politics of those interactions. Particularly, this chapter notes that the level and type of attention given to different situations by scholars *means something*—and not only in the sense that it is politically important that conflict research sometimes ignores queer lives and queer structures and neglects queer methods. Instead, when (and how) LGBTQ+ subjects are addressed in conflict research also has a politics, which Serrano-Amaya suggests merits analysis.

In particular, Serrano-Amaya argues that 'it is important to discuss why violence against LGBTIQ individuals and collective has sometimes been rendered invisible while in other times made a matter of consideration'. Other scholars doing queer conflict research have suggested that hypervisibility of queer lives has often been a tool of pinkwashing or neoliberal imperium, and Serrano-Amaya argues that these and other possible frameworks are important to consider, given that both silence *and* recognition carry political implications for scholars of and scholarship in conflict research. As Serrano-Amaya explains, 'regimes of representation' can 'intersect to create a system of expertise' on LGBTIQ *people* and *issues* in global politics. Rather than taking that system of expertise as a given, Serrano-Amaya encourages queer conflict research scholars to consider, and interrogate, the political implications of *who* focuses on LGBTIQ issues and *how*, both in the policy world and in the academic world.

Jamie J. Hagen's Chapter 3, in important ways, takes up that challenge, asking how LGBTQ-focused conflict research would be affected by analytically centring queer women, and why queer women are often neglected by both feminist research on women in conflict and queer research on LGBTQ+ persons in conflict. As Hagen notes, 'queer women continue to fall between the cracks in both research about women in conflict as well as research about LGBTQ (lesbian, gay, bisexual, transgender, and queer) experiences in conflict'. As a result, Hagen is interested in thinking about what it would mean to make queer women *representationally* more visible, and what that increased representation might mean for the empirical and theoretical substance and politics of queer conflict research. Particularly, Hagen challenges readers to think about the ways that 'queer thinking challenges what security looks like, especially if committed to decolonial, anti-militaristic practices'. Putting Hagen's challenge together with Serrano-Amaya's might even generate thinking about the unique role of queer women in militarisms and anti-militarisms. Hagen's chapter suggests that there are also important theoretical lessons to be learned, including combining feminist concerns about gender essentialism and queer concerns about pinkwashing to move 'beyond the dangerous narratives of rescuing queers' to make room for complex, multidimensional, and intersectional research interested in the pursuit of epistemic and practical justice in global politics, rejecting sexisms, cisheteronormativities, and their intersections.

My takeaway from reading this group of chapters is a combination of aspirations and cautions about mapping the field of conflict research—many things (good and bad, if the world were that simple) that queer conflict research *can* be, both in 'the field' of conflict research and in the 'world' in which conflict is being researched (putting aside for a second the false dichotomy required to make that distinction). Some are aspirational: queer conflict research *can* make 'conflict research' broader, more accountable, and more comprehensive; it can take account of genders, sexualities, and intersectionalities in key ways; it can contribute to (more) complicated thinking about the positionalities of researchers (with)in research; and it can highlight exclusions within inclusions, and the complex relationships between exclusion, inclusion, and cisheteronormativities—to name a few. Others, though, are cautionary—queer conflict research is not (and cannot be forced to carry the burden of being) a panacea answer to all of the (raced, sexed, classed, gendered, colonial) problems of research(ing) (in/of) global politics generally and conflict specifically. Any way of doing/writing about queer conflict studies is likely to address some problems with conflict studies as such which reifying either those same problems or others, and likely to have silences, engage in (epistemic) violences, and remain 'incomplete' even as it might criticize and attempt completeness all at the same time. Queer approaches, then, are important to discuss—and perhaps the substance in those discussions *is* the queer conflict research, rather than some idealized understanding that whatever queer approach or queer approaches are constituted in those discussions are some sort of formula for what 'good' research ought to be and/or look like.

Queer methods of conflict research

Nowhere are these questions more crucial than when we talk about how to perform queer conflict research. If the first part talks about approaching and experiencing conflict research through/in/of queer perspectives, the next part of this book is interested directly in what it looks like to *do* that research. Rather than looking to provide a comprehensive manual of all possible methods that can be used to perform queer conflict research, the four chapters in this part provide considered, well-designed, and well-executed examples while walking the reader through the methodological considerations made in putting together the research project. As such, they are not made to be emulated, but instead to be learned from, and, as a reader, I really enjoyed learning from each of them in different ways.

Dean Cooper-Cunningham's Chapter 4, 'The visual as queer method', situates queer conflict research in/with the 'visual turn' in global politics, suggesting that the visual can be an appropriate and helpful method for doing queer conflict research. As a number of the theoretical and auto-ethnographic contributions to this volume have related, Cooper-Cunningham observes that 'queerness has always had a close and complex relationship with (in) visibility'. Given this, what is and is not seen has always been a question in queer research in and across global politics. Cooper-Cunningham suggests that this means that visual methods for queer conflict research might be a good fit.

Cooper-Cunningham clarifies that visual methods are not always and necessarily queer, however. Citing Lauren Berlant and Michael Warner, Cooper-Cunningham argues that nothing is inherently queer per se. Instead, Cooper-Cunningham argues that visual methodologies can be made queer, and productively so. He suggests that, 'since our methodologies are invariably inflected by our queer theorizing and thinking, they become queer the moment they are put in service of queer research or queer political projects'. Cooper-Cunningham then argues that it is both intellectually interesting and politically important to deploy visual methodologies in service of queer research and queer political projects. This pairing is central to Cooper-Cunningham's view that the international politics of sex is appropriately studied at least in part by thinking of how it is and can be seen.

Andrew Delatolla's Chapter 5, 'Poetry as a queer epistemological method', starts with the argument that traditional ways of knowing are often paired with and related to traditional expressions of knowledge. Delatolla points out that traditionally constituted textual academic knowledge often 'is generated by White (Western) and hetero-masculine bodies, traditionally for White (Western) and heteronormative-masculine bodies'. Sourcing knowledge differently is related to thinking differently about what knowledge is, and Delatolla argues that this extends to thinking about queer method as rising from thinking about queer knowledges—links between lived experiences, ontologies, epistemologies, and methods are essential to understanding what it means to *do* queer conflict work. While there are a variety of ways in which this could be approached by scholars in the field, Delatolla focuses on one that has been an expression in his own research—thinking about knowing conflict studies through poetry and literature.

As Delatolla explains, 'poetry and literature can also act as a queer methodological tool to intervene, question, reinterpret, and transform how we think about issues, and, in particular, conflict and war'. On the one hand, this seems like a fairly straightforward point when thinking about knowledge broadly—the poetry and literature of war(s) and conflict(s) have played a fairly significant role in making up the corpus of knowledge that any collective 'we' feel like 'we' have about the past as such. On the other hand, two aspects of the application of poetry and literature in the context of queer conflict studies make Delatolla's argument both novel and important. The first aspect of this application is the disciplinary context—where conflict studies has systematically delegitimized knowledge that does not take a particular (White, heteronormative, 'scientific') form by the regular promotion and reification of a set of particular forms of journal article and book processes which use exclusive forms and standards to keep 'our' ways of knowing war(s) and conflict(s) that have otherwise been commonplace in many contexts across time and place. In this sense, the (re)introduction of poetry and literature *as knowledge in conflict studies* is transgressive of the narrowing of knowledge key in constituting the inherited field. Here, Delatolla's emphasis that poetry and literature can play a key role in 'revealing multiplicities and disrupting linear logics of conflict' is an important intervention—not because it is telling 'us' something necessarily new, but because it is pushing to (re-)expand the ways of knowing that the field legitimizes. The second aspect of this application is the things that particularly queer deployment of poetry and literature have to offer. In particular, using the case of Adnan's *The Arab Apocalypse*, Delatolla suggests that a 'queer feminist epistemic engagement' has unique contributions to disrupting linearity, temporality, and inherited accounts of trauma. Delatolla both shows that the text being analysed is queer conflict research *itself* with key insights about conflict that cannot be sourced elsewhere, *and* that Delatolla's textual analysis is another form and layer of queer conflict research. As Delatolla explains, Adnan interrupts inherited knowledge about the Lebanese Civil War, and I would add that Delatolla's analysis of Adnan's work adds a key dynamic to that disruption. With Delatolla, I think that this has important implications not only for how to think about the Lebanese Civil War or even how to think about doing queer conflict research, but also (and perhaps most importantly) how to think about doing conflict research better.

The importance of developing methodologies for queer conflict research to do conflict research better is also a key theme in Patricio Simonetto's Chapter 6, 'Queer tools for the ruthless archive'. The title of this chapter is itself important and innovative, simultaneously arguing for queer and trans methodologies for archival work and arguing (perhaps contra implicit or even explicit understandings in conflict research) that historical work is (and is central to) conflict research. In this chapter, Simonetto argues against a number of inherited assumptions about queer histories and their place in conflict research. One of the key assumptions that Simonetto contradicts is the idea that doing queer histories of conflict is somehow (no more and no less than) an exercise in revealing what is hidden by heteronormative histories of those same conflicts. As Simonetto explains, 'there is a widespread belief that queer history is a work against invisibility' where 'we usually start our research projects convinced that we will set light on all the lives erased by the heterosexual gaze'.

With Simonetto, I think that it is important to note that doing queer conflict history work cannot be reduced to making visible (or, perhaps problematically, promoting the hypervisibility of) the queer in conflict. Using the example of the archival production of the Medicine College at the University of Buenos Aires, Simonetto demonstrates that, *methodologically*, queer historians are confronted with a wide variety of ethical questions from what to make visible, how to treat historical subjects that do not necessarily fit neatly into the categories that 'we' might use 'today' (with both concepts showing a unity they do not have), and how to make sure that queer scholarship is about *reading history differently* instead of adding 'new' subjects (who frequently are not that new to begin with). These complexities are methodological, but they are also substantive, where how these questions are dealt with have implications for what history is, what conflict is, and even what queerness is. Simonetto then suggests that a 'queer sensibility' might be a good way to think about how to *do queer history* well, and therefore *do history well*.

Citing Kadji Amin's *Disturbing Attachments*, Simonetto explains that 'queer historians have contributed to developing a sensibility that helps us know the risks of the demand for stability in historical writing' among other risks.

Rather than look for a coherent, streamlined, linear narrative with fixed concepts and actors, approaching historical analysis with a queer sensibility rethinks history as such. As Simonetto explains, such a queer sensibility can produce an 'uncomfortable feeling that boosts the formulation of questions to distrust stable and teleological narratives', which means archival research is not looking to 'add' new people or tell the stories of the previously invisible (or previously hypervisible) in terms of the previous norm. Instead, it is looking to tell the different, disjointed, complex, and fraught stories that one sees when one thinks about histories of/with/in the queer. While, on the one hand, '"queer sensibility" should help us be aware of the limits and potence of our position as writers of historical narrative', the same work that Simonetto does showing these limits also shows the potentialities of queer historical research to see and think conflict otherwise.

A wide variety of ways to do queer conflict research then arise—varieties of media, varieties of forms of analysis, varieties of lenses looking at different phenomena, and varieties of ways to disseminate results of research (however conceptualized). A few takeaways from this part come to the surface for me. First, with multiple chapter authors, what queer conflict research is *about* influences the methods used to do it at every turn: from thinking differently about interview methodologies because of queer vulnerabilities to deploying queer temporality in analysis of poetry, *queer research needs queer methods*. Second, also with a number of the chapter authors, no method is inherently queer (and perhaps no method is inherently incompatible with queer research, though this may be more hotly contested)—instead, as Simonetto notes, applying a 'queer sensibility' to all possible research tools is important to make sure that they work for queer (conflict) research. Third, and perhaps most complexly, there is no one queer approach to conflict research, no one queer experience of conflict research, and no one queer method for conflict research—nor are all possible approaches compatible or fellow travellers. On the one hand, this is an opportunity—to take queer critiques of understandings of knowledge cumulation into understandings of the research field as such. On the other hand, it is a challenge—to look to understand futures of queer conflict research in plural ways.

Queer experiences of conflict research

This might be all the more important for questions involving queer experiences of conflict research, which are necessarily both broad and contextual, both fundamental and unresolvable. These are the questions that the third substantive part of this book asks, focusing on addressing questions about how queer conflict research is experienced by researchers, and engaging some of the challenges of doing research inspired by what can be thought of as queer lenses. Though each of the researchers writing in this part take slightly different views of what it means to do (and therefore to experience) queer research, they share taking 'this emerging field of research seriously, as well as the legacy of queer and feminist research those queering conflict research are in conversation with today' (Hagen, Ritholtz, Delatolla) and therefore asking what roles queerness plays in research practices. The same way that there are multiple (both complementary and contradictory) views of what taking 'a' queer approach to conflict research might be, there are multiple, intersecting and diverging, experiences of (and views of experiences of) queer conflict research. This part addresses questions of how to talk about queer lives (in conflict and in researching conflict), navigating the complexities of lived experiences for researcher and researched, and the intimate/lives of research/researcher in the field, among other key questions of experience.

Chitra Nagarajan, in her chapter, 'Researching queer lives in the shadow of north-east Nigeria's conflict', discusses the many concerns that need to be taken into account in mapping methodologies for studying queer lives in conflict contexts. Noting that 'despite our efforts, very few queer people in north-east Nigeria whom we contacted were willing and able to be involved', Nagarajan elaborates on the importance of looking at methods to address power, ensure safeguarding, and maximize benefit to queer people. These methodological concerns are sharpened in queer conflict research because queer research subjects can 'face specific harms' including but not limited to discrimination, fear, less access to institutionalized resources, and less ability to report conflict sexual violence. As such, it is ever more important to 'identify and provide areas of support required' rather than doing research that ends up being extractive. In the face of a number of state and non-state actors which often dismissed or actively opposed queer rights, Nagarajan and her research team found the need to balance multiple concerns about the safety of research subjects, urgent needs in conflict zones, and complicated social situations. Nagarajan's chapter brings up important questions about how to talk about researching queer lives, how to do ethically responsible research, and how to do that research in a way that is productive for, rather than extractive of, those people whose lives are being researched. Recognizing that both researcher and researched live queer conflict research, Nagarajan shows both several key directions that effort can, should, might and even must go to address experiencing research through/in/as queer, and the necessary incompleteness of any strategy to address these complexities in heteronormative conflict contexts in/across global politics and the study thereof.

Chapter 8, Ahmad Qais Munhazim's 'Entangled intimacies, queer attachments', integrates the positionality of the researcher into discussions about experiencing queer conflict research. Resisting the reduction of queer conflict research to research about queer people's lives, Munhazim engages questions of gender, sexuality, nationality, and positionality among and between queer researcher and the research. Munhazim's chapter explores ways to 'decolonize intimacies and queerly re-imagine relationships, attachments, friendships, and chosen kinships that are formed as a result of shared experiences of violence and surveillance, displacement, and war'. While traditional conflict researchers suggest that doing their research can be separated from the personal, feminist and queer researchers have long argued that disentanglement is not only impossible but also undesirable. Munhazim notes that the neoliberal imperium that is academia, confronting homophobia and racism both in its institutions and in its texts. Explaining that they were trained in an academy that asked them to assume that their own people were homophobes who would never accept them, Munhazim writes about un-learning their heritages as a survival mechanism. Finding queer conflict research more complicated and multi-layered than the inherited discipline accounts for it as, Munhazim discusses delicately claiming queer space, finding a 'queerness informed by Afghanness', and doing research grounded in 'critical intimacies and feminist care'. Munhazim's chapter provides insight into (queer) conflict research as multidimensional, multi-layered, intimate, affective, and entangled. The messy world that Munhazim sees, lives, and writes about is one that shows the importance of queer approaches and queer methods in this chapter and across the parts of this book, as they are unfathomable without (and difficult to navigate with) the many complex and contingent tools of queer research.

In the conclusion conversation piece, Zeynep Pınar Erdem, Charbel Maydaa, Henri Myrttinen, and Helena Berchtold also discuss the dynamics of doing research into queer lives in conflict, with particular attention to NGO research with diverse SOGIESC refugees in Lebanon, Syria, and Turkey. The authors explain that, despite academic interest in queer lives in conflict, most research continues to be conducted by NGOs. When the queer refugees they study face 'already-difficult situations' exacerbated by the multiple complexities in their host country, the authors noted that NGOs have many advantages in adapting to complex research situations, including direct local contacts, greater flexibility, and a greater possibility to give back. At the same time, NGOs have some disadvantages, including a lack of the infrastructure present in academic institutions and common funding limitations. Whoever is doing the research, Erdem, Maydaa, Myrttinen, and Berchtold emphasize 'the need for intersectionality and understanding different vulnerabilities' to do queer conflict research both responsibly and well. Their chapter goes over many of the dimensions that are necessary to take into account when doing queer conflict research, and gives some insight into the complexities of doing research in this field, as well as the complexities of queer experiences of conflict. In many ways, this part can be seen as a microcosm of some of the complexities in, and debates within, queer conflict research: does researching queer/SOGIESC/gender and sexual minority communities make conflict research queer? What does queer conflict research mean for queer bodies in/of conflict? In what ways are queer bodies in/of conflict *war bodies* in Swati Parashar's (2014) accounts of what it means to live wars? What are the multiple ways that we can think about the queer in conflict and in conflict research, in theory and in practice? These are all important questions, and a number of the contributions in this volume reckon with them in indispensable ways. In the end, it may be about multiple answers to these questions rather than about one answer or even a set of answers—but they are crucial to ask.

Futures of/for queer conflict research

Overall, I think this edited collection shows exciting futures of and for queer conflict research. The research contained and discussed in this book shows queer conflict research as both diverse and vibrant. From queer conflict research, it is possible learn about the entangled intimacies of doing queer conflict research as a part of/in a 'diaspora of war' (Munhazim) and to learn about SOGEISC rights work done by NGOs in Turkey (Erdem et al), among many other different aspects, locations, and views of queerness in/of conflict research. The theoretical and empirical contributions that this field of research has made are only surpassed by the contributions it will continue to make as it grows—and this collection is a testament to the existing and future strength of the many research programmes that can be thought of as queer conflict studies.

Perhaps even more than that, though, the ways in which this collection can serve as instructive for the development of research in the field are very exciting. Each of these chapters offers experiences with, perspectives on, and advice about doing queer conflict research that can serve to guide the future research plans of not only the contributors in this book but also scholars and students who pursue queer conflict research in the future. Across this volume, whether in analysing poetry (Delatolla), doing archival work (Simonetto) or interviewing in the field (Nagarajan), the contributors lead by both example and instruction. The lessons included both in their research and in their presentation of that research can help to navigate difficult practical, ethical, theoretical, and epistemological questions. Researchers building on this work can both take lessons from that work and build methodologically in conversation with it—such that conversations about the possibilities for queer conflict research are a key part of queer conflict research.

The futures of queer conflict research, then, are multiple and potentially transformative, and can reach beyond the traditional performances of conflict research across the field. There are many things that queer conflict research *can* be, all of which have strengths and limitations, promises and silences, 'answers' and incompleteness—all stakes in choices about what queer approach and what queer methods are used to do conflict studies research. The more one explores those multiple possibilities, the more one can see high levels of complexity and contingency, alongside many tough questions about queer researchers, queer experiences of researching, queer experiences of being researched, and queer experiences of conflict(s), either narrowly or broadly understood. Next to these varieties of approaches and multiple contingencies are questions of method, necessarily linked to but not the same as questions of ontologies, epistemologies, and politics. The combination of tough questions and multiple forms of knowledge making and knowledge sharing mean that queer conflict studies is in for tough conversations—about how to *think about* queer research, about how to *plan* queer research, about how to *do* queer research, and about how to *evaluate* queer research. At the core of those tough conversations, though, is a commitment to both *telling queer stories* and (relatedly and beyond that) thinking about conflict differently.

In my view, the ability to accomplish both of those things is *in* the conversation, the debate, the disagreement, and the unresolvable nature of some of the key tensions across this volume. Queer conflict studies is also in the feeling, the awkwardness, the difficulty, the impossibility, and the intimacy of queer approaches to and experiences of conflict research. Rather than some idealized understanding that whatever queer approach or approaches one scholar or one chapter here uses, queer conflict studies is best seen in their intersection, conversation, and perhaps even divergence. In this way, a volume set to discuss epistemologies, methods, and even ontologies of queer conflict research might be *necessarily* multiple and inconclusive—and that might be among the contributions of queer approaches, queer experiences, and queer methods. What the contributions to this volume share is queer questions (Rao, 2014) and queer intellectual curiosities (Weber, 2016)—the multiple different approaches that they find are the appropriate result of those two commonalities, rather than a set of debates that need to be resolved to find one preferred path.

Note

[1] Cohn (2011) suggests that 'feminist security studies' as such is different depending on which two of the three words are grouped together, where 'feminist security' studies would be led by feminist commitments, and feminist 'security studies' is led by the existing field understood to be 'security studies'.

Bibliography

Cohn, C. (1987) 'Sex and death in the rational world of defense intellectuals', *Signs: Journal of Women in Culture and Society*, 12(4): 687–718.

Cohn, C. (2011) '"Feminist security studies": toward a reflexive practice', *Politics & Gender*, 7(4): 581–86.

Enloe, C. (1989) *Bananas, Beaches, and Bases: Making Feminist Sense of International Relations*, Berkeley, CA: University of California Press.

Enloe, C. (2000) *Maneuvers: The International Politics of Militarizing Women's Lives*, Berkeley, CA: University of California Press.

Parashar, S. (2014) *Women and Militant Wars: the Politics of Injury*, London: Routledge.

Rao, R. (2018) 'The state of "Queer IR"', *GLQ: A Journal of Lesbian and Gay Studies*, 24(1): 139–49.

Walt, S. (1991) 'The renaissance of security studies', *International Studies Quarterly*, 35(2): 211–39.

Weber, C. (2015) 'Why is there no queer international theory?', *European Journal of International Relations*, 21(1): 27–51.

Weber, C. (2016) *Queer International Relations: Sovereignty, Sexuality and the Will to Knowledge*, New York: Oxford University Press.

RESOURCE GUIDE I

Guide for Good Practices for Researching Queer and Trans Communities in Highly Sensitive Contexts

Cristian González Cabrera, Erin Kilbride, Kyle Knight, Yasemin Smallens and Rasha Younes

Human Rights Watch's LGBT Rights Program

Outline

Introduction	219
1. Deciding to conduct research	220
2. The spectrum of sexual and gender minority experiences	221
Case study 1: Where are the lesbians?	222
3. Interview process and selection	223
Part 1: Interview design	223
Case study 2: Syria: supporting interviewees during research on sexual violence against men, boys, and trans people	225
Part 2: Interview outreach	226
Part 3: Interview encounter	228
Case study 3: Iraq: remote interviewing and security guidelines	230
4. Context-specific security planning	232
Case study 4: Aceh: leaving a hostile environment to improve safety	234
5. Trauma-informed research techniques	235
Case study 5: Saint Vincent and the Grenadines: engaging trauma on interviewees' terms	236
Conclusion	239

Introduction

Sexual and gender minority (or LGBT) populations in contexts affected by political violence, conflict, and other crises—which we refer to as 'highly sensitive contexts'—face a range of safety, security, and retraumatization risks that researchers should consider and address at all stages of the research process: in training, design, implementation, and review. This guide draws on the experience of the authors, who are Human Rights Watch (HRW) researchers, in conducting investigations with LGBT populations in different situations around the world. It makes recommendations based on HRW's core standards and protocols[1] for human rights investigations, including in highly sensitive contexts.

The guide is not meant to be exhaustive or comprehensive; instead, it intends to offer insights into key considerations researchers should undertake when working with sexual and gender minority populations in highly sensitive contexts. The subjectivity of trauma can overlap with the subjectivity of queerness in particular ways, some of which this guide attempts to unpack in examples researchers have encountered. Adopting ethical good practices in engaging with LGBT people in such situations is particularly important given the levels of trauma they experience as queer people that are further exacerbated during crises.

The core methodologies discussed are grounded in general HRW standards, which have been developed over 40 years of practice documenting human rights abuses in virtually every context around the world. For this guide, we translate the general standards, principles, and practices in HRW's research guidance, which has been used to train researchers for several years, to focus on issues of sexual orientation, gender identity, and gender expression as they relate to research participants' identities and experiences of abuses that may or may not be based on their sexual orientation or gender identity. In other words, our discussion is applicable to conducting research with queer and trans people whether or not the research is specifically focused on queer or trans experiences.

This guide begins by addressing the importance of analysing how sexual orientation and gender identity occur in unique contexts, and will provide guidance on factors to consider when doing this analysis, such as understanding the interaction between pre- and post-crisis contexts, the shifting individual and communal priorities, and the dynamics of survival, resilience, and informality. The guide then suggests steps to take in designing interview projects, including tips on how to reach out to potential research participants, anticipate criticisms from perpetrators or sceptics, take account of biases in 'snowballing sampling', and other methodological concerns. Lastly, the guide delves into planning for security issues that impact researchers, participants, and third parties such as interpreters, and shares guidance on conducting research with a trauma-informed approach grounded in the 'do no harm' principle. The guide is interspersed with case studies of HRW research projects to illustrate the tips and guidance shared.

HRW works for LGBT peoples' rights, and with activists representing a multiplicity of identities and issues.[2] We document and expose abuses based on sexual orientation and gender identity worldwide, including torture and other ill-treatment, killing and extrajudicial executions, arbitrary arrests, unequal treatment, censorship, medical abuses, discrimination in health and jobs and housing, domestic violence, abuses against children, and denial of family rights and recognition. We advocate for laws and policies that will protect everyone's dignity.

1. Deciding to conduct research

The visibility that HRW investigations bring to violations against LGBT people is both a critical tool that can be utilized by local activists leading struggles for rights and justice, and a potential risk that could result in retribution. While this guide focuses on mitigating these risks, an equally important analysis for each potential project is whether to embark on the research. The decision to pursue an investigation with LGBT communities should centre their own assessment on both the benefits and risks associated with visibility. The decision-making process should include:

- An honest exchange about the power dynamics at play (for instance, between an international non-governmental organization (NGO) and a local human rights organization), and a plan to mitigate these dynamics should the local organization wish to pause, cancel, or withdraw from the project at any stage.
- A thorough risk assessment.
- A comprehensive advocacy strategy that maps the rationale and feasibility of a project.

At the same time, LGBT rights defenders have raised concern that international NGOs often deem visibility for local queer activists 'too dangerous' in a particular context, including when visibility is being explicitly sought by the activists as part of their advocacy and security strategy. In 2022, for example, several lesbian, bisexual, and queer (LBQ+) rights defenders interviewed as part of a global scoping on the rights of queer women told HRW they faced rejection by international NGOs who declined to feature them in reports and campaigns for liability concerns, overriding the activists' own risk assessment and desire to make visible their work. This denial of visibility thwarted the queer women activists' ability to secure funding and strategic partnerships, making their movements less secure, sustainable, and resilient in the long run. The analysis and expertise of local LGBT activists is central not only to how to conduct research, but also whether to conduct it at all.

2. The spectrum of sexual and gender minority experiences

It is critical that researchers analyse how sexual orientation and gender identity, as facets of individual and communal lives, interact with social, political, and material contexts. This is particularly important as situations shift from ordinary and 'stable' to extraordinary and violent. Individuals, and even whole communities, do not have static priorities; instead, their priorities shift in line with resilience and survival strategies for specific circumstances. In this calculus, when discrimination and violence is heightened, and social structures that provided a modicum of safety and security are disrupted and eroded, queer and trans people may be forced to conceal their sexuality and gender or alter their gender expression in order to survive.[3]

With this framework in mind, researchers seeking to engage networks of sexual and gender minority populations in knowledge production should strive to unpack the nuances of 'political violence' or 'conflict'. Political violence can build very quickly or over time. At times, the antecedents of acute sensitivity or fragility were part of daily life long before the circumstances garnered broader attention. As a marginalized group in many contexts, sexual and gender minority populations often experience discrimination and unequal access to services and opportunities regardless of—though certainly partially determined by—broader political circumstances. Paying careful attention to not only the 'extraordinary' context, but also the 'ordinary' pre-crisis one, will help the researcher determine the additional effects of political violence or conflict to LGBT people. For example, armed conflict or humanitarian crises put LGBT people at heightened risk; however, these risks often exacerbate pre-existing ordinary risks due to colonial-era criminalization and ongoing political homophobia (HRW, 2008).

It is also very important to acknowledge survival, resilience, and informality. Research necessarily assumes a certain level of formality. While design and preparedness are critical to ethically undertaking research, fluid sexual and gender minority experiences in highly sensitive contexts may clash with the rigidity of structured questionnaires or evidentiary hierarchies inherent in research endeavours. Instead, researchers should provide research participants the space to share stories of how they creatively navigated anti-LGBT political violence and resilience that rigid methodologies may obscure. Researchers should consider less restrictive methodologies in their research design, which may be crucial to informing security protocols, behaviours, and even research outcomes.

Case study 1: Where are the lesbians?

In 2022, HRW undertook its first global investigation on violence and discrimination against lesbian, bisexual, and queer (LBQ+) women. The research was motivated by the severe lack of LBQ+ data in most human rights areas, and the urgent need for documentation and recommendations specific to their experiences. The research demonstrated how existing LGBT research has typically poorly captured the human rights abuses most affecting LBQ+ women and non-binary people. Key takeaways included:

- *LBQ+ women are not safer than other queer people.* The report found that despite immense physical, sexual, and economic violence, there is a 'persisting myth' in the human rights field that LBQ+ women and girls have 'more space, safety, and freedom in society than queer men and boys, including to explore their sexuality' (Human Rights Watch, 2023). This stems, in part, from the fact that many anti-sodomy laws do not explicitly criminalize same-sex conduct between women. But the idea that LBQ+ women are somehow safer for being ignored discounts how sexist and patriarchal violence impacts every aspect of their lives.

  More than two-thirds of our LBQ+ interviewees referenced and critiqued that myth, noting that these alleged freedoms stem from the devaluation of women, their sexuality, and their intimacies. Legal regimes around the world deny women full personhood; in fact, the lack of explicit criminalization of queer women's sexual conduct proves this point. LBQ+ sex decenters the traditional prominence of men, so it is delegitimized to the extent of not qualifying as sex at all. It falls outside the knowable bounds of criminalization in many homophobic contexts, not because LBQ+ women are accepted, but because they are radically devalued. Colloquially, this implies that LBQ+ lives are somehow 'easier' for being neither visible nor legitimate enough to criminalize or regulate. (Human Rights Watch, 2023)

- *LBQ+ women and non-binary people face unique forms of violence and discrimination.* Very few interviewees raised the criminalization of same-sex conduct, gender affirmation laws, or same-sex marriage. Instead, across 66 interviews in LBQ+ activists, human rights defenders, lawyers, and community leaders in 26 countries, some of the most common themes were: forced and coerced marriage; women's land and property rights; violence by security forces against masculine-presenting women, regardless of their sexual orientation or gender identity; and the need to visibilize and protect LBQ+ human rights defenders.

- *Interviewees are the experts.* Victim and survivor testimonies should dictate, not merely inform, researchers' framing, analysis, and key findings. Given adequate space, interviewees can teach you how to frame your research. The research for this report would have looked radically different if HRW researchers had approached interviews with a pre-set list of LGBT topics in mind, and simply asked about how lesbians

experience those violations. Women's property rights and sexist inheritance practices, for example, would likely not have been included.
- *LBQ+ activism comes in many forms. It may not match what you think you're looking for.* LBQ+ activists are leaders in a wide range of environmental, economic, gender, political, minority rights, Indigenous, and racial justice movements. Many of the names or stated objectives of LBQ+ organizations are outside the bounds of what is typically conceptualized of as 'LGBT rights' work. A bisexual woman in Indonesia told HRW that her collective focuses on minority rights, and building solidarity between queer, Indigenous, and ethnic minority groups. It is not safe or strategic to market this work as 'LGBT rights', but is fundamentally queer in its approach. In conflict zones, LBQ+ women are often found on the front lines of humanitarian support, but do not advertise themselves as LGBT activists.
- *Structural barriers prevent LBQ+ organizations from registering.* LBQ+ organizations are unlikely to be formally registered with their governments, due not only to discriminatory legal restrictions or security concerns faced by all LGBT people, but also because women often have less access to formal education, legal support, and funding needed to register an NGO. LGBT rights researchers can help close this gap by ensuring that formal registration with the government is not a prerequisite for partnership.

3. Interview process and selection

This section describes good practices gleaned from HRW's approach to designing the interview, soliciting participants, and conducting the interview itself.

Part 1: Interview design

Constructing an interview requires accounting for information about the highly sensitive context, methodological and ethical requirements, and security concerns. To that end, the researcher should:

A. *Create a list of interview topics and a questionnaire.* While most HRW interviews are semi-structured and flexible, a questionnaire helps ensure consistency across interviews to establish patterns of experiences or abuses or to corroborate an event. Discuss and vet these questions with your relevant colleagues and partners.
B. *Translation.* Translate the interview questionnaire into the local language(s) where the interviews will be conducted and ensure that terms related to sexual orientation and gender identity reflect the nuances of the local language(s).
C. *Anticipate criticisms from perpetrators or sceptics.* Where feasible from a methodological and security perspective, seek information from

perpetrators and sceptics to include in the data set. Include questions that will provide you with relevant information to respond.
D. *Leave no one behind.* Include perspectives of all people, and design questions to uncover a range of experiences and intersectional identities. Security permitting, contact local LGBT leaders, activists, or networks ahead of the research project to learn how the crisis is affecting their communities. This will help researchers know what to look for, without demanding disclosures from interviewees that may be dangerous, intrusive, or traumatic.

Examples include:
- When interviewing forcibly displaced women, consider how to frame questions that capture their unique experiences or relevant protection gaps without requiring an interviewee to disclose their sexual orientation or gender identity.
- Ask whom they travelled with. Try to ascertain if they are travelling without a male partner, as this exposes them to additional risks. Do not assume that a particular marital status indicates sexuality, or vice versa.
- If they have children, ask what their main concerns about their children's futures are. Try to ascertain what their legal relationship to their children might be.
- Ask questions about care responsibilities. Understanding the guilt, shame, and societal pressures a woman is under regarding leaving her family is critical to unpacking her experience of displacement.

E. *Conduct mock interviews with a colleague.* This is a good way to get constructive feedback on your ability to address sensitive, complex, or painful topics while helping you become more comfortable with conducting such interviews. If you are working with an interpreter, do the mock interviews with your interpreter so they are equally prepared. Do these mock interviews until you are comfortable discussing and receiving information about the topic.

F. *Adopt a trauma-informed approach.* You may be interviewing someone who is revealing an abusive episode or other distressing information for the first time. The process of participating in the interview may be distressing to the interviewee.

To reduce the risk of harm and retraumatization, you should:
- Adequately prepare and plan for the interview, including by assessing risks (noting that sometimes it may be unethical to interview an individual due to the risks) and preparing a referral list.
- Ensure the interviewee has a sense of control over the interview, including when to take a break or stop.
- Avoid probing into graphic or specific details unless critical for the research *and* the survivor is willing to discuss them.
- End the interview in a 'safe space' and the present moment, including by asking about their hobbies, children, or plans after the interview.
- Provide a referral list.

G. *Create a referral list.* As a researcher, you are likely unable to provide direct assistance to interviewees. However, you can—and should—share a referral list of service providers and details (such as location and contact information), translated into the interviewees' local language(s), and connect interviewees to services if they wish. It is thus essential to build time into your preparation to identify service providers and into the research phase to explain the referral list and provide contact details to interviewees. The list should include, at minimum, well-regarded service providers of psychosocial and medical healthcare, legal aid, housing or shelters, children's services, and advocacy groups.

Other factors to keep in mind when preparing and sharing the referral list:
- *The availability of informal services.* Include community-based support groups.
- *The accessibility (physically and economically) and quality of services.* Avoid making referrals to services that are far away, costly, or have a reputation for being discriminatory or insensitive.
- *The appropriateness of services.* For example, if LGBT NGOs are primarily run by men, consider whether their services are appropriate and non-discriminatory for LBTQ people and what alternative services may be necessary.
- *Safety and appropriateness of leaving a referral list with the participant.* If it is unsafe or inappropriate to leave the list, explore other options, such as designating a local contact (often an NGO or activist) who can provide this information as needed. In some situations, it may be appropriate to ask participants for their permission so you can refer their case to a trusted NGO worker or counsellor.

H. *Follow up with the interviewee after the interview to provide additional referrals as necessary.* If the interviewee indicates a specific, unforeseen need that the services on your list are unable to address, we believe researchers have an ethical obligation to explore potential services for those unforeseen needs afterwards and provide additional referrals in a safe and secure manner through a local contact or secure messaging.

Case study 2: Syria: supporting interviewees during research on sexual violence against men, boys, and trans people

In 2018 and 2019, HRW researched sexual violence against men and boys in the Syrian armed conflict (Human Rights Watch, 2020). The interview part of the project, which occurred almost exclusively in Lebanon, was inherently complex and sensitive at every stage.

During the initial outreach, researchers encountered difficulties gaining the trust of potential interviewees. Given these challenges, researchers took extra steps to ensure the comfort and safety of interviewees and also shared a referral list that had been prepared beforehand.[4]

Three lessons learned:

1. *Understanding and acknowledging that, due to various sensitivities for men and boys in disclosing experiences of sexual violence,[5] outreach and interviewee recruitment would face limitations.* Specifically, it became clear that contacting cisgender heterosexual men would be more challenging than contacting gay and bisexual men, trans women, or non-binary people. We believe this is because existing civil society infrastructure, via LGBT NGOs, allowed for more expeditious and safer contact with these communities than for straight men, some of whom were involved in torture survivor groups but were by and large unwilling to participate in this type of research.
2. *Allowing interviewees to request the presence of a social worker they knew during the interview.* This added level of comfort and control was critical given the subject matter.
3. *Arranging for a psychologist on retainer for interviewees and mentioning this service during the informed consent process.* This decision was taken after a careful assessment of service availability in Lebanon, which was limited, and barriers to services, which were primarily financial.

Part 2: Interview outreach

Research outreach approaches vary across methodologies, and in fragile contexts, they may be heavily determined by pragmatic considerations such as feasibility and security. For example, survey methods that include formal 'snowballing' utilize ticketing systems that generate respondent-driven interviewee samples. Such 'snowballing' informs HRW's outreach, which largely relies on networks of contacts mediated through NGOs, individual activists, lawyers, allied reporters, and academic researchers.

Because COVID-19 movement restrictions altered the way HRW conducted investigations in general, the organization has moved towards using more remote, online strategies for recruiting. In one project, researchers used an online survey to recruit interviewees by allowing them to answer a series of questions in order to familiarize themselves with the research topic and then share their contact information at the end if they wish to participate in an oral semi-structured interview (Human Rights Watch, 2016). This approach is becoming increasingly common because it reduces the burden on NGO interlocutors or 'fixers', and may increase the number of respondents who prefer the survey format to meeting an unknown researcher, or have access to an online survey but not a space or network run by an NGO.

The communications method you choose will impact your ability to reach LGBT people of different genders, social groups, and ages. Consider how to best access four specific communities of people:

1. *People who are older or are living in rural areas* and may not have consistent access to email or the internet to read emailed requests or participate in online surveys. Be sure to work with activists who know the phone numbers, home addresses, or social gathering spaces of older, rural community members.
2. *People who live in countries with low rates of literacy*, as relying only on written communication to arrange interviews would limit participation. Security permitting and accounting for privacy concerns, consider individual or group sessions where participants can hear the text of the study read aloud and provide their consent to participate orally.
3. *People who are linguistic minorities.* Be sure to work with an interpreter who speaks not only the official language of the country, but also local languages, to facilitate the participation of queer Indigenous people.
4. *People who are LBQ+.* Be sure to work with LBQ+, trans, and non-binary activists to ensure representation from these particularly marginalized communities.

In designing outreach strategies that account for literacy and language, local LGBT organizations can assist you in developing tactics to effectively and safely contact potential research participants. As illustrated, there are different outreach and recruitment methods. However, regardless of which approach is chosen, you should follow the same nine core principles apply to engaging with intermediaries and potential participants:

1. Explain in plain language who you are, what your research team or organization does and does not do, and what you will do with the information provided by the interviewee.
2. Explain clearly to intermediaries what your research project covers and what you are seeking so intermediaries do not arrange interviews with individuals who do not have relevant information.
3. Emphasize the voluntary nature of the interview and convey to potential interviewees that, in the case of HRW, we are only gathering information and cannot provide assistance, services, or compensation.
4. Do not pressure anyone who is reluctant to participate.
5. Explain and emphasize the confidential nature of the interviews.
6. Explain to intermediaries that they are bound to respect confidentiality.
7. Explain that we want to avoid retraumatization, which can occur when trauma survivors tell, or retell, their story. Inform intermediaries and potential participants if any researchers on your team have undergone trauma-informed interview technique training and apply their skills to the interview process.
8. Discuss any security risks.
9. Agree with intermediaries on mitigation measures relevant to their partnership with you and to any liaising work they are performing.

Part 3: Interview encounter

HRW uses interviews to document first-hand and witness accounts of human rights abuses as well as to obtain other forms of evidence, such as photographs, videos, medical records, court documents, and the names of other people to interview. During the interview, bear in mind the necessary security considerations for requesting and reviewing documentation. When requesting other relevant documentation, such as legal or medical records, consider whether you have the expertise and time to sufficiently analyse them in the moment or whether you will need to photograph or copy them to take with you for analysis. Both processes require a re-engagement on the terms of consent as the document reveals private information about an interviewee, some of which may not be relevant to your interview topic. If you need to copy documents, you also need to explain how you will securely copy, store, and use your records of the file.

At the same time, you must be aware of security and bias considerations in your snowball sampling. Requesting that interviewees suggest other people to interview can be a fruitful and meaningful way to 'snowball' interviewees—especially since drawing on social networks among sexual and gender minority populations is often critical to undertaking research—requires security considerations. As a non-random sampling technique, it also introduces self-selection biases. First, consider whether it is safe to have an interviewee initiate a conversation with their contacts to explain the research and ask their contacts to share, for example, their email or phone number with a researcher. Second, consider digital security concerns in your outreach method. Use end-to-end encrypted platforms for outreach. Do not include identifying information about the interviewee during outreach. Instruct the interviewee not to share information about the interview, the interviewer, or research team with others without the research team's permission.

As snowballing introduces self-selection biases, consider how to structure the interview to account for potential biases inherent to snowball sampling. For example, if the police detained and mistreated Interviewee A, Interviewee A may suggest Interviewee B as a witness to the human rights violations against Interviewee A. While interviewing Interviewee B, you should not only gather details of the Interviewee A's experience (location, date/time, specific actions and words, attributes of perpetrator, and so on) to corroborate their account, but you should also ask Interviewee B about other information that may be unrelated to this incident but relevant to your research. It is also important to consider gaps that may result from snowballing. Because many LGBT networks are historically led by gay men, the first contact may lead to a contact pool in which LBQ+ people and trans men are underrepresented. In that case, specifically ask for contacts who are LBQ+ women and transgender men. Interviewees are often able to suggest contacts of different sexualities and genders if the researcher expresses a clear desire to document a range of experiences.

The possibility of remote interviews opens important opportunities for research. Remote interviews allow the researcher to reach interviewees in different parts of a country who would not necessarily be included in an in-person mission because travelling around a highly sensitive context may be prohibitively dangerous for either the researcher or interviewee. The remote option also helps some survivors struggling with stigma and shame to feel more comfortable sharing their stories, as they are not physically with the interviewer. In addition, interviewing by phone or other remote means provides the best mode of contact from the interviewee's perspective, since it can be the only accessible, safe, or comfortable mode for interviewees with limited mobility.

At the same time, remote interviews pose distinct challenges in terms of information accuracy, information security, and the safety and well-being of interviewees during and after the interview. During remote interviews, researchers could not perceive contextual or non-verbal cues that are often perceptible when meeting in person. This lack of physical proximity and signs also renders it more difficult to assess the interviewee's credibility and feelings, including whether they were in distress and would be safe after the interview. Location is no longer shared between researcher and interviewee, so researchers need to ensure that the interviewee is not in the presence of others who might intimidate or otherwise inhibit them from speaking freely. In general, it is more difficult to establish rapport and trust with an interviewee when communicating remotely, so researcher should anticipate greater difficulties in raising sensitive topics. While remote interviews expand research opportunities hindered by the lack of ability or capacity to travel and conduct interviews, they also pose distinct challenges in terms of information accuracy, information security, and the safety and well-being of interviewees during and after the interview.

For remote interviews, we recommend researchers:

1. Partner with an institution or organization with in-depth contextual knowledge and contacts with LGBT people in the target research location(s).
2. Conduct a risk assessment before each interview to determine possible risks and a mitigation strategy regarding each interviewee.
3. Securely approach interviewees through trusted individuals who could verify their identity.
4. Build trust with interviewees by communicating at least twice before the interview itself to introduce yourself, your organization, and your project; obtain informed consent; explain the content of the interview; and assess the potential for retraumatization.
5. Provide a referral list, including to psychosocial services, at the end of the interview.
6. Provide a secure and accessible way for interviewees to contact your institution or organization with any feedback, concerns, and complaints or any additional information related to the research.

Case study 3: Iraq: remote interviewing and security guidelines

In 2021, HRW conducted entirely remote interviews on the killings, abductions, torture, and sexual violence of LGBT people by armed groups in Iraq (Human Rights Watch, 2022). The research involved numerous complexities, including an inherently high-risk context where violence against LGBT people is ongoing, difficulties in accessing affected individuals and corroborating evidence of abuses, and increased digital security needs given the remote nature of the interviews.

Risk mitigation strategy

The researcher conducted extensive internal and external consultations to determine the viability of doing remote interviews. In partnership with an Iraqi LGBT rights organization, HRW conducted a risk assessment before each interview to determine possible risks and a mitigation strategy. All interviewees were approached securely through trusted individuals who could verify their identity.

For many interviewees, this was the first time they had ever spoken about the abuses they had experienced. To establish trust, the researcher spoke to most interviewees twice, on separate occasions, before the interview itself. In the first call, the researcher introduced the organization, the people involved, and the project and obtained informed consent. In the second, the researcher familiarized the individuals with the content of the interview and determined what level of retraumatization might result from the interview. The final and third call was the interview itself, during which the researcher reminded individuals that they could take a break or stop the interview at any time.

To circumvent interference, most interviews were conducted late at night to accommodate interviewees who could only speak when their family members were sleeping. The researcher and each interviewee decided on a safe word that the interviewee would use if they were interrupted, could no longer speak freely, or had to immediately stop the interview.

The researcher provided each interviewee with a list of referrals to available services, including psychosocial support, at the end of the interview. The researcher also provided individuals with a secure and accessible way to contact HRW to report any consequences from their participation in the interview, make complaints regarding the interview, including any negative consequences of being interviewed, or provide any other feedback or information.

Surveillance risks and mitigation strategies

There are several threats that may increase the risk to the research participant, and it is important to understand each and how to respond.

<u>Actor-based threats</u> use physical access to the people involved in the remote interview to identify, intercept, or disrupt the integrity of the interview. For example, a family member or partner in the room during a call poses a threat.

Mitigation strategies: If the interview was done via audio only, interviewers made sure to verify the identity of the interviewee by asking for a five-second video to see the interviewee's face and confirmed that they were the same person throughout the interview phases. Interviewees were instructed to take the call from a private location.

<u>Logistic-based threats</u> use access to information about the interview, short of observing the interview itself, to identify the interview's existence or topic or the people involved in the interview. For example, if the interview is done using a traditional phone call, other people may have access to the call history, either on the phone itself or on a phone bill.

Mitigation strategies: Interviewers did not share locations, full names, or other identifying information or locators with interviewees so that interviewers could not be physically located. Interviewers deleted any record of interview calls and notes from their devices. Disappearing messages were enabled on mediums of communication. Interviewees were instructed to delete any record of the call from their devices afterwards.

<u>Device-based threats</u> use physical or digital access to the device of any of the people involved in the remote interview to identify, intercept, or disrupt the interview. They can be used to target the content of a remote interview or the operational information around it. For example, sensitive information about who participated in a call, a phone number or username, or the length or timing of a call.

Mitigation strategy: Interviewees were cautioned against sharing information about their interview with others.

<u>Account-based threats</u> use access to the online accounts, such as email or social media, of any of the people involved in the remote interview to identify, intercept, or disrupt the interview. For example, a partner who coerces access to online accounts or an external attacker who gains access to their attacks through phishing. These threats can target operational information by looking at contacts, calendar events, or call logs. They may also target the remote interview itself by accessing the account to intercept or disrupt the interview.

Mitigation strategies: All online accounts used for communication before, during, and after the interviews were secured with a strong password and multi-factor authentication. The researchers implemented security protocols throughout the research process to avoid entrapment of interviewers and interviewees. This was particularly important in the Iraqi context, where LGBT activists had been entrapped by bad actors on online dating sites.

<u>Service-based threats</u> use access to the services, such as social media platforms or phones, being used for the remote interview to identify, intercept, or disrupt

the interview. These threats are most commonly used by law enforcement and intelligence services.

Mitigation strategy: Only end-to-end encrypted communication channels (Signal, WhatsApp, Wire, JitsiMeet) were used to conduct interviews.

Connection-based threats use access to the connection used during the interview to identify, intercept, or disrupt the interview. Threats to connections can occur at a variety of levels. At the most basic level, an attacker may simply call into a conference call and listen to a remote interview. For example, law enforcement may require local network operators or service providers to intercept calls from and to a specific actor's numbers and accounts.

Mitigation strategy: Staff used VPNs throughout the research phase. A VPN—or Virtual Private Network—is a mechanism that can be used on a computer or smartphone to create a secure connection between two users for communications. There are free VPNs available for download, and they offer an added layer of protection for communications; they are highly recommended for activists and researchers of all types.

4. Context-specific security planning

It is critical to robustly unpack the sensitivities of the context, especially since situations of political violence, conflict, and other crisis have both overlapping and different risks attached. Ask yourself: Does the political situation create a climate of fear, persecution, and abuse with impunity for LGBT people? Are your planned activities likely to contribute to the already heightened risks faced by LGBT people?

HRW's guidelines for working with LGBT communities instruct as follows. Given the systemic, often politicized nature of violence against LGBT people, researchers should intimately understand the context in which violence occurs. Researchers should:

1. *Evaluate how their research institution is perceived in the field site* (by the general population and by LGBT people more specifically) and accompanying security considerations.
2. *Understand that sexuality and gender are rooted in time, place, and culture and are not universal.* Researchers should educate themselves about social and cultural norms, vocabularies, and potentially contested identity categories.
3. *Understand the difference between sexual practice and identity, and do not impose identity categories based on practice.* For example, some men may not identify as gay but routinely have sex with other men. Many LBQ+ women are married to and have children with men due to societal

expectations, norms, and pressures. Quantitative research methods have considered this phenomenon and how to distinguish between identity, practice, and attraction when asking questions (Badgett et al, 2009). In the research preparation phase, the researcher should ask LGBT activists and organizations about language, sexual practice, and signals of sexual identity. For example, some women may publicly identify as a lesbian while other women who have sex with women identify as heterosexual because they are married to a man.

4. *Be aware of barriers that might prevent individuals from reporting violence and be prepared to give appropriate advice about remedial courses of action that may not involve reporting to authorities.* In countries where same-sex conduct is illegal, the risks of reporting a homophobic crime are high because it effectively exposes the individual as gay. This is also true of other non-SOGI-specific incidents due to LGBT people's lack of trust in the authorities and vulnerability to secondary victimization, including from inappropriate questioning.

5. *Proactively establish connections with LGBT organizations, including those focusing on LBQ+ and trans people, or LGBT-friendly NGOs that may be able to provide assistance to survivors of violence*, which will help you create an appropriate referral list. Consider the sexualities and genders of the leadership of the organizations you speak with, particularly how this may skew the representation of sexuality and gender in your research.

6. *Create a safe and comfortable environment for interviews or other data collection experiences to promote disclosure.* Part of this involves understanding that there are often tensions among groups and individuals and how they might impact your research and your participants' experiences. Be sensitive to the fact that even where same-sex conduct is legal, individuals may fear social stigma and keep silent about abuses.

7. *Learn the lingo in the context you are researching.* Understand what it means to be lesbian, gay, bisexual, or transgender—and that none of those terms may be liked or used, including consistently, in a particular context. Understand, for example, if 'butch' and 'stud' are terms used exclusively by lesbians or if they are also used by trans men, as failing to understand these terms could lead to misgendering someone. This is important for background knowledge and to signal your understanding and knowledge, which are pivotal to creating a safe environment and building a rapport based on trust.

8. *Work with interpreters who understand the concerns and issues of the LGBT community you are working with.* The 'LGBT community' is not a monolith. Women interviewees may still be uncomfortable sharing some details with researchers and interpreters who are men; transgender interviewees may feel unable to fully communicate their experience with a cisgender

research team, even if they are all queer. If you cannot hire interpreters who are endorsed by LGBT organizations, search for interpreters within feminist networks that have close ties to the queer community and may be qualified to interpret. Regardless of who is hired, budget time to discuss stigma, stereotypes, social norms, terminology, and ethical interviewing techniques with your interpreters. Bear in mind that your interviewees will consider every member of your team, including interpreters, as a representative of you, your institution, or your organization.

> **Case study 4: Aceh: leaving a hostile environment to improve safety**
>
> Aceh is the only province in Indonesia that has been allowed to develop its provincial laws in accordance with sharia (Islamic law). Due to a peace agreement ending a decades-long armed conflict that granted Aceh semi-autonomous status, its local government has unique laws and law enforcement methods, including a sharia police that, in cooperation with other security forces, has targeted minority populations, including LGBT people, for violating sharia.
>
> In early 2016, HRW researchers were invited by Acehnese activist groups to interview LGBT people in the province and document anti-LGBT incidents as well as the atmosphere created by sharia ordinances that specifically allowed for up to 100 lashes in public as a sentence for those convicted of same-sex behaviour. HRW had on staff two non-Acehnese researchers who had experience working in Aceh. Their visible outsider status was a critical security factor in this highly sensitive context because interviewees observed to be engaging with outsiders were at higher risk of surveillance and violations.
>
> HRW's security and feasibility assessment determined that it was neither safe nor ethical to undertake in-person research in Aceh, but that it was possible to safely conduct interviews in a remote location to which participants travelled for the interviews. HRW identified a safe city outside Aceh with available hotels, relatively simple and affordable transportation, and a local LGBT activist group to provide additional support.
>
> Four lessons learned:
>
> 1. *Outreach to affected individuals should be discrete and may need to happen through several layers of interlocutors who should be reimbursed for their reasonable out-of-pocket expenses.* HRW contacted various individuals, including Acehnese activists who were aware of incidents and could learn specific details through their social networks. Partners inside Aceh were instructed to speak obliquely about the project and, as much as possible, have in-person conversations to avoid introducing security risks from phone surveillance. HRW reimbursed activists willing to undertake such outreach for their fuel expenses related to this extra travel, which sometimes required several hours on motorcycles.

2. *Be mindful of potential hurdles related to the need for legal names and legal genders for travel purposes.* Some participants gave names to staff that were not their legal names; consequently, their airplane tickets were booked under their chosen name, not the name reflected on their travel documents. In some cases, this also occurred with gender markers on ID documents. Indonesia has no formal procedure for legal gender recognition, but the courts have approved some gender recognition cases, so the researchers could not assume that any particular person had or did not have documents reflecting their gender identity. As a result, the staff needed to sensitively and safely re-contact participants to get their legal names and legal genders to adjust the bookings and avoid security incidents at the airport. All these logistical hurdles were weighed against the security risks that would have been introduced by wiring money to individuals inside Aceh so they could book their own tickets.
3. *Have a reasonable cover story for participants.* Once the logistical arrangements, including flights and hotels, were in place, the staff and partners in Aceh developed a cover story for the 16 people who were travelling so they did not arouse suspicion in their own communities when departing or at the airport. It was decided that, based on recent history, it would be reasonable for participants to say they were travelling to the nearby non-Acehnese city for either a 'workshop' or shopping related to their businesses. Partners in Aceh communicated this strategy to participants, some of whom raised concerns regarding the sheer numbers in the group. As a result, half of the group was re-booked on a different flight, and participants' seats were deliberately purchased apart from each other to reduce any suspicion or attention while travelling.
4. *Provide participants with autonomy in coordinating all or parts of their travel.* Some participants raised concerns about the lodging HRW had selected in the destination city and wanted to stay at a place where they felt more comfortable. HRW agreed, cancelled the hotel bookings, and obtained cash equivalent to the cost of the cancelled bookings in appropriate denominations (an effort that took two days due to bank limitations) to give to participants when they arrived. After the research was completed, the partners in Aceh told HRW that allowing participants to coordinate their own journey to an extent made them feel safer and that the process was more genuine. It is important to note that this level of freedom was possible because the security situation for participants was stable outside Aceh. Interviews were conducted over four days, in the researcher's hotel room or an empty hotel restaurant, depending on each interviewee's comfort level.

5. Trauma-informed research techniques

A traumatic event is an event or series of events that causes an individual a lot of stress.[6]

Trauma-informed research methods are critical to working with sexual and gender minority populations, particularly in contexts of heightened sensitivity where experiences of traumatic events may be higher. The research encounter, while important for knowledge creation, advocacy, and other goals, should be guided by 'do no harm' principles as much as possible.

A thorough discussion of trauma-informed research techniques is beyond the scope of this resource guide. However, we have provided tips and resources to help you create a trauma-informed research protocol and establish relevant practices.[7]

Case study 5: Saint Vincent and the Grenadines: engaging trauma on interviewees' terms

HRW researchers investigated the hostile environment that the laws criminalizing consensual same-sex conduct create in Saint Vincent and the Grenadines for LGBT people. Researchers documented cases of physical violence, harassment, sexual violence, and other forms of discrimination. Interviewees were contacted through local human rights organizations. As part of this project, researchers interviewed a 22-year-old gay man whose story illustrates the importance of engaging with interviewees on their own terms regarding the documentation of traumatic events.

All the LGBT people that researchers had interviewed before meeting the gay man had recounted multiple incidents of violence or discrimination and had expressed that Saint Vincent and the Grenadines is deeply homo- and transphobic. However, when researchers asked the interviewee if he had ever experienced direct or indirect homophobia, he said he had not. Researchers politely asked the question in different ways, but the interviewee gave the impression that the situation for LGBT was not at all difficult in the country, which contradicted other interviewees' accounts. The interviewee had a similar socio-economic and racial background as the other interviewees and resided in the same area.

After asking all the relevant questions, researchers began to close the interview, considering that this person's experience was an outlier in the pool of interviewees. At the end, researchers enquired about the interviewee's future, aspirations, and whether he was happy in his country. The tone of the conversation changed dramatically after that point. He began to express a belief that conditions for LGBT people are better elsewhere, and that his ability to live 'comfortably' in Saint Vincent and the Grenadines was limited. When asked if he would leave the country, he responded affirmatively because abroad he 'could get to do more'.

The interviewee never explicitly shared information about what discrimination he or others suffered, but his later comments made clear that the situation for LGBT people in the country was not positive. There could be a host of reasons why he did not offer clearer information and researchers prying could have had a negative impact, such as retraumatization. However, phrasing questions in a more positive manner by discussing his dreams and desires, and thereby engaging with the interviewee on his own terms, led to some insights into what the reality is for LGBT people in the country.

Ultimately, this interview prompted researchers to consistently ask about interviewees' futures and desires for emigration, which revealed a consistent practice on the part of all interviews to envision their futures outside the country and never therein. This was an important finding of the research, highlighting the dire situation of discrimination against LGBT populations.

Three key takeaways:

1. *Be aware that traumatic incidents and experiences are highly subjective.* Some interviewees will not want to share details of these difficult moments, even if they want to support the research.
2. *Respect the boundaries that the interviewee is setting.* While it is good to reformulate questions to make sure you are being clear, do not pry excessively or belabour a particular point.
3. *Do not make assumptions about what is 'useful' testimony during a research encounter.* It may be helpful to explore what interviewees do want to speak about, even if it may not at first appear relevant for the research, to learn more about people's lived realities. This could lead to new insights while centring interviewees' wishes and dignity.

HRW believes a guiding principle to ethical research engagement and trauma-informed techniques is a thorough, consistent, and comprehensible informed consent process. The following 12-step process is adapted from the HRW Interview Manual:

1. *Choose an appropriate location.* Ask the interviewee ahead of time where the safest, most comfortable place to meet is. Consider if the person's partner or family members will be home. Do not make assumptions about who the interviewee wants in the room during the interview or about what 'privacy' looks and feels like to a queer person in this context. For example, a married LBQ+ interviewee may not be out to her husband and may thus want to meet outside her home. At the same time, she may wish to hold her infant child during the interview. Consider your own clothing, transport method, and time of day of the interview, and ask in advance how each of these will impact the interviewee's security.
2. *Introduce yourself (and anyone else present).* Explain what you do, explain what you are doing in this research project, give examples of your work (physical copies in relevant languages are ideal), and ask participants if they have questions. Also explain what you do not do—for example,

tell participants if you cannot provide legal advice or other services—especially if participants may be concerned about the material or personal benefits of participating in your project.
3. *Explain the scope and purpose of the interview.* Explain the topic(s) to be covered in the interview and the aims in collecting the information. Provide an estimate of how long the interview will take.
4. *If you want to record, ask the interviewee for permission to do so.* If you plan to record audio or video, show the interviewee which devices you would use, discuss which portions of their body you can record, and how you would record. Recognize that even if the interviewee consents, it may affect what they say in the interview. Consider how particular devices may be retraumatizing to survivors. Some hand-held audio recorders, for example, appear similar to tasers (stun guns), which may be retraumatizing to survivors of police violence.
5. *Describe how you will disseminate the information gathered.* If you can anonymize the information, explain anonymization, but be realistic and transparent about risks even with anonymization.
6. *Emphasize the voluntary nature of the interview, that participants can stop the interview at any time, and that they can withdraw their testimony at any point.* In some cases, it may help to explicitly describe an example of when another one of your interviewees stopped an interview in order to stress that you were not personally offended and that you will not pressure any participant into continuing their involvement.
7. *Clarify compensation (or the lack thereof) for participation.* HRW researchers clearly state that we do not provide compensation for participation in an interview. If you are operating in a situation where you will reimburse travel expenses, you should emphasize that the interviewee will be reimbursed regardless of how much of the interview they complete.
8. *Discuss potential risks, including any weaknesses in anonymity protection.* For example, if you are interviewing LGBT refugees who live in a refugee camp, clarify whether your publication will name the camp and explain risks that come with that. Show participants how you are recording their names; we recommend using codes for each unique interview and recording real names in a separate document that you store securely apart from your interview notes. If the interview may touch on traumatizing material, mention risks of retraumatization.
9. *Agree on safety measures to mitigate risks, including those to protect identity.* Discuss cover stories (see Aceh case study). Consider asking participants to choose their own pseudonym because this grants a greater sense of control and often helps ensure pseudonyms are culturally appropriate. At the same time, you should ask them why they chose a name (in case they choose a name that introduces security risks of its own, such as

a sibling's name). It may help to show examples of other publications where you have protected identities in photos or with pseudonyms. Discuss how you will record information during the interview (for example, notes, audio recording, and so on).
10. *Discuss referrals.* Have a list of referrals to service providers ready, and mention this as part of the consent process. If it is unsafe or inappropriate to give them the list, explore other safer options (see the relevant point under 'Part 1: interview design').
11. *Provide opportunities for questions and revisit consent.* Both at the outset and again at the end of the interview, ask questions to gauge whether a participant understands the basics of the interview; namely, that it is voluntary, they can withdraw their testimony, and you will protect their identity in certain agreed upon ways.
12. Record consent. Your interview notes should explicitly mention that the person gave consent to be interviewed. HRW does not require written consent for all interviews, but we do for some that come with heightened risk, such as recorded video interviews.

Conclusion

Engaging in research with sexual and gender minority populations in highly sensitive contexts requires attention to the overall situation, potential individual trauma, and security risks and mitigation strategies. Researchers should ensure their research projects account for security risks and are safely implemented in all phases of the research. Carefully designed research acknowledges risks (which always exist), benefits participants (who are better protected) and researchers (who are acting ethically), and allows knowledge production to occur attentive to and minimizing risks of retraumatization or other harm.

We hope this guide, based on our experiences and drawing off of principles that have been developed based on the work of hundreds of HRW researchers, can provide some grounding. It is also critical that researchers working on difficult topics and in difficult contexts protect themselves from vicarious trauma (see Resource Guide II) and other mental health impacts of doing this kind of work. While it is beyond the scope of this guide to discuss effective methodologies, we strongly recommend research institutions and supervisors invest in supporting researchers' mental health.

Notes

[1] Many of the research standards and practices discussed in this guide were consolidated in internal guidance documents for HRW staff by Sagaree Jain and Nisha Varia in 2019. That guidance is not publicly available but reflected here in part.
[2] For a full running list of our publications on LGBT rights, visit: www.hrw.org/lgbt
[3] For example, in research conducted by CARE and UN Women, some queer participants described how their desire for survival took precedence over their desire for free expression

of their sexual orientation and gender identity. One interviewee said: "Based on my personal experience of communicating with friends and acquaintances, I would say that at the moment, the question of survival is still higher than any personal preferences regarding one's way of life or sexual orientation. This is a temporary dynamic that needs to be addressed in peacetime" (CARE and UN Women, 2022).

4   For more on trauma-informed interview techniques, see the 'Trauma-informed research techniques' section later in this resource guide and Resource Guide II in this volume.

5   Conflict-related sexual violence against men and boys is often recorded in surveys, studies, and legal proceedings only as torture or other forms of violence, thereby obscuring the degree to which they experience it and hindering provision of appropriate and specialized services linked to the sexual nature of the crime. Researchers have written extensively on how these cases have been obscured, and how methodologies are now attempting to gather information on this type of sexual violence in a more nuanced way.

6   Centers for Disease Control and Prevention, *Mass Trauma Fact Sheet*, www.cdc.gov/masstrauma/factsheets/public/coping.pdf, p 1.

7   Further resources that provide important starting points for developing a trauma-informed research protocol—one that should integrate a nuanced and context-specific understanding of sexual orientation and gender identity—include: Stanford University's Center for Human Rights and International Justice: Human Rights in Trauma Mental Health Program (Stanford University); UNITAD's *Trauma-Informed Investigations Field Guide* (UNITAD); Bellevue/NYU Program for Survivors of Torture (Center for Survivors of Torture).

Acknowledgements

This resource guide benefited immensely from reviews by Anji Manivannan and Graeme Reid.

Bibliography

Badgett, L., Goldberg, N., Conron, K. and Gates, G. (2009) 'Best practices for asking questions about sexual orientation surveys (SMART)', *The Williams Institute*, [online]. Available from: https://williamsinstitute.law.ucla.edu/publications/smart-so-survey/

Bellevue/NYU Program for Survivors of Torture (n.d.) 'Center for survivors of torture'. Available from: www.survivorsoftorture.org/

CARE and UN Women (2022) 'Rapid gender analysis: Ukraine', *UN Women*, [online] 4 May. Available from: www.unwomen.org/sites/default/files/2022-05/Rapid-Gender-Analysis-of-Ukraine-en.pdf

Human Rights Watch (2008) 'This alien legacy: the origins of "sodomy" laws in British colonialism', *Human Rights Watch*, [online] 17 December. Available from: www.hrw.org/report/2008/12/17/alien-legacy/origins-sodomy-laws-british-colonialism

Human Rights Watch (2016) "The Nail That Sticks Out Gets Hammered Down": LGBT Bullying and Exclusion in Japanese Schools, *Human Rights Watch*, [online] 5 May. Available from: https://www.hrw.org/report/2016/05/05/nail-sticks-out-gets-hammered-down/lgbt-bullying-and-exclusion-japanese-schools

Human Rights Watch (2020) '"They treated us in monstrous ways": sexual violence against men, boys and non-binary people in the Syrian conflict', *Human Rights Watch*, [online] 29 July. Available from: www.hrw.org/report/2020/07/29/they-treated-us-monstrous-ways/sexual-violence-against-men-boys-and-transgender

Human Rights Watch (2022) '"Everyone wants me dead": killings, abductions, torture, and sexual violence against LGBT people by armed groups in Iraq', *Human Rights Watch*, [online] 23 March. Available from: www.hrw.org/report/2022/03/23/everyone-wants-me-dead/killings-abductions-torture-and-sexual-violence-against

Human Rights Watch (2023) ' "This is why we became activists": violence against lesbian, bisexual, and queer women and non-binary people', *Human Rights Watch*, [online] 13 February. Available from: www.hrw.org/report/2023/02/14/why-we-became-activists/violence-against-lesbian-bisexual-and-queer-women-and-non

Human Rights in Trauma Mental Health Program (Stanford University) 'Human rights, mental health, and trauma', *Stanford University*, [online]. Available from: https://humanrights.stanford.edu/human-rights-trauma-mental-health

United Nations Investigative Team to Promote Accountability for Crimes Committed by Da'esh (UNITAD) and the Human Rights in Trauma Mental Health Program (Stanford University). 'Trauma-informed field investigations field guide', *UNITAD*, [online]. Available from: www.unitad.un.org/sites/www.unitad.un.org/files/general/2104429-trauma-informed_investigations_field_guide_web_0.pdf

RESOURCE GUIDE II

'The Emotional Work is Part of the Work': Strategies to Maintain Researcher Emotional and Psychological Safety During Challenging Fieldwork

Maureen Freed

Acknowledging and addressing the emotional and psychological challenges of research is important if queer researchers operating in conflict settings are to remain healthy, functional, and well.

It is increasingly recognized that social science research can place exceptional emotional and psychological demands on the researcher. Over the past 10 to 15 years, many individual researchers have written reflexively about this aspect of their work (for example, Weiss, 2014; Drozdzewski, 2015; Moussawi, 2021). Meanwhile, attention has been given to the experiences of researchers within specific academic disciplines (for example, Loyle and Simoni (2017) on political science; Pollard (2009) on anthropology) and fields of study (for example, Maček (2014) on genocide/mass atrocities; Williamson (2020) and Schulz et al (2022) on gender-based violence).

Some hazards are obvious: the researcher observing suffering, deprivation, cruelty, or injustice day after day is vulnerable to a darkening of worldview. This is exacerbated by feeling increasingly helpless and hopeless in the face of what can seem overwhelming and intractable social and political problems. It can be hard to sustain belief that there is goodness in the world, and value in the work done as researchers. Those who work in difficult and trying fields discover that it is vital to offset negative experiences by balancing them with positive experiences, if the work is to be sustainable.

But in addition, researchers whose work entails engaging directly with *traumatized* research subjects—those whose experiences have overwhelmed their coping capacities and left them with a profound sense of powerlessness—may be at risk of developing symptoms of vicarious trauma (VT), a variant of PTSD arising in response to hearing about and empathizing with traumatized others in a professional capacity (McCann and Pearlman, 1990; American Psychiatric Association, 2013). These symptoms are distressing for many and debilitating for some. They can also be detrimental to the quality and integrity of the academic work: a traumatized researcher's emotional responses can get in the way of seeing their research subjects clearly (Loyle and Simoni, 2017; Shesterinina, 2019). It is therefore very important for researchers to be aware of the risks of VT and to manage this dimension of their research experience in a proactive and thoughtful way.

For queer researchers working in conflict settings, research challenges may be amplified and compounded by both internal and external factors. Internally and intra-psychically, many queer researchers must contend not only with VT, but also with the after-effects of trauma in their personal histories, and with the complex interplay between personal and VT which may leave them feeling that no place is 'safe'; while externally chaos, unpredictability, and ever-present possibility of violence may tax coping resources.

I write not as a queer researcher, but as a White, heterosexual, cisgender woman bringing two perspectives: first, that of a practising psychotherapist specializing in trauma, and working predominantly in a university setting where many of my clients struggle with the issues just described; and, second, as the developer of what as far as I am aware is the only established, university-based training to equip student and staff researchers with the tools to manage the impact of trauma exposure resulting from fieldwork and other sensitive research. This training, offered termly at the University of Oxford since 2016, and more recently at other universities and think tanks, is designed to meet the needs of social scientists researching topics such as genocide, mass displacement of populations, and gender-based violence; scientists studying impacts of climate change, destruction of habitats and extinction of species; medics studying experiences of illness and death; and researchers working on a broad range of issues in conflict and post-conflict settings.

I feel a strong personal commitment to this training because I believe wholeheartedly that for researchers whose work brings them into contact with difficult human experiences, *the emotional work is part of the work*: not a side issue, but a necessary and integral part of the work, if they are to withstand the emotional and psychological impacts and remain solid and strong. It is also essential for the quality and the integrity of the work.

My involvement in this work began in 2015, when the University of Oxford Counselling Service (where I was Deputy Head until 2021) set up a specialist clinic to treat students with trauma-related symptoms. We expected to see students following sexual assault, accident, injury, and the like, but were taken aback by the numbers of students who were social science researchers, both masters and doctoral students, presenting with post-traumatic symptoms arising in response to fieldwork. In some cases, the connection to fieldwork was immediately evident, as when a researcher seeking an appointment wrote on their registration form: 'I've been having nightmares and intrusive images relating to stories I heard during my fieldwork. I'm having a hard time transcribing interviews because I cry uncontrollably and start feeling like I can't breathe.'[1] In other cases, researchers might initially describe symptoms of depression ('In general, I feel very flat and have lost interest in most things') or anxiety ('I feel highly anxious and on edge all the time, am struggling to sleep and I am exhausted and stressed') but when we explored the context in which their symptoms had emerged it became clear that they were related to fieldwork, and in particular fieldwork which entailed vicarious exposure to trauma.[2]

The need for preventative intervention was clear. Our response was to develop training drawing together input from three sources: the collective wisdom of researchers; an understanding of the neurobiology of response to traumatic stress; and finally, insights and approaches from the world of trauma psychotherapy, including those used by therapists to help their clients, and those used by therapists to take care of themselves. Over time the training has grown organically, enriched by the contributions of more than 300 workshop participants and from trauma therapists who have come from a variety of contexts to act as guest co-facilitators.

My hope is that with time this kind of training will become established alongside other research methods training at universities. Meanwhile, many of the resources produced for the benefit of other professional groups recognized to be at risk of VT (including psychotherapists, humanitarian aid workers, and caring professions such as nurses and social workers) are useful resources. These include Saakvitne and Pearlman's *Transforming the Pain: A Workbook on Vicarious Traumatisation*; Françoise Mathieu's *The Compassion Fatigue Workbook*, and the resources on the websites of the Headington Institute[3] and Tend Academy[4]. Valuable guidance on trauma-informed self-care can be found in *Hell Yeah Self-Care: A Trauma-Informed Workbook* by Alex Iantaffi and Meg-John Barker. Achilles[5] provides psychological resilience training for people working in conflict zones.

Broad recommendations for maintaining researcher emotional and psychological safety during challenging fieldwork informed by the Oxford workshops include the following:

1. *Do thoughtful and thorough preparation ahead of fieldwork.*
    a. Acknowledge (and, if necessary, address) past traumas. Your history as a queer individual may be an asset—a rich source of insight and an invaluable wellspring of motivation—but if earlier traumatic experiences

are unprocessed you may be more vulnerable as a result. Reflect honestly on what you need: is it enough to be aware of your vulnerabilities, or would you benefit from some counselling or therapy to get you research-ready? Even two or three sessions of counselling at a university counselling service, many of which now have staff members versed in trauma, may be sufficient to help you think about how to 'hold' your own trauma history as you do your research. If you need more therapy, a book such as *The Body Keeps the Score* (van der Kolk, 2014) may help you to be a more informed and confident consumer and the Free Psychotherapy Network[6] can help you identify affordable options.

b. Identify some elements of a self-care routine that you can really commit to and ensure that these are well adapted to the conditions of your field site. For example, if you normally run for exercise but will not be able to do so in the field, establish an exercise routine you can perform in the confines of your room, or on a yoga mat. Having a routine helps researchers working in precarious or unsettled external environments to hold on to a sense of agency. This is a useful antidote to the feelings of powerlessness that are the essence of trauma.

c. Commit to yoga, meditation, or a breathing practice to enhance your resilience to stress, including traumatic stress. The combination of close interaction with traumatized others and observing/experiencing the realities of life disrupted by conflict can leave researchers in a chronically hyper-aroused state (described colloquially as 'fight-flight' response), which can be debilitating. Using these practices regularly to reduce arousal and reinstate normal function can transform resilience. Breathing practices are especially accessible to novice practitioners, and Brulé (2017) offers a good introduction.

d. Acquire some tools you can use to help you stay clear-headed and functional in a crisis, including: simple grounding techniques; 'box' breathing (routinely used by military personnel); and activation of the 'mammalian diving reflex' via facial immersion, to restore calm and clarity in 30 seconds. You can easily learn about all these techniques online. Other tools and techniques can be explored in texts that provide guidance on trauma interventions and mitigation practices (see, for example, the work of Baranowsky and Gentry (2015) and Curran (2013)).

e. Make sure adequate breaks are built in to your plans. This may be especially important for queer researchers who feel they need to mute their identities—for example, circumscribing gender expression and performance—to maintain safety in the field. Regular access to environments in which authentic expression is safe and welcome are likely to be very helpful in maintaining a strong sense of self under pressure.

2. *Regulate exposure to disturbing stimuli.*
   a. Plan intelligently so that exposure to difficult or disturbing material is paced and recovery time is built in to the programme of work. Monitor your 'distress saturation' (Wray, 2007) and be prepared to have flexible plans if you are at risk of exceeding your distress tolerance.
   b. Be clear about your professional role and remain within it—not only when interacting with others, but whenever you are engaging with potentially challenging or disturbing material. Like a wetsuit, it gives you a layer of protection while supporting your professional function.
   c. Deploy empathy safely and skilfully. This may be especially challenging for queer researchers who are researching experiences which resonate with their own, and who may have intense emotional responses as a result. The capacity of a researcher to respond to stories of interlocutors with authentic engagement and to empathize with their experiences is essential to the integrity of a qualitative research process, but over-empathizing can heighten the risk of VT. Master the art of 'exquisite empathy' (Harrison and Westwood, 2009) to get close while remaining separate and on solid ground.
   d. Minimize repetitive listening to or reading distressing research materials. Take special care when exposed to visual material; for example, following the standard operating protocol recommended by the Dart Centre for Journalism and Trauma (Reese, 2017).
   e. Minimize non-work-related trauma exposure; for example, via news and social media. Repeated checking of (usually negative) news is a problem area for many; consider checking news only once a day or every other day, and where possible only in print form (that is, without images or sound).
   f. Distinguish clearly between work/non-work time and work/non-work space so that there are always zones in which you can relax and feel safe. Many find it helpful to have rituals of transition between work and non-work (for example, taking a shower or changing clothes). Have an area near your bed that has NO reminders of your work, but only objects that connect you with a sense of safety and home. Do not read or think about your research materials in your pyjamas, or in bed.
3. *Commit to regular and active processing of disturbing or unbalancing experiences, where helpful borrowing tools from the trauma therapist's toolkit.*
   a. Resolve to turn towards and acknowledge difficult feelings, rather than trying to cope by cutting off from feelings. Embrace the idea that emotions are a valuable source of intelligence.
   b. Capture thoughts and feelings regularly (for example, in field notes) so that they can be processed intentionally at an appropriate time and place. Note that writing them down also enables you to stop

thinking about them for the present, without fear of forgetting anything important.
   c. Notice what your body wants to do following exposure to anything difficult or disturbing—run? punch a pillow? curl into a ball? make some noise?—and allow this if possible. If you feel you are carrying trauma or tension in your body, try Dr David Bercelli's Tension & Trauma Releasing Exercises[7] to achieve a dramatic one-off release.
   d. Return to thinking about any especially difficult experiences when you feel safe and have adequate time. Bear in mind that processing trauma entails: *knowing* what you know, *feeling* what you feel, and *attending* to implications. Deploying some trauma therapy techniques may be helpful to this process; for example, gentle tapping on acupressure points (see 'Emotional Freedom Technique' in Curran (2013)). If it feels overwhelming to think about an experience on your own, debrief with a therapist who can help you to remain sufficiently calm and grounded to do useful processing.
   e. Consciously expand your personal perspectives to embrace new complexities, recognizing that this process may have intellectual, spiritual, and philosophical dimensions. Try not to leave rhetorical questions hanging for too long. For example, you may find yourself asking 'What's the point (of life, of your research, of caring)?' Make space to discover your authentic response to those questions—through your own reflection but also, where possible, in conversation with others who have grappled with similar questions.
4. *Maintain and develop relationships.*
   a. Be honest with yourself about the limits of your existing support networks and consider establishing new relationships to fill any gaps—for example, a research buddy or a peer support group. For queer researchers, it is very valuable to form connections with other queer researchers whose experiences may resonate powerfully with your own.
   b. Value and invest in your most important relationships, even if you don't feel like it. Give your loved ones your full attention and catch yourself if you start to feel their concerns are 'too small to count'.
   c. Beware the tendency to displace anger (with the world? with the political system? with others' apparent indifference to suffering?) onto loved ones.
   d. If concern about upsetting or damaging others inhibits you from communicating with colleagues or others about your work, learn 'Low-Impact Debriefing' techniques (Mathieu, 2012).
5. *Balance trauma with the positive.*
   a. Pay attention to small moments of beauty, acts of kindness, and so on. Notice and value what is good in people and in the world.

b. Actively recall experiences from your past that have helped you to trust that there is goodness in the world. Reimagine these engaging all your senses, in line with good practice in therapeutic use of imagery (Naparstek, 1994).
c. Remind yourself of the importance and value of your work and do it as effectively as you can (but keep your aims modest and grounded).
d. Adopt a stance of active optimism. Commit yourself to maintaining faith and trust in the self as 'good enough'; the idea that something worthwhile (even if small) can come from the interaction we have with each other; and that the world is a place of beauty and potential despite and in addition to the pain and suffering. It may be helpful to explore the idea of 'radical hope' (Lear, 2006; Solnit, 2016).

Many of these things will be easier to do if they are recognized and affirmed as important by departments, research groups, supervisors, and relevant others. Being open about steps you are taking to look after yourself, and encouraging others to be similarly proactive, may help to shape a more positive research culture in which the emotional and psychological challenges of research are more openly acknowledged.

★ ★ ★

Twelve questions to help researchers gauge readiness for sensitive research:

1. Have you been completely honest with yourself about any areas of anxiety or apprehension you have in relation to your research, including about the way it may make you *feel*?
2. Have you reflected on areas of personal, familial, and community trauma that may give rise to vulnerability as you do your research? Do you know how to manage yourself if you are 'triggered'?
3. Do you have clarity regarding your role and its boundaries and limitations? Have you thought about what degree of self-disclosure is appropriate and why? How readily accessible should you be to your respondents? What responsibilities do you have to them?
4. When thinking about planning and logistics for your project, have you considered your psychological needs—for example, opportunity to orient and feel sufficiently safe/in control in a field environment, spacing of challenging interviews to enable emotional processing, balancing of trauma-intensive and non-trauma-intensive tasks?
5. Are you confident that you can deploy empathy deliberately and safely? Do you know how to moderate the intensity of the emotional connection between yourself and another (for example, in an interview setting), while remaining present and engaged?
6. Have you identified spatial and temporal 'safe zones' in your life?

7. Do you have people with whom you can talk openly about your experience, both in your personal life and in your professional life? Do you have the skills to discuss difficult experiences without traumatizing others?
8. Do you know how to recognize when you are in a state of sympathetic nervous system arousal (or, colloquially, 'fight-flight')? Do you know what steps to take to restore parasympathetic nervous system function (colloquially, 'rest and digest') so that you can think more clearly and access more of your coping resources?
9. Have you committed to regular, active acknowledgement and processing of distressing (whether or not obviously 'traumatic') experiences in the course of your research? Have you established disciplines and procedures to support this?
10. Do you know who you would contact if you were seriously worried about your emotional or psychological well-being or functioning in the course of your research? Have you identified some red flags that would help you to recognize the need to do this?
11. Do you have regular activities or practices that help you to reconnect with your knowledge of what is good, trustworthy, moving, beautiful in humanity and in the world?
12. Have you forgiven yourself in advance for the limitations in what you will achieve?

Notes

[1] Form quoted with permission.
[2] Quotes are illustrative, not taken from actual registration forms.
[3] www.headington-institute.org/
[4] www.tendacademy.ca/
[5] www.resiliencetraining.eu
[6] www.freepsychotherapynetwork.com
[7] https://traumaprevention.com/

Bibliography

American Psychiatric Association (2013) *Diagnostic and Statistical Manual of Mental Disorders* (5th edn).

Baranowsky, A.B. and Gentry, J.E. (2015) *Trauma Practice: Tools for Stabilization And Recovery* (3rd edn), Oxford: Hogrefe & Huber.

Brulé, D. (2020) *Just Breathe*, New York: Atria Books.

Curran, L. (2013) *101 Trauma-Informed Interventions: Activities Exercises and Assignments to Move the Client and Therapy Forward*, Ashland: PESI.

Drozdzewski, D. (2015) 'Retrospective reflexivity: the residual and subliminal repercussions of researching war', *Emotion, Space and Society*, 17(2015): 30–6.

Harrison R.L. and Westwood M.J. (2009) 'Preventing vicarious traumatization of mental health therapists: identifying protective practices', *Psychotherapy* (Chic), 46(2): 203–19.

Iantaffi, A. and Barker, M.J. (2021) *Hell Yeah Self-Care! A Trauma-Informed Workbook*, London: Jessica Kingsley.

Lear, J. (2006) *Radical Hope: Ethics in the Face of Cultural Devastation*, Cambridge, MA: Harvard University Press.

Loyle, C. and Simoni, A. (2017) 'Researching under fire: political science and researcher trauma', *PS: Political Science & Politics*, 50(1): 141–5.

Maček, I. (2014) *Engaging Violence: Trauma, Memory and Representation*, London: Routledge.

Mathieu, F. (2012) *The Compassion Fatigue Workbook*, London: Routledge.

McCann, L. and Pearlman, L. (1990) 'Vicarious traumatization: a framework for understanding the psychological effects of working with victims', *Journal of Traumatic Stress*, 3(1): 131–49.

Moussawi, G. (2021) 'Bad feelings: on trauma, nonlinear time, and accidental encounters in "the field"', *Departures in Critical Qualitative Research*, 10(1): 78–96.

Naparstek, B. (1994) *Staying Well with Guided Imagery*, New York: Warner Books.

Pollard, A. (2009) 'Fields of screams: difficulty and ethnographic fieldwork', *Anthropology Matters*, 11(2): 1–24.

Reese, G. (2017) 'Handling traumatic imagery: developing a standard operating procedure', *Dart Centre for Journalism and Trauma, Columbia University*, [online]. Available from: https://dartcenter.org/resources/handling-traumatic-imagery-developing-standard-operating-procedure

Saakvitne, K.W. and Pearlman, L.A. (1996) *Transforming the Pain: A Workbook on Vicarious Traumatization*, New York: W.W. Norton.

Schulz, P., Kreft, A.-K., Touquet, H., and Martin, S. (2022). 'Self-care for gender-based violence researchers: beyond bubble baths and chocolate pralines', *Qualitative Research*, 0(0).

Shesterinina, A. (2019). 'Ethics, empathy, and fear in research on violent conflict', *Journal of Peace Research*, 56(2): 190–202.

Solnit, R. (2016) *Hope in the Dark: Untold Histories, Wild Possibilities*, Chicago, IL: Haymarket Books.

van der Kolk, B.A. (2014) *The Body Keeps the Score: Brain, Mind, and Body in the Healing of Trauma*, New York: Viking Press.

Weiss, N. (2014) 'Research under distress: resonance and distance in ethnographic fieldwork', in I. Maček (ed) *Engaging Violence: Trauma, Memory, and Representation*, London: Routledge.

Williamson, E. et al (2020) 'Secondary trauma: emotional safety in sensitive research', *Journal of Academic Ethics*, 18: 55–70.

Wray, N., Markovic, M., and Manderson, L. (2007) 'Researcher saturation: the impact of data triangulation and intensive-research practices on the researcher and qualitative research process', *Qualitative Health Research*, 17(10): 1392–402.

Index

References to endnotes show both the page number and the note number (231n3).

A
abilities 65
Abou, Selman Ibrahim 116
academia
  activism, relationship with 43–4, 207
  citations 124n5
  English as primary language of publication 46, 55
  epistemologies preferred by 25
  NGO research, compared to 190, 194, 200n2, 214–15
  queer research scholars, challenges faced by 21–3
  See also knowledge production
activism
  academia, relationship with 43–4, 207
  AIDS 85, 86, 88, 90, 95
  criminalization of LGBTIQ+ 158
  LBQ+ 222, 223
  queer 86, 95, 102n5, 220
activist scholarship 43
ACT UP New York 95
Adnan, Etel 107–8, 110–11, 112–13, 114–19, 119–23, 124n1, 210–11
advocacy
  organizations 77–8, 191, 195
  queer and trans, challenges faced by 67–9, 74
  research, role of in 20–1, 35n2
  as research goal 173
Afghanistan 180
AIDS activism 85, 86, 88, 90, 95
Albarracín, Mauricio 8, 48
Alianza Cinco Claves (5 Claves) 70
Amin, Kadji 211
Amnesty International 51
Andersen, Rune Saugmann 94
Aniquilar la Diferencia (CNMH) 50
antisociality 88, 102n3
AOGs (armed opposition groups) 157, 158, 161, 165, 167, 171, 175n3

approaches, queer conflict research
  about 2, 5–6, 30–3
  best practices (*See* Human Rights Watch (HRW))
  See also constructivism; *critical* approaches; epistemologies; feminist approaches; humanist(ic) approaches (postmodernism); interpretivism; *mainstream* approaches; postpositivism (critical realism); qualitative approaches; quantitative approaches
Arab Apocalypse, The (Adnan) 107–8, 112–13, 114–19, 119–22, 123, 210–11
Aradau, Claudia 92
Aragón, Arturo de 143–6, 149
archives
  about 130–1
  AIDS activism 86
  challenges with 128–9
  creation of queer 46, 56n3
  gender / sexuality in 140–1
  grassroots-based 149
  language in 132, 140–3, 148
  Medicine College library (University of Buenos Aires) 132–3, 140, 211
  power dynamics of 131–2
  queer sensibilities to understand 129, 130, 146, 211–12
Archivos de Criminología, Medicina Legal y Psiquiatría 135–6
Argentina
  Medicine College archive (University of Buenos Aires) 132–3, 140, 211
  military service, mandatory 135–6
  National Archive 131
  'public morality' legislation 135
  sexuality, role of in 147–8
  sexual practices, decriminalization of 134–5
armed opposition groups *See* AOGs (armed opposition groups)
art 107–8, 123, 210

Ashe, Fidelma 8
Assaf, Dib 116
Assi, Joseph Abu 116
assumptions, queer conflict research 3, 23, 29, 33, 204–5, 211, 237
Astraea Lesbian Foundation for Justice 75n5
Atlantic, The 4
Ayoub, Phillip 21, 26, 31, 35n5
Azoulay, Ariella 139

B

Bardall, Gabrielle 31
Barker, Meg-John 244
Barthes, Roland 84, 94
Belbey, José 133–40
Beltrán, Laura 66–7, 69
benefits, research 28, 172–4, 194, 195, 199
Bercelli, David 247
Berchtold, Helena 9, 191, 214
Berlant, Lauren 88, 89, 185, 209
best practices, research *See* Human Rights Watch (HRW); research
biases
 cisheteronormative in refugee studies 32
 heterocentric in research 28–9
 queer epistemology to explore 27
 self-selection 228
 traditional research 3
binaries
 deconstruction of 90, 110
 gender / sexuality 88
 masculine positionalities and 111
 queer feminist workshops to push beyond 64
bisexuals 164, 196
 See also LGBTIQ+ people; SOGIESC, people of diverse
bodies
 as epistemic sites 91, 95–6, 98–9
 metaphors of body parts 148
 visual impact of 85–6, 100, 101
Body Keeps the Score, The (van der Kolk) 245
Boesten, Jelke 21
Boko Haram 157, 159, 160, 175n3
 See also AOGs (armed opposition groups)
'boomerang strategy' 47
Boym, Svetlana 185–6
breathing exercises 245
Brettschneider, Marla 21–2
Brim, Matt 19, 140
Browne, Kath 4, 29, 33, 63, 93
Brown III, Alan 29
Brulé, Dan 245
Bueno-Hansen, Pasha 73
Bus Massacre (1975) (Beirut) 116
Búsqueda de Víctimas (*Unidad de Búsqueda de Personas dadas por Desaparecidas*) (Search Unit for Missing Persons) 71
Buxton, Rebecca 33

C

Canadian High Commission 162, 167, 170
Cano, Gabriela 150n14
Caras y Caretas 143–4
Caribe Afirmativo (Colombia) 8, 65–6, 75n11
 Casas de Paz (houses of peace) (Colombia) 66
Catholicism 78, 110–11
Católicas por el Derecho a Decidir (Catholic Women for the Right to Decide) 78
censorship 46–7
Centro Nacional de Memoria Histórica (CNMH) (National Centre for Historic Memory) 45, 50
Chanaga, Ximena 57n7
Chauncey, George 142
Chomsky, Noam 47
cisheteronormativity
 biases, addressing research 3, 27, 29, 32
 binaries, deconstruction of 90–1, 99
 gender analysis approaches 62
 perpetuation of 88
 research, and traditional 203
 and security 85–6, 101–2
cissexism 48, 62
citations 124n5
class 65
Cohen, Cathy 91, 93, 102n5
Cohen, Dara Kay 21, 30
Cohn, Carol 203, 207, 216n1
Coleman, Kevin 139
collective identities *See* identities
collective memories *See* memories
Collins, Patricia Hill 21
Colombia
 censorship 46–7
 identity-based language 72–3
 Peace Agreement (2016) 45–6, 53
 'politics of not knowing' 45, 51
 queer conflict experiences in, documenting 8, 45–6, 48–9, 53
 queer feminist workshops 65–7, 67–9, 74
 report on violence during conflict 50–1
 security risks for LBTQ women 69–72
 WPS NAP development 65, 66–7, 76n16
Colombia Diversa 65, 66, 67, 68–9, 70, 72–4, 76n12, 76n16, 77
colonialism 52, 55, 64, 72, 88, 109–10, 122, 132
Combahee River Collective 65
coming out 3, 4, 52
complaints 229, 230
condoms 148, 150n19
configuration of relations 186
conflict
 about 5–6, 96
 research (*See* research)
 trauma as a tool to understand 108–9, 113–14

INDEX

conflict sensitivity 163, 175n3
consent 169, 171, 226, 227, 228, 229, 237–9
constructivism 25, 26, 32
  See also approaches, queer conflict research; research
continuums of violence 193
  See also violence
Cooper-Cunningham, Dean 7, 42, 209–10
Corbetta, Piergiorgio 24
Corporación Humanas (Humans Corporation) 77
cover stories 235, 238–9
COVID-19 pandemic
  people of diverse SOGIESC, experiences during 162, 192–3
  research during, challenges with 163–4, 168, 195–6, 226
Criminal Code Act (CCA) (Nigeria) 161
criminalization
  of LGBTIQ+ rights activism 158
  of sexual practices 134–5, 161–2
critical approaches 3, 11n3, 27
  See also approaches, queer conflict research; research
critical intimacy 187, 188, 214
  See also intimacies
critical realism *See* postpositivism (critical realism)
critical security studies 32, 33, 94
cuirizar 72, 76n19

D

Dafne *See* Aragón, Arturo de
data 25, 48, 51, 52, 55, 63, 93, 158, 162–4, 170–1, 173
de Beauvoir, Simone 124
decision-making process, research 220–1
decolonize 47, 52, 185, 187, 188, 203, 206, 207, 208
deductive research 24, 25
  See also approaches, queer conflict research; research
DeJusticia (Organization of Justice) 68–9, 77
Delatolla, Andrew 7, 203, 210–11
Della Porta, Donatella 23, 24–5
departments *See* academia
Derrida, Jacques 131
diasporic intimacy 185, 186
disability 2, 159, 161, 163, 164, 168, 197
disidentification
  about 130
  queer histories 146–9
Disturbing Attachments (Amin) 211
diversity 64
documentation
  of anti-homosexual violence, challenges with 48–9
  oral knowledge, at expense of 131
  See also archives; data; interviews

Donovan, Thom 108
Dotson, Kristie 27
Duggan, Moira 8
Dyke March 72, 76n20

E

Eddé, Emile 124n9
emotional safety of researchers 242–9
endosexism / endosexist 3, 165
English
  primacy of, challenging 56, 66
  publications, as primary language of 46, 55
Enloe, Cynthia 202
Epic of Gilgamesh 115–16
epistemic injustice 27, 57n7
epistemic violence 27, 209
epistemological bases 24
epistemologies
  about 23–4
  bridging different 31–2
  conflict research 23–5, 27–30
  critical 27
  queer as a method 30, 32–4, 206
  queer as a structure 30, 32, 206
  queer as a subject 30–2, 206
  types of 24–5
  visual, lack of in 92–3
  See also constructivism; feminist approaches; feminist standpoint theory; humanist(ic) approaches (postmodernism); interpretivism; poetry; positivism; postpositivism (critical realism)
Erdem, Zeynep Pınar 9, 191, 195, 196–7, 198, 199, 214
ethics
  images, use of 139–40, 211
  informed consent process 237–9
  of queer conflict research 2, 36n15, 48–9, 53, 166–7, 169–72, 190
ethnicity 28, 163, 186
ethnographic research 64, 180, 185, 186, 187–8
exploitation, sexual 172, 192
extraction 64

F

femininity 3, 111, 134, 135, 140, 142, 145, 149
feminist approaches
  intersectional 163
  LBTQ women, prioritization of experiences of 63, 69
  men, how and when to include 73–4
  poetry as (*See* poetry)
  workshops 63, 64, 67–9
  WPS agenda 61–2
feminist security studies 203, 216n1
feminist standpoint theory 27–8, 29, 36n11
Fierke, Karin 98, 124n4

253

forced migrants *See* migrants, forced; refugees
Forum CIV 77
Foucault, Michel 20, 29, 33, 131
France 110–11
Freed, Maureen 10
Fricker, Miranda 27
Fujii, Lee Ann 32
Fundación Artemisas (Artemis Foundation) 77
fundamentalism, religious 159, 175n5

G

García, Camila 66
Gay Clown Putin memes 85, 98
gay men
  inclusion of in WPS spaces 73–4
  invisibility of abuses 52
  social homophobia, as targets of 97, 102n2
  visibility of 63
  See also LGBTIQ+ people; SOGIESC, people of diverse
Gay New York (Chauncey) 142
Gayropa 89, 97, 100, 101, 102n2
GBV *See* gender-based violence (GBV)
gender
  assumptions, destabilization of 3
  cis/heteronormative approaches to 62, 88
  conflict research and 28–30, 36n12, 43–4
  historical experiences of, understanding 146–9
  identities (*See* gender identities)
  in images 136, 139–40, 145–6
  impact on subject of study 32
  intersectional research and 65, 206
  re-inscription 136
  as social structure organizer 110
  transformation 163
Gender, Justice and Security Hub 191
Gender, Violence and Security (Shepherd) 33
gender-based violence (GBV) 65, 164, 166, 171
  See also violence
gender identities
  binary approach to 62, 64, 136
  discrimination based on 193
  Human Rights Watch (HRW) standards and 10, 219–20, 221, 223, 224, 235
  sexuality, sexual desire and 142–3
  terminology for 72–3, 158–9
  violence related to 49, 54, 196
  See also SOGIESC, people of diverse
Ghaziani, Amin 140
Gide, André 110–11
Gilgamesh 116, 121
Global North
  academia and activism, relationship 43, 55
  queer feminist workshops 64
  rights abuses in 198–9
  See also specific countries (e.g. United States)
Global South
  academia and activism, relationship 43, 55–6
  NGO research challenges in 194
  queer feminist workshops 63, 64, 74
  SOCIESC rights in 198
  suffering in, Global North's attraction to 48
  See also specific countries (e.g. Colombia)
Gómez, María Mercedes 52–3, 65
Good Friday Agreement (Northern Ireland) 4
governance 33–4, 41, 111, 159, 160–1
grounded-theory approach 163
Grovogui, Siba 124n3

H

Hagen, Jamie J. 6, 36n12, 203, 208
hair 136–7
Halim, Haji 186–7
Halperin, David 141
Hammers, Corie 29
Hansen, Lene 91, 94–5, 102n2
Harding, Sandra 21, 28
Hartsock, Nancy 28
Hay, C. 35n8
healthcare 160–1, 164, 173, 193
hegemonic orders 28–30, 88, 206
heteronormative internationalism 83, 87, 97, 98
heteronormativity
  about 51, 102n1
  biases of 27
  coming out and 3
  perpetuation of 84, 88
  women and gender, approach to 62
heterosexism 63, 208
hierarchies
  of activism 55
  of expertise in peacebuilding 67–9
  of knowledge 45–7, 48
  of power 11n3, 110, 111, 131–2, 138–9
homophobia
  about 102n1
  political 88–9, 97, 102n6, 221
  state-sponsored 83, 85, 87, 98–9, 102n2
  violence and 44, 49, 86, 101
Hoover Green, Amelia 30
HRW *See* Human Rights Watch (HRW)
humanist(ic) approaches (postmodernism)
  about 24, 26–7
  anti-LGBTIQ+ violence, studies of 31
  gender, approaches to 30
  See also approaches, queer conflict research; research
human rights
  'boomerang strategy' 47
  discrimination based on gender identity 193
  homonationalism 199
  pinkwashing 207, 208

Human Rights Watch (HRW)
  consent 226, 227, 228, 229, 237–9
  core standards and protocols 219
  gender identity / sexual orientation and research 10, 219–20, 221, 223, 224, 235
  interviews, best practices 223–5, 226–7, 228–9
  LGBT Rights Program 10
  referral lists 224–5, 229, 230, 233, 239
  risk assessments 220, 229, 230
  risk mitigation strategies 230–2
  security planning, context-specific 232–5
  trauma-informed research techniques 220, 224, 227, 235–9, 244
Husseini, Antoine 116
Hutchings, Kimberly 124n3
Huysmans, Jef 92

I

Iantaffi, Alex 244
identities
  categories, imposing of 232–3
  collective 49, 55
images
  as epistemic sites 91, 95–6, 98–9
  gender as binary 136, 139–40, 145–6
  interpretations of 97–8
  power relationships in 138–9
  See also visual, the
Indonesia 234–5
inductive research 24
  See also research
The Initiative for Equal Rights (TIERs) *See* TIERs (The Initiative for Equal Rights) (Nigeria)
injustice, epistemic 27, 57n7
International Alert 75n7
international relations (IR)
  heteronormativity in 84–5, 202–3
  queer 26–7, 89–90, 91–2, 203–4
  visual 93–4
interpreters 66, 224, 227, 233–4
interpretivism
  about 24, 26
  gender, approaches to 30
  queer as a structure approach 32
intersectionality
  approach to research 28–9, 65, 163, 206
  and coping / adapting ability 164
  refugees of diverse SOGIESC 192–3
  violence and 2
intersex 163
interventions 3, 10, 27–8, 41–2, 44–5, 55, 101, 161–2, 166–8, 172–4
interviewees *See* research participants
interviewers *See* researchers
interviews
  case study 225–6
  design 223–5

  encounter 228–9
  outreach 226–7, 228–9, 234
  remote 229, 230–2
intimacies 182, 184, 185–6, 187–8, 214, 215
invertidos sexuales 136, 142–3, 146
Investigación Acción Participativa 43
invisibility
  passing as cisgender / heterosexual 85
  'politics of not-knowing' 45, 51
  queer experiences of 3
  of queer women 63, 208
  in research 207
  trans histories 141–3, 145–6
  visibility, moving to 51–4
  the visual, to address 209–10
  See also visibility
IR *See* international relations (IR)
Iraq 230–2
Islamophobia 180, 188
ISWAP (Islamic State West African Province) 160

J

Jablonka, Ivan 147
JASDJ (Jama'atu Ahl al-sunna li-l-Da'wa wa-l-Jihad) 160
'Jon and Alex' 99–100

K

Keating, Michael 23, 24–5
knowledge production
  about 43–4
  evolution of 41
  hierarchies 45–7, 48
  methods used as critical to 92
  'normal' / 'standard' methods, critiques of 109–12
  queer knowledges 92, 210
  See also academia
Krafft-Ebing, Richard von 133, 150n5
Krystalli, Roxani 51, 53

L

Lake, Milli 30, 36n14
La Larga, Juana 141
language
  in archives 132, 140–3, 148
  common terminology, challenges with 158–9
  context-specific in research 233
  identity-based 72–3, 76n19
  italics, words in 175n2
  See also English; interpreters; Spanish
LBQ+ women (lesbian, bisexual, queer, and others) 222–3, 227, 228, 232–3, 237
  See also LGBTIQ+ people; SOGIESC, people of diverse; women
Lebanon
  Civil War (1975–90) 107–9, 111–12, 116–20, 122–3
  refugees of diverse SOGIESC in 191–3

lesbians 52, 67, 69–70, 71, 72–3, 76n20, 88, 150n1, 164, 222–3
  See also LBQ+ women; LGBTIQ+ people; SOGIESC, people of diverse
Ley de Víctimas (The Victims Law) 44, 45
LGBTIQ+ people (lesbian, gay, bisexual, transgender, intersex, queer, and others)
  about 11n1
  acronym, use of 11n1, 47, 52, 56n2, 72
  rights of (*See* rights)
  violence against (*See* violence)
  See also Corey (queer person)
liberalism 134
Liga Internacional de Mujeres por la Paz y la Libertad (LIMPAL) 77
linearity 108, 112–13, 114–19, 124n3, 210–11
literature 107–8, 123, 210
  See also poetry
Love, Heather 36n11
Luker, Kristin 34n1

M

mainstream approaches 3, 11n3, 21, 30, 33–4, 35n4, 203
  See also approaches, queer conflict research; research
Maira, Sunaina 186
maricas 76n19, 141–2
mariconear 72, 73, 76n19
Martinez, Elena 131, 138, 141
Marxism 28, 36n11
masculinity 3, 109, 110, 111, 112, 143, 145, 148, 149, 181
Mathieu, Françoise 244
Maydaa, Charbel 9, 191, 193–4, 195–6, 197–8, 199, 214
Mayolo, Carlos 47–8
McKee, Lyra 4
Medicine College Library archive (University of Buenos Aires) 132–3, 140, 211
memories, collective 49–50
men 73, 165
  See also gay men; LGBTIQ+ people; SOGIESC, people of diverse
MENA region (Middle East and North Africa) 9, 191, 194
methodological bases 24
methodologies
  about 2, 6–7, 23–4, 103n8
  challenges with 140–1
  importance of 92–3
  See also approaches, queer conflict research; epistemologies; research; snowball sampling; trauma-informed research techniques; tripartite word–image–body model
microaggressions 197

migrants, forced 191, 192, 198
military
  gender dynamics in 202
  mandatory service 135–6
minority burden 31
missing persons 71, 113, 183
Mohammed, Bala 158, 168–9, 170, 171–2, 174
Mohammed, Xeenarh 158, 168, 169, 172
MOSAIC 9, 191, 194, 195, 197
Moussawi, Ghassan 198–9
Mujeres al Borde 56n5
Mujeres-hombres (Women-men) 143–5
Munhazim, Ahmad Qais 9, 213–14
Munt, Sally R. 182
Muslims
  bans 188
  ethnographic research challenges 180–2
  Lebanese Civil War 111–12
  research with 182–4
  state-sponsored surveillance of 181
  targeting of 160
Myrttinen, Henri 9, 191, 194–5, 197, 198–9, 214

N

Nagarajan, Chitra 8, 213
NAPs *See* WPS National Action Plans (NAPs)
narratives
  conflict 111–12
  victim, focus on 53
Nash, Catherine 4, 29, 33, 93
National Action Plans *See* WPS National Action Plans (NAPs)
New York Lesbian Avengers 76n20
NGO research 190–1, 193–9, 214–15
Nigeria
  AOGs (armed opposition groups) 157, 158, 161, 165, 167, 171, 175n3
  Boko Haram 157, 159, 160, 175n3
  conflict in north-east 157, 159–62
  language, SOGIESC terminology 158–9
  LGBTQI+ rights activism, criminalization of 158
  research in, addressing risks of 169–72
  same-sex sexual relations, criminalization of 161, 165
  sharia codes 159, 161, 165
  SSMPA (Same Sex Marriage Prohibition Act) 161, 162, 165
9/11 180, 186
Nissen, Mads 98, 99, 100
non-governmental organizations *See* NGO research
normality
  logics of in conflict resolution studies 41
  male heterosexuality as standard of 110–11
normalization of violence 55

Northern Ireland 4, 8
  See also Good Friday Agreement

O

objectivity 26, 109, 110, 112–13, 207
ontological bases 24
ontologies 23–4, 35n8, 90, 91, 92, 206, 216
Ordoñez, Juan Pablo 46–7
Ospina, Luis 47–8
outreach strategies 226–7, 228–9, 234
Oxfam 192–3

P

pandemic *See* COVID-19 pandemic
Panos Pictures 97
'parachute research' 55
Parkinson, Sarah 30, 36n14
Parra, Valentina 66
participatory research 8–9, 63, 168, 169, 199
passing 85
Patel, Sonali 184
patriarchy 61, 62, 63, 87, 98, 159, 198
Patriotic League 137
peace
  about 7–8
  temporality of as queered 118–19
Peace Agreement (2016) (Colombia) 45–6, 53
peacebuilding
  gender perspectives in 61, 62–3, 65–7, 73–4
  hierarchies of expertise in 67–9
  LGBTIQ+ research in Colombia 45–6, 49, 52–3, 55–6
Pearlman, L.A. 244
Peralta Ramón, María Susana 66, 67, 73
Perón, Juan Domingo 147, 150n16
Phalange 116, 124n10
photographs *See* images
pictures *See* images
pink triangles 85
pinkwashing 207, 208
Planeta Paz 56n5
poetry 107–9, 112–13, 114–19, 123, 210–11
political ontology 35n8
politics of knowledge *See* knowledge
'politics of not-knowing' 45, 51
Pornomiseria—Misery Porn (Ospina and Mayolo) 47–8
positionalities
  conflict, of individuals who experienced 113–14, 123
  intersectional 4, 68
  masculine 111
  queer feminist 108, 110, 111
  of researchers 2, 3, 7, 35n6, 42–3, 109–10, 213–14
positivism 24, 25
postmodernism *See* humanist(ic) approaches (postmodernism)

postpositivism (critical realism)
  about 24, 25–6
  sexual violence, approaches to study of 30
power
  hierarchies of 11n3, 110, 111, 131–2, 138–9
  in research 166–9
prejudice
  -based violence targeting LGBTIQ+ people 65–6
  collective identities and 50
  visibility and 52–3
production, knowledge *See* knowledge
protection 148, 150n19
pseudonyms 169, 170, 235, 238–9
psychological safety of researchers 242–9
Psychopathia Sexualis (Krafft-Ebing) 150n5
Puar, Jasbir 27
Putin, Vladimir 89, 97

Q

qualitative approaches
  examples of 64, 163, 180
  inductive research and 24
  postpositivism (critical realism) 25–6
quantitative approaches
  deductive research and 24
  identity categories 233
  postpositivism (critical realism) 25–6
queer
  about 88–91
  See also LGBTIQ+ people; SOGIESC, people of diverse
queer as a method / subject / structure *See* epistemologies
queer conflict research
  about 1–2
  See also approaches, queer conflict research; epistemologies; Human Rights Watch (HRW); methodologies; research
queer entanglements 187
queer epistemologies *See* epistemologies, queer
queer feminist approaches *See* feminist approaches
queering (v)
  about 32–3, 72–3
  challenges with in conflict research 48–9
  pillars of WPS 67
  politics of knowledge 43–4
  of security 64
  trauma as 119–23
Queering Atrocity Prevention (Protection Approaches) 75n7
'Queering Women, Peace and Security (WPS)' 76n13
Queer International Relations (Weber) 1, 26–7, 109
queer research *See* research
queer sensibilities 129, 130, 146, 211–12

queer women
  invisibility / marginalization of 63, 208
  security risks for 69–72
  visibility, denial of in research 220–1
  See also LBQ+ women; LGBTIQ+ people; SOGIESC, people of diverse; women

R

race
  images and 145
  intersectionality and 8, 28, 65, 141–2
  positionality and. 35n6, 109–10
  shared experiences and. 186
rainbow flags 85, 95, 98, 185
Ranawana, Anupama 76n13
Rao, Rahul 27
Rasool 179, 180, 181
readiness gauge for researchers 248–9
Red Nacional de Mujeres (National Women's Organization) 77
referrals / referral lists 170, 171–2, 173, 224–5, 229, 230, 233, 239
refugees 182–3, 191–3, 195, 196, 197, 198, 200n5, 214, 238
refugee studies 32, 33
re-inscription, gender 136
religious fundamentalism 159, 175n5
representation
  forms of 50–1
  regimes of 47–8, 49, 207–8
research
  about 4
  advocacy grounded in 20–1, 35n2
  assumptions 3, 23, 29, 33, 204–5, 211, 237
  benefits of 172–4
  best practices (*See* Human Rights Watch (HRW))
  decision-making process 220–1
  dissemination of 198
  ethics (*See* ethics)
  fatigue 198
  impacts of 199
  NGO research 190–1, 193–9, 214–15
  power imbalances in 166–9
  process 23–4
  risks, addressing in 169–72
researchers
  best practices (*See* Human Rights Watch (HRW))
  emotional / psychological safety of 242–9
  experiences / challenges faced by 213–15
  positionality of 109–10
  readiness gauge for 248–9
  trust, building of 64, 171, 180–2, 229, 230, 233
research participants
  good practices 223–5
  outreach strategies 226–7, 228–9, 234

risk mitigation strategies 230–2
  See also Human Rights Watch (HRW)
rights
  awareness training for LGBTIQ+ people 173
  backlashes against LGBTIQ+ 54
  LGBTIQ+ people 3
risks
  assessments 220, 229, 230
  mitigation strategies, research 230–2
  research, addressing in 169–72
Ritholtz, Samuel 6, 32, 33, 203, 204, 205–6
Rolin, K. 29
Russia
  Gay Clown Putin memes 85, 98
  gay propaganda / anti-homopropaganda law 26, 83, 87, 95, 97, 98
  Gayropa 89, 97, 100, 101, 102n2
  heteronormative internationalism 83, 87, 97, 98
  political homophobia 88–9
  Ukraine, justification for war in 89
'ruthless archives' 131–2
  See also archives

S

Saakvitne, K.W. 244
safe spaces 8, 193, 224
safety of researchers, emotional / psychological 242–9
Said, Edward 180
Saint Vincent and the Grenadines 236–7
Salsa Dancing in the Social Sciences (Luker) 34n1
Sánchez, Camila 66, 74
San Miguel Asylum 135
sectarianism 111, 119, 120–21, 123, 124n14
security
  about 96
  context-specific research guidelines 232–5
  feminist studies 203, 216n1
  images, study of 94–5
  for LGBT women 69–72
  'passing' as a strategy for 85
  risk mitigation strategies, research 230–2
  training for LGBTIQ+ people 173
Sedgwick, Eve Kosofsky 33
self-care 197, 244–5
self-selection bias 228
September 11 180, 186
Serrano-Amaya, José Fernando 6, 35n4, 206–8
sex
  images of 99–100
  international politics of 88–9
sexual exploitation 172, 192
sexuality
  assumptions, destabilization of 3
  cis/heteronormative approaches to 88, 147–9
  conflict research 28–30, 36n12, 43–4

historical experiences of,
understanding 146–9
impact on subject of study 32
intersectional research and 65, 206
as social structure organizer 110
sexual orientation
Human Rights Watch (HRW) standards and 10, 219–20, 221, 223, 224, 235
See also LGBTIQ+ people; SOGIESC, people of diverse
sex workers 132, 134, 135, 147–8
Shamash 115–16
sharia codes 159, 161, 165, 234
Sharpe, Christina 186
She Called Me Woman (Mohammed, Nagarajan and Aliju) 175n7
Shekau, Abubakar 160
Shepherd, Laura 33, 36n16
silencing
in archives 131–2
of lived experiences 27
speech, moving to 52–4
Simonetto, Patricio 7, 56n3, 211–12
Sjoberg, Laura 9
Smith, Valerie J. 180
snowball sampling 163, 169, 219, 226, 228
social inclusion 163
SOGIESC, people of diverse (sexual orientations, gender identities and expressions, and sex characteristics)
about 11n1
benefits to, research-identified 172–4
continuums of violence faced by 193
NGO research with 190–1, 193–9
Nigerian conflict 157–9, 161–2
participatory research with 168–9
refugees 191–3
research, issues of power in 166–9
risks, addressing research-related 169–72
study of in Nigeria 162–6
Spanish 66
Special Jurisdiction for Peace (Jurisdicción Especial para la Paz) (JEP) 66
speech *See* voice
Spivak, Gayatri Chakravorty 21, 27, 187
SSMPA (Same Sex Marriage Prohibition Act) (Nigeria) 161, 162, 165
standpoint theory *See* feminist standpoint theory
Stanley, Liz 27
Stein, Gertrude 114
subjectivity
humanistic approaches 26–7
interpretivism 26
of linearity and temporality 114
postpositivism 25
of traumatic experiences 219, 237
sun 114, 115–16, 117
survivor's guilt 113

Syria 111, 118, 124n14, 191–2, 195, 214, 225–6

T

Ta'if Agreement 118, 124n11
Taylor, Diana 131
Tel al-Zataar siege and massacre 124n1
temporality 108, 114–19, 124n3, 210–11, 212
Terrorist Assemblages (Puar) 27
testimonial quieting 27
testimonial smothering 27
testimonies *See* narratives
theory-building (inductive research) 24
theory-testing (deductive research) 24
threats *See* risks
TIERs (The Initiative for Equal Rights) (Nigeria) 158, 162, 163, 168, 173–4, 175
Tilly, Charles 108
tolerance 71
Tortorici, Zeb 131–2
trans people
advocacy 67–8, 73
archives 131, 132, 135–7, 139–42, 145–6
missing 71
outreach strategies, research 227, 228
security for 70
term, use of 11n1
See also LGBTIQ+ people; SOGIESC, people of diverse
transphobia / transphobic 6, 21, 56, 66, 87, 97, 136, 192, 197, 236
travestismo 133, 136, 137
trauma
about 124n4
as queering 119–23
conflict, as tool to understand 108–9, 113–14
ethical good practices for 219
guilt, survivor's 113
temporality and 116
vicarious (VT) 243–4, 246
trauma-informed research techniques 220, 224, 227, 235–9, 244
tripartite word–image–body model 87, 91, 95–6, 98–9, 101
Trump, Donald 188
trust-building by researchers 64, 171, 180–2, 229, 230, 233
Tschantret, Joshua 25
Turkey 191–3

U

Ukraine
queer organizations / individuals targeted 97
war in, Russian justification for 89
United States
Islamophobia 180, 188

259

LGBTIQ+ people, violence against 11n3
military, gender dynamics in 202
Muslim bans 188
universities *See* academia
UN Security Council 35n3, 61, 66, 68, 73, 75n7
Usman, Kaka 184, 186, 187

V

vicarious trauma (VT) 243–4, 246
 See also trauma
victims
 LGBTIQ+ as collective 55
 narratives of 53
 partners in same-sex relationships as 44
violence
 causes of, gender identity / sexual orientation as 196
 continuums of 193
 documentation of, challenges with 48–9
 epistemic 27, 209
 gender-based (GBV) 65, 164, 166, 171
 intersectionality and 2
 LGBTIQ+ people, against 11n2, 221
 microaggressions 197
 normalization of 55
 prejudice-based 65–6
 sexual 30, 213, 225–6, 240n5
 (in)visibility of 44
 visual representations of 86–7, 97–8, 100
visibility
 denial of in research 220–1
 invisibility to, from 51–4
 of research subjects 63
 risks of 3, 54, 55
 See also invisibility
visual, the
 about 85, 86–7
 AIDS activists' use of 86
 bodies as 85–6
 in critical security studies 94–5
 gender as binary 136, 139–40
 images, effects of 83–5
 invisibility, to address 209–10
 knowledge production, lack of in queer 92–3
 queer (in)security, seeing 97–100
 tripartite word–image–body model 87, 91, 95–6, 98–9, 101
Visual IR 93–4
 See also international relations (IR); visual, the

voice
 archives, silencing of in 131–2
 silence to, moving from 52–4
Vuori, Juha 94

W

Waites, Mathew 47
Walsh, Catherine 44
Walt, Stephen 207
war
 causes of 205
 temporality of as queered 114–19
Warner, Michael 88, 89, 103n7, 209
Weaver, Kathleen 110
Weber, Cynthia 1–2, 26–7, 109, 123, 203
Wedeen, Lisa 32
Weiss, Margot 187
When States Come Out (Ayoub) 26
Wilkinson, Cai 26, 36n10
Wise, Sue 27
women
 heteronormative approaches to 62
 LBQ+ women 222–3, 227, 228, 232–3, 237
 LGBT, WPS workshops 65–9
 Nigerian, experiences of 164
 pinkwashing 207, 208
 risks faced by 69–72
 in US military 202
 See also LBQ+ women; lesbians, LGBTIQ+ people; queer women; SOGIESC, people of diverse
Women, Peace, and Security (WPS) agenda
 about 61, 62
 deconstructing 33
 NAP-development workshops 63, 66–7
 pillars of, queering 67
Wood, Elisabeth J. 21, 30
word–image–body model *See* tripartite word–image–body model
words as epistemic sites 91, 95–6, 98–9
WPS *See* Women, Peace, and Security (WPS) agenda
WPS National Action Plans (NAPs)
 about 63, 75n3
 drafting of Colombia's 65, 66–7, 76n16
 LGBTIQ+ mentions in 63, 75n4, 75n7

Y

yan daudu 158, 163, 164, 165, 175n6
yan yusufiyya 160
Young, Iris Marion 21
Yusuf, Mohammed 159–60

www.ingramcontent.com/pod-product-compliance
Lightning Source LLC
Chambersburg PA
CBHW051532020426
42333CB00016B/1889